Computational Intelligence

Scrivener Publishing
100 Cummings Center, Suite 541J
Beverly, MA 01915-6106

Publishers at Scrivener
Martin Scrivener (martin@scrivenerpublishing.com)
Phillip Carmical (pcarmical@scrivenerpublishing.com)

Computational Intelligence

Theory and Applications

Edited by

T. Ananth Kumar

E. Golden Julie

Venkata Raghuveer Burugadda

Abhishek Kumar

and

Puneet Kumar

Scrivener Publishing

WILEY

This edition first published 2024 by John Wiley & Sons, Inc., 111 River Street, Hoboken, NJ 07030, USA and Scrivener Publishing LLC, 100 Cummings Center, Suite 541J, Beverly, MA 01915, USA

For more information about Scrivener publications please visit www.scrivenerpublishing.com.

Wiley Global Headquarters
111 River Street, Hoboken, NJ 07030, USA

For details of our global editorial offices, customer services, and more information about Wiley products visit us at www.wiley.com.

Library of Congress Cataloging-in-Publication Data

ISBN 978-1-394-21422-8

Front cover images supplied by Adobe Firefly
Cover design by Russell Richardson

Set in size of 11pt and Minion Pro by Manila Typesetting Company, Makati, Philippines

Printed in the USA

10 9 8 7 6 5 4 3 2 1

Contents

Introduction

Chapter 1 encompasses computing paradigms inspired by nature and cognition, rooted in evolution, fuzzy systems, and neural networks. Computational intelligence (CI) underpins potent AI systems, notably deep learning, a cornerstone of modern AI technology. It is the bedrock of highly effective AI systems, driving advancements like video games and cognitive development.

Chapter 2 handles merging evolutionary computation, neural networks, and fuzzy systems decades ago. Nature-inspired algorithms have evolved, proving more adaptable for optimization. Various types of these algorithms, particularly those centered on self-organizing natural communities, are actively developed. This article compares state-of-the-art optimization techniques with established gradient-based and gradient-free methods. It also identifies unresolved issues in optimization and meta-heuristics for future research.

Chapter 3 demotes AI's significance in modern industries for its robust computing capabilities, which process extensive data, yielding valuable insights and aiding decision-making. AI customizes experiences through user data analysis. Computational intelligence research benefits individuals and society, enhancing data processing for intelligent AI systems. This chapter explores various dimensions of computational intelligence, driving societal development and economic progress. It delves into hybrid models, ensemble techniques, and practical AI applications, offering insights for future researchers and scholars in advancing computational intelligence.

Chapter 4 delves into an AI system based on cognitive mechanisms for visual data processing. It explores the relationship between this model and cognitive processes, focusing on selective attention. AI is viewed as a transformative force in human–machine interaction, impacting organizational dynamics, communication, and ecosystems. While AI research can be complex, the information systems field is pivotal. The paper suggests that AI technology may surpass human instructors within a decade.

Chapter 5 deals with groups of spatial co-location patterns. This work introduces a computational intelligence method employing a grid clustered technique, enhancing pattern detection. The Top-K co-location technique is used for generating highly co-located spatial patterns. Implemented on the MapReduce framework, it accelerates the processing of large spatial datasets, improving efficiency. Experimental results confirm the algorithm's effectiveness across various data sizes.

Chapter 6 introduces an efficient method for early detection and classification of plant illnesses using machine learning. Early detection of plant diseases is crucial in agriculture for increased profitability and yield protection. The approach involves capturing leaf images with a camera sensor, extracting essential features through segmentation, and utilizing SVM for disease categorization. The system's effectiveness is evaluated for both detection and classification.

Chapter 7 predicts that protein structure, a deep learning challenge, has seen notable progress, yet room for improvement remains. Deriving tertiary, secondary, and quaternary structures from the primary is complex. Convolutional neural networks (CNNs) model interactions using features like amino acid sequences. Employing data from a protein data bank, we developed CNN-CA-P, augmenting cellular automata. Achieving high accuracy (96.56% secondary, 91.2% tertiary, and 86.32% quaternary), it outperforms baseline methods, evaluated on parameters like accuracy, AUC, precision, F1 score, and recall.

Chapter 8 explores the application of artificial intelligence techniques, specifically artificial neural networks (ANNs) and expert systems (ES), in modeling and forecasting renewable energy effectiveness. It presents various problems in renewable energy engineering to showcase how these systems operate. The research demonstrates the potential of AI as a design tool across different aspects of renewable energy engineering, affirming the efficacy of neural networks in this domain.

Chapter 9 presents health informatics and a surge in data analytics driven by diverse multimodal data. This has sparked interest in tailored machine learning (ML) models. Deep learning (DL), rooted in neural networks, has emerged as a potent tool in AI, promising transformative impacts. Its capacity for complex feature enhancement and semantic analysis, coupled with computational advancements, fuels its prominence. This chapter comprehensively assesses DL's advantages, potential limitations, and prospects, particularly in health-related contexts. The investigation focuses on critical applications, spanning bioinformatics, continuous sensing, medical imaging, and public health.

Chapter 10 tackles real-world issues using nature-inspired methods, distinct from formal models. CI plays a crucial role in human activity recognition (HAR), capturing activities via sensors and processing them. HAR holds vital information on identity, personality, gestures, and more, impacting interpersonal interactions. This chapter delves into CI paradigms for HAR, like fuzzy logic, artificial neural networks, swarm intelligence, evolutionary computing, and artificial immune systems. Researchers are advancing HAR with CI algorithms, showcasing CI's versatility and discussing its benefits and drawbacks in various research contexts.

Chapter 11 deals with AI with healthcare. Biomedical image processing employs image analysis, machine learning, and cloud technology. Fuzzy logic, Bayesian inference, and statistics aid medical disease detection. Overcoming challenges of high dimensionality, class imbalance, and limited databases, modern technology provides superior results. Cloud computing enables global accessibility for data storage and processing, improving diagnostic accuracy for connected diseases. AI strives for precise, comprehensive solutions in biomedical processing.

Chapter 12 deals with computational intelligence (CI) methods, including sample augmentation, feature extraction, categorization, indexing, fusion, normalization, and anti-spoofing, which are crucial in creating biometric identities and addressing dataset challenges. CI enables complex nonlinear calculations and model development from training data, employing supervised and unsupervised training. This chapter explores CI-based biometric recognition methods.

Chapter 13 deals with hyperspectral imaging (HSI), which has gained prominence, especially in biomedical fields like cancer detection. Breast cancer (BC) is a significant global health concern, with over 1.3 million cases in India. Early detection improves survival rates. Various optical techniques are employed, each with its advantages and drawbacks. Biopsies, the current validation method, are invasive. Non-invasive methods like HSI show promise. This chapter comprehensively reviews HSI for breast cancer detection, covering advanced deep-learning frameworks for automated diagnosis.

Chapter 14 also deals with healthcare and AI. Oral cancer (OC) is particularly prevalent in India, accounting for a significant percentage of cases and deaths. Early detection is crucial for survival. Various imaging techniques exist, with drawbacks. Emerging methods like hyperspectral imaging (HSI) show promise for non-invasive, safe, and precise diagnosis. HSI combined with deep learning techniques like CNNs and 3DCNNs holds potential for early OC detection. This chapter outlines these advancements and suggests future research directions.

Chapter 15 deals with image processing, which plays a crucial role in human eye recognition. Prolonged computer use can lead to visual problems. Optic disc (OD) is vital for diagnosing retinal diseases. It is characterized by high fractal dimensions due to blood vessels. OD's location helps diagnose conditions like glaucoma. This screening system aids in glaucoma detection through OD segmentation. Glaucoma is a chronic eye disease causing irreversible vision loss. Retinal image features like OD, optic cup (OC), and neuro retinal rim (NRR) are crucial for disease identification. This work aims to enhance OD detection using multiple segmentation algorithms. The method involves directional matched filtering, vessel detection, and cup boundary assessment for OC segmentation. Machine learning algorithms further aid in glaucoma diagnosis. This method shows promising potential with a solid correlation to ground truth segmentation results.

Chapter 16 revolutionized AI in marketing, providing innovative ways to engage customers. It processes vast data, offering insights for tailored marketing strategies. Social media and placement automation streamlines operations, saving time and enhancing plans. AI-powered chatbots handle basic inquiries, freeing marketers. Predictive analytics use client data to forecast behavior and refine products and services. Embracing AI ensures a competitive edge in the digital landscape, enabling customized, effective marketing tactics. This chapter explores AI's role in marketing, presenting opportunities and challenges. It is a valuable resource for marketing professionals, educators, and students keen on understanding AI's impact in the field.

1

Computational Intelligence Theory: An Orientation Technique

S. Jaisiva[1]*, C. Kumar[2], S. Sakthiya Ram[3], C. Sakthi Gokul Rajan[1] and P. Praveen Kumar[4]

[1]*Electrical and Electronics Engineering, Sri Krishna College of Technology, Coimbatore, Tamil Nadu, India*
[2]*Electrical and Electronics Engineering, Karpagam College of Engineering, Coimbatore, Tamil Nadu, India*
[3]*Electronics and Instrumentation Engineering, Bannari Amman Institute of Technology, Sathyamangalam, Tamil Nadu, India*
[4]*Department of Information Technology, Sri Manakula Vinayagar Engineering College, Pondicherry, India*

Abstract

The ability of a system to change its behavior to reach its objective in a variety of settings is intelligence. In reality, a different definition of computational intelligence (CI) is that it entails real-world adaption in challenging and shifting situations. In other words, it serves as a precise illustration of a notion. Adaptation and computational intelligence are intimately linked concepts. The concept, design, implementation, and advancement of computing paradigms driven by natural and cognitive motivations is known as CI. Evolutionary computation, fuzzy systems, and neural networks have historically been the three major foundations of CI. However, over time, various computing models that were inspired by nature have emerged. Sustainable smart information system, such as the creation of video games and cognitive developmental systems, heavily relies on CI. Deep learning study, especially that on deep convolutional neural networks, has exploded in recent years. Deep learning is currently the main approach for artificial intelligence. Deep learning has become the main technology for AI. In reality, CI is the foundation of some of the most effective AI systems.

**Corresponding author*: jaisiva1990@gmail.com

T. Ananth Kumar, E. Golden Julie, Venkata Raghuveer Burugadda, Abhishek Kumar and Puneet Kumar (eds.) Computational Intelligence: Theory and Applications, (1–24) © 2024 Scrivener Publishing LLC

Keywords: Computational intelligence, artificial intelligence, biological intelligence, neural networks, fuzzy systems, optimization, evolutionary computation

1.1 Computational Intelligence

Intelligence is a trait shared by all decision-makers with a goal. An analysis paradigm known as an artificial neural network (ANN) is loosely framed on the basis of the human brain massively parallel architecture [1]. It replicates a massively parallel, linked computing framework with a large number of very straightforward individual processing components (PEs). The phrases artificial neural network and neural network will now be used equally throughout this chapter. Fuzzies are non-statistical inexactitude and ambiguity in info, as used in this article. The majority of notions used or expressed in the real world are hazy. For instance, the sentence "It's somewhat misty outdoors right now" combines the notions of being pretty and, even before, a long period of time. (One may even contend that the term is ambiguous and inaccurate enough to be hazy.) Fuzzy sets simulate the characteristics of estimation, ambiguity, and inaccuracy. Fuzzy membership values in a fuzzy set represent the membership dimensions (or grades) of the set's components. It will be demonstrated that the fundamental concept of fuzzy set theory is a membership function, which is the same as a fuzzy set [2].

Crossover, mutations, and the survival of the fittest are examples of natural evolutionary phenomena that are incorporated into genetic algorithms, which are search algorithms. They are utilized for categorization as well as optimization more frequently. While genetic algorithms incorporate crossover, evolutionary programming approaches do not. Instead, they depend on mutation and the survival of the fittest. Comparable to genetic algorithms, evolution tactics frequently employ a distinct kind of mutation in addition to using combination to share data across members of population rather than crossover [3]. Computer programs can evolve using a technique called genetic programming. Hierarchical tree topologies are frequently used to manipulate structures. Potential solutions are dispersed throughout the problem space by particles in particle swarm optimization. The issue space's chosen locations where prior fitness values have been high are where the particles are pushed. The term "computational intelligence" refers to a computing-based methodology that gives a system the capability to gain knowledge of novel situations, giving the system the appearance of possessing one or more rational qualities including generalization, discovery, connection, and abstraction. They are frequently made to resemble one or more characteristics of natural intelligence. In the illustration of a neural network paradigm is back-propagation, which presupposes a particular set of characteristics, such as the design and the learning algorithm [4]. A certain collection of options for each characteristic constitutes a paradigm. Introducing a separate paradigm includes putting together a group of characteristics that describe the desired behavior of the CI tool.

There are some words that should only be used with care. One such instance is neural networks, where it is important to be clear if we are taking about analytical tools for artificial neural network wetware. Let us explore the conceptual and technological underpinnings of computational intelligence tools and component approaches after providing the fundamental definitions [5]. We utilize and mention the caveat mentioned before. The creation of algorithmic models to address ever-more-complex issues is a key focus of algorithmic innovation. These clever algorithms are a subset of artificial intelligence, along with deductive reasoning, expert systems, case-based reasoning, and symbolic machine learning systems (AI). AI can be seen as a synthesis of various scientific areas, such as computer science, physiology, philosophy, sociology, and biology, just by looking at the broad range of AI methodologies [6].

Yet what exactly is intelligence? Definitions of intelligence continue to spark heated discussion. Dictionary definitions of intelligence include the capability for cognition and reason, as well as the capacity to perceive, comprehend, and benefit from experience (especially to a high degree). Innovation, ability, awareness, empathy, and instinct are other terms used to characterize characteristics of intelligence.

Can computers think for themselves? Even now, there is more disagreement over this issue than over how to define intelligence. Alan Turing gave this issue a lot of study in the middle of the 20th century. He thought it was possible to build devices that could duplicate the functions of the human brain. Turing firmly felt that a well-designed computer could perform every task that the brain was capable of. His predictions are still prophetic more than fifty years later. Smaller biological neural system components have been successfully modeled, but the complicated task of modeling is an essential component of mankind intelligence and remains unsolved [7].

The Turing test, created by Turing in 1950, is a measurement of computing intelligence. The test involved asking questions of both a person and a machine using a keyboard. The computer might be thought to be smart if the interviewer was unable to tell the computer from the person.

Turing anticipated that by the year 2000, a system will be able to compete with the testing and training of 70% chance. Has his conviction been realized? In order to avoid jumping into yet another argument, the reader is left to choose the solution to this issue. However, the information in this book may help to clarify some aspects of the response [8].

The IEEE Neural Networks Council of 1996 gave a more modern version of artificial intelligence as the research of how to get computers to perform tasks that people are good at. These processes include the AI paradigms that can generalize, synthesize, discover, and connect as well as learn novel contexts. While specific approaches and techniques from various CI paradigms have been effectively used to address issues in the real world, the current trend is to create hybridization of models because no one model is always better than the others. By doing this, we strengthen the areas where each component of the hybrid CI system excels and do away with those where it falls short. Swarm intelligence is a category of the CI concepts, despite the fact that many investigators believe they should only fall within the category of synthetic biology [9].

1.2 Application Fields for Computational Intelligence

There are applications for which every computational intelligence element technique is particularly well suited. A particular problem might be solvable by either a neural network or a fuzzy system, but at varying standards of achievement; therefore, consider the fact that main applications may intersect. It might not even be typical of all the important application fields. It is intended to give some insight into the variety of issues that have been addressed by using CI's component techniques.

1.2.1 Neural Networks

Generally speaking, neural networks are best suited for five types of applications. The first three have a connection.

1.2.1.1 Classification [10]

This section examines which of a number of predefined classes most accurately captures an input sequence. Usually, there are not many classes compared to the quantity of inputs. One illustration determines whether a specific EEG data section represents an epileptiform spike waveform. Another type of clustering is the creation of nonlinear mappings between high-dimensional spaces by neural networks. This application area includes several forms of video image processing (such as tumor diagnosis).

1.2.1.2 Clustering or Compression

Although categorization is a part of this field, compression algorithm can also be used to describe it. Think of natural language processing as an example of how the complexity of a source is considerably decreased. Lowering the number of bits necessary to represent a data block within a specific allowed error range is another. In other words, less bytes than in the source information can be used to reproduce the original block of data within the allowed mistake.

1.2.1.3 Generation of Sequences or Patterns

In contrast to the first three, this fourth area does not entail any classification. Using examples as training data, a network creates these patterns [11]. At an instant, to duplicate a particular kind of harmonious progression, the network may be able to create "original" renditions of that style of music. Another option is to train a neural network to emulate or model anything. There may not be any "correct" solutions because the system being replicated has inherent unpredictability, yet the system can perhaps be quantitatively defined. These statistical characteristics can then be incorporated into the network simulation.

1.2.1.4 Control Systems

Among the quickest-evolving application areas for neural networks is control systems. It is being used extensively for a number of reasons. An ANN-based control system can first handle all sets of nonlinear effects. (An approximate linearity of the system is not required.) Second, when building the control system, the chaotic system can be modeled using a network. Third, compared to other, more conventional methods, developing a neural network control system often takes a lot less time. For each of the five uses, there appear to be more and more emerging every day. Some implementations are unique to a field of study [12]. EEG waveform classification and appendicitis diagnosis are two examples of fields such as medicine. Neural networks are used in accounting and commerce to process loan applications from financing companies and to trade options on commodity futures contracts. Neural networks are able to govern the locations of several cars on an interstate at once in the automotive sector.

1.2.1.5 Evolutionary Computation

Optimization and categorization are the two basic applications of evolutionary algorithms. Since optimization is the subject of the majority of engineering disciplines for evolutionary computation, optimization is the main topic of discussion in this theme.

1.2.2 Fuzzy Logic

Numerous engineering fields, including robotics and control, modeling, and geotechnical sciences, use fuzzy logic in a variety of applications. Medicine, management, decision analysis, and computer science are further application fields. Similar to neural networks, new applications pop up practically every day. Fuzzy expert networks and adaptive logic are two of the key application domains [13].

1.2.2.1 Fuzzy Control Systems

Fuzzy control systems have been used in traffic signal circuits, household appliances, video cameras, metro systems, cement kilns, and a number of automotive subsystems, along with the gearbox and emergency systems. The circuitry within a video camera that stabilizes the image despite the user's shaky hand placement is one technology that many people are familiar with. Fuzzy expert systems have been used in a variety of fields, including corporate strategy selection, industrial automation, medical diagnosis, planning, and currency trading.

1.2.2.2 Fuzzy Systems

According to conventional set theory, a component may either be a member of a set or it cannot. Similar restrictions apply to the results of an implicit learning procedure in binary-valued logic, which calls for model parameters to be either 0 or 1. Unfortunately, human logic is rarely this precise. Normally, there is a level of ambiguity in both our perceptions and thinking [14].

Probabilistic thinking is made possible by fuzzy sets and fuzzy logic. When using fuzzy sets, an element can be quite assured that it conforms to a range. Fuzzy logic enables inference of actual revelations from these ambiguous facts, each of which has a degree of certainty attached to it. In a way, rational thinking can be modeled using fuzzy sets and reasoning.

Fuzzy systems have been effectively used to regulate traffic lights, lifts, cog shifting and brake mechanisms in automobiles, and many other systems.

1.2.2.3 Behavioral Motivations for Fuzzy Logic

Fuzzy systems are lacking a physiological rationale or foundation at the subcellular and cellular levels. It manifests itself in the way the creature behaves, or in how the creature engages with its surroundings. The methodologies before have a strong biological foundation, but fuzzy logic mostly works with uncertainty and vagueness. We do not exist in a universe of truth and untruth, ones and zeros, black and white, or other objective facts. Our emotions, interactions, and perceptions almost always contain a significant amount of unpredictability [15].

There are two primary categories of ambiguity. One is quantitative and is based on the probabilistic laws. The other kind of uncertainty is nonstatistical and relies on ambiguity, inaccuracy, or both. Fuzziness is a term used to describe nonprobability unpredictability. Fuzzy logic's capacity to effectively collect and manage these hazy, disorganized thoughts is one of its key characteristics.

A system's essential characteristic is fuzziness. By inspection or measurement, it is neither changed nor resolved. The representation of a complicated system can be made more tractable to analysis by accounting for some unpredictability. Thus, fuzzy logic offers a structure for the definition, description, and analysis of descriptive unpredictability. According to him, fuzziness results from a verbal lack of precision [16].

1.3 Computational Intelligence Paradigms

Artificial neural networks (NN), evolutionary computation (EC), swarm intelligence (SI), artificial immune systems (AIS), and fuzzy systems are the five basic paradigms that computational intelligence (CI) takes into account (FS). Figure 1.1 illustrates how deterministic methods are typically combined with CI approaches in addition to CI paradigms. The arrows show how different paradigm approaches can be merged to create architectures. Every CI paradigm has biochemical pathways at its foundation.

1.3.1 Artificial Neural Networks

A sophisticated, chaotic, and simultaneous computer is the nervous system. Even if events happen in the range of nanoseconds for semiconductor

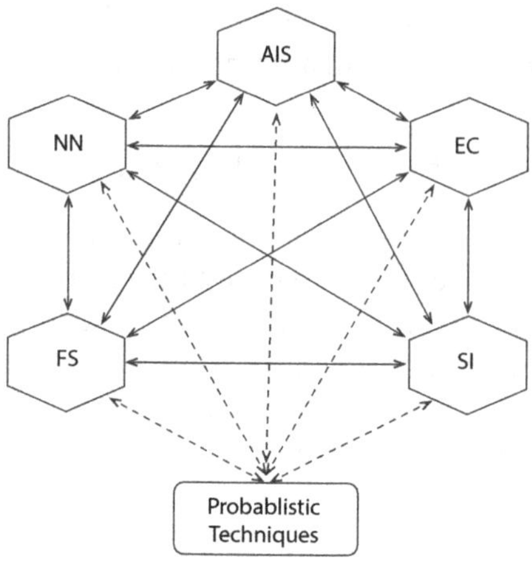

Figure 1.1 Computational intelligence paradigms.

gates and milliseconds for brain systems, it can accomplish tasks like analytical thinking, vision, and motor control much more quickly than any computer. Investigation into algorithmic modeling of biological brain systems, also known as artificial neural networks, was stimulated by these traits as well as others like the capacity to learn, memorize, and still generalize (NN) [17].

The cerebral cortex is thought to contain 60 trillion interconnections and between 10 and 500 billion axons. Each of the 1000 primary modules that make up the arrangement of the neurons has about 500 neural networks. The most successful artificial neural networks (NNs) used in neural modeling today are tiny, task-specific NNs. As long as you are limited by the limits of current processing capacity and memory size, challenges are handled rather feasible with reasonable NNs. Conversely, the intellect has the capacity to solve many issues at once by utilizing different brain regions.

Neurons, often known as nerve cells, are the fundamental components of biological brain networks. A neuron comprises of an axon, dendrites, and the cell body as represented in Figure 1.2. Neurons are incredibly linked, with connections often occurring in between axon and dendrite of two different neurons. The term "synapse" refers to this link. From the synapses, signals travel to the axon and cell body, from where they spread to all associated filaments. When a nerve cell fires, a signal travels to the axon of the unit. A pulse can be either excited or inhibited by a cell. The following Figure 1.3 shows the representation of an artificial neuron, which

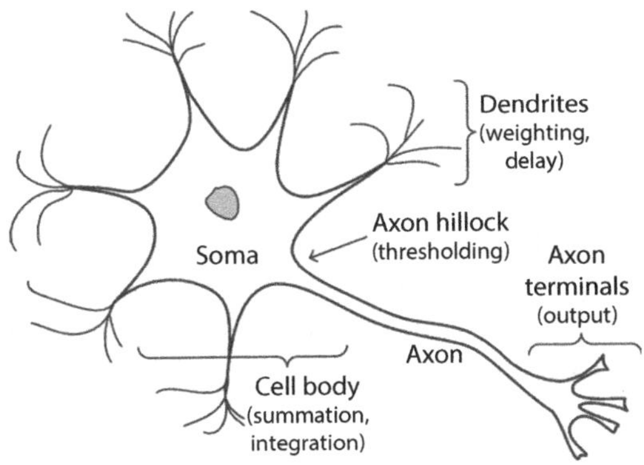

Figure 1.2 A biological neuron.

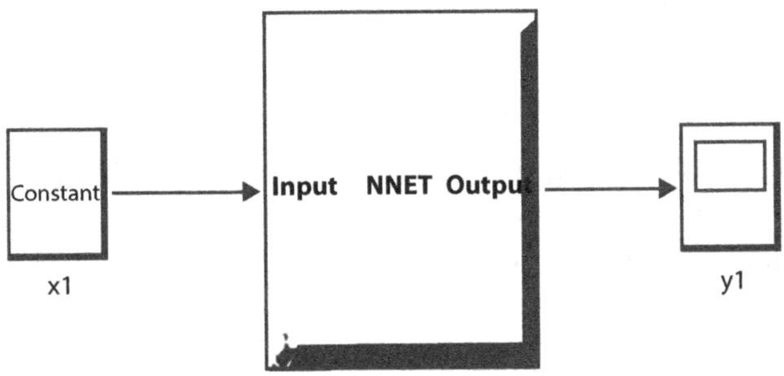

Figure 1.3 An artificial neuron.

comprises of three different layers namely as input layer, middle layer and an output layer.

Stacked networks of neural networks make up an artificial neural network (ANN). All the feasible ones are response linkages to earlier layers. Figure 1.4 shows an illustration of a typical NN construction.

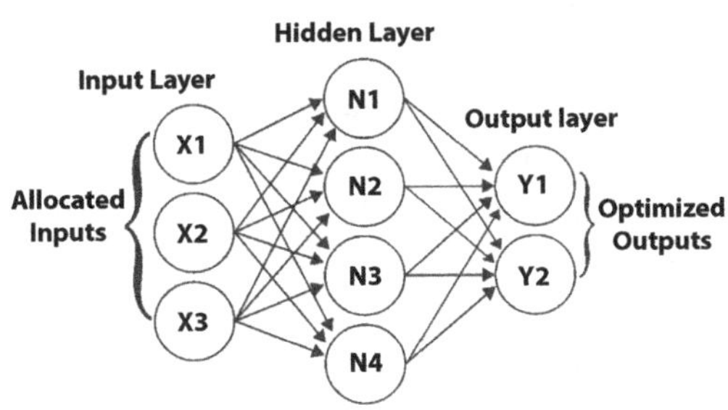

Figure 1.4 Structure of ANN.

There have been numerous distinct NN types produced:

- The Hopfield system is an example of a single-layered NN.
- Multilayer feedforward NNs, such as conventional backpropagation.
- Functioning link and number of units networks are examples of deep neural NNs.
- Controlled and uncontrolled NNs are integrated to each other with similar operations.

These NN types have been applied to a variety of tasks, such as diagnostic techniques, natural language processing, data analysis, music composition, computer graphics, face recognition, strategy development, and decompression, among others.

1.3.2 Evolutionary Computation (EC)

The goal of EC is to replicate ordinary evolutionary changes, where the principle of the strongest surviving species dictates that the weak must perish. In gradual evolution, procreation is the means of ensuring survival. Offspring with two parents (or more, in rare cases) carry the genetic information of all their parents, presumably inheriting the greatest traits from each. People who inherit negative traits are feeble and fail in their attempts to stay alive. This is skillfully demonstrated in some living species, whereby a particularly strong individual succeeds in obtaining more food, becomes stronger, and ultimately drives its siblings off the nest where they will perish [18].

The community of humans used by evolutionary algorithms is known as the chromosomal populace. The traits of a person in a group are determined by a gene. A gene is used to describe each trait. An allele is a gene's variation in value. Individuals strive to create offspring within each cycle. The most likely candidates to multiply are those with the best chances of survival. Crossover is the process of creating offspring by fusing elements of the parents. Every member of the population has the potential to experience mutation, which changes some of the chromosome allele. An individual's sustenance strength is calculated using a fitness function that represents the goals and limitations of the issue at hand. Individuals may be eliminated after each cycle or they may live to breed another time.

Evolutionary algorithms (EAs) have been created in several classes, including the following:

- Genetic algorithms that simulate the evolution of DNA.
- Programming that is based on evolutionary development and simulates adaptive behavior.
- Evolutionary approaches that are focused on simulating the variables involved in the activation that regulates variation.
- Differential evolution, which differs in its generation method and is comparable to genetic algorithms.
- Cultural evolution, which simulates how a society's demographic changes over time and how this affects how people's phenotypes and genetics evolve.
- Co-evolution, in which formerly "stupid" people develop the traits they need to exist by cooperating or competing among themselves.

There have also been additional spontaneous evolution-related aspects modeled, for instance, dispersed (island) learning algorithm and extinction event, which maintain various populations while allowing genetic evolution to occur in each group. Additionally, factors like population movements are modeled. The improvement of evolutionary approaches has also benefited from the modeling of parasitic behavior. In this instance, people are infected with parasites. Those who are too frail pass away.

Information extraction is one of the examples of real-world scenarios where evolutionary programming has been effectively employed.

1.3.3 Optimization Method

The effectiveness of NNs is strongly influenced by the optimization technique used to compute weight adjustments. GD is a very well-liked optimization technique; however, it suffers from delayed convergence and is vulnerable to local minima. To solve these issues, GD has been improved, for instance, by including the acceleration term. Additionally, weight updates have been calculated using the objective function's second-order derivatives. Using global optimization strategies, such as optimization, in place of local optimization algorithms is another way to enhance NN training.

1.3.3.1 Optimization

The regulation of gas pipeline transmission was one of the earliest uses of genetic algorithms that gained popularity. Multiple-fault detection, robot track identification, itinerary optimization, conformational DNA analysis constitute some of the applications of evolutionary algorithms. The emergence of neural networks is one of the computational intelligence approaches that are covered, together with other classification techniques, such as classifier systems for high-level semantic networks and mandated machine learning systems, which are used to learn regulation of pipeline processes.

1.4 Architecture Assortment

In accordance with axioms, the network with the fewest weights will, on aggregate, have the best generalization ability if multiple networks match the training set equally well. A network with an excessive number of free components may be able to accurately fit the noise present in training data as well as memorize the learning algorithm, which would result in poor generalization. Thus, overfitting can be avoided by shrinking the network by getting rid of particular weights. Therefore, the goal is to strike a compromise between the network's intricacy and the genuine function. Architecture picking is the term used to describe this procedure. To choose the best architecture, a number of strategies, including regularization, network building, and trimming, have been devised.

Identifying the ideal structure is also considered to be part of training, in addition to determining the ideal weight values. The recognition for good is not often immediately apparent, though. A search of all feasible structures is necessary to identify the absolute optimum architecture. Meta-heuristic algorithms are employed to condense the search area. Choosing the model with the least generalization error as determined by the generalized prediction error or the network information criterion is a straightforward procedure that involves training several networks with various architectural designs.

To lessen the likelihood that the ideal design will not be discovered, several designs must be evaluated as part of this costly strategy. Alternately, the NN design can be improved through trial and error. The efficiency of a chosen structure is assessed. An alternative structure is chosen in the event that the performance is unacceptably poor. This procedure is repeated until an architecture is identified that generates an overfitting that is reasonable.

Three forms of alternative sampling techniques for design are presented:

i. ***Regularization:*** The mathematical formulation that must be minimized is given a penalty term as part of the regularization process for neural networks. A number of penalty phrases have been created to dynamically lower bandwidth throughout training. Although it is an easy system to use, it is lacking in terms of penalizing large weights equally to tiny weights. In their more complex soft scale factor method, Nowlan and Hinton combined many different Rayleigh distributions to represent the distribution of weight values. Small masses are caused by narrow Gaussians, and big weights are caused by broad Gaussians.

ii. ***Growing:*** When the network is stuck at a minimum during development, hidden units are progressively added by network development techniques. An approximation model of a portion of the training set is created by a tiny network. To prevent resuming the function of the sampling techniques, training is essential to the success of development algorithms. Ad hoc treatment of these problems could lead to overfitting and longer training sessions.

iii. ***Network Pruning:*** With an enormous network as a starting point, pruning techniques for neural networks eliminate extraneous connection weights. All three types of network parameters—individual weights, hidden units, and input units—are taken into consideration for elimination. Based on metric, the choice to reduce a network property is made. Each parameter's significance is calculated, and a pruning heuristic is employed to determine whether or not a variable is deemed an irrelevant system that can converge quite quickly with a big starting design.

The goal of every algorithm for selecting an architecture is to perform the nature of the work. Smaller networks have the following benefits in enhancing generalization benefits and reducing the fitting problem. The number of training patterns necessary to achieve a specific generalization capability depends on the generalization restrictions and the network design. Therefore, mesh nodes require fewer training examples. Additionally, a set of more basic principles can more readily characterize the information that is contained in subnetworks. Pruning networks result in fewer rules being derived from local networks or from bigger networks. Additionally, it is simpler to visualize the function of each concealed unit in subnets. Choice threshold recognition methods' difficulty has also decreased. Due to the small test set sizes, NNs are frequently hampered by large volatility. By creating bias with network architectural reduction, this variation is decreased.

Compact systems are biased because there are fewer units that can match the information because the hypothesis space is narrower.

1.4.1 Swarm Intelligence

The study of hives or swarms of social beings is where swarm intelligence (SI) got its start. Very effective optimization and clustering algorithms were developed as a result of research into the behavior of creatures in swarming. The creation of the particle swarm optimization algorithm, for instance, was inspired by simulated investigations of the elegant but erratic ballet of bird flocks, while the creation of optimizing ant colonies methods was inspired by research on the gathering habits of ants. In order to position the particles toward an ideal solution, a particle must tend to make use of both its own perfect situation and the best positions of its neighbors. The result is that particles "fly" toward an ideal state while still looking in many different directions for the best available answer. Each particle's effectiveness (i.e., its "closeness" to the global minimum) is evaluated using a predetermined fitness value that is connected to the issue at hand.

Numerous ant colony studies have been influenced by the modeling of ant pheromone deposition in their pursuit of the quickest routes to feedstuffs. Ant colony optimization is also used to solve the multi-objective issue, color graphs, optimize routing in network technologies, and schedule tasks. Algorithms for clustering and structural optimization were created as a result of research into the construction of ant and bee nests.

1.4.2 Artificial Immune Systems

Impressive pattern recognition skills are utilized by the natural immune system (NIS) to discriminate between body-belonging particles and external particles that are ingested. The NIS's adaptive character is on display as it interacts with antigens, learning the antigen's composition to respond to it more quickly.

There are four types of the NIS that have been studied:

- According to the traditional understanding of the immune system, cytokines generated in the lymphoid organs are used to discriminate between individuality. These cells acquire the ability to attach to an antigen.
- The replication process used by an active B-cell to create antibodies under the search and optimization paradigm. The clones that are created are likewise altered.

- The danger theory, which postulates that the immune system can tell a risky antigen apart from a non-threatening one.
- Network theory, where a system of B-cells is presumptively formed. A B-cell reacts to an antigen that is associated with the system and gets active.

An artificial immune system (AIS) is primarily used to address information processing issues, carry out classifiers, and aggregate datasets. An AIS simulates some of the characteristics of a NIS. A detection system, including fraud and software malware, is one of the key applications for AISs.

1.5 Myths About Computational Intelligence

There are some misconceptions about computational intelligence. First, contrary to what some private vendors claim, using CI technologies does not require a supercomputer, a large number of money, or a multidisciplinary team in order to get results. It is not necessary to have a supercomputer or a parallel processing device in order to use CI technologies effectively. The hardware foundation for the majority of operational and interface initiatives is a computer. Therefore, issues that would ordinarily be impractical to tackle can be handled using very simple hardware and software techniques. Some issues can be tackled using machine learning technologies that cannot be solved by conventional methods.

The idea that CI tools can handle the majority of issues by themselves is a misconception as well. They frequently are not suitable for issues needing exact computations. For instance, it is improbable that the neural network is going to be adequately balanced. The claim that artificial neural networks may be used without any scripting is another one that falls under the category of largely myth. This is, at best, deceptive. The training of a neural net is not merely asserting designs; rather, it trains and runs on incoming data and is in accordance with a set of rules that update the weights connecting the processing units or nodes.

However, computing is necessary in the reality of neural network implementations to move from the specification of the problem to a solution. The need for rebooting is greatly reduced by neural network technologies. Once the issue has been identified, it is not uncommon to reuse the network code multiple times while adjusting to the network real-time settings for data preparation.

In addition, it is truly the case that computational intelligence techniques like neural networks can be crucial in solving a variety of types of difficulties that are challenging or difficult to resolve using currently available methods. Most of the code is often used during filtering and other number crunching methods to create pattern files for presentation to the network. Some other substantial portion is frequently taken up by interpreting and displaying the results. Another misconception concerning implementations of neural networks and soft computing is that you need to comprehend neural biology or biological genetics in order to comprehend them.

Neural network and evolutionary computation methods can actually be viewed as a suite of features in the CI analytics arsenal by the majority of architects and computer scientists. Additionally, there is a strong case to be made for the idea that neural networks are technically related to analog technology in the same way that they are related to neurology. It is a misconception that fuzzy logic is genuinely fuzzy or inaccurate. Case formulation for process variables serve as the inputs to a fuzzy system. Similar to sharp outcomes, information from a fuzzy system can, for example, be used as accurate inputs to control systems.

The idea that fuzzy logic is only an additional form of probabilities is another misconception about it. It is not. Fuzzy logic is related to nonstatistical uncertainty, whereas likelihood deals with empirical unpredictability. The idea that optimization occurs is fiction, to sum up. Although I'm saying this somewhat jokingly, it is vital to understand how infrequently a real-world CI implementation finds the complete best of everything. If the maximum is known, a decision to arrive inside a specific area of it is supported. If there are several optima, the design involves the process of locating the ideal one or, in that case, all of the multiple optima.

1.6 Supervised Learning in Computational Intelligence

All species might be motivated by competence. The quality of life will not increase if functionality is not improved. According to this, when designing an ANN, functionality is the most crucial factor to take into account. The effectiveness of an ANN is evaluated not only by the steadiness attained by the system, but also by factors like computational complexity and convergence properties. These metrics, along with others that evaluate the effectiveness, specifically mention supervised nodes. Numerous aspects that affect connection speeds must be carefully taken into account while designing NNs for optimum level. The neural network-based research enables one to design the system mostly carried out by adhering to the rules of the spontaneous impressions of the experienced systems. It was important to better comprehend how NNs functioned and to open the "black box" thanks to the numerous theoretical analyses of NNs that have been conducted. These discoveries aided in the development of more effective NNs.

1.6.1 Performance Measures

Complexity, accuracy, and convergence are the three categories under which NN evaluation metrics are presented in this section.

1.6.1.1 Accuracy

A crucial component of neural network learning is generalization. The eventual aim of NN acquisition is to create a learning with minimal generalization error. For multiclass classification, an additional error measure is necessary because the MSE is not a reliable indicator of accuracy on its own. The proportion of successfully categorized patterns is used as an efficiency indicator for classification tasks. The structure may be accurate across the quantity of right categories despite the somewhat high results, which is why the MSE is not an appropriate measure.

Performance of the model is a crucial component of NN efficiency. The NN memorizes the learning algorithm when a supervised learning is overfit, which impairs its capacity to generalize. That is, overfit NNs are unable to forecast accurate results for large datasets that were not visible during learning. The parameters, as a result, obtain too many unimportant input components and hidden units. The learning algorithm, as well as the noise in the learning algorithm of the NN, is taught for an excessively long time.

To identify the moment of overfitting, estimates of generalization error throughout retraining might be used. Studies of training and generalization profiles led to the development of the most straightforward method for determining data of overfitting. A typical representation of learning and extension errors as a consequence of training iteration is shown in Figure 1.5. Beginning with the first training session, both the training and generalization defects start to decline—typically dramatically. There is a moment, especially for large NNs, where the learning rate continues to go down while the generalization error begins to go up. As soon as a generalization mistake increases, learning should end.

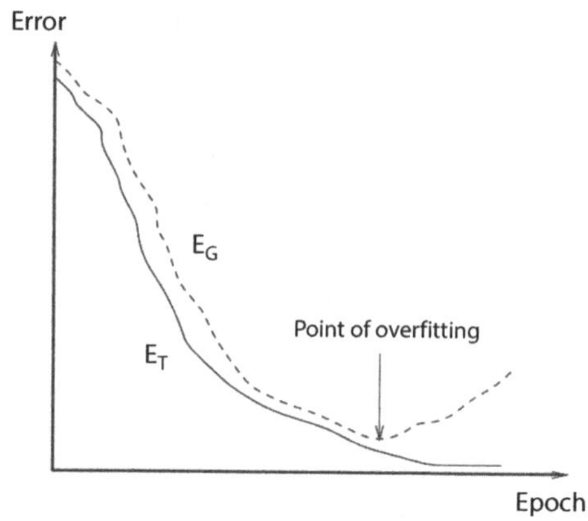

Figure 1.5 Illustration of overfitting.

When the learning rate and the error diverge, overfitting is present because the prediction error grows while the learning rate decreases. The learning rate should be higher than unity for categorization situations where the proportion of correctly categorized sequences is used as a gauge of performance. It is significant to highlight that measuring the accuracy of an NN solely on the basis of training error is insufficient. These two mistakes must be taken into account.

1.6.1.2 Complexity

1. **The network architecture:** This factor directly affects how complicated an NN is to compute. The broader the structure, the more teaching parameters are required for each pattern display required to anticipate outcomes of the learning rate.
2. **The size of the training set:** More designs are made available for the learning rate of the system. As a result, learned computations are done overall per epoch.
3. **Complexity of the optimization method:** To enhance the accuracy and convergence properties of NNs, numerous complexes that focus on the key have been devised. However, the intricacy comes at the expense of more difficult computations to calculate weight adjustments. The amount of training time required to reach a certain training or generalization error is typically expressed in terms of the number of epochs. The calculation time is typically not

a reliable indicator of training time or computing cost when comparing various learning techniques.

1.6.1.3 Convergence

The capacity of the network to converge to predetermined erroneous levels can be used to explain the convergence characteristics of an NN. The structure accomplished in attaining a certain error is used to represent a network's capacity to converge to that mistake. Although this is an empirical technique, several network topologies have undergone comprehensive theoretical research.

1.6.2 Performance Factors

This section examines a variety of factors that affect how well-directed NNs function. Learning parameters, data manipulation architectural choice, and optimization techniques are some of these components.

1.6.2.1 Data Preparation

The collection and processing of information into an appropriate form for the NN is a crucial task in using an NN to resolve practical issues. Making a decision about the endpoints is the initial stage. Inputs that are absolutely relevant should be included, and the NN can determine which inputs are irrelevant on their own. The data must next be processed in order to manage missing information, convert quasi data to numerical information, and identify redundant data.

1.6.2.2 Scaling and Normalization

The scaling model parameters are not required, and efficiency can be enhanced by scaling inputs. Take the backpropagation algorithm, for instance. The dynamic region that corresponds to the regions of input values produces a large set of output, according to straightforward complex equations. Weight adjustments are barely impacted by values close to the logistic function's exponential endpoints. Changes in these values have a very slight impact on the output. Additionally, weight upgrades are roughly zero since variations close to the asymptotes are approximately zero.

1.6.2.3 *Learning Rate and Momentum*

The learning rate and the duration of NN adaptation are directly inversely related. The momentum element that is introduced to the weight updates with regard to probabilistic GD also aims to speed up resolution.

1.6.2.4 *Learning Rate*

The magnitude of each movement toward the optimum of the goal functional is controlled by the learning algorithm. When learning rates are too low, weight modifications are also too low. The number of learning repetitions needed to reach a local minimum then increases. Early resolution will be quick, but ultimately the process will fluctuate without achieving the minima. Additionally, a training algorithm that is excessively high may result in "jumping" over a good local minimum and moving in the opposite direction of a poor local minima. There is no way to leave the first minima and travel to the second, better lowest one; thus, the search path descends it. The exploration direction is, of course, dependent on the beginning point. The NN will reach the second beginning point if it is used.

For training, a number of algorithms have been created to continuously change the learning algorithm. Making the assumption that each component learns at varying rates is one of the easiest strategies. The position where the inaccuracy has already been incremented is the same as the direction in which it reduces at these weight fluctuations. The orientation for which the inaccuracy reduction is governed by model displays, rather than just the most recent alteration, is typically taken into account. An approach is to progressively decrease a greater cognitive rate to a low value using an ablation strategy. This permits huge first steps but guarantees simple actions across the area.

1.6.2.5 *Noise Injection*

Controlled injection of noise aids in the creation of novel training sets for situations with a finite set of labeled training sequences. It can be expected that the modifications in the multilayer perceptron that come from sampling noise will have no meaningful effects. Additionally, the level process is convolutionally smoothed as a consequence of the channel noise, which shortens training time and improves accuracy. The creation of novel training patterns for higher results is realized through the insertion of noise at nonlinear decision.

1.7 Training Set Manipulation

In order to manage the sequence in which images are given for learning, the training time and accuracy were both improved as a result of these strategies. The approach called partial demonstration, which divides the original training set into two training sets, provides a brief review of similar training dataset manipulating strategies. The first group features familiar designs, whereas the second batch is made up of perplexing patterns. The authors use the terms "general pattern" and "perplexing pattern" to describe patterns that are distant from nonlinear decision and patterns that are close to a border. During training, the two training sets are made once. The creation of these training sets presupposes understanding of the topic, namely, the location of the grid points in the embedding space.

1.8 Conclusion

The computational intelligence technique has the issue of being inappropriate for specific tasks due to the issue dependence of the complexity measure of training data. Next, there are progressive training techniques, such as incremental increased complexity training and cumulative subgroup development. In incremental subset training, the initial subgroup is chosen at random. Random subsets from the initial training set are mixed with the learning subset itself during learning. The difficulty of adding multiple subsets is preserved in an incremental increased complexity training method, but retraining is not conducted on every single complication subset. The alternative is to reduce each difficulty grouping into more manageable randomized subgroups.

References

1. P.J. Angeline. Adaptive and Self-Adaptive Evolutionary Computation. In M. Palaniswami and Y. Attikiouzel, editors, *Computational Intelligence: A Dynamic Systems Perspective*, pages 152–163, 1995.
2. R.C. Eberhart, P.K. Simpson, and R.W. Dobbins. *Computational Intelligence PC Tools*. Academic Press Professional, first edition, 1996.
3.. T. Back and U. Hammel. Evolution Strategies Applied to Perturbed Objective Functions. In *IEEE World Congress on Computational Intelligence, Proceedings of the IEEE Conference on Evolutionary Computation*, volume 1, pages 40–45, 1994.

4. Kumar Chandrasekaran, Jaisiva Selvaraj, Felix Joseph Xavier and Prabaakaran Kandasamy, "Artificial Neural Network Integrated with Bio-Inspired approach for Optimal VAr Management and Voltage Profile Enhancement in Grid System", *Energy Sources Part A*, vol. 43, no.21, pp. 2838-2859,2021.
5. Kumar, T. Deva, TS Arun Samuel, and T. Ananth Kumar. "Transforming Green Cities with IoT: A Design Perspective." In *Handbook of Green Engineering Technologies for Sustainable Smart Cities*, pp. 17-35. CRC Press, 2021.
6. J-P. Chiou and F-S. Wang. A Hybrid Method of Differential Evolution with Application to Optimal Control Problems of A Bioprocess System. In *IEEE World Congress on Computational Intelligence, Proceedings of the IEEE International Conference on Evolutionary Computation*, pages 627–632, 1998.
7. C-J. Chung and R.G. Reynolds. A Testbed for Solving Optimization Problems using Cultural Algorithms. In L.J Fogel, P.J. Angeline, and T. B¨ack, editors, *Proceedings of the Fifth Annual Conference on Evolutionary Programming*, pages 225–236, Cambridge, M.A., 1996. MIT Press.
8. D. Cohn and G. Tesauro. Can Neural Networks do Better than the Vapnik-Chervonenkis Bounds? In R. Lippmann, J. Moody, and D.S. Touretzky, editors, *Adv. Neural Inf. Process. Syst.*, volume 3, pages 911–917, 1991.
9. J. Conradie and A.P. Engelbrecht. Training Bao Game-Playing Agents using Coevolutionary Particle Swarm Optimization. In *Proceedings of the IEEE Symposium on Computational Intelligence in Games*, pages 67–74, 2006.
10. Akhatov, A., I. Himmatov, Christo Ananth, and T. Ananth Kumar. "System of Persons Identification Based on Human Characteristics." In *International Conference on Data Management, Analytics & Innovation*, pp. 1029-1046. Singapore: Springer Nature Singapore, 2023.
11. Kumar, Abhishek, Swarn Avinash Kumar, Vishal Dutt, S. Shitharth, and Esha Tripathi. "IoT based arrhythmia classification using the enhanced hunt optimization-based deep learning." *Expert Syst.* (2023): e13298.
12. R. Fletcher. *Practical Methods of Optimization*. John Wiley & Sons, 1987.
13. J.E. Dennis and R.B. Schnabel. *Numerical Methods for Unconstrained Optimization and Nonlinear Equations*. Prentice-Hall, 1983.
14. Srivastav, Arun Lal, Markandeya, Naveen Patel, Mayank Pandey, Ashutosh Kumar Pandey, Ashutosh Kumar Dubey, Abhishek Kumar, Abhishek Kumar Bhardwaj, and Vinod Kumar Chaudhary. "Concepts of circular economy for sustainable management of electronic wastes: challenges and management options." *Environ. Sci. Pollut. Res.*, 30, no. 17 (2023): 48654-48675.
15. Kumar Chandrasekaran, Jaisiva Selvaraj, Clement Raj Amaladoss and Logeshwari Veerapan, 'Hybrid renewable energy based smart grid system for reactive power management and voltage profile enhancement using artificial neural network', *Energy Sources Part A*, vol. 43, no.19, pp. 2419-2442, 2021.
16. R. Durbin and D.E. Rumelhart. Product Units: A Computationally Powerful and Biologically Plausible Extension to Backpropagation Networks. *Neural Comput.*, 1:133–142, 1989.

17. W. Durham. *Co-Evolution: Genes, Culture and Human Diversity*. Stanford University Press, 1994.
18. Burri, Srinivasa Rao, Sachin Ahuja, Abhishek Kumar, and Anupam Baliyan. "Exploring the Effectiveness of Optimized Convolutional Neural Network in Transfer Learning for Image Classification: A Practical Approach." In *2023 International Conference on Advancement in Computation & Computer Technologies (InCACCT)*, pp. 598-602. IEEE, 2023.

2

Nature-Inspired Algorithms for Computational Intelligence Theory—A State-of-the-Art Review

B. Akoramurthy*, K. Dhivya and B. Surendiran

Department of CSE, National Institute of Technology Puducherry, Karaikal, India

Abstract
The history of computational intelligence can be traced back to several decades ago. Several technologies such as evolutionary computation, neural networks, and fuzzy systems were fused together to be called CI technologies. Nature-inspired algorithms, which are more adaptable and effective at addressing optimization issues, have changed over time. Many different types of nature-inspired algorithms are now being developed, and the majority of them are focused on self-organizing communities of nature and optimization issues. This article gives a state-of-the-art assessment of a few popular optimization techniques. Its key traits have been examined and compared to other established methods like gradient-based and gradient-free algorithms. Additionally, certain unresolved issues with optimization and metaheuristics methods were identified, which should be helpful for further work.

***Keywords*:** Genetic algorithms, optimization, nature-inspired computing, gradient based algorithms, algorithmic features, open recommendations

2.1 Introduction

Solving real-life problems by using traditional methods of computing is not an easy task because the problems may not be properly defined in nature, with their uncertainty and complexity level. Sometimes, the complexity of

**Corresponding author*: akor.theanchor@gmail.com

T. Ananth Kumar, E. Golden Julie, Venkata Raghuveer Burugadda, Abhishek Kumar and Puneet Kumar (eds.) Computational Intelligence: Theory and Applications, (25–52) © 2024 Scrivener Publishing LLC

the problem may not be an issue to deal with, but the feasibility of converting the real-world problems into computer-understandable format may be a hindrance. To deal with such a problem, the opposite or hard side of conventional computing is required, which is known as computational intelligence or soft computing. Having said that, it is ever needed to find out the optimal solutions to various real-time problems in the range of any complex level problem with defined constraints. To achieve an optimal solution, we need a technique called optimization, which is important in many applications like business planning, engineering design, and artificial intelligence. Its major purpose is to maximize and minimize anything. For any work, the cost of the product or process, overall time taken, waste, energy consumption, and impact on the environment or surroundings should be minimized. Maximization includes the performance, profits, efficiency, outputs, and sustainability of the project. In a real-time scenario, the availability of time, human resources, or any other physical resources and money are limited constraints, which makes us unable to find the optimum solution for any range of constraints for real-time problems.

For an optimum solution, one must need the best model or architecture, which, in turn, needs a mathematical way of solving things. As real-time problems are much more complex to represent, it is always necessary to construe the information about the problem and simulate the various behaviors of the objects or elements in the problem that help to produce the optimal solution. Several areas, such as machine learning [36], deep learning [17], business process management [47], operation research, and many industrial applications, demand a mathematical way of representing the problem.

In order to compare and evaluate the various design templates, it is important to decide the function constraints, whether they should be maximized or minimized. The function that has to be maximized or minimized is called the cost-objective function (CO), or simply criterion. The problem solved here is called an optimization problem [56]. Any optimization problem will have one or more optimal solutions, which is represented as OP+, where, with constraint, maximization or minimization can be done for the objective function.

Having said that, the modeling or formulation of objective functions takes more time for certain problems like large-scale business planning, aerodynamic problems, machine learning, scheduling problems, network design and flow, drug designing, and many more. To solve such levels of complex problems, better algorithms are needed to fit in the space. These algorithms are specifically called optimization algorithms. Along with these algorithms, we need erudite tools for optimization as most real-time problems are not in the form of linearity with respect to the definition of objective functions.

It is not possible to achieve optimal solutions by deploying brute force methods to any problem, though we are powered by modern computers. Thus, this shows that algorithms are very important to almost all real-time applications. There has been an emergence of numerous algorithms from traditional algorithms, which are more effective and efficient in nature. Additionally, there has been a significant increase from the dawn of the century to the present, and this article will present a synopsis of current advancements in the field of metaheuristics algorithms, with a focus on optimization algorithms.

2.2 Related Works

Nature has served as the biggest foundation of motivation and or starting point for several scholars in a multitude of ways. At present, most brand-new algorithms are nature activities based, and that is the way it was created based on the inspiration. Based on the quantity of information and the number of substitute or alternate sources we want to employ, we may still categorize things inversely even when the stimulus's foundation is tinted. For the sake of brevity, we will be holding on to most progressive fields such as biochemistry or social sciences.

With that said, nature serves as the primary muse, to use the broadest possible definition. As a result, it is possible to classify practically all new algorithms as being nature-inspired [1]. The large proportion of algorithms that draw inspiration from nature are built on a few effective traits of natural systems. Accordingly, natural science, for sure, accounts for the majority of metaheuristics algorithms [9, 26]. A unique bundle or package of bio-inspired algorithms was created by taking spur from nature's self-organized systems. Consequently [31, 33, 34, 41], swarm-intelligence-based algorithms may be used to describe some bioinspired algorithms. In fact, nature's self-organized systems-based processes are among the largely applied. Firefly method [5, 23, 37, 40], ant colony optimization [7], cuckoo search [19, 42, 55], the bat algorithm [14, 15, 39, 41, 51], and the particle swarm optimization [16, 22] are all good examples.

It goes without saying that not all algorithms are derived from biological systems. The development of many algorithms has drawn inspiration from far and few processes of nature [29]. They can even be influenced on music in certain cases [13]. We shall swiftly arrange all algorithms into various groups in the future portions of the research, although this is not asserted as the sole group. This is an admirable effort to deliver sources that are appropriately comprehensive.

2.3 Optimization and Its Algorithms

2.3.1 Definition

It is a step, process, an act or a methodology of doing things (such as a system, a design, or even a decision) as a functional, effective, and perfect working model.

Any complications would be framed as optimization [20, 21] because of its complexity, for instance, network routing issues, Job Scheduling, Software designs, Capacity Planning, Cash Management, Inventory Management, Transportation Model, Fleet Routing and Assignment, Cutting Stock Problems, etc.

Even the problems in contemporary areas such as AI (machine learning, deep learning), data analytics, and science can be framed into optimization problems, which is completely functional. If any problem, based on some constraints, tends to be maximized or minimized, an appropriate optimization problem can be framed out. Converting a real-time problem into optimization problems will fetch much more insights into the problems that help in finding the way to the solution. However, some optimization problems are very tough to solve such as travelling salesmen problem (TSP) as it is solved in non-deterministic polynomial time, which shows that no efficient algorithm is available to solve the NP hard problems. However, alternatives are available such as heuristic methods [30], approximation algorithm, and lucky algorithm.

2.3.2 Mathematical Notations

This section exhibits the mathematical side of optimization problems. It consists of a set of decision variables or design parameters denoted as x_k, where $k = 1,2,3......i$, which tell about the working space such as design or decision by means of vector.

The vector range is in the form of $x = (x_1, x_2, x_3 .... x_i) \in R^i$

Here, the objective or cost function will be either maximized or minimized based on inequality or equality constraints. It is of the form z = ax+y, where x and y are decision variables.

The solution obtained from the objective function should be satisfying the constraints defined in the problem, which may be either maximized or minimized, in which we can say that it is an optimum solution.

Overall, an optimization constraint would be articulated as

$$\text{Maximize (Max(y)) or Minimize function (Min(y))}, \tag{2.1}$$

subject to

$$f_a(y) \geq 0, (a = 1, 2,3,4 \dots i), \tag{2.2}$$

$$g_b(y) \leq 0, (b = 1, 2,3,4 \dots,j), \tag{2.3}$$

where f_a and g_b are the impartiality and disparity constraints, respectively.

If the Objective function is multiplied by −1 (if the problem is maximization), it can be easily converted into minimization problems, so any optimization statements can be outlined or expressed by way of minimization.

In some exceptional cases, where all the notations or functions defined become linear, we can say that it is a linear optimization. These linear problems will be unravelled effortlessly by deploying the Dantzig's simplex algorithm or method. Since the issue definition conversion can happen only in a very few cases, the functions defined in the problem will be mostly nonlinear in nature, which makes the problems tougher to crack. Furthermore, if only discontinuous values are accepted by objective functions, i.e., values based on counting, then the optimization problem will be called a discrete-oriented optimization problem. If the decision variable is applied with integer values, which tends to show the unknown information in the population with the possible combinations of constraints on it, such a problem could be called "integer programming. Adding to that, if part of the decision variables accept discrete data and the rest of the variables accept continuous data based on some constraints, then the problem is called mixed integer programming. Although optimization programming techniques are diverse in nature, the aforementioned new problems are extremely difficult to solve. Linear programming, non-linear programming, combinatorial optimization, network optimization, optimal control, multi-criteria optimization, stochastic optimization, and many other techniques are examples of optimization techniques. Due to the lack of effective methods for addressing combinatorial difficulties (large-scale), they are solved with approximation algorithm methods and metaheuristic methods.

However, for solving optimization problems, we started using nature-inspired algorithms or methods, which are now considered to be the most efficient.

2.3.3 Gradient-Based Algorithms

Since GBA is having a rock-hard background of mathematics, even for a local minimal solution, first derivative tests are required, which can be done by Karush–Kuhn–Tucker conditions. If suppose the cost function or objective function are defined on convex set, in which it is a convex function, then these conditions are also sufficient for attaining minimal optimal solution. It is always noteworthy to mention the findings of the Leng 2015 to get more insights into gradient-based algorithms for optimization.

- ✓ Though KKT conditions are useful in finding local minimal solutions, its equations or functions are non-linear, which makes it a little bit harder for the process involved to obtain the solution, which will in turn affect the cost of the cost function gradually.
- ✓ Classical problems of unconstrained optimizations are involved only in estimation of stationary points of function, which is nowhere near the objective function. Two popular strategies can be deployed to overcome the abovementioned, which creates a quadratic model near the objective function value or a point.
- ✓ For constrained non-linear optimization problems, Sequential Quadratic Programming can be more effective since it is having a profound theoretical basis and provides commanding algorithmic gears for the solution of comprehensively relevant issues.
- ✓ Duality theory talks about the two sides of the linear optimization's problems, whereas one is primal and the other is dual. Primal deals with the maximization of the problem and dual deals with a minimization problem formulation. Because of the primal–dual team, it is able to produce an optimization solution, even though it requires a gradient-based method to be applied.
- ✓ Finally, another important finding is that, a gradient-based approach is required for optimized solution, but it is lagging in its analytical structure representation. Also, its approximation side involves a greater number of evaluations of the cost function, which makes it computationally costly for the solution to be produced.

The crux of gradient-based algorithms is that the future value or the new solution is generated from the current solution involving a random number of iterations, by using an increment operator. These can be evaluated by the slope of the cost function, which is represented as tails:

$$\text{New optimal solution} = \text{Current solution} + \text{Increment vector} \tag{2.4}$$

An increment or modification vector is a function of slope or gradient along with the step size parameter that can change during any iterations.

Getting into the deeper part, a modification vector usually shows the negative value for the minimization problems that means positive value for the maximization problems.

In the case of deep learning, especially for large-scale problems, gradient calculations seem to be much expensive; hence, partial evaluation or approximation methods are preferrable for the gradient vector calculation. For instance, a stochastic method evaluation of gradients involves sporadically a portion of data, which may be chosen randomly. A selection of randomized data might add great advantage to nature-inspired algorithms, which will be discussed in a subsequent section; in fact, it increases the range or diversification of the solution.

2.3.4 Gradient-Free Optimizers or Algorithms

Another way to solve the optimization problems, which is flexible and easier, is through gradient-free algorithms. Though it is slower, it does not involve any derivative method.

Table 2.1 Comparison of gradient-based and gradient-free algorithms.

Gradient based	**Gradient free**
Derivatives needed	No derivates needed
When traversing parameter(s), we may become stuck in a local minimum or maximum.	No such faults and no guarantee of optimal solution
Newton–Raphson algorithm Gradient descent Stochastic gradient descent Frank–Wolfe algorithm	Exhaustive search [46] Simulated Annealing [35, 43] Nelder-Maed Ant colony algorithm Nature-inspired algorithms
Search direction Step size Convergence check	Slow for larger problems
Requires smooth gradients	Gradients not required here

Table 2.1 compares the gradient-based and gradient-free algorithm to understand more about their concepts and cases.

2.4 Metaheuristic Optimization Methods

The following are the nature-inspired methods that is capable of solving the optimization problems.

2.4.1 Ant Colony Algorithm

The Ant Colony Algorithm draws its sole inspiration from the foraging strategies of ant colonies. Therefore, in the 1990s, Marco Dorigo came up with the family name Formicidae to define ants. As eusocial insects, ants put the well-being of the colony before that of any individual member. Pheromones, physical contact, and sound are all forms of communication used by ants. Pheromones, another product of chemical synthesis, are produced by ants and trigger social responses in members of the same species. These chemicals may act on the recipients in a manner similar to that of hormones generated by the external organs of the people who are receiving them. Despite spending most of their time on the ground, ants use the ground to lay down scent tracks that other ants can detect by smell. Ants live in colonies known as "brotherhoods," and the primary idea of ACO is to follow the ants as they forage for food outside their homes. At first, ants forage aimlessly around their nest areas in search of food. With this search method, you have a few options for getting from your house to your food supply. Because of this, ants only bring back a certain amount of food with the necessary pheromone strength, which varies according on the quantity and quality of the meal they have just consumed. These pheromone tests would determine the viability of various routes to the food source, increasing or decreasing the likelihood that following ants would take a given path. This probability, obviously, is related to the potency of the pheromone and its rate of evaporation. Therefore, the rate of concentration of the pheromone should also be taken into account. The average frequency of each route can be easily determined.

2.4.1.1 Ant Colony Optimization Algorithm

A numerical method to solve challenging optimization issues is found using the ant colony optimization (ACO) technique, which is based on metaheuristic optimization. Software agents, sometimes referred to as "artificial ants," are used in ACO to look for workable alternatives to the provided optimization issue. The optimization issue [50] is converted into the task of locating the optimal route on a weighted network in order to implement ACO. In addition to building solutions by moving on graphs, the artificial ants (hereafter ants) A pheromone model, or collection of criteria linked to network components (either nodes or edges) whose quantities are changed instantaneously by the ants, biases the probabilistic resolution helps fuel. Besides constructing solutions by navigating through graphs, the artificial ants, also known as ants, use a pheromone model, which is a collection of criteria linked to network components (either nodes or edges), whose quantities they instantaneously change, to bias the probabilistic resolution.

There are two possible paths that have been considered from source (food) to destination (nest). There are four stages:

> Level 1: Every ant is in its colony. The atmosphere is devoid of any pheromone content. (In computational design, excess pheromone quantity can indeed be taken into account sans taking probabilities into account.)
> Level 2: With a probability density function of 0.5 for each path, ants start their exploration at this point. The triangular route is obviously the longer one, and as a result, ants take longer to reach the supply (food) than is shown (nest).
> Level 3: In the third stage, the ants travel the quickest route to the food supply. Of course, they now confront a comparable selection problem, but this time, the likelihood of choice is greater since a pheromone trail already exists along the fastest route.

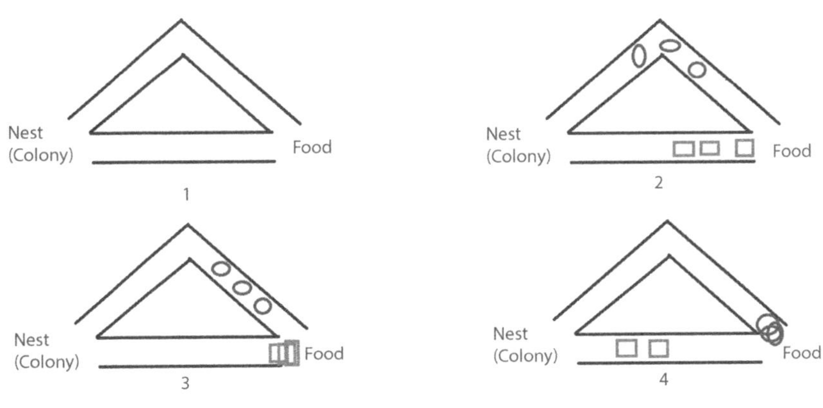

Figure 2.1 Optimization process of an ant colony.

Level 4: Many ants arrive via the quickest route, and pheromone levels start rising as well. The pheromone intensity on the longest side also falls as an outcome of evaporation. Figure 2.1 depicts all these optimization processes of the ant colony algorithm. That lowers the confidence interval of choosing this option in later phases. As a result, the shortest route is progressively used by the entire ant colony with a greater probability distribution. Finally, we arrive at the route of optimization. All these optimization process of ant colony algorithm has been depicted in Figure 2.1.

2.4.2 Flower Pollination Algorithm

Because angiosperms have indeed been evolving for about 130 millennia, plants require pollinators in addition to being responsible for 93% of bloom fertilization. Pollinating insects, including insects and birds, come in more than 200 different species [6]. The Floral Pollen Algorithm [49] is a metaheuristics algorithm that yields the best outcomes when used to solve real-world issues in a variety of fields, including video gaming, wireless sensing networks, worldwide feature enhancement, and both automatic and operational business optimization. Figure 2.2 exhibits the flower pollination process.

Each method has certain drawbacks in addition to their benefits, so they must be altered to provide superior efficiency [2]. There are multiple different ways to express flowering in FPA, including limitation, hybridization with other methods, cross-variations, and s-parameters. FPA has gained traction in recent years as a result of its relevance to contemporary issues.

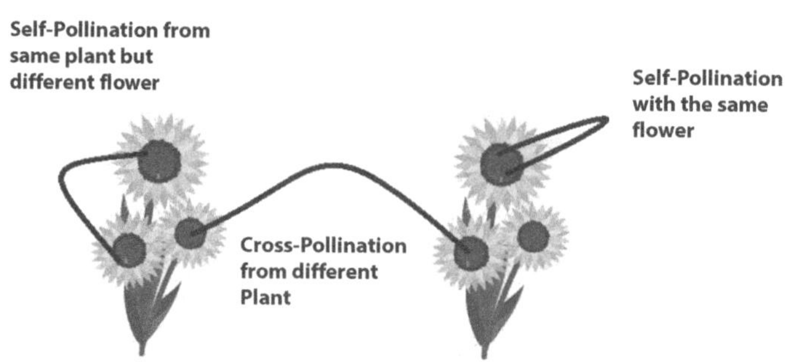

Figure 2.2 Flower pollination process.

Directions of FPA

Decree 1: To follow Levy's laws of motion, universal pollen merges with biological and cross-pollination by pollinators.

Decree 2: Pollen is the method used for biogenic and selfer (self-pollinated).

Decree 3: The floral constancy concept states that the likelihood of reproduction is inversely correlated with floral resemblance.

Decree 4: By selecting a switching rate, specifically one that falls between zero and one, the local or worldwide pollinating receptacles may be managed.

2.4.3 Genetic Algorithms

Responsive heuristic search techniques include genetic algorithms (GA) [28]. They are a major component of evolutionary algorithms. The concepts of natural evolution [44] through selection and genetics serve as the foundation for genetic algorithms. They are intelligent solutions that use a probabilistic approach as long as there is historical data to guide the search into the area of improved performance in solution space. They are typically employed to produce excellent solutions for search and optimization issues. Genetic algorithms mimic the natural selection process, which results in the more adaptable species having a higher chance of surviving, procreating, and carrying on to the next age. Simply put, they applied the concept of "survival of the fittest" among people's descendants to find a solution. Every generation consists of a group of individuals, and each person chooses a location in the search area and a potential answer. Each person is represented by a string of letters, integers, floats, and bits. This chain resembles a gene.

The genetic organization and function of cells in a population can be compared to genetic algorithms. Using this comparison as a premise, GA was founded.

- ✓ People struggle for commodities in the ecosystem and partner; those who succeed (are the fittest) mate to produce more children than other progeny.
- ✓ Each successive generation is more suited to its habitat because genes from the "fittest" parent proliferate throughout the generation, multiplying several times the parents to produce kids that are more like each of the mother and father.

GA Method

1) Seed the population arbitrarily.
2) Ascertain the population's level of fitness.
3) Perform the following procedure up to the idealized influence again:

    a) Choose the mom and dad from the crowd.
    b) Use recombination to create new populations.
    c) Apply the mutation to the new offspring.
    d) Determine the viability of a new population.

4) Get all the ideal response (after step 3).

2.4.4 Evolutionary Algorithm

Adaptive computing is based on the natural evolutionism of engineering and optimization, where answers are built rather than derived by Darwinian evolution from fundamental problems [4]. One of the most common techniques is evolutionary computation, sometimes known as "metaheuristics computing." To differentiate something from symbolic AI technology, metaheuristics methods, including ANN, SI, and fuzzy logic, are sometimes known as "computational models" or "intelligent systems" [48]. In terms of science, evolutionary computation is an illustration of a heuristic search approach, or exploration by trial-and-miss techniques, where, in EC, the "trials" are termed candidate solutions and the "miss" is defined as the quantification of how far away an experiment is from the intended conclusion. The error is used to decide which attempts should be used to create the additional attempts. According to a general rule of thumb, creating fresh attempts by making improvements to the prior attempts with the least mistakes has the best probability of reducing failure.

In evolutionary computation, the evolutionary method is the key goal. There exists a challenge that needs to be addressed, and the answer is thought to reside within the state space among possible contender answers. Through using the following format, the algorithm looks for the best answers inside the state space (process or steps of EA).

1. **Beginning**: Create a population from the target region at random.
2. **Reiteration:**

    (a) Calculate the value of the goal function for every instance as a part of the assessment.

(b) Optimizer: Choose the data that will be utilized in step 2 using the values of the fitness function that were derived for the projected values (c).
(c) Application of modification agents will transform the collected data into data observations from the search space.

Diagram for EA

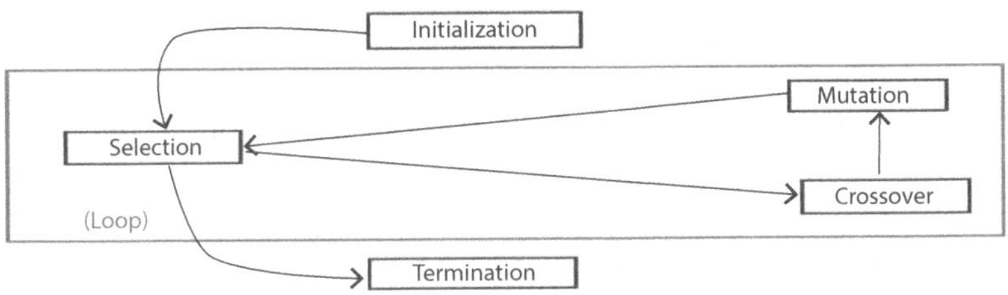

Figure 2.3 Evolutionary algorithm steps.

3. **Ending:** Halt the operation if all of the deletion requirements have been met; otherwise, go back to step 2 (a).
4. Get all the optimum answers right away from the search space area. All these above mentioned steps are indicated in the Figure 2.3.

2.4.5 Method Based on Bats

The "B" algorithm is a cutting-edge method for heuristic techniques that mimics bats' sound waves' ability to provide the world's finest answers [3] as depicted in Figure 2.4. The echo sounding (sound wave) of bats [8] serves as the basis for the Bat algorithm [25]. Bats use a compelling sonar signal called auditory cues to discover prey and, in some mysterious ways,

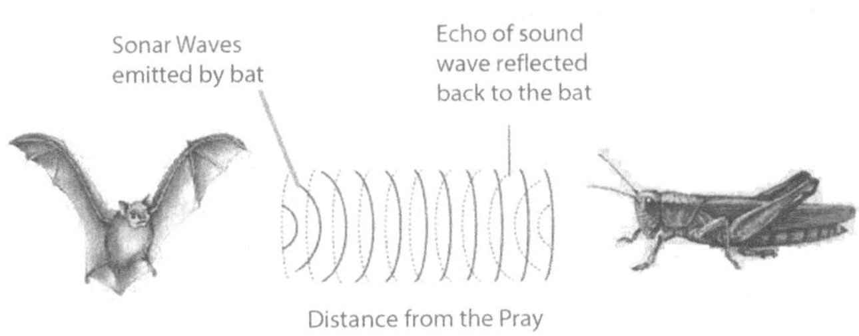

Figure 2.4 Echo location behavior of BAT.

to recognize various types of obstacles or hazards on the approach to the hunt in the full night.

The large acoustic waves are emitted by the bats, which then react to the reverberation that is deflected from the adjacent surroundings.

For simplicity, this employs some rules.

- ✓ Bats use acoustic signals to detect food, attackers, and any other obstructions in their way.
- ✓ Bats glide with location and momentum. To get to their prey, they employ frequencies (f) and decibels (d). They are able to change the pulse emission frequency.
- ✓ The bats became louder and their heartbeat quickened as they approached the victim.

2.4.6 Cuckoo Searching Method

The Cuckoo method is inspired by a cuckoo bird's daily activities. This optimizing technique is designed specifically for cuckoo bird breeding and egg production. In this motif, mature cuckoos and babies are used. The primary purpose of cuckoos is to hatch mature eggs in the host nests of other birds. If the ova are not discovered and discarded by the host birds, they develop and turn into cuckoos. Clusters of cuckoos are reliably guided to cluster and choose the ideal location for hatching an offspring by the relocation of clusters and the environment. For a cuckoo's egg, the goal function is the ideal location. With inspiration from the natural world, Yang and Deb launched Cuckoo Optimization in 2009. Rajabioun created the Cuckoo Optimization Algorithm in 2011. The Cuckoo Optimization Algorithm (COA) is a brand-new, continuing morpho that is built on the everyday reality of a cuckoo bird. COA starts with a primary population in a cuckoo group. Several eggs are deposited by these cuckoos in the houses of those other host birds. We create a set of random possible solutions that reflect the COA ecosystem.

Mechanism for Cuckoo Mating Behavior

The CS method was inspired by the obligatory brood parasitism of a few cuckoo taxa, in which they hatch their "zygote" in host bird nests (as depicted in Figure 2.5). Many cuckoos have suggested that female parasitic cuckoos may mimic the various hues and egg-arrangement patterns of a few selected host organisms. This lowers the likelihood that the embryos will go bad, thus increasing the new competition more. It is indeed crucial to note that several host birds directly compete against trespassing cuckoos. If the host birds discover the zygotes are not their own, they will either discard the eggs or retain them in their homes while building fresh ones. The host bird alone lays all of the eggs in the nest, which is a common choice for parasitic cuckoos. The cuckoo eggs often develop a little bit earlier than the host eggs. When the first cuckoo chick is fabricated, one of his first basic actions is to knock the host ova out of the brood in a haphazard manner. As a consequence of all this success, the cuckoo chick receives a larger proportion of the food offered compared to its host bird.

All the eggs in a brood have a unique characteristic, and a cuckoo egg has a brand-new characteristic. The key aim is to use the freshest and maybe best solutions (cuckoos) to send the subpar solutions back to their brood. A solitary home contains a single egg in the most basic design. The technique may be expanded to handle highly complicated situations, so each brood contains numerous eggs that stand in for a collection of answers.

The CS is built on three tenets:

- ✓ Every cuckoo deposits an egg into a nest that is chosen at random.
- ✓ The greatest homes pass them down to the succeeding generations together with the finest offspring (answers).
- ✓ The number of host nests that may be accessed is restricted, and a host has a chance of finding an unusual egg.

Representation of Cuckoo's Nest:

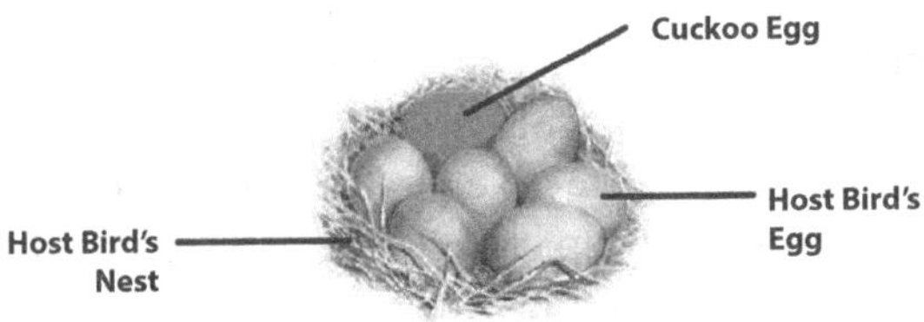

Figure 2.5 Cuckoo's nest.

2.4.7 Firefly Algorithm

Bugs or wingless insects called fireflies emit a glow and flicker in the dark. Chemiluminescence, as opposed to infrared or ultraviolet wavelengths, is the term used to describe the light that is organically created from the belly [5]. To lure prey or mates, they specifically employ the flash signal. By alerting others to the possible predatory animals, the flashing signal is also employed by the fireflies to protect themselves as depicted in Figure 2.6.

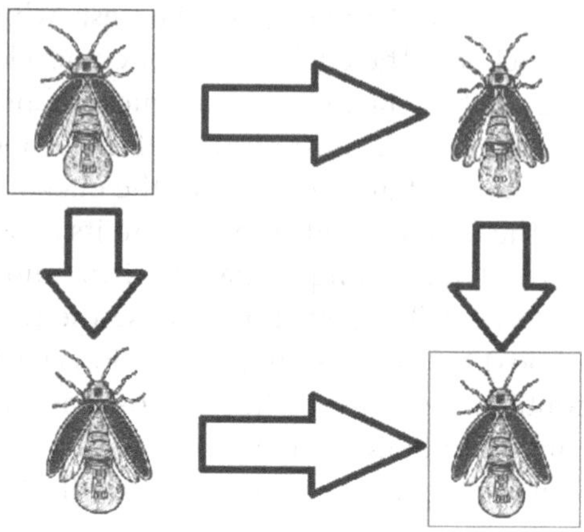

Figure 2.6 Novel method for firefly algorithm (attracts by light).

Yang developed the Firefly algorithm, an evolutionary algorithm inspired by the luminescent signaling phenomena and the flickering characteristic of fireflies.

The steps listed below are for the Firefly Algorithm with these presumptions:

- ✓ Due to their being unisexual, fireflies will be attracted to one another regardless of their sexual orientation.
- ✓ As long as the less dazzling firefly is drawn to the more brilliant firefly, their attractiveness is proportionate to their luminosity. The more space existing between points 1 and 2, though, the less appealing they are.
- ✓ The movement of fireflies in actuality is unpredictable if their luminosity is identical.

The lure of the firefly and unplanned walks are what generate innovative solutions or local responses. The goal function must be related to the firefly's luminosity. They can separate into the tiniest units thanks to their attraction, and each one congregates around the neighborhood figures. In the context of the Nature Inspired Optimization methodology, the Firefly Algorithm (FFA) is an effective method for resolving restricted optimization issues as well as NP-hard problems. Although often employed, the FFA has been widely utilized to solve continuous mathematical functions. The method must only be a straightforward mathematical and logical solution in pragmatic arithmetic. Because FFA has a simple behavior, it is appropriate for solving continuous mathematical problems.

Based on the statistical performance assessed using common stochastic test functions, this is relatively well-organized and may surpass other traditional approaches. The method relies on the firefly's interplanetary communication to function. As a result, it is applied to discover both global and local optimum solutions at once. Actual random variables are the major use of FFA. Fireflies of various kinds function independently, and thus, it is appropriate for the simultaneous construction of operations. FFA is one of the methods that academics have lately employed to resolve optimization issues in a dynamic context.

2.4.8 Particle Swarm Optimization Algorithm

One approach that takes cues from nature and employs a stochastic programming technique is known as particle swarm optimization (PSO), which helps find the most effective solution in a problem space. It differs from previous optimization techniques in that it does not rely on the slope or any other differential form of the cost functions; instead, it simply requires the cost function. There are also not many hyper-parameters.

In PSO, the notion of social contact is necessary for issue resolution. It uses an enormous number of elements (agents) that act as a swarm and move around the search space in quest of something like the best answer. In order to find the best solution that has been reached thus far by that component, each member of the swarm searches for its geolocation dimensions in the related optimal solution. It is known as the Pbest swarm or the Career High Hive. The PSO keeps track of another best value called the "gbest hive" or "global best swarm" [45]. This represents the best outcome that any element that is closest to that element or component has been able to achieve thus far.

Procedure for the PSO algorithm:

- ✓ Generate an equally dispersed "population" of the agents (particles) across X.
- ✓ The fitness function takes into account the location of each particle while evaluating it.
- ✓ Recase a particle if its current location is superior to its prior prime location.

Diagram:

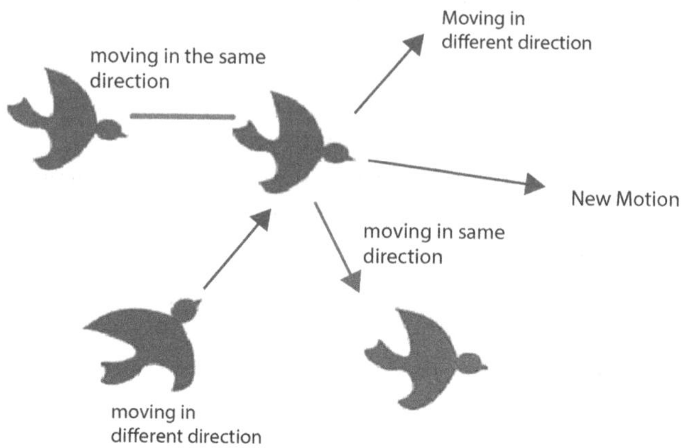

Figure 2.7 Particle swarm optimization.

- ✓ Find the top element in search space.
- ✓ Update particle speed (Particle Swarm Optimization - speed/velocities).
- ✓ The components should now be at their new locations (as depicted in Figure 2.7).
- ✓ Continue till the scenario meets the PSO requirements by moving on to step 2.

2.4.9 Krill Herd Algorithm

The major goal of the suggested new method is to solve optimization issues. The program mimics krill's herding behavior [52] (a small fish found in all oceans). The design of the cost function is based on the remoteness among every krill and the herd compactness. There are three factors available for calculating the time-dependent position of the krill fish:

- ✓ If another krill fish is present, its movement will be completely induced
- ✓ Hunting activity
- ✓ Physical diffusion at random

Krill swarms exhibit both underlying and quasi-herding behavior. The krill herds are collections of animals that occur across time periods of minutes to days and over distance lengths of 10 seconds to 100 seconds in the sea. As a result, the krill's primary characteristic is that they are found in vast groupings.

Pseudocode for Krill Herd:

```
Initial: Krill Herd
Variables or Parameter Definition
Pre-Processing
Krill's Initial Position and Movements
For Every Iterations
    Population counts
    For Every Krill
    -  Induced Movement
    -  Hunting Motion
    -  Random Physical Diffusion
    -  Mutation and Crossover
    -  Updating of Krill Positions
Updating Current Optimal Solution
```

Predators including larger fish, seals, penguins, and seagulls often isolate krill fish before attacking them, which lowers the density of the krill herd. Numerous factors, including the characteristics of the attack, will affect the krill herd composition after the attack. The gathering of krill is a procedure with two basic objectives: (1) increase in the abundance of krill and (2) acquiring nutrition.

2.4.10 Artificial Bee Colony (ABC) [53]

An additional nature-inspired algorithm is the artificial bee colony (ABC) algorithm [53], which is based on an evolutionary approach. As the name indicates, the algorithm is an inspiration of honey bees' behavior in finding a food source that is of high quality. The algorithm is set up so that the fake bees change where they are in relation to where the food is. Here, artificial honey bees are the computational agents that help to produce the optimal solution.

The computational agents can be of three types: (i) active, (ii) observer, and (iii) scout. The active agent senses the position of nutrition, while the observer agent will be holding in a line for info about the position and the amount of food available. Based on the information, the observer bees select the particular food position and will start exploiting the selected food.

Finally, the scout bees will keep searching for new locations of food. Each and every solution will have their respective optimization parameters from the search space, which is actually a representation of the position of the food source. The number of agents deployed is directly related to the number of feedstuffs, and the fitness function represents the value of the food supply.

Since its inception in 2005, the ABC optimization method has been credited to Karaboga. The solution search equation used by the ABC method is powerful in exploration but weak in exploitation [53]; therefore, while it may outperform other traditional computational learning algorithms in some optimization tasks, most ABC algorithms still fall short. The ABC algorithm's swarm size and limit are just two of many settings the user must play around with. If the parameters are not optimized for this use case, the algorithm may converge too quickly or not at all. With the help of the fitness value, the trailing error can be brought down to a manageable level [54].

2.5 Computational and Autonomous Systems

Various approaches to methods are applied for analysis, based on real viewpoints and perspectives. We will mostly discuss computational properties and autonomy in this section. In the subsequent chapter, we will undertake a deeper study.

2.5.1 Computational Features of Nature-Inspired Computing

The following section will examine the key components of metaheuristics, such as search (moves and procedures), inquiry and exploitation, and formulation update or volatility. Additionally, they will be examined as autonomous systems in this section. The methods can be summarized as follows:

- ✓ The computational properties [10] considered are population-oriented, meaning they consist of multiple agents. The vector of solutions for the optimization problems is the position and formation of every agent in the search state space. Based on some local rules defined under problems, the agents present in the search state space have interaction among themselves and exist contemporaneously. The agents can be bats, bees, cuckoos, ants, particles, fireflies, etc.
- ✓ Starting with a population of random candidates, the evolution [24, 27] can be made possible by means of two different

and important operators of genetic algorithms. First of all, mutation permits the growth of un-inherited features in the population. As a result, the mutated population will have diversity or variety among itself, allowing for offspring. Secondly, the crossover involves the creation of new solutions from the entire population. In order to preserve the variety, random perturbations will be followed in the population, or else they will end up in a local optimal solution. Along with it, two other abilities of the algorithm, such as exploration and exploitation, are possible in the population.

- ✓ The former entails discovering new solutions in new regions of population state space, whereas the latter entails improving fitness by modifying existing solutions.
- ✓ In a search space, some level of population has to be maintained, where each sample from the population is a partaker in the pursuit of the survival of the fittest. With the help of fitness scores, the capability of the discrete chromosomes to vie with the other chromosomes in a populace is determined. The idea is to find the fittest member of the populace, which can be passed on to future generations.
- ✓ In the early stage of population iterations, the diversity or variety of the population seems to be high enough with respect to the randomness of the candidate selection. The population's variety declines as the number of repetitions rises. In other words, diversity is indirectly balanced to the iterations of the population.

$$\text{i.e., diversity} \propto \frac{1}{no.\ of\ iterations\ in\ the\ population}$$

Once all the solutions of every individual candidate reach an analogous state, the whole system will get into a self-organized criticality state. In this state, the population has a strong and similar structure among themselves, but with minimum diversity.

2.5.2 Comparison with Legacy Algorithms

Metaheuristics methods utilize multiway or multiple path solutions as opposed to conventional or legacy methods like gradient-based approaches, which use local information to arrive at a local optimal solution that only

Table 2.2 Comparing metaheuristics and legacy methods' key features and characteristics.

Features	Metaheuristics	Legacy methods
Agent	Multiple	Single
Iteration	More	Less
Gradient	Rare case	Mostly cases
Hessian	No	Yes (mostly used)
Randomness	Frequently Used	No
Hyperparameter	A far and few times	One time
Selection	Elitism	Ever and always

reveals one way or single path solution. The evaluation of essential attributes and features between standard optimization [38] methods and techniques derived from nature is shown in Table 2.2.

2.5.3 Autonomous Criticality Systems

Another clever strategy is to consider algorithms derived from natural phenomena as an autonomous criticality system. According to the methodology, there are clear parallels between the characteristics of algorithms and the actions of autonomous systems. The comparability of computational characteristics and self-organizing systems, in addition to their functions or characteristics, is shown in Table 2.3.

From the table, it is obvious that there are some substantial differences as well. Having said that, we need some cases to get a better picture, but the research side is missing in that part, because the transition of the self-organization system [32] is still unclear. In the case of algorithms (nature-inspired), the evolution of populations and any updates seems to be clear. The time factor is very crucial in algorithms because of the practical importance of the rate of integration of algorithms. According to Wolpert and Macready's (Wolpert and Macready's 1997-Research Paper) NFL theorem, no algorithm or model is best for working in any situation. Thus, it is advisable to identify what kind of algorithm can be applicable to a particular problem and what type of problem an algorithm can be able to solve.

Table 2.3 Nature-inspired algorithmic components vs. self-organization systems role.

Features of nature-inspired algorithms	Its role
Multi-population	Diversity
Ettism	Based on the candidate selection
Selection	Prime mover, leads to integration of algorithms
Crossover	Diversity, combined solutions
Mutation	Solution modification for other parameters
Derivates	Fitness improvement
Iteration	Gradual development of population
Randomization	New solutions from new regions, avoids local optimum solution

2.6 Unresolved Issues for Continued Study

Nevertheless, metaheuristics methods are gaining more popularity nowadays among researchers, but a number of areas have to be explored, such as the need for in-depth understanding of theoretical aspects and more concentration on mathematical frameworks, which shows a big gap separating knowledge from reality. Multiple trials, for example, have shown that metaheuristics methods can unravel stimulating optimization issues, although a thorough understanding of why and how the algorithms are solved is still lacking. It is too early to say whether the nature-inspired algorithms will work on newer problems until we try them. Adding to that, the integration of algorithms seems to be clandestine for some problems.

It might not be feasible to aggregate all open issues. Below, we shall showcase a few outstanding issues in order to stimulate further study.

1. **Computational Structure**

A computational structure will permit a demanding examination of various processes, which will give us a much deeper understanding of the algorithm properties and their exploration methods that will allow us to use these methods more efficiently and successfully in such a way to design more intelligent and competent algorithms. These analyses can be in terms of stochastic models such as Monte Carlo simulation, Markov chains and systems, pure interactive systems, and many more. An interdisciplinary strategy should produce better results, as is expected.

2. **Integration of Methods**
To get optimized performance, it is necessary to combine different algorithms together, and their study will be helpful in finding a new optimized algorithm [18]. This might help researchers to identify when to integrate and what types of algorithms can be converged, which avoids convergence errors. The algorithms can be fine-grained to achieve an extreme level of integration for better performance, but the area of fine-graining an algorithm for convergence is still untouched.

3. **Solidity (Stability) and Strength (Robustness)**
The efficiency of an algorithm is completely different from the stability of an algorithm. The former is a well-defined sum of computational resources used and then the entire period was taken to produce the result, whereas the latter is the relative order of the equal sorted elements that will be preserved. On the other hand, the robustness of an algorithm is the property that exemplifies how effective an algorithm is while being tested on a new dataset. The defined properties are of much importance; those can be controlled by adjusting and setting the parameters defined in the system based on the type of the problem being dealt with. The algorithms, which are not stable, cannot be used in any applications as they will produce only insensible and unhealthy solutions. As many real-time systems are nonlinear in nature, it is advisable to have nonlinear stability algorithms for problem solving.

4. **Unbiased Comparison**
In the literature, there are not only different types of algorithms but also an "n" number of variants of the same algorithm. Internal comparison among the variants of the same algorithm is also needed to get unbiased results. In order to avoid biased results, we will be considering several performance measures such as hit rate or success rates, the number of functions deployed and their evaluations, accuracy of the results, fault tolerance, mean value, overall computation time taken, optimal value or solution, and standard deviations, among others. The performance measures defined here may not be enough for the unbiased comparison of the systems, and the results are always grim. As a result, more studies and research in a mathematical modeling approach are required.

References

1. Yang, Xin-She (2014). *Nature-Inspired Optimization Algorithms || Genetic Algorithms., (), 77–87.* doi:10.1016/b978-0-12-416743-8.00005-1
2. Xin-She Yang, Chapter 11 - Flower Pollination Algorithms, *Nature-Inspired Optimization Algorithms*, Elsevier, 2014, Pages 155-173, ISBN 9780124167438, https://doi.org/10.1016/B978-0-12-416743-8.00011-7.
3. Xin-She Yang,Chapter 10 - Bat Algorithms, *Nature-Inspired Optimization Algorithms*, Elsevier, 2014, Pages 141-154, ISBN 9780124167438, https://doi.org/10.1016/B978-0-12-416743-8.00010-5.
4. Xin-She Yang, Chapter 6 - Differential Evolution, *Nature-Inspired Optimization Algorithms*, Elsevier, 2014, Pages 89-97, ISBN 9780124167438, https://doi.org/10.1016/B978-0-12-416743-8.00006-3.
5. Xin-She Yang, Chapter 8 - Firefly Algorithms, *Nature-Inspired Optimization Algorithms*, Elsevier, 2014, Pages 111-127, ISBN 9780124167438, https://doi.org/10.1016/B978-0-12-416743-8.00008-7.
6. Alam, D.F., Yousri, D.A., Eteiba, M.B., 2015. Flower pollination algorithm based solar PV parameter estimation. *Energy Convers. Manage.*, 101 (2), 410–422.
7. Jessintha, D., Kenjaev Sanjar Sobirovich, Christo Ananth and T. Ananth Kumar. "Design of Optimized low-power GPS-Yagi Antenna using Machine Learning techniques." In *2022 5th Int. Conf. Contemp. Computing Inf. (IC3I)*, pp. 619-624. IEEE, 2022.
8. Altringham, J.D., 1996. *Bats: Biology and Behaviour*. Oxford University Press, Oxford, UK.
9. Alyasseri, Z.A.A., Khader, A.T., Al-Betar, M.A., Awadallah, M.A., Yang, X.S., 2018. Variants of the flower pollination algorithm: a review. In: Yang, X.S. (Ed.), *Nature-Inspired Algorithms and Applied Optimization*. Springer, Cham, pp. 91–118.
10. Arara, S., Barak, B., 2009. *Computational Complexity: A Modern Approach*. Cambridge University Press, Cambridge, UK.
11. Ashby, W.A., 1962. Principles of the self-organizing systems. In: von Foerster, H., Zopf Jr., G.W. (Eds.), *Principles of Self-Organization: Transactions of the University of Illinois Symposium*. Pergamon Press, London, pp. 255–278.
12. Kumar, Abhishek, Pramod Sing Rathore, Ashutosh Kumar Dubey, Rashmi Agrawal, and Kanta Prasad Sharma. "LTE-NBP with holistic UWB-WBAN approach for the energy efficient biomedical application." *Multimed. Tools Appl.*, (2023): 1-15.
13. Zong Woo Geem, Joong Hoon Kim, and GV Loganathan. A new heuristic optimization algorithm: harmony search. *Simulation*, 76(2):60–68, 2001.
14. Selvaraj, Jaisiva, Kumar Chandrasekaran, Ananth Kumar Tamilarasan, Mehdi Gheisari, Christian Fernández-Campusano, Yang Liu, and Naser Khodabakhshi-Javinani. "Design of advanced Aalborg inverter for extracting

maximum power from renewable energy sources tied with autonomous grid system." *IET Power Electron.*, (2023).
15. Chen, S., Peng, G.H., Xing-Shi Yang, X.S., 2018. Global convergence analysis of the bat algorithm using a markovian framework and dynamic system theory. *Expert Syst. Appl.*, 114 (1), 173–182.
16. Clerc, M., Kennedy, J., 2002. The particle swarm: explosion, stability, and convergence in a multidimensional complex space. *IEEE Trans. Evol. Comput.*, 6 (1), 58–73.
17. Srivastav, Arun Lal, Markandeya, Naveen Patel, Mayank Pandey, Ashutosh Kumar Pandey, Ashutosh Kumar Dubey, Abhishek Kumar, Abhishek Kumar Bhardwaj, and Vinod Kumar Chaudhary. "Concepts of circular economy for sustainable management of electronic wastes: challenges and management options." *Environ. Sci. Pollut. Res.*, 30, no. 17 (2023): 48654-48675.
18. Burri, Srinivasa Rao, Sachin Ahuja, Abhishek Kumar, and Anupam Baliyan. "Exploring the Effectiveness of Optimized Convolutional Neural Network in Transfer Learning for Image Classification: A Practical Approach." In *2023 Int. Conf. Advancement Comput. Comput. Technol., (InCACCT)*, pp. 598-602. IEEE, 2023.
19. Davies, N.B., 2011. Cuckoo adaptations: trickery and tuning. *J. Zool.*, 284 (1), 1–14.
20. De Jong, K., 1975. *Analysis of the Behaviour of a Class of Genetic Adaptive Systems*. Ph.D. Thesis. University of Michigan, Ann Arbor, MI, USA.
21. Dorigo, M., 1992. *Optimization, Learning, and Natural Algorithms*. Ph.D.
22. James Kennedy and Russell Eberhart. Particle swarm optimization. In *Neural Networks, 1995. Proceedings., IEEE Int. Conf.* on, volume 4, pages 1942–1948. IEEE, 1995.
23. Fister, I., Fister Jr, I., Brest, J., Yang, X.S., 2013. A comprehensive review of firefly algorithms. *Swarm Evol. Comput.*, 13 (1), 34–46.
24. Fogel, L.J., Owens, A.J., Walsh, M.J., 1966. *Artificial Intelligence Through Simulated Evolution*. Wiley, New York, USA.
25. Gandomi, A.H., Yang, X.S., 2014. Chaotic bat algorithm. *J. Comput. Sci.*, 5 (2), 224–232.
26. Geem, Z.W., Kim, J.H., Loganathan, G.V., 2001. A new heuristic optimization algorithm: harmony search. *Simulation*, 76 (2), 60–68.
27. Glover, F., 1986. Future paths for integer programming and links to artificial intelligence. *Comput. Oper. Res.*, 13 (5), 533–549.
28. Goldberg, D.E., 1989. *Genetic Algorithms in Search, Optimization and Machine Learning*. Addison- Wesley, Reading, MA, USA.
29. Holland, J., 1975. *Adaptation in Nature and Artificial Systems*. University of Michigan Press, Ann Arbor, MI, USA.
30. Judea, P., 1984. *Heuristics*. Addison-Wesley, New York, USA.
31. Karaboga, D., 2005. An idea based on honeybee swarm for numerical optimization. Technical report. Eriyes University, Turkey.

32. Keller, E.F., 2009. Organisms, machines, and thunderstorms: a history of self-organization, part ii. Complexity, emergence, and stable attractors. *Hist. Stud. Natural Sci.,* 39 (1), 1–31.
33. Kennedy, J., Eberhart, R., 1995. Particle swarm optimization. In: *Proc. IEEE Int. Conf. Neural Networks. IEEE,* Piscataway, NJ, USA, pp. 1942–1948.
34. Kennedy, J., Eberhart, R.C., Shi, Y., 2001. *Swarm Intelligence.* Academic Press, London, UK.
35. Kirkpatrik, S., Gellat, C.D., Vecchi, M.P., 1983. Optimization by simulated annealing. *Science,* 220 (4598), 671–680.
36. LeCun, Y., Bengio, Y., Hinton, G.E., 2015. Deep learning. *Nature,* 521 (7553), 436–444.
37. Marichelvam, M.K., Prabaharan, T., Yang, X.S., 2014. A discrete firefly algorithm for the multi-objective hybrid flowshop scheduling problems. *IEEE Trans. Evol. Comput.,* 18 (2), 301–305.
38. Nelder, J.A., Mead, R., 1965. A simplex method for function optimization. *Comput. J.,* 7 (4),308–313.
39. Osaba, E., Yang, X.S., Diaz, F., Lopez-Garcia, P., Carballedo, R., 2016. An improved discrete bat algorithm for symmetric and asymmetric traveling salesman problems. *Eng. Appl. Artif. Intell.,* 48 (1), 59–71.
40. Benkhaddra, Ilyas, Abhishek Kumar, Mohamed Ali Setitra, and Lei Hang. "Design and Development of Consensus Activation Function Enabled Neural Network-Based Smart Healthcare Using BIoT." *Wirel. Pers. Commun.,* 130, no. 3 (2023): 1549-1574.
41. Osaba, E., Yang, X.S., Fister Jr., I., Lopez-Garcia, P., Vazquez-Paravila, A., 2019. A discrete and improved bat algorithm for solving a medical goods distribution problem with pharmacological waste collection. *Swarm Evol. Comput.,* 44 (1), 273–286.
42. Padmapriya, N., T. Ananth Kumar, R. Rajmohan, M. Pavithra and P. Kanimozhi. "Secure Vehicular Communication Using Blockchain Technology." In *Blockchain, Artificial Intelligence, and the Internet of Things,* pp. 141-162. Springer, Cham, 2022.
43. Pavlyukevich, I., 2007. Lévy flights, non-local search and simulated annealing. *J. Comput. Phys.,* 226 (2), 1830–1844.
44. Price, K., Storn, R., Lampinen, J., 2005. *Differential Evolution: A Practical Approach to Global Optimization.* Springer, Berlin, Germany.
45. Rango, F.D., Palmieri, N., Yang, X.S., Marano, S., 2018. Swarm robotics in wireless distributed protocol design for coordinating robots involved in cooperative tasks. *Soft Comput.,* 22 (13), 4251–4266.
46. Reynods, A.M., Frye, M.A., 2007. Free-flight odor tracking in drosophila is consistent with an optimal intermittent scale-free search. *PloS One,* 2 (4), e354–e363.
47. Storn, R., Price, K., 1997. Differential evolution: a simple and efficient heuristic for global optimization. *J. Global Optim.,* 11 (4), 341–359.

48. Turing, A.M., 1948. *Intelligent machinery*. Technical report. National Physical Laboratory, London, UK.
49. Waser, N.M., 1986. Flower constancy: definition, cause and measurement. *Am. Nat.*, 127 (5), 596–603.
50. Wolpert, D.H., Macready, W.G., 1997. No free lunch theorems for optimization. *IEEE Trans. Evol. Comput.*, 1 (1), 67–82.
51. Yang, X.S., 2010. A new metaheuristic bat-inspired algorithm. In: Cruz, C., González, J.R., Pelta, D.A., Terrazas, G. (Eds.), *Nature Inspired Cooperative Strategies for Optimization (NISCO 2010). In: Studies in Computational Intelligence*, vol. 284. Springer, Berlin, Germany, pp. 65–74.
52. Amir Hossein Gandomi; Amir Hossein Alavi (2012). Krill herd: A new bio-inspired optimization algorithm. , 17(12), –. doi:10.1016/j.cnsns.2012.05.010
53. Zhu G, Kwong S. Gbest-guided artificial bee colony algorithm for numerical function optimization. *Appl. Math Comput.*, 2010;217:3166e73.
54. Shah, Habib (2016). *Applied Computing in Medicine and Health || Swarm Based-Artificial Neural System for Human Health Data Classification.* , (), 287–309. doi:10.1016/B978-0-12-803468-2.00014-X
55. Xin-She Yang and Suash Deb. Cuckoo search via l´evy flights. In *Nat. Biologically Inspired Computing, 2009. NaBIC 2009. World Congress* on, pages 210–214. IEEE, 2009.
56. X.S. Yang. A new metaheuristic bat-inspired algorithm. *Nat. Inspired Cooperative Strategies for Optim. (NICSO 2010)*, pages 65–74, 2010.

3

AI-Based Computational Intelligence Theory

Jana Selvaganesan[1], S. Arunmozhiselvi[2*], E. Preethi[3] and S. Thangam[4]

[1]*Department of Electronics and Communication Engineering, Veltech Rangarajan Dr Sagunthala R&D Institute of Science and Technology, Chennai, India*
[2]*Holycross Engineering College, Vagaikulam, Thoothukudi, India*
[3]*Department of Computer Science and Engineering, Holycross Engineering College, Vagaikulam, Thoothukudi, India*
[4]*Department of Computer Science and Engineering, Amrita School of Computing, Bengaluru, Amrita Vishwa, Vidyapeetham, India*

Abstract

AI has increased in importance in the modern world due to its computing capacity and ability to transform a variety of industries. AI systems can process and analyze large amounts of data to produce intelligent insights and lead deliberations. It provides tailored experiences by analyzing user data and activity patterns. It includes a range of methods and procedures intended to use computational models to resolve challenging real-world issues. Computational intelligence research has several advantages for both individuals and society as a whole. Technical advancements in this field aid in data processing, extracting useful insights that may be quickly utilized by intelligent systems powered by AI, giving organizations a competitive edge and enabling them to make decisions based on facts. This chapter deals with discovering various dimensions of computational intelligence servicing for the society development and transforming business strategies that in turn helps in achieving economic advancements. This chapter focuses on the different aspects of computational intelligence that serve to enhance society and change corporate tactics, which, in turn, promotes economic growth. Hybrid models and ensemble techniques adapted by organizations are explored that contribute to improve predictive analytics tasks for automated machines. Explore the practical uses of computational intelligence methods based on AI, including robotics, speech and image recognition, natural language processing, optimization issues,

**Corresponding author*: heyaruna@gmail.com

T. Ananth Kumar, E. Golden Julie, Venkata Raghuveer Burugadda, Abhishek Kumar and Puneet Kumar (eds.) Computational Intelligence: Theory and Applications, (53–96) © 2024 Scrivener Publishing LLC

and data analytics. The practical applications of computational intelligence techniques based on AI are examined in this chapter, including robotics, speech and image recognition, natural language processing, optimization problems, and data analytics. This chapter will open up the views of future researchers and scholars that help to advance computational intelligence to the next level.

Keywords: Computational intelligence, artificial intelligence, machine learning, applications

3.1 Computational Intelligence

Computational intelligence (CI), a research area, combines elements of artificial intelligence (AI), machine learning (ML), and other computational methodologies to produce intelligent systems that are capable of handling difficult problems. To guide the development of AI-based intelligent systems, CI has developed a number of ideas and techniques. Computational intelligence methods like machine learning and expert systems, which rely on data and pre-established rules, enable computer decision-making. By evaluating enormous amounts of data, machines may discover patterns, identify trends, and reach justifiable conclusions without the need for human intervention. This is especially helpful when instantaneous judgments must be made, as in the case of automated cars or industrial automation.

Application examples include recommendation algorithms used by online platforms, customized marketing efforts, and virtual assistants that provide specific guidance and support. Voice assistants such as Siri, Alexa, and Google Assistant employ AI to understand human commands and questions. It acts as the brain of autonomous vehicle technology, helping vehicles to perceive their surroundings, make real-time decisions, and navigate safely [3]. When detecting diseases like cancer, AI-powered medical imaging tools can increase precision and speed, while AI-driven drug discovery can quicken the development of new medications.

By employing techniques like genetic algorithms, particle swarm optimization, or reinforcement learning, machines can iteratively explore and evaluate a variety of options to deliver the optimal results. Resource allocation, logistics optimization, and production planning can all benefit from this. It enables machines to recognize patterns and classify things or data. Methods that reliably identify patterns in huge datasets by learning from examples include deep learning models, neural networks, and support vector machines. Many automated systems, including those that detect fraud, recognize speech, and identify images, require this capability. By analyzing patterns and trends, machines are able to predict events and take preventative action [4]. Using techniques such as reinforcement learning, machines may interact with their surroundings, gather input, and adjust their behavior to achieve desired outcomes. This versatility is critical in automation systems that must respond to changing circumstances or unexpected events.

Computational intelligence can increase human–machine collaboration in automation systems. Machines can assist humans in performing complex tasks by giving intelligent recommendations, automating repetitive duties, or augmenting human abilities. This collaborative method boosts production and efficiency by combining the talents of humans and machines.

3.2 Designing Expert Systems

An expert system can be conceived of as a computer simulation of a human expert. It can also be defined as a computer code that simulates the decision-making and actions of an individual or group with substantial training and expertise in a certain industry. In such a system, a knowledge base containing accumulated experience and a set of rules for applying the knowledge base to each unique situation presented to the program are often provided. Expert systems, in addition to employing human knowledge, can address difficulties that would normally require human intellect. These expert systems reflect expertise knowledge using computer data or rules. These data and guidelines can be applied to solve an issue. Books and manual guides have a tremendous amount of knowledge but a human has to read and interpret the knowledge for it to be used. A system uses human knowledge captured in a computer to solve problems that ordinarily require human expertise.

A computer program is designed to model the problem solving ability of a human expert. Expert systems make extensive use of specialized knowledge to solve problems at the level of a human expert [5]. An expert is a person who has expertise in a certain area; i.e., the expert has knowledge or special skills that are not known or available to most people. An expert can much more efficiently solve problems that most people cannot solve. Thereby, hardware, software, and special expert system languages may all be included in expert system technology, which is used to create and run expert systems. Expert systems may use knowledge that is specialized or generally accessible through publications like books and journals and knowledgeable people.

3.2.1 Characteristics

- Functions as an interactive system by answering queries and requesting clarifications.
- Tools have the ability to sift (filter) knowledge, such as knowledge storage and retrieval systems and mechanisms for continuously growing and updating knowledge bases.
- Draw conclusions logically from information and ability to explain reasoning.
- Possibility of defining confidence values.

3.3 Core of Computational Intelligence

3.3.1 Artificial Intelligence (AI)

Acknowledge the fundamental values, goals, and multiple methodologies used in the design of artificially intelligent systems. Ontologies, semantic networks, and rule-based systems are examples of AI strategies for arranging knowledge representation. As a result of their representations, intelligent systems may reason, infer new knowledge from previously known information, and solve difficult problems. The purpose of the artificial intelligence branch known as natural language processing (NLP) is to use human language to communicate with computers [6]. It enables intelligent machines to understand, compose, and translate human language. NLP techniques such as sentiment analysis, machine translation, and text summarization enable artificial intelligence by extracting information from textual input and allowing human-like interactions.

The field of computer vision combines AI techniques with image processing to enable robots to see and analyze visual data from images or films. It can be used by machines with AI to analyze and grasp visual input, such as object recognition, image categorization, image segmentation, and scene comprehension. Robots, surveillance, surveillance systems, and medical imaging are among sectors that use computer vision. Computational intelligence is enhanced by AI-powered robotic systems [7]. AI-powered robotics advances computational intelligence. AI approaches such as sensing, reasoning, and planning enable robots to interact with their surroundings, reason, and behave freely. Examples of robotics applications include medical care, factory automation, support robots, and self-driving cars.

3.3.2 Machine Learning (ML)

Discover supervised learning, unsupervised learning, deep learning, and other machine learning methods. Study terms like feature selection, dimensionality reduction, model evaluation, and optimization in greater detail. Decision-supporting models and algorithms are provided by machine learning, which benefits systems that support decisions [8]. Machine learning algorithms can forecast outcomes, assess risks, and offer suggestions to enhance human decision-making in industries like healthcare, finance, and logistics by learning from historical data and trends. They can do hidden relationship discovery, dimension reduction, hyperlink identifying, aggregation, and reduction in dimensionality. By learning the expected behavior from labeled or unlabeled data, machine learning algorithms may find anomalies or outliers in datasets [9]. This is helpful for systems for network intrusion detection, fraud detection, and problem diagnosis. The advancements in machine learning techniques, along with the availability of large datasets and computing power, have greatly increased the potential of computational intelligence [10]. Many smart computer applications depend on machine learning methods because they enable intelligent systems to learn from data and adapt and improve on it.

Deep learning, a subclass of machine learning, includes training deep neural networks with many layers in order to learn hierarchical representations of input. By outperforming earlier methods in a number of areas, such as speech and image recognition, natural language processing, and recommender systems, the use of deep learning has revolutionized computational intelligence. Deep learning models such as convolutional neural networks (CNNs) and recurrent neural networks (RNNs) allow for advanced data processing and decision-making.

3.3.3 Neural Networks

Neural networks are the interrelated cells that collectively make up computer-generated neurons or neurons. Neurons compute, process inputs, and generate outputs. Neurons have a layer structure in which an input layer receives the initial data, one or more hidden layers execute intermediate computations, and an output layer delivers the final results [11]. A weight is assigned to each neuron–neuron link in a neural network. To increase network performance, these weights, which represent connection strength, are modified over time.

A bias term is frequently present in each neuron, accounting for any offset or bias in the computation. Learn about the various neural network topologies, including convolutional networks, feedforward networks, recurrent networks, and deep neural networks (DNNs). Recognize regularization methods including activation functions, gradient descent, and backpropagation. They are a crucial component of computational intelligence and machine learning because they can draw patterns from complex data and learn from it.

3.3.4 Evolutionary Computation

Examine developmental approaches, genetic programming, and other evolutionary algorithms. Acknowledge ideas such as efficiency assessment and mutation, crossover phenomenon, and selection operators [12]. The principles of biological evolution and natural selection serve as the foundation for the intelligent computing branch known as evolutionary computation. It consists of a group of computational methods for figuring out the optimum course of action within a given search area, streamlining responses, and addressing difficult issues [13].

3.3.5 Fuzzy Systems

Recognize ideas like fuzzy rules, fuzzy membership operations, and fuzzy logic [14].

Important ideas related to fuzzy systems:

- ✓ **Fuzzy Sets:** By allowing elements to have degrees of membership ranging from 0 to 1, fuzzy sets generalize classical sets. Fuzzy sets allow for incremental membership depending on degrees of truth as opposed to rigorous membership (0 or 1). A fuzzy set's membership function describes the degree to which each element is a part of the set.
- ✓ **Linguistic Variables and Fuzzy Membership Functions:** Fuzzy systems employ linguistic variables to express qualitative notions or linguistic labels. Temperature symbols in language include terms like "hot," "cold," and "warm." Fuzzy membership functions use degrees of membership to associate numerical data with linguistic descriptors.
- ✓ **Fuzzy Rules:** Fuzzy systems use a collection of fuzzy rules to perform reasoning or make judgments. An antecedent (via

input variables) and a consequent (the production action) make up fuzzy rules. The consequent describes the output action or choice based on the evaluated degree of truth, whereas the antecedent evaluates the degree to which the input variables satisfy the requirements using fuzzy logic.

- ✓ **Fuzzy Inference:** Fuzzy inference is the process of arriving at a clear output or decision by using fuzzy rules and input data. Fuzzy logic operations such as fuzzy AND, fuzzy OR, and fuzzy implication are utilized by fuzzy inference mechanisms such as the Mamdani and Sugeno models to combine fuzzy rules and determine the overall degree of truth for the outcome.
- ✓ **Defuzzification:** The process of defuzzification involves turning the fuzzy output into a clear value that may be used for control or decision-making. To extract a single representative value from the fuzzy output, a number of defuzzification techniques are used, including centroid, mean of maximum, and weighted average.

3.3.6 Swarm Intelligence

Discover ant colony optimization, particle swarm optimization, and bee algorithms, among other swarm intelligence techniques. Recognize how interactions and collective behavior among simple agents can result in clever problem-solving. It is a method of computational intelligence that investigates the collective intelligence that results from the interaction of several people inside a group [15]. Swarm intelligence systems mimic the interactions and behaviors seen in natural swarms to solve complicated problems. Swarm intelligence is concerned with how basic individual interactions lead to the formation of intelligent behavior at the group level. Individuals may have limited skills or knowledge, but the collective behavior of the swarm exhibits attributes such as resilience, flexibility, and problem-solving abilities that are superior to those of the individual agents [16]. Swarm intelligence approaches have been utilized successfully in a variety of disciplines, including optimization, data clustering, image processing, network routing, workload distribution, and pattern recognition. Because of their ability to explore vast solution spaces, adapt to changing environments, and manage difficult situations, they are a significant tool in computational intelligence.

3.3.7 Bayesian Networks

Learn about probabilistic graphical models and Bayesian networks. Discover probabilistic thinking, belief propagation, and Bayesian inference. They offer a mathematical and graphical framework for modeling and examining intricate interactions between variables and for drawing probabilistic conclusions from the facts at hand [17]. A random variable is represented by each node in a Bayesian network. Each node has a conditional probability distribution (CPD) that determines the probabilities of its prospective values in respect to the values of its parent nodes. CPDs represent the probabilistic dependencies in the network. Bayesian networks are used in a variety of areas, including healthcare, banking, natural language processing, picture recognition, and defect detection. They are especially useful when dealing with uncertainty, inadequate data, and intricate probabilistic linkages between variables.

3.3.8 Optimization Techniques

Investigate optimization strategies used in artificial intelligence such as gradient descent, stochastic optimization, metaheuristics, and evolutionary algorithms. The genetic algorithm is an example of a search and optimization approach inspired by natural evolution. Maintaining a population of potential solutions, producing new solutions via genetic operators like crossover and mutation, and measuring the fitness of those solutions using an objective function are all part of the process [18]. GA iteratively produces the population to identify optimum or nearly ideal solutions to a specific problem.

3.3.9 Data Mining and Pattern Recognition

Recognize approaches such as association rule mining, classification, and regression for eliminating information and useful patterns from large datasets. Data mining is the process of extracting patterns, connections, and insights from massive databases. It combines methods from statistics, machine learning, and database systems to uncover hidden patterns and knowledge [19]. The primary purpose of pattern recognition is to detect and categorize patterns in data using previously developed models or templates. It entails using algorithms to identify and decipher patterns across a range of fields. The goals of data mining and pattern recognition, two related sciences, are knowledge extraction from data and pattern recognition. While pattern recognition focuses on the discovery and classification of patterns based on predetermined models, data mining especially focuses on finding insights and linkages within massive datasets.

3.3.10 Decision Support Systems

Learn about decision-making approaches in the face of uncertainty, such as Bayesian decision theory, decision trees, and probabilistic reasoning. Decision support systems (DSS) are computer-based solutions that provide relevant data, models, and tools to decision-makers [20]. DSS integrates artificial intelligence tools, data analysis, and interactive interfaces to aid in difficult decision-making scenarios. Models and algorithms are used by DSS to study and evaluate decision-making possibilities. These models could be based on methodologies such as mathematics, statistics, simulation, or artificial intelligence. They let those in charge investigate numerous scenarios, conduct sensitivity studies, and examine the consequences of alternative options. They provide what-if analysis, optimization, and quantitative analysis resources. Decision-makers can examine trade-offs, evaluate options, and make sound decisions based on objective criteria. Such systems can provide rapid insights and suggestions because of their capacity to interface with real-time data sources [21]. Dynamic DSS can learn from earlier decisions and user feedback to improve the precision and applicability of the support provided over time.

3.3.11 Hybrid Approaches

Look at combining the machine learning methods with other methods of intelligence, including neuro-fuzzy systems, evolutionary neural networks, and swarm-based optimization. The integration and fusion of several techniques or algorithms from diverse disciplines of AI and computational intelligence are referred to as computational intelligence hybrid approaches [22]. By combining the benefits of multiple methods, hybrid designs aim to overcome the shortcomings of individual approaches and improve performance and robustness. Hybrid techniques can tackle multi-objective optimization problems by combining different optimization methods or methodologies. This means balancing multiple competing goals at the same time. Hybrid multi-objective optimization techniques may use evolutionary computation, mathematical programming, or swarm intelligence approaches to search the solution space and find a set of Pareto-optimal solutions.

3.4 Research and Development

Despite a slowing rate of collaboration, the United States and China had the most cross-country partnerships in AI articles between 2010 and 2021. Since 2010, the number of AI research collaborations between the US and China has about quadrupled, and this number is roughly 2.5 times more than that of the next closest country pair, the UK and China. However, the rate of growth for all US–China relationships between 2020 and 2021 was the slowest since 2010. It accounted for only 2.1% of the total. All areas of AI research are expanding. Since 2010, the overall number of papers on AI has more than doubled. Pattern recognition, machine learning, and computer vision are the specific AI areas that continue to rule research [23]. The majority of important machine learning models were published by academia up until 2014. Enterprise has since seized control. In contrast to the three significant machine learning models generated by academia in 2022, there were 32 significant models produced by the industry. Modern AI systems require enormous volumes of data, computing power, and capital—resources that business actors naturally hold in higher quantities than non-profits and academia [24].

3.4.1 Government Plans in Enriching AI-Based Computational Intelligence Theory

Government involvement in AI-based computational intelligence theory is essential in determining how AI technologies are developed, regulated, and used. Aspects of government involvement in this area are listed below [25].

3.4.1.1 Funding and Research Initiatives

Governments routinely subsidize and support attempts to perform AI research. They offer grants to colleges, research institutes, and industry collaborations in order to advance the computational intelligence theory based on AI. Such courses foster innovation, knowledge exchange, and the development of cutting-edge AI technologies.

3.4.1.2 Policy and Regulation

It is to ensure the moral and responsible use of AI; governments play a role in creating legislation and regulations. They could create standards and frameworks for the creation and use of AI as well as for the protection of user privacy, algorithmic transparency, and fairness. The possible social, economic, and legal ramifications of AI technology are also a concern for governments.

3.4.1.3 *Standards and Interoperability*

The development of standards and interoperability frameworks for AI systems may involve government involvement. These standards aid in ensuring interoperability, data exchange, and collaboration between various AI platforms and technologies. They encourage uniformity and compatibility, facilitating widespread acceptance and incorporation of artificial intelligence-based intelligent computing systems.

3.4.1.4 *Education and Workforce Development*

Governments invest in education and workforce development initiatives because they understand how important it is to cultivate AI talent. They might sponsor programs that offer chances for study of AI, training, and specialized instruction in the theory of intelligence in computers. This promotes the development of a skilled labor force that can advance AI technology and spur innovation.

3.4.1.5 *Industry Collaboration and Partnerships*

To speed up AI research and development, governments encourage collaboration between academia, industry, and government agencies. They promote public–private collaborations to make the most of the knowledge and assets of various parties. Such partnerships may result in the implementation of AI-based computational intelligence theory and positive social effects.

3.4.1.6 *Ethical Guidelines and Responsible AI*

The development of moral standards and frameworks for the ethical application of AI technologies is a goal of governments. They address issues with prejudice, privacy, responsibility, openness, and the social effects of AI [26]. Governments establish ethical criteria to make sure that AI-based computational intelligence theory is used in a way that respects social norms, human rights, and the greater good.

3.4.1.7 International Collaboration and Governance

To address global issues related to AI-based computational intelligence, governments work together internationally. They take part in events, programs, and organizations that promote global norms and laws for AI technology as well as information exchange and international cooperation.

To promote creativity, handle ethical issues, assure responsible installation, and establish a setting that fosters the positive application of AI technology for society, government engagement in AI-based computational intelligence theory is crucial. Governments may influence the advancement and use of AI-based computational intelligence for the good of all through strategic policies, rules, and investments.

3.5 New Opportunities and Challenges

3.5.1 Explainable AI (XAI)

The purpose of explicable artificial intelligence is to provide methods and tools for explaining AI system decisions and outputs. It aims to increase interpretability and transparency, allowing people to understand how AI models get their conclusions. Everything in the current world is data-driven, with artificial intelligence taking center stage. XAI's architecture and tool set enable companies and developers to add a transparency layer to a given AI model, allowing customers to understand the reasoning behind the prediction. When AI is employed in many ways, it enhances the organization's ecosystem since it improves the accuracy, outcomes, and accessibility of the AI [27]. Figure 3.1 shows the working of XAI that serves as a useful tool that helps businesses understand fully the reasoning behind each decision-making step taken by a particular AI model. XAI assists you in keeping track of everything and receiving precise justifications for

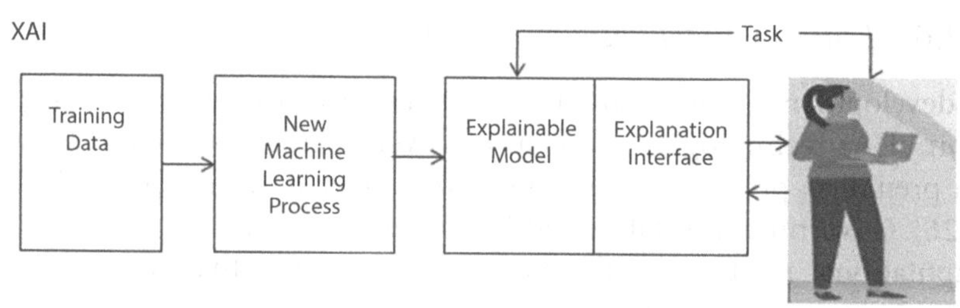

Figure 3.1 Working of explainable AI.

each choice, from comprehending machine learning algorithms to assessing neural networks and deep learning networks. When you use XAI, it becomes easier to evaluate the precision as well as responsibility of each AI decision and decide whether it is appropriate for your organization.

XAI is a vital part as it is in control of establishing and maintaining a responsible AI model in your company's ecosystem that will deliver fair and correct decisions. Furthermore, XAI helps to maintain user trust while limiting privacy and regulatory challenges.

3.5.2 Adversarial Machine Learning

Analyzing AI models' defenses against adversarial attacks is the focus of adversarial machine learning. To shield AI systems from harmful manipulation, researchers are creating defenses and countermeasures. Adversarial attacks use carefully constructed inputs, perturbations, or adjustments to the data to influence or trick machine learning models.

Adversarial examples are samples used as input that are intended to trick machine learning algorithms [28]. These instances are frequently invisible to humans, yet they can lead to inaccurate predictions or classifications from the model. Techniques like the Fast Gradient Sign Method (FGSM), the Jacobian-based Saliency Map assault (JSMA), or the Carlini-Wagner assault can be used to create adversarial examples.

To strengthen the resistance of machine learning models to hostile attacks, a variety of defense mechanisms have been developed, including:

- ✓ Feature squeezing
- ✓ Defensive distillation
- ✓ Input sanitization
- ✓ Ensemble methods
- ✓ Gradient masking

Adversarial machine learning research seeks to understand the vulnerabilities of machine learning models and develop effective defense mechanisms to mitigate the impact of adversarial attacks. It plays a crucial role in improving the security and trustworthiness of AI systems deployed in real-world applications.

3.5.3 AI for Edge Computing

Machine learning (ML) and optimization techniques are combined in edge computing AI techniques to enable effective and intelligent processing at the edge devices. In order to reduce latency and bandwidth needs, edge computing refers to executing computation and AI processing closer to the data source or device. For edge devices, AI approaches are being modified and improved, offering real-time processing and inference capabilities. In general, edge devices have little storage and computational power [29].

- ✓ Model compression techniques are used to minimize the size and complexity of AI models without significantly sacrificing accuracy and they are:
- ✓ quantization
- ✓ pruning
- ✓ knowledge distillation

It enables the deployment of more compact models on edge devices, making them more practical for on-site processing.

- ➢ **Federated learning:** Federated learning is a distributed machine learning technique in which training is done on the edge devices themselves as opposed to having data sent to a centralized server. With the use of this method, a common model may be jointly trained by a number of edge devices while protecting data privacy. Federated learning is especially helpful in situations where it is difficult to upload information to a centralized server because of connectivity or confidentiality constraints.
- ➢ **Transfer learning:** It entails using knowledge obtained from pre-training a model on a large dataset and applying it to a related but smaller dataset available at the edge. By sharing information, edge devices can take advantage of the pre-trained model's ability to generalize, minimizing the requirement for intensive device-specific training and conserving computational resources.
- ➢ **Inference:** Running models that were trained on fresh data to draw conclusions are known as inference. Edge-based inference is the practice of inference on the edge device itself, independent of servers located in the cloud. For effective and quick inference on resource-constrained edge devices, methods like optimized model architectures, hardware acceleration (e.g., GPUs and TPUs), and runtime optimization are used.

- **Edge-Cloud Collaboration:** To offload computationally demanding tasks or use cloud-based AI services, edge computing can be supplemented with cloud resources. This method involves offloading more sophisticated operations to the cloud while still performing some processing at the edge device. When it comes to edge data analytics, task partitioning, load balancing, and adaptive resource allocation are used to achieve the best possible balance between edge and cloud processing. Since edge devices produce enormous amounts of data, real-time analytics on these data are essential for AI applications. By enabling effective analysis and the extraction of valuable insights from the data generated at the edge, edge data analytics techniques including stream processing, anomaly detection, and data aggregation support real-time decision-making.

3.5.4 Continual Learning

Continual learning aims to enable AI systems to learn from a continuous stream of data over time, without forgetting previously learned knowledge. It addresses the challenge of adapting models to new data while retaining knowledge acquired from past experiences. Continual learning, also known as lifelong learning or incremental learning, is the ability of an AI system to learn from a continuous stream of data over time, without forgetting previously learned knowledge [30].

Real-world environments are often dynamic, with data distribution changing over time. Continual learning allows AI systems to adapt and continuously update their models to incorporate new information and handle changes in the environment. This is particularly valuable in applications like autonomous driving, robotics, and online recommendation systems, where the system needs to keep learning and improving as new data arrives. Concept drift refers to the phenomenon where the statistical properties of data change over time. Continual learning allows AI systems to address concept drift by adapting their models to the evolving data distribution. This is crucial in domains like fraud detection, anomaly detection, and cybersecurity, where the concept of normal behavior might change, and the system needs to continuously update its understanding to detect new patterns. Catastrophic forgetting occurs when an AI system forgets previously learned information as it learns new knowledge. Continual learning techniques mitigate this issue by employing strategies such as regularization, rehearsal, and knowledge distillation, which preserve and consolidate past knowledge while learning new tasks.

Continual learning is crucial in the real world as it enables AI systems to continuously improve, adapt to changing environments, handle concept drift, optimize resource usage, and retain previously learned knowledge. It helps bridge the gap between static batch learning and the dynamic nature of real-world applications, making AI systems more capable, efficient, and reliable.

3.5.5 Meta-Learning

To enable AI models to learn how to learn is the main goal of meta-learning. It investigates algorithms and architectures that, by utilizing transfer learning and prior knowledge, can swiftly adapt to new tasks or domains with little training data. The area of meta-learning, commonly referred to as "learning to learn," focuses on developing approaches and algorithms that help AI systems learn new tasks or domains more quickly and effectively. Meta-learning algorithms acquire knowledge from a variety of tasks or domains, enabling the system to generalize to other tasks that are comparable and to learn new tasks quickly and effectively from small sample sizes. When data are scarce and quick adaptability is necessary, like in the case of personalized recommendation systems or autonomous robots, this skill is essential. Transfer learning, a form of learning in which skills acquired by learning one activity are applied to another related one, is facilitated by meta-learning. Meta-learning algorithms can extract and transfer the pertinent information by learning the similarities between tasks, resulting in more effective learning and improved generalization on new tasks.

Hyperparameter optimization for machine learning algorithms is aided by meta-learning. Hyperparameters like learning rate, regularization strength, and network design control how well learning algorithms perform and behave. In order to boost performance and minimize manual tinkering, meta-learning algorithms are able to develop the search for the appropriate hyperparameters for a variety of tasks. It can be challenging and time-consuming to find the right hyperparameter values for large-scale deep learning applications. Meta-learning algorithms are able to recommend or automatically select the best algorithm for a new task by studying the results of various algorithms on a set of tasks. By automating the algorithm selection process, it is possible to create custom learning algorithms that are tailored to the specifics of the current challenge [31]. AI systems may learn from just one or a small number of examples thanks to meta-learning. Meta-learning algorithms are able to generalize to new instances or classes with little data by learning the underlying structure or patterns across tasks and extracting pertinent information. In applications like medical diagnosis or the detection of unusual events, when labeled data are scarce or obtaining new labeled samples is expensive, this is especially advantageous.

3.5.6 AI for Cybersecurity

AI is being used to improve cybersecurity because of the sophistication of cyber-attacks. In domains like intrusion detection, malware analysis, and network security, AI techniques aid in the detection and mitigation of assaults, the identification of abnormalities, and the improvement of security defenses. Due to the complexity and sophistication of cyberthreats, AI for cybersecurity has gained more and more importance in current research. The capability of conventional rule-based and signature-based cybersecurity techniques to identify novel and complex cyberthreats is constrained. AI methods, like machine learning and deep learning, can analyze enormous volumes of data, find patterns, and spot anomalies that could be signs of sophisticated dangers, such as malware, insider threats, and zero-day assaults. AI systems can adapt to new attack vectors and learn from prior data, improving the capabilities of detection and protection. By continuously monitoring and examining network traffic, system records, and user behavior, AI can allow real-time threat intelligence. AI systems may identify possible threats as they occur by utilizing techniques like anomaly detection and behavior analysis, enabling proactive defense measures and prompt response to reduce risks.

Security analysts struggle to manually handle the sheer number and complexity of security warnings and incidents. AI can automate a number of security operations processes, including alert triage and prioritization, log file analysis, incident investigation, and even action suggestion. This increases the effectiveness of security personnel and frees them up to concentrate on more important and difficult jobs. AI models can update and improve their skills over time, increasing their effectiveness in fighting off new threats, by analyzing changing patterns and input from security occurrences. Machines that are dynamic and learn on their own offer a benefit in the dynamic world of cybersecurity.

User and Entity Behavior Analytics (UEBA): AI might be very effective in evaluating user behavior and identifying anomalous actions that could indicate compromised accounts or insider threats. By learning typical patterns of human activity, AI systems can detect differences and raise red flags for further investigation. UEBA approaches enable the early identification of unauthorized access, data breaches, and insider attacks.

Through automated vulnerability evaluations and breach detection, AI can help in finding vulnerabilities in software systems and networks. Algorithms based on artificial intelligence are capable of simulating attacks, identifying flaws, and making security improvement suggestions. This aids organizations in proactively identifying and fixing flaws before bad actors can take advantage of them. By examining vast amounts of security logs, network traffic, and other data sources, AI can help with security analytics and threat hunting. Security analysts can find hidden risks and sophisticated attack operations that may have eluded conventional security measures by using AI algorithms to extract valuable insights, spot trends, and correlate events. AI has a lot of promise to improve cybersecurity practices by reducing response times, bolstering defenses, and shielding vital systems and data from new threats.

3.5.7 AI for Healthcare

With services including disease detection, medication discovery, personalized treatment, and tracking of patients, AI is revolutionizing the healthcare industry. AI-powered robotic surgery, personalized medicine, and genomics are some of the burgeoning fields.

Artificial intelligence (AI) can analyze a large quantity of patient data, including genetic information, electronic health records (EHRs), medical imaging, and scientific papers, to help in properly identifying disorders and proposing the best course of action. In order enhance clinical precision, more precisely target therapies, and improve patient outcomes, AI systems can identify trends, forecast illness risks, and make personalized suggestions.

1. **Enhanced Efficiency and Productivity:** Data input, documentation, and administrative procedures can all be automated by AI, freeing up the time of healthcare professionals to work on more important and difficult duties. AI increases efficiency, streamlines operations, and makes it possible for healthcare providers to give treatment more effectively by eliminating manual burdens.
2. **Personalized Healthcare:** Utilizing unique patient data, such as genetic information, lifestyle characteristics, and medical history, AI enables personalized medicine by customizing interventions and therapies. Biological marker

identification, response to treatment prediction, and personalized care plan recommendation are all made possible by AI algorithms, which results in more precise treatments, better patient experiences, and better health outcomes.

3. **Data Analysis and Insights:** Because of the enormous amounts of complicated data generated by the healthcare industry, it can be difficult for healthcare practitioners to glean insightful information. Large-scale healthcare information can be analyzed using AI techniques like machine learning and natural language processing to find hidden patterns and produce useful insights. This data-driven strategy aids healthcare personnel in making wise choices, spotting patterns, and improving the effectiveness and quality of patient treatment.
4. **Remote Monitoring and Telemedicine:** Outside of conventional healthcare settings, real-time patient data can be collected and analyzed by AI-enabled devices and remote monitoring systems. AI algorithms are able to spot anomalies, keep an eye on vital signs, and notify medical professionals of any health dangers. In order to improve access to care, particularly for those living in remote or underserved areas, telemedicine platforms driven by AI can permit remote consultations, allowing patients to obtain medical advice and treatment without visiting a healthcare center.
5. **Drug Discovery and Development:** AI is essential for expediting the procedures of identifying and developing drugs. Huge collections of scientific information available, patient information, and biochemical databases can be analyzed by AI algorithms to find novel drug candidates, foretell drug interactions, and improve medication formulations. This increases the opportunities for personalized medicine while also assisting in cutting down on the time and expense involved in bringing new therapies to market.
6. **Public Health and Disease Surveillance:** By examining population-level data, social media feeds, and environmental factors, AI can support public health initiatives and disease surveillance by identifying outbreaks, forecasting the spread of diseases, and directing public health measures. AI systems are able to spot trends, keep tabs on vaccination rates, and assist in making decisions about how to allocate resources and prepare for emergencies.

7. **Patient Engagement and Education:** Consumers can receive personalized health education, prescription notifications, and assistance with the self-management of chronic illnesses from artificially intelligent systems like AI-powered assistants and chatbots. These innovations support healthier lifestyles, enable people to take charge of their health, and improve patient involvement.

3.5.7.1 AI for Healthcare-Based Recommendation System

Healthcare professionals may receive clinical decision support from AI recommendation systems. These systems can help physicians identify diseases, forecast outcomes, and provide suitable interventions by examining patient data, symptoms, test findings, and medical literature. To find particular biomarkers, forecast illness risks, and direct focused medicines for better patient outcomes, recommendation systems can incorporate multi-omics data, including genomics, proteomics, and metabolomics. When recommending relevant pharmaceuticals and treatment choices, these algorithms may analyze enormous drug databases, clinical trials, and research publications, taking into consideration variables like efficacy, safety, side effects, and patient preferences. These technologies can improve clinical trial enrollment and hasten medical research by automating the trial identification and patient eligibility screening processes.

It is important to note that data privacy, security, and ethical issues must come first in the development and application of AI in healthcare. To earn the trust of healthcare practitioners, patients, and regulatory agencies, it is essential to ensure the AI algorithms are transparent, interpretable, and accountable.

3.5.8 Responsible AI

The goal of responsible AI is to create AI systems that are moral, impartial, and fair. It addresses issues with algorithmic bias, data security, responsibility, and the social effects of AI technologies. Responsible AI encourages AI systems' capacity for explanation and transparency. It involves creating algorithms and models that offer clear justifications for their judgments and forecasts so that people may comprehend the thinking behind AI-driven outcomes [1]. It entails abiding by privacy laws, receiving informed consent, and putting in place strong security measures to protect sensitive data. Clear governance frameworks and lines of accountability are necessary for responsible AI. Establishing procedures for AI system monitoring, dealing with unforeseen outcomes or mistakes, and defining accountability for the decisions or actions taken by AI systems are all included.

The human race are at the focus of AI development and application in responsible AI. It requires considering the effects on individuals, communities, and society as a whole, as well as ensuring that AI systems are designed to improve human welfare and benefit society as a whole. It requires ensuring that AI systems are reliable, secure, and capable of dealing with unexpected events or adversarial attacks without endangering users or jeopardizing their safety. Responsible AI requires collaboration from a wide range of stakeholders, including researchers, policymakers, corporate leaders, and the general public. It entails bringing together a diverse set of perspectives and expertise to address the tough issues and moral quandaries posed by AI.

3.5.9 AI and Robotics Integration

Robotics and AI fusion is a rapidly developing field. Intelligent robots that can see and interact with their surroundings, learn from data, and carry out complicated tasks in fluid and unstructured environments are currently being developed by researchers [2]. Robots are equipped with sophisticated perception abilities thanks to AI techniques like machine learning and computer vision. Robots' engagement and adaptability in dynamic situations are improved by their capacity to analyze sensor data, such as visual, auditory, or tactile inputs, to recognize objects, detect barriers, understand human gestures, or interpret natural language orders. Robots can understand and respond to human intentions, emotions, and commands with the help of AI algorithms, enabling interactions that feel intuitive and natural. This enables uses like cooperative assembly, help in hospital settings, and co-working situations.

Robotics and AI algorithms can be used together to automate a variety of jobs. Robots are more productive and can take on jobs that are physically taxing or repetitious with more accuracy and efficiency. Manufacturing, logistics, and agricultural businesses all benefit greatly from this integration. Robots can learn from their experiences and adjust to new circumstances thanks to AI. Robots may adapt their actions depending on feedback and pick up new skills through continual training and iteration thanks to reinforcement learning and other AI techniques. The versatility and effectiveness of robotic systems are improved by this adaptability. Robotic system safety is improved thanks to AI. Robots can detect anomalies in real-time monitoring, prediction, and anomaly detection using AI-based algorithms, which allows them to recognize possible dangers or hazardous conditions and take the necessary precautions to reduce them.

Self-organizing systems, in which individual robots interact and work together to do challenging tasks collectively, can be designed with the use of AI algorithms. Applications for swarm robots can be found in distributed sensing, environmental monitoring, and search and rescue activities. Addressing the ethical and social ramifications of combining robotics and AI is necessary. Research focuses on ensuring that AI-powered robots behave responsibly and accountable, taking into account factors like transparency, fairness, privacy, and ethical decision-making to avoid any potential hazards or biases in interactions between humans and robots. Future developments and expanded applications of integrating AI and robots are anticipated to result from ongoing research and improvements in this area.

3.5.10 AI for Sustainability and Climate Change

AI is being used to tackle ecological issues and stop global warming. It aids in resource management, climate modeling, environmental monitoring, and energy optimization to enable more sustainable practices. AI models can increase the accuracy of climate modeling, forecast extreme weather occurrences, and evaluate the long-term effects of climate change by spotting complex patterns and correlations within the data. Natural catastrophe management and prediction can benefit from AI. Its algorithms can assist in the forecasting of floods, hurricanes, wildfires, and other natural calamities by examining historical information as well as real-time sensor data. This makes it possible to issue prompt warnings, plan for evacuations, and allocate resources for disaster response and recovery. AI-powered algorithms can examine patterns of energy use, anticipate times of peak demand, and recommend plans to improve energy distribution and cut waste. Real-time monitoring, load balancing, and demand response can be made possible by smart grids and energy management systems that use AI. This will result in more sustainably consumed energy. These algorithms can allocate and schedule energy production from renewable resources like solar and wind while taking into account variables like weather and demand fluctuations. This increases the use of renewable energy, lessens the reliance on fossil fuels, and improves grid stability.

This makes it possible to issue prompt warnings, plan for evacuations, and allocate resources for disaster response and recovery. AI-powered algorithms can examine patterns of energy use, anticipate times of peak demand, and recommend plans to improve energy distribution and cut waste. Real-time monitoring, load balancing, and demand response can be made possible by smart grids and energy management systems that use AI. This will result in more sustainably consumed energy. These algorithms can allocate and schedule energy production from renewable resources like solar and wind while taking into account variables like weather and fluctuations in demand. This increases the use of renewable energy, lessens the reliance on fossil fuels, and improves grid stability.

AI models may examine traffic data, public transit trends, and urban infrastructure to optimize travel routes, reduce emissions, and improve urban planning decisions. AI-enabled robots and computer vision systems can distinguish and classify diverse types of waste, allowing for more effective recycling and reduced landfill waste. AI can also aid with garbage collection route optimization to cut fuel consumption and carbon emissions.

3.5.11 Quantum Computing and AI

By delivering quicker and more efficient computation for specific problems, quantum computing has the potential to revolutionize AI and computational intelligence. The study looks into how quantum algorithms and quantum machine learning can improve AI capabilities. Quantum computers use quantum bits, or qubits, which are capable of representing and processing information in superposition and entangled states. As a result, quantum computers can do some calculations orders of magnitude quicker than classical computers. Complicated AI algorithms involving large-scale optimization, pattern recognition, and simulation can thus be conducted more efficiently, resulting in faster and more accurate outcomes. Quantum machine learning methods, such as quantum support vector machines and quantum neural networks, have been proposed to exploit the processing potential of quantum computing for pattern identification, categorization, and problems related to regression.

The superior ability of quantum computers to represent quantum systems enables the study of complex physical, chemical, and biological processes. Quantum computing can help with data analysis tasks including grouping, dimensionality reduction, and optimization of large datasets. Quantum algorithms such as quantum singular value decomposition and quantum clustering algorithms have been proposed for more effective data processing and pattern detection. Quantum annealing and quantum optimization algorithms can simultaneously investigate a large number of candidate solutions, potentially discovering the optimal ones more quickly. This has an impact on tasks such as resource allocation, portfolio optimization, and route optimization.

3.5.12 Human–AI Collaboration

The goal of human–AI cooperation is to create AI systems that can communicate and collaborate with humans in a variety of disciplines. AI-powered virtual assistants, decision support systems, and human–robot interaction are all examples of this. Humans can help AI algorithms improve by providing accurate and dependable annotations and labeling for training data. Human judgment and expertise aid in the refinement and creation of datasets, eliminating biases and assuring high-quality inputs for AI models. This collaboration ensures that AI algorithms learn from a varied and well-annotated set of data, resulting in better computational intelligence. Human intelligence is essential in the design and development of AI algorithms. Human knowledge in fields such as machine learning, mathematics, and computer science is required for the development of novel algorithms and architectures that can improve the intelligence of computers.

People supply the imagination and insight required to devise novel ways and tailor AI solutions to specific issues. AI systems frequently make complex and illogical conclusions. Collaboration between humans and AI aids in making AI algorithms more interpretable and explainable. Humans may collaborate with AI systems to get relevant insights, comprehend the thinking behind AI-driven decisions, and detect any biases or inaccuracies. This collaboration ensures that AI models are liable, translucent, and trusted. Humans have domain-specific expertise and contextual understanding that can be used to supplement AI skills. Better insights into complicated topics can be acquired by combining AI's computing capacity with human knowledge. Human input adds context, intuition, and reasoning to AI systems, guiding them to more accurate and contextually relevant judgments. They can spot and fix any biases, flaws, or inconsistencies that an AI system may have with its algorithms.

For AI algorithms to be reliably and robustly improved over time, human feedback and oversight are essential. To solve ethical issues and make sure AI-based computer intelligence is in line with human values and society standards, human engagement is required. In situations where AI systems face ethical conundrums or complex trade-offs, humans can establish ethical standards, provide oversight, and make value-based judgments. Collaboration between humans and AI ensures ethical and responsible usage of AI technologies. Humans may improve models, fix errors, and direct AI systems towards higher computational intelligence through iterative feedback loops. This cooperative strategy makes it easier for AI systems to continuously learn and adapt to shifting requirements and developing data.

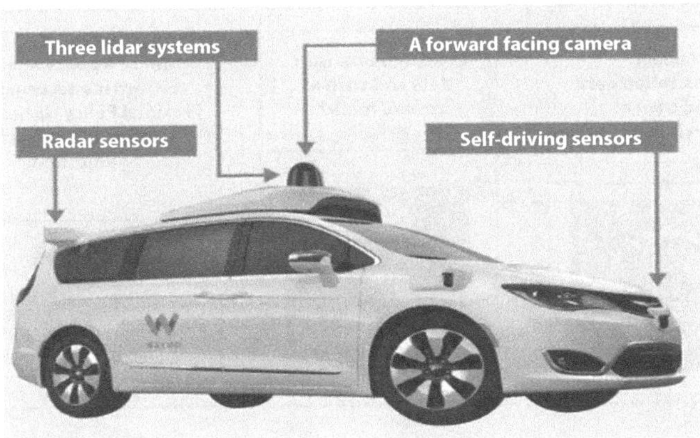

Figure 3.2 Waymo—autonomous car.

These new fields represent fascinating study and creation opportunities in AI-based computer intelligence. Figure 3.2 shows the prototype of Waymo-autonomous car. As scholars attempt to improve the capabilities, dependability, and ethical considerations of AI systems in use cases, they present fresh opportunities and difficulties.

3.6 Applications

3.6.1 Google-Waymo Car

Waymo vehicles are fitted with a range of sensors, including radar, cameras, cameras, high-precision GPS, and LIDAR (Light Detection and Ranging), which can be seen in Figure 3.3. These sensors give the automobile a thorough view of its surrounds, allowing it to recognize objects, people, cars, road signs, and traffic signals. Advanced computer vision and machine learning techniques are used to process the sensor data that Waymo cars collect. These algorithms do a real-time analysis of the sensor data, recognizing and categorizing objects, forecasting their behaviors, and building a complete 3D map of the surrounding area.

The Waymo Driver's decision-making algorithms evaluate the current driving scenario based on perception of the environment and plan the necessary actions. These algorithms take into account things like traffic laws, road conditions, other drivers' behaviors, and pedestrian movements. The algorithm generates the best possible navigation judgments, including turning,

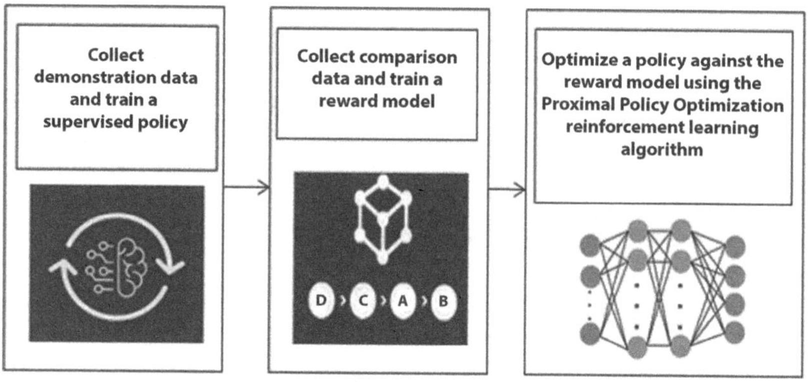

Figure 3.3 Overall working of ChatGPT.

merging, changing lanes, and stopping. The decision-making algorithms are translated into precise actions by the Waymo Driver's control system. To carry out the predetermined driving maneuvers, it manages the vehicle's acceleration, braking, and steering. The car's control system makes sure it stays on course, maintains a safe speed, and reacts to environmental changes.

Safety is a top priority for Waymo. To ensure fail-safe operation, the self-driving system has redundant hardware and software components. The redundant systems can step in to preserve the safety and functionality of the vehicle if a sensor or system component fails. It tests and validates its autonomous driving technology in-depth. Testing in various real-world situations, controlled settings, and simulation platforms are all included in this. The objective is to guarantee that the system operates dependably and safely in a variety of environments and driving circumstances. To continually enhance the effectiveness of its self-driving system, Waymo gathers enormous volumes of actual driving data. Machine learning algorithms are trained using these data, enabling them to learn from real-world examples and adapt to various driving circumstances.

The Waymo app is compatible with screen readers for mobile devices. In accordance with their accessibility choices and requirements, riders can also alter their app settings. For instance, see and alter the following riding choices by going to Account > Accessibility:

1. Show button to honk horn—Enabling this function enables you to tap the button during pickup to sound the horn and make it easier to locate the vehicle.
2. Assistive in-car audio—With this feature, you can listen to audio that describes buttons in the car, announces some

of the actions of the automobile, and recounts significant moments while you drive.
3. Reduce walking distance—This function makes sure that Waymo will pull up on the same side of the roadway as the rider.
4. Order a wheelchair accessible car by tapping a phone symbol.

3.6.2 ChatGPT

Based on the concepts of computational intelligence, ChatGPT is an application of artificial intelligence. Built on a deep learning model known as the Transformer architecture, ChatGPT can comprehend and produce writing that is human-like based on the input it gets. The model learns patterns, linguistic structures, and contextual information through training on a substantial amount of text data.

Input-output pairs—in which the input is a prompt or a message and the output is the associated response or completion—are fed to ChatGPT during the training phase. By adjusting its internal parameters in response to the patterns and correlations it finds in the training data, the model learns to produce responses.

Simply making use of this artificial intelligence strategy, ChatGPT is able to produce logical and environmentally appropriate answers to user inquiries or prompts. It uses its trained parameters to make predictions and produce writing that mimics natural human language after learning from a sizable corpus of text data. Millions of parameters in the deep learning model must be changed during this procedure in order to capture intricate correlations between words and phrases.

The response to be provided by the model is written using a sampling prompt and then provided by a human as training data to the most recent version of GPT-3, GPT-3.5. These data are used to train the transformer model that GPT-3.5 uses to try to generate new responses based on future prompts that are similar to those used during the training process. Be aware that the model will not generate exactly the same response for exactly the same prompt as if it were a database. Following the use of a prompt and responses produced by the GPT-3.5 model, the responses are ranked by a human from best to worst, and this information is then provided to the reward model. The ultimate stage of the process is rather intricate to elucidate. Proximal Policy Optimization (PPO) is an algorithm utilized by the model to optimize its learning process by incorporating feedback to enhance its performance on the given task. The objective at hand pertains to the production of a coherent reply in response to a designated prompt.

While ChatGPT has the potential to enhance productivity and streamline various tasks, it is not infallible and may commit errors like any other technological tool. Therefore, it is crucial to exercise caution and refrain from relying solely on its responses as the definitive solution for our daily activities. Figure 3.3 illustrates overall working of ChatGPT. The current AI model remains limited in scope, as it is primarily designed to facilitate text-based communication. The system lacks a comprehensive cognitive ability and a profound comprehension of concepts and contexts beyond the confines of its training dataset.

3.6.3 Boston Dynamics' Atlas

Boston Dynamics is a technology company that specializes in the creation of sophisticated robotics and self-governing systems. The dimensions of Atlas are reported to be approximately 1.5 meters in height, which is equivalent to 4.9 feet, and a weight of approximately 80 kilograms, which is equivalent to 176 pounds. The entity in question exhibits anthropomorphic characteristics, featuring a cranial region, a central trunk, bilateral upper appendages, and bilateral lower appendages. Atlas is outfitted with a variety of sensors that enable it to detect and traverse its surroundings. The system employs a combination of cameras, LIDAR, and various sensors to collect both visual and depth data, thereby facilitating its capacity to identify and classify objects, barriers, and individuals within its environment. The entity possesses remarkably adept appendages equipped with sensory receptors, facilitating its ability to delicately seize and maneuver items with accuracy. The appendages of this entity possess the ability to execute a diverse array of actions, such as grasping items, accessing entryways, and manipulating equipment. The robot exhibits semi-autonomous behavior by executing tasks based on top-down directives, while also demonstrating adaptability to its surroundings and prompt decision-making abilities.

Atlas is a humanoid robot that exhibits bipedal locomotion and is capable of performing diverse tasks. Figure 3.4 shows the Atlas robotic system that is equipped with 28 joints that are operated by hydraulic mechanisms, thereby enabling it to exhibit a diverse array of motion and flexibility. The robot is equipped with a range of sensors such as LIDAR, stereo cameras, and an IMU, which facilitate its ability to comprehend and navigate its environment. The advanced control system of Atlas facilitates versatile and nimble locomotion, while intricate algorithms analyze intricate dynamic interactions that encompass the entire body and surroundings to strategize movements. The recent advancements in Atlas have brought the robot

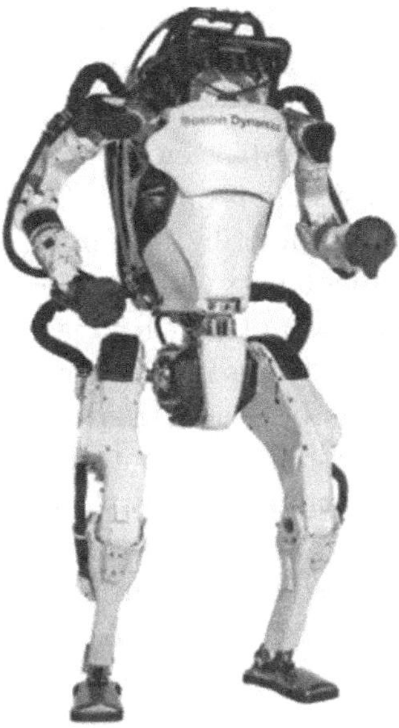

Figure 3.4 Atlas.

closer to being a practical instrument for various purposes such as rescue operations, construction, and production.

3.6.4 Netflix

Netflix serves as a notable illustration of the utilization of AI-driven computational intelligence within the entertainment sector, particularly in the domain of content suggestion and customization. The organization employs sophisticated algorithms and machine learning methodologies to furnish individualized recommendations to its clientele. Netflix utilizes collaborative filtering algorithms to examine user behavior and preferences. Netflix is capable of generating personalized recommendations by gathering user interaction data, which includes search queries, viewing history, and ratings. This methodology involves the comparison of a user's preferences with those of other users who exhibit similar interests, with the aim of providing recommendations for content that is congruent with their preferences. Netflix employs deep learning methodologies, including neural networks, to augment its recommendation algorithm. Deep learning algorithms possess the ability to acquire intricate patterns and representations from vast quantities of data, thereby enabling Netflix to discern subtle user preferences and furnish more precise recommendations. As an illustration, Netflix has the capability to conduct an analysis of the audio and visual attributes of its content in order to provide recommendations for comparable movies or shows that share similar audiovisual characteristics. The recommendation system is optimized through online learning by adapting bandit algorithms. The utilization of algorithms by Netflix facilitates the ongoing experimentation with diverse recommendation strategies and the prompt evaluation of user feedback. Netflix employs bandit algorithms to dynamically adjust its recommendations in response to user feedback, thereby enhancing the overall user experience.

The algorithms employed in this context undertake an analysis of various attributes of movies and TV shows, including but not limited to genre, director, cast, and plot keywords, with the aim of comprehending the content in question. Netflix utilizes user preferences in conjunction with these data to suggest content that aligns with the individual's personal preferences.

3.6.5 Trinetra

The mobile application "Trinetra" utilizes advanced artificial intelligence technology, specifically facial recognition, visual search, machine learning, and deep learning, developed by Staqu. It boasts a database of 500,000 individuals with criminal records, each accompanied by a photograph, address, and criminal history. According to data from 2016, Uttar Pradesh (UP) exhibited the highest prevalence of criminal activity, as evidenced by a crime rate of 128.7 per 100,000 individuals. The Uttar Pradesh Police expressed concern regarding their inability to expeditiously and effectively resolve criminal cases. Consequently, law enforcement agencies have sought to enhance their operational effectiveness through the utilization of diverse technological tools, including crime mapping analytics and predictive systems. The mobile application "Trinetra" was launched by the Director-General of Police, Om Prakash Singh, in December 2018. The application is powered by artificial intelligence. Trinetra maintains a database of 500,000 offenders, comprising their photographic identification, residential location, and criminal record. The aforementioned data have been gathered through the contributions of the district police, prison department, and Government Railway Police. The system is propelled by Staqu's facial recognition, visual search, machine learning, and deep learning technologies, and exhibits high performance even when processing low-resolution images and videos. The utilization of AI-powered Gang Identification Technology enhances the precision of the application.

Trinetra is capable of not only detecting and identifying a perpetrator of a crime, but also locating and identifying their accomplices who may be operating in various regions within the state. The mobile application is integrated with data from various correctional facilities, including DCRBs, SCRB, and CCTNS, to generate unambiguous and non-redundant information on criminal activities within the state. Furthermore, it is associated with the current Under Trial Management System (UTMS), which monitors the condition of all undertrials throughout the state. The aforementioned data can be promptly retrieved by any authorized personnel utilizing the designated software in a live setting. This application facilitates the registration and search of criminals for law enforcement officials through the utilization of basic biometric characteristics, such as images or videos. Trinetra aided law enforcement in apprehending a notorious offender who was charged with engaging in a daylight gun battle in Lucknow. It is anticipated that Trinetra will extend its coverage to encompass 75 districts, 6 GRP, ATS (Anti-Terrorist Squads), and STF (Special Task Force). The aforementioned application is intended for utilization by a total of 1,464 station house officers within the state, 65 GRP inspectors, as well as all other senior police officials.

3.6.6 Voice-Activated Backpack

Jagadish K. Mahendran, an artificial intelligence (AI) developer, and his team have developed an AI-based backpack that is activated by voice and can assist individuals with visual impairments in navigating and comprehending their surroundings. The system is contained within a compact backpack that accommodates a primary computing unit, such as a laptop. The utilization of a vest jacket for concealing a camera and a fanny pack for accommodating a pocket-sized battery pack that has the potential to offer nearly eight hours of usage is observed. The Luxonis OAK-D spatial AI camera has the capability to be mounted onto either a vest or fanny pack and subsequently linked to the computing unit located within the backpack. The OAK-D, affixed to the interior of the vest, can be viewed through three small apertures present on the vest. The OAK-D device is a highly adaptable and potent artificial intelligence tool that operates on the Intel Movidius VPU and the Intel Distribution of OpenVINO toolkit for on-chip edge AI inferencing. The device exhibits the ability to execute sophisticated neural networks, alongside furnishing expedited computer vision capabilities and a live depth map derived from its stereo pair. Additionally, it captures color information through a solitary 4k camera. The utilization of a Bluetooth-enabled earphone facilitates user interaction with the system through voice queries and commands, with the system reciprocating by providing verbal information. As the user navigates their surroundings, the system provides auditory feedback regarding prevalent obstructions such as signage, foliage, and individuals on foot. Additionally, it provides alerts regarding imminent crosswalks, curbs, staircases, and entryways. The backpack is equipped with the capability to identify and address prevalent obstacles such as traffic signals, suspended barriers, pedestrian crossings, mobile entities, and fluctuating altitudes, all while operating on an energy-efficient, interactive apparatus. The system can be utilized by individuals with visual impairments for both indoor and outdoor navigation, as well as for enhancing their comprehension of the surrounding environment.

3.7 Case Study: YOLO v7 for Object Detection in TensorFlow

The aforementioned applications serve as a clear demonstration of the significance of object detection in the realm of AI-based computational intelligence theory. This technology plays a pivotal role in a multitude of applications, thereby propelling the field of computer vision forward. The utilization of object detection enables the examination of extensive visual data through the provision of valuable insights pertaining to object frequencies, distributions, and relationships. The utilization of these data can facilitate the recognition of regularities, tendencies, and deviations, culminating in enhanced decision-making capabilities and the acquisition of commercial insights. The application of object detection technology has been shown to enhance automation and efficiency across diverse industries. The technology facilitates the mechanization of procedures that are dependent on the identification of objects, such as the supervision of stock, assurance of quality, and examination of products. Artificial intelligence (AI) systems have the potential to enhance operational efficiency, minimize errors, and boost productivity by effectively and precisely identifying objects.

3.7.1 YOLO v7

The YOLO model is categorized as a member of the one-stage detectors group and is widely recognized as a state-of-the-art object detection system. The YOLO architecture comprises of 24 convolutional layers and two fully connected layers. The YOLO v7 model is readily available for public use and offers a convenient Python-based implementation, rendering it easily accessible to a diverse community of developers and researchers. The YOLO v7 model employs a one-stage object detection methodology, wherein it performs the prediction of both bounding boxes and class probabilities in a single network pass. The employed architecture involves a convolutional neural network (CNN) that comprises a backbone network, typically derived from the EfficientNet architecture, and supplementary detection heads.

The software repository comprises comprehensive documentation, exemplar scripts, and pre-existing models that facilitate straightforward utilization. The methodology integrates sophisticated training methodologies, including data augmentation, focal loss, and multi-scale training. The application of these techniques serves to augment the model's capacity to effectively manage diverse object sizes, enhance the precision of localization, and mitigate the challenges associated with class imbalance. Postprocessing techniques, including non-maximum suppression (NMS), are employed by YOLO v7 to effectively filter and refine the detected bounding boxes. This process involves the elimination of duplicates and the selection of the most confident predictions. The YOLO v7 model demonstrates a commendable level of accuracy and simultaneously sustains real-time inference speeds on contemporary GPUs, thereby establishing its competitiveness. The various sizes of models provide a spectrum of trade-offs between speed and accuracy, catering to diverse use cases.

3.7.2 Working and Its Features

The YOLO algorithm employs a basic deep convolutional neural network to identify objects within an image, following the input of said image. The initial 20 convolutional layers of the model have been pre-trained with ImageNet through the implementation of a provisional average pooling and fully connected layer. Subsequently, the pre-existing model is transformed to execute detection, as prior studies have demonstrated that incorporating convolution and connected layers into a pre-trained network enhances its efficacy. The ultimate fully connected layer of YOLO is responsible for predicting the probabilities of different classes and the coordinates of the bounding box.

The YOLO algorithm partitions an input image into a grid of dimensions S × S. In the event that the centroid of an entity is situated within a particular grid cell, it is incumbent upon the said grid cell to detect said entity. Every individual grid cell makes predictions for B bounding boxes and their corresponding confidence scores. The confidence scores are indicative of the level of confidence exhibited by the model with regard to the presence of an object within the box, as well as the degree of accuracy associated with the predicted box.

The YOLO algorithm is designed to generate multiple bounding boxes for each grid cell. During the training phase, it is desirable to assign the responsibility of detecting each object to a single bounding box predictor. The YOLO algorithm designates a singular predictor as the "responsible" entity for object prediction, determined by the highest current intersection over union (IOU) value with the ground truth. This phenomenon results in specialization among the bounding box predictors. The performance of each predictor in predicting specific sizes, aspect ratios, or object classes is enhanced, leading to an overall improvement in the recall score.

Non-maximum suppression (NMS) is a prominent technique employed in YOLO models. Non-maximum suppression (NMS) is a computational technique utilized as a postprocessing step to enhance the precision and efficacy of object detection. Multiple bounding boxes are frequently generated for a single object in an image during object detection. The bounding boxes may exhibit overlap or disparate positioning, yet they are all indicative of a singular object. Non-maximum suppression (NMS) is a technique employed in object detection to effectively eliminate superfluous or inaccurate bounding boxes, thereby generating a solitary bounding box for each object present in the image.

The utilization of anchor boxes is a significant enhancement in YOLO v7. Anchor boxes refer to a predetermined collection of boxes that possess varying aspect ratios and are utilized for the purpose of detecting objects of diverse shapes. The utilization of nine anchor boxes in YOLO v7 enables the detection of a broader spectrum of object shapes and sizes in comparison to its predecessors. This feature contributes to the mitigation of false positives. An essential enhancement in YOLO v7 pertains to the implementation of a novel loss function, denoted as "focal loss." Former iterations of YOLO employed a conventional cross-entropy loss function, which has been acknowledged to exhibit lower efficacy in detecting diminutive entities. The problem at hand is addressed by the focal loss technique, which involves reducing the weight of the loss for accurately classified examples and prioritizing the challenging examples, i.e., the objects that pose a difficulty in detection.

The YOLO v7 iteration exhibits an increased resolution in comparison to its antecedent versions. The image processing capability of the system is conducted at a resolution of 608 by 608 pixels, surpassing the 416 by 416 resolution employed in YOLO v7. The enhanced resolution of YOLO v7 facilitates the detection of diminutive objects and augments the overall precision of the model. The primary benefit of YOLO v7 is its rapid processing capability. The algorithm exhibits a high processing speed of 155 frames per second for image processing, surpassing other contemporary object detection algorithms. The YOLO model in its initial form exhibited a processing capacity of up to 45 frames per second. The aforementioned characteristic renders it appropriate for delicate real-time applications such as surveillance and autonomous vehicles, wherein faster processing rates are of utmost importance.

3.7.3 Configuration to Deploy YOLO V7

a. Setup and Installation:

- The initial step is to install TensorFlow and any other essential dependencies.
- Retrieve the YOLO v7 model weights and configuration files.

b. Preprocessing:

- Rescale the input image to correspond with the specified input dimensions of the YOLO v7 model.
- The process of standardizing the pixel values of the image to a common scale is referred to as normalization.
- The task at hand involves transforming the image into the suitable input format that can be utilized by TensorFlow.

c. Model Architecture:

- The YOLO v7 model architecture is loaded through the utilization of TensorFlow's API.
- Establish the input and output layers of the model.
- The pre-existing weights are to be loaded into the model.

d. Object Detection:

- Utilize the YOLO v7 model to analyze the preprocessed image.

- Retrieve the anticipated bounding boxes, classification labels, and levels of confidence.
- The implementation of non-maximum suppression can be utilized to eliminate overlapping bounding boxes that may contain redundant information.

e. Postprocessing:

- The transformation of the anticipated bounding box coordinates obtained from the model's output to the dimensions of the initial image is required.
- Eliminate entities that fall below a specific level of confidence.
- Illustrate the bounding boxes and class labels obtained on the image.

f. Inference and Evaluation:

- Execute the object detection pipeline on test images or video frames.
- Assess the efficacy of the YOLO v7 model through a comparative analysis of the predicted bounding boxes and the ground truth annotations.

3.8 Results

Photographs captured from the sea are utilized for experimental purposes, as they frequently exhibit diminished image quality owing to various factors, including water reflections, waves, and weather conditions. This phenomenon may lead to a decrease in the level of clarity and visibility of objects, thereby posing a greater challenge in terms of detecting and distinguishing them from the surrounding background.

The intricate backgrounds may cause interference and diversions, thereby impeding the ability of object detection algorithms to distinguish between the targeted objects and the encompassing surroundings. The detection of the Crown-of-thorns starfish, a challenging task due to its similarity in color to the surrounding coral reef, was accomplished through the utilization of YOLO v7 in TensorFlow. Figure 3.5a shows COTS detected in a good resolution image and Figure 3.5b illustrates COTS that are identified precisely though it is a blurred image, which proves the efficiency of

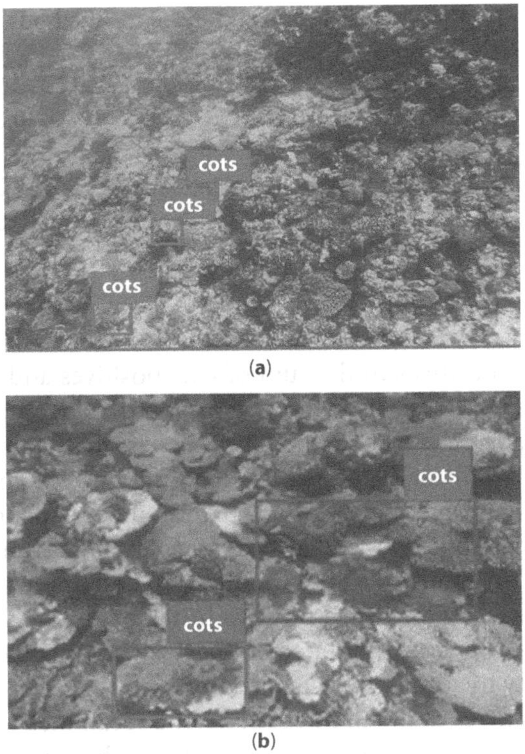

Figure 3.5 (a) COTS detected at coral reefs. (b) COTS identified in blur image.

the system. The resulting output effectively distinguishes the presence of the Crown-of-thorns starfish from the surrounding environment, which was previously difficult to discern in the provided images.

3.9 Performance Analysis

The comparative evaluation of YOLO v7 with other object detection methodologies, including Detection Transformers (DETR) and EfficientDet, has been conducted with regard to crucial factors such as speed and real-time inference. The evaluation metrics of precision and recall have been adopted. The metric of precision quantifies the ratio of true-positive instances, which are correctly identified as positive, to all instances predicted as positive. The statement pertains to the quantification of the system's capacity to accurately recognize pertinent instances while reducing the occurrence of false positives. The precision metric can be calculated as

Table 3.1 Comparison table of object detection methods.

	DETR	EfficientDet	YOLO v7
Recall	0.69	0.7	0.85
Precision	0.71	0.91	0.93
Average Inference Time	3.4	0.1	0.05
Accuracy	75%	95%	90%

the ratio of true positives to the sum of true positives and false positives. Table 3.1 shows the comparison table of proposed Yolov7 algorithm vs previously used algorithms. Stated differently, precision pertains to the degree of correctness in affirmative forecasts, denoting the system's adeptness in circumventing false positives. A high precision score denotes a reduced occurrence of false positives and an increased level of certainty in the positive forecasts. The metric of recall is utilized to determine the ratio of true positives, or correctly identified positive instances, to the total number of actual positive instances. The statement pertains to the quantification of a system's capacity to accurately detect all pertinent occurrences while minimizing the occurrence of false negatives. The recall metric can be calculated by dividing the number of true positives by the sum of true positives and false negatives. Figure 3.6 is the performance graph of transformer, EfficientDet, and YOLO v7 across various parameters from which it proves

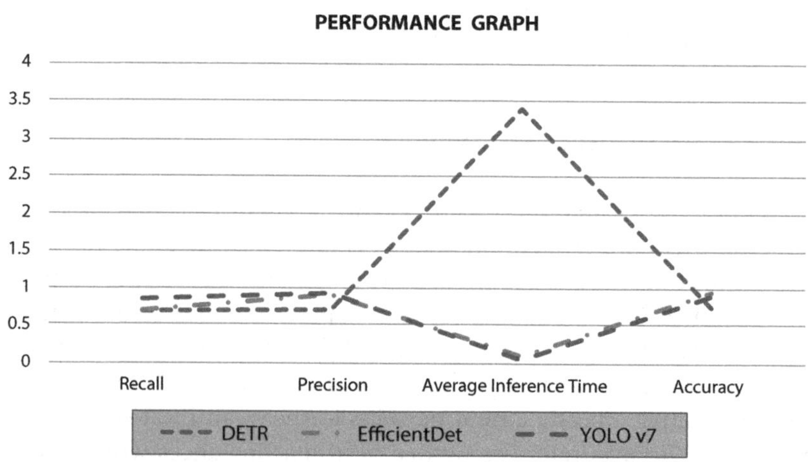

Figure 3.6 Performance analysis.

that both EfficientDet and **YOLOv7** are far better than transformer. The concept of recall underscores the extent to which positive predictions are exhaustive, thereby reflecting the system's efficacy in minimizing false negatives. A high recall score denotes a reduced frequency of false negatives and an enhanced capacity to apprehend all affirmative occurrences.

3.10 Challenges in Automation

- Facial recognition algorithms have been found to display bias, particularly towards individuals of color and women, as evidenced by multiple studies. The presence of bias may result in erroneous identification and probable prejudicial treatment in diverse contexts, such as the domain of law enforcement.
- Algorithmic hiring bias has been a subject of criticism directed towards certain companies that employ algorithms in their recruitment procedures, which may result in unintentional discrimination against specific categories of candidates. The algorithms in question may exhibit a bias towards candidates belonging to certain demographics or educational backgrounds, thereby reinforcing pre-existing disparities.
- Accidents involving autonomous vehicles have elicited apprehension regarding their safety and dependability. One of the most prominent instances pertains to the lethal incident that occurred in 2018, wherein a pedestrian lost their life due to a collision with a self-driving Uber vehicle.
- The emergence of deepfake technology has raised significant concerns due to its ability to produce manipulated or synthesized media content, such as videos or images, that can convincingly appear authentic. Social media platforms have the potential to disseminate false information, exert influence over the perceptions of the general public, and pose a risk to the credibility of individuals.
- The implementation of artificial intelligence and predictive algorithms in the realm of law enforcement has generated discussions concerning issues of privacy, surveillance, and potential biases. Detractors contend that the implementation of these technologies may result in inequitable profiling

practices and excessive law enforcement targeting specific societal groups.

- The escalating dependence on AI and automation frequently entails the gathering and manipulation of extensive quantities of personal data, thereby raising concerns regarding data privacy and breaches. The Cambridge Analytica scandal and similar occurrences have brought to the forefront the dangers associated with data privacy violations and the possibility of personal information being misused.
- Instances of market disruptions and "flash crashes" have been attributed to algorithmic trading glitches in high-frequency trading. The aforementioned occurrences give rise to apprehensions regarding the stability and equity of financial markets.
- The escalating automation of diverse industries has generated apprehensions regarding job displacement and its ramifications on the labor force. Discussions have arisen regarding the necessity of implementing retraining initiatives and policies as a means of mitigating potential economic disparities that may arise from the advent of automation.

The ethical ramifications of artificial intelligence (AI) are a topic of ongoing discussion and dispute, encompassing concerns such as accountability, transparency, and decision-making responsibility.

3.10.1 Marching Towards Solution

It is advisable to adopt cross-functional collaboration and actively pursue prospects to collaborate with experts from diverse disciplines. The development and implementation of AI and automation frequently necessitate specialized knowledge from multiple fields, including but not limited to data science, engineering, psychology, and business. Interdisciplinary collaboration facilitates the acquisition of novel viewpoints, the utilization of varied expertise, and the enhanced resolution of intricate issues. The implementation of automation and artificial intelligence necessitates the establishment of suitable governance and regulatory frameworks. It is advisable to remain updated on policy deliberations and actively participate in the discourse. It is recommended to actively involve policymakers, industry experts, and advocacy organizations in the process of formulating policies that can effectively tackle the issues arising from automation and foster an optimistic and all-encompassing future. It is imperative to prioritize human-centric design in the development of AI systems. It is imperative to contemplate the ethical ramifications, potential predispositions, and inadvertent outcomes of automation. It is imperative to pursue inclusivity and equity in the context of algorithmic decision-making. Through prioritizing human welfare and ethical principles in the development of artificial intelligence, it is possible to minimize potential hazards and optimize the advantages of automated systems. It is advisable to maintain agility and consistently modify one's skills and strategies to align with changing demands. One should perceive challenges as prospects for personal development and exhibit resilience when confronted with obstacles.

The obstacles presented by the implementation of automation in the field of artificial intelligence are not insuperable. Individuals can successfully adapt and flourish in an AI-driven world by adopting a mindset of perpetual learning, nurturing distinctive human abilities, promoting teamwork, and endorsing ethical principles.

3.11 Conclusion

Artificial intelligence-based intelligent systems have the capability to efficiently handle and evaluate vast amounts of data originating from various sources, while operating in real time. It facilitates the process of informed decision-making by extracting valuable insights and patterns. The capacity of computational intelligence-adapted systems to recognize patterns and produce forecasts is advantageous for companies across various sectors, including finance, healthcare, and manufacturing, among others, as it enables them to maintain a competitive edge, which is clearly explained in this chapter. This study presents an application of object detection utilizing the YOLO v7 algorithm, which incorporates the EfficientDet structure in TensorFlow. The study also includes a performance analysis of analogous AI-based tools, along with their respective results across different parameters.

References

1. Cao, Lianjun, Xinyu Zheng, and Luming Fang. "The Semantic Segmentation of Standing Tree Images Based on the Yolo V7 Deep Learning Algorithm." *Electronics*, 12, no. 4 (2023): 929.

2. Lund, Brady D., and Ting Wang. "Chatting about ChatGPT: how may AI and GPT impact academia and libraries?." *Libr. Hi Tech. News*, 40, no. 3 (2023): 26-29.
3. Bala, P. Manju, S. Usharani, R. Rajmohan, T. Ananth Kumar and A. Balachandar. "Bioinspired CNN Approach for Diagnosing COVID-19 Using Images of Chest X-Ray." In *Smart Computer Vision*, pp. 181-201. Cham: Springer International Publishing, 2023.
4. Tan, Mingxing, Ruoming Pang, and Quoc V. Le. "Efficientdet: Scalable and efficient object detection." In *Proceedings of the IEEE/CVF conference on computer vision and pattern recognition*, pp. 10781-10790. 2020.
5. Sallam, Malik. "ChatGPT utility in healthcare education, research, and practice: systematic review on the promising perspectives and valid concerns." In *Healthcare*, vol. 11, no. 6, p. 887. MDPI, 2023.
6. Mekhalfi, Mohamed Lamine, Carlo Nicolò, Yakoub Bazi, Mohamad Mahmoud Al Rahhal, Norah A. Alsharif, and Eslam Al Maghayreh. "Contrasting YOLOv5, transformer, and EfficientDet detectors for crop circle detection in desert." *IEEE Geosci. Remote Sens. Lett.*, 19 (2021): 1-5.
7. Li, Ronghui, Jinshan Wu, and Liang Cao. "Ship target detection of unmanned surface vehicle base on efficientdet." *Syst. Sci. Control Eng.*, 10, no. 1 (2022): 264-271.
8. Subbulakshmi, N., R. Manimegalai, G. Rajakumar, T. Ananth Kumar, and Umadevi Kosuri. "A novel design of low-cost hearing aid devices using an efficient lifting filter bank with a modified variable filter." *Expert Rev. Med. Devices*, 19, no. 12 (2022): 991-999.
9. Wang, Yanfeng, Tao Wang, Xin Zhou, Weiwei Cai, Runmin Liu, Meigen Huang, Tian Jing et al. "TransEffiDet: aircraft detection and classification in aerial images based on EfficientDet and transformer." *Comput. Intell. Neurosci.*, 2022 (2022).
10. Liu, Shu, Lu Qi, Haifang Qin, Jianping Shi, and Jiaya Jia. "Path aggregation network for instance segmentation." In *Proceedings of the IEEE conference on computer vision and pattern recognition*, pp. 8759-8768. 2018.
11. Afzaal, Hassan, Aitazaz A. Farooque, Farhat Abbas, Bishnu Acharya, and Travis Esau. "Computation of evapotranspiration with artificial intelligence for precision water resource management." *Appl. Sci.*, 10, no. 5 (2020): 1621.
12. Toscano, Piero, Annamaria Castrignanò, Salvatore Filippo Di Gennaro, Alessandro Vittorio Vonella, Domenico Ventrella, and Alessandro Matese. "A precision agriculture approach for durum wheat yield assessment using remote sensing data and yield mapping." *Agronomy*, 9, no. 8 (2019): 437.
13. Mekhalfi, Mohamed Lamine, Carlo Nicolò, Ivan Ianniello, Federico Calamita, Rino Goller, Maurizio Barazzuol, and Farid Melgani. "Vision system for automatic on-tree kiwifruit counting and yield estimation." *Sensors*, 20, no. 15 (2020): 4214.
14. Shafaei, S. M., M. Loghavi and S. Kamgar. "Reliable execution of a robust soft computing workplace found on multiple neuro-fuzzy inference systems

coupled with multiple nonlinear equations for exhaustive perception of tractor-implement performance in plowing process." *Artif. Intell. Agric.*, 2 (2019): 38-845.

15. Cao, Liangben, Xixin Zhang, Jingyu Pu, Siyuan Xu, Xinlin Cai, and Zhiyong Li. "The field wheat count based on the efficientdet algorithm." In *2020 IEEE 3rd International Conference on Information Systems and Computer Aided Education (ICISCAE)*, pp. 557-561. IEEE, 2020.
16. Kumar, Abhishek, Swarn Avinash Kumar, Vishal Dutt, S. Shitharth, and Esha Tripathi. "IoT based arrhythmia classification using the enhanced hunt optimization-based deep learning." *Expert Syst.*, (2023): e13298.
17. Ghiasi, Golnaz, Tsung-Yi Lin, and Quoc V. Le. "Nas-fpn: Learning scalable feature pyramid architecture for object detection." In *Proceedings of the IEEE/CVF conference on computer vision and pattern recognition*, pp. 7036-7045. 2019.
18. Alhijawi, Bushra, and Arafat Awajan. Genetic algorithms: Theory, genetic operators, solutions, and applications. *Evol. Intell.*, 17, 3, 1245–1256, 2024.
19. Cavalcante, Rodolfo C., Rodrigo C. Brasileiro, Victor LF Souza, Jarley P. Nobrega, and Adriano LI Oliveira. "Computational intelligence and financial markets: A survey and future directions." *Expert Syst. Appl.*, 55 (2016): 194-211.
20. Srivastav, Arun Lal, Markandeya, Naveen Patel, Mayank Pandey, Ashutosh Kumar Pandey, Ashutosh Kumar Dubey, Abhishek Kumar, Abhishek Kumar Bhardwaj, and Vinod Kumar Chaudhary. "Concepts of circular economy for sustainable management of electronic wastes: challenges and management options." *Environ. Sci. Pollut. Res.*, 30, no. 17 (2023): 48654-48675.
21. Alam, Ashraf. "Should robots replace teachers? Mobilisation of AI and learning analytics in education." In *2021 International Conference on Advances in Computing, Communication, and Control (ICAC3)*, pp. 1-12. IEEE, 2021.
22. Chu, Shih-Ting, Gwo-Jen Hwang, and Yun-Fang Tu. "Artificial intelligence-based robots in education: A systematic review of selected SSCI publications." *Comput. Educ.: Artif. Intell.*, (2022): 100091.
23. Kurrek, Philip, Firas Zoghlami, Mark Jocas, Martin Stoelen, and Vahid Salehi. "Q-model: An artificial intelligence based methodology for the development of autonomous robots." *J. Comput. Inf. Sci. Eng.*, 20, no. 6 (2020): 061006.
24. Sumantri, Viony Kresna. "Legal responsibility on errors of the artificial intelligence-based robots." *Lentera Huk.*, 6 (2019): 337.
25. Bousdekis, Alexandros, Gregoris Mentzas, Dimitris Apostolou, and Stefan Wellsandt. "Evaluation of AI-Based Digital Assistants in Smart Manufacturing." In *Advances in Production Management Systems. Smart Manufacturing and Logistics Systems: Turning Ideas into Action: IFIP WG 5.7 International Conference, APMS 2022, Gyeongju, South Korea, September 25–29, 2022, Proceedings, Part II*, pp. 503-510. Cham: Springer Nature Switzerland, 2022.

26. Benkhaddra, Ilyas, Abhishek Kumar, Mohamed Ali Setitra, and Lei Hang. "Design and Development of Consensus Activation Function Enabled Neural Network-Based Smart Healthcare Using BIoT." *Wirel. Pers. Commun.*, 130, no. 3 (2023): 1549-1574.
27. Alsamhi, Saeed H., Ou Ma, and Mohd Samar Ansari. "Survey on artificial intelligence based techniques for emerging robotic communication." *Telecom. Syst.*, 72 (2019): 483-503.
28. Maedche, Alexander, Christine Legner, Alexander Benlian, Benedikt Berger, Henner Gimpel, Thomas Hess, Oliver Hinz, Stefan Morana, and Matthias Söllner. "AI-based digital assistants: Opportunities, threats, and research perspectives." *Bus. Inf. Syst. Eng.*, 61 (2019): 535-544.
29. Brill, Thomas M., Laura Munoz, and Richard J. Miller. "Siri, Alexa, and other digital assistants: a study of customer satisfaction with artificial intelligence applications." *J. Mark. Manage.*, 35, no. 15-16 (2019): 1401-1436.
30. Buhalis, Dimitrios, and Iuliia Moldavska. "In-room voice-based AI digital assistants transforming on-site hotel services and guests' experiences." In *Information and Communication Technologies in Tourism 2021: Proceedings of the ENTER 2021 eTourism Conference, January 19–22, 2021*, pp. 30-44. Springer International Publishing, 2021.
31. Akkaya, Cigdem, and Helmut Krcmar. "Potential use of digital assistants by governments for citizen services: The case of Germany." *In Proceedings of the 20th Annual International Conference on Digital Government Research*, pp. 81-90. 2019.

4

Information Processing, Learning, and Its Artificial Intelligence

P. Praveenkumar*, Pragati M., Prathiba S., Mirthulaa G., Supriya P., Jayashree B. and Jayasri R.

Department of Information Technology, Sri Manakula Vinayagar Engineering College, Madagadipet, Pondicherry, India

Abstract

This chapter provides a thorough analysis of the artificial intelligence (AI) system that is based on cognitive mechanisms for processing visual data. For the purpose of demonstrating the relationship between a generic model of an intelligent system and cognitive mechanisms, we investigate the processing of visual information with selective attention. Many would contend that artificial intelligence signifies a fundamental shift in how people and machines interact, not just a technological advancement. The majority of the literature makes the assumption that AI-powered practices significantly alter organizational structure, communication, affordance, and ecosystem. However, research in AI is sometimes hazy and illegible. There is a need for a defined direction that outlines how information systems can contribute and what are to be the main research issues and questions, even if the information systems (IS) field can play a crucial role in the development and usage of AI. The paper concludes that artificial intelligence (AI) technology may overtake or replace human instructors in the next ten years.

***Keywords*:** Information processing, deep learning, artificial intelligence, virtual reality, data processing, and management of learning

**Corresponding author*: prhsel@gmail.com

T. Ananth Kumar, E. Golden Julie, Venkata Raghuveer Burugadda, Abhishek Kumar and Puneet Kumar (eds.) Computational Intelligence: Theory and Applications, (97–116) © 2024 Scrivener Publishing LLC

4.1 Introduction—Artificial Intelligence

Artificial intelligence (AI) has ushered in a new era of technological advancement, endowing machines with the remarkable ability to learn from experiences, adapt to novel inputs, and execute tasks akin to human capabilities. This transformative power of AI extends its influence to the realm of education, where it emerges as a potent tool for facilitating learning processes. In the following discourse, we will expound upon the multifaceted applications of AI in the field of education, delving into its nuanced implications. Prior to delving into the specifics, it is imperative to comprehend the essence of AI technology, which serves as the cornerstone of these transformative applications. AI can be succinctly described as an emulation of human cognitive functions, realized through machine-based processes. This encompasses a wide spectrum of capabilities that can be further categorized based on their intellectual prowess. Of particular resonance is the paradigm of deep learning, a facet within the AI domain that empowers computer programs to autonomously acquire knowledge, engage in reasoning, and rectify errors, all without explicit human intervention. This dimension of AI becomes profoundly pertinent within the context of automated data extraction, exemplifying the potential to streamline and enhance data management processes [1]. AI's synergy with robotic technology is illustrative of its capacity to mirror human behavior and imitate the learning trajectory. Robots, harnessed by AI, possess the dexterity to learn from their mistakes, adapt to changing circumstances, and thus replicate human-like learning curves. The integration of these principles underscores AI's potential as a potent enabler in the learning journey. This perspective sets the stage for a comprehensive examination of AI's contributions to the educational landscape, as it navigates uncharted territories with the promise of optimized learning outcomes [2].

Artificial intelligence (AI) assumes a pivotal role in reshaping the landscape of learning, ushering in a new era of personalized, efficient, and adaptive educational experiences. AI's influence is multifaceted and encompasses various aspects of the learning journey. It tailors educational content and pacing to cater to the individual needs and learning styles of students, while AI-driven assessments provide real-time feedback and evaluation, adapting to students' performance levels. AI generates engaging and immersive learning materials, facilitates language learning, and ensures 24/7 accessibility to resources. By analyzing educational data, AI offers insights into student performance and trends, informing instructional strategies. Additionally, AI streamlines administrative tasks, offers virtual tutoring, promotes education equity, and supports lifelong learning. Overall, AI's integration in learning enhances the educational landscape, creating dynamic, learner-centric environments that empower both educators and students for success in a rapidly evolving world [3].

AI's impact extends beyond customization, delving into real-time assessment and feedback. By constantly analyzing student interactions and performance, AI-driven assessments adapt and evolve, offering timely insights into comprehension levels and learning trajectories. This responsive evaluation fosters a growth-oriented mindset, encouraging students to refine their understanding and bridge knowledge gaps.

The fusion of AI and education goes beyond conventional classroom boundaries. AI-generated learning materials, often enriched with immersive technologies like virtual reality, spark engagement and creativity, enabling learners to explore complex concepts through interactive simulations and visualizations. Moreover, AI-powered language learning platforms harness natural language processing to facilitate nuanced language acquisition, catering to diverse linguistic backgrounds [4].

4.2 Artificial Intelligence and Its Learning

Artificial intelligence (AI) is a groundbreaking force that is fundamentally reshaping the landscape of learning and education. At its core, AI leverages advanced algorithms and computational power to simulate human cognitive processes, allowing machines to emulate learning, reasoning, and problem-solving abilities. This intersection of technology and education has given rise to a multitude of innovative applications that are revolutionizing traditional learning paradigms. One of the most significant contributions of AI to learning lies in its ability to personalize educational experiences. Through intricate data analysis and sophisticated machine learning models, AI can discern individual student patterns, preferences, and strengths. This enables educators to tailor learning materials, content delivery, and instructional strategies to cater to each student's unique learning style, thereby enhancing engagement and comprehension. One of AI's most transformative roles in learning lies in personalization. By harnessing intricate data analysis and sophisticated machine learning models, AI discerns individual learning patterns, preferences, and strengths. This ability enables educators to tailor learning materials, instructional strategies, and content delivery to cater to each student's unique style, fostering deeper engagement and comprehension [5].

AI's prowess extends to assessment and feedback. AI-driven assessments provide real-time insights into student performance, adapting to individual learning trajectories. This facilitates targeted interventions, enabling educators to address areas of weakness and refine teaching strategies for optimized learning outcomes.

Moreover, AI orchestrates immersive and dynamic learning experiences. Through language processing, AI facilitates language learning, offering interactive platforms that enhance linguistic skills. AI-generated content engages students with simulations, interactive modules, and virtual environments, augmenting traditional learning methods and stimulating active participation. AI also leverages analytics to provide educators with nuanced insights into student engagement and performance. By analyzing data on interactions with learning materials, AI unveils patterns and trends that inform instructional decisions, driving continuous improvement and fostering data-informed pedagogy [6].

The integration of AI extends beyond the confines of the classroom. AI-driven administrative automation alleviates educators' burdens, enabling them to focus on teaching rather than administrative tasks. Virtual tutoring, aided by AI, promotes education equity by offering personalized support to learners, regardless of geographic location or resources.

4.3 Artificial Intelligence's Effects on IT

The infusion of artificial intelligence (AI) into the realm of information technology (IT) has catalyzed a profound transformation, reshaping the very fabric of IT practices and ushering in a new era of innovation and efficiency. The effects of AI on IT are far-reaching and multi-dimensional, fundamentally altering the way businesses and organizations operate in the digital landscape. AI empowers IT systems with the capability to process and analyze colossal volumes of data with unparalleled speed and accuracy [7].

This data-driven approach revolutionizes decision-making, enabling organizations to extract valuable insights, identify patterns, and make informed choices that drive strategic initiatives. AI's predictive and prescriptive analytics fuel proactive problem-solving, minimizing downtime, optimizing resource allocation, and enhancing overall operational performance.

Cybersecurity, a paramount concern in the digital age, witnesses a significant transformation with the integration of AI. AI-powered cybersecurity solutions fortify digital fortresses by autonomously detecting and mitigating threats, responding to breaches in real time, and adapting defenses to evolving attack vectors. The amalgamation of AI and cybersecurity cultivates a robust defense mechanism that safeguards sensitive data and digital assets.

The landscape of customer experience and engagement is profoundly enriched by AI's capabilities. Chatbots, virtual assistants, and AI-driven recommendation systems enhance user interactions, providing personalized support, and anticipating customer needs. This not only enhances user satisfaction but also contributes to fostering lasting customer relationships, thereby augmenting business success [8].

The workforce ecosystem undergoes a paradigm shift with AI's introduction, as intelligent automation streamlines routine tasks, liberating human resources to focus on strategic, creative, and value-added endeavors. AI-driven process automation expedites workflows, minimizes errors, and enhances overall efficiency, yielding substantial gains in productivity and cost optimization.

Nevertheless, the integration of AI in IT is not without challenges. Ethical considerations surrounding AI's decision-making processes, data privacy concerns, and the need for transparency necessitate robust governance frameworks. Additionally, the need for upskilling the workforce to harness AI's potential emerges as a critical imperative to fully exploit its transformative power.

4.4 Examples of Artificial Intelligence

Here are 4 ways that AI is transforming the teaching profession:

1) Smart learning content
2) Intelligent tutoring system
3) Virtual facilitators and learning environment
4) Content analytics

4.4.1 Smart Learning Content

AI is revolutionizing learning materials by creating adaptive and dynamic content. Through AI-driven algorithms, educational content can be tailored to individual student's learning styles, preferences, and progress. This smart content adjusts its complexity, format, and pace, ensuring optimal engagement and comprehension.

It allows educators to offer personalized, interactive, and engaging materials that cater to a diverse range of students, making the learning process more effective and impactful [9].

1. Personalized Learning

Personalized learning aims to modify training to each student's talents and strengths because every learner is different and progresses at a different rate. One way to do this is through one-on-one tutoring, but it may be expensive and time-consuming. AI can create a personalized learning trajectory for each learner that automatically receives feedback, adapts, and offers the best course of action. An illustration of a customized learning tool is Duolingo. One of the best examples of individualized instruction is Duolingo. You may enroll in quick online courses in more than 30 different languages on the language-learning website Duolingo. To ensure that each student advances at the right pace and level, Duolingo's lessons are individually tailored. Duolingo uses linguistics and artificial intelligence to evaluate each student's progress.

2. Intelligent Tutoring System

Figure 4.1 shows the evidence of AI-driven intelligent tutoring systems provide students with personalized and real-time guidance. These systems analyze student performance, identify areas of weakness, and offer targeted exercises, explanations, and feedback. Educators can leverage these systems to supplement their teaching, offering students additional support and resources outside of the classroom. The continuous monitoring and adaptive nature of these systems lead to more effective learning outcomes and skill development. These platforms will eventually be able to support a

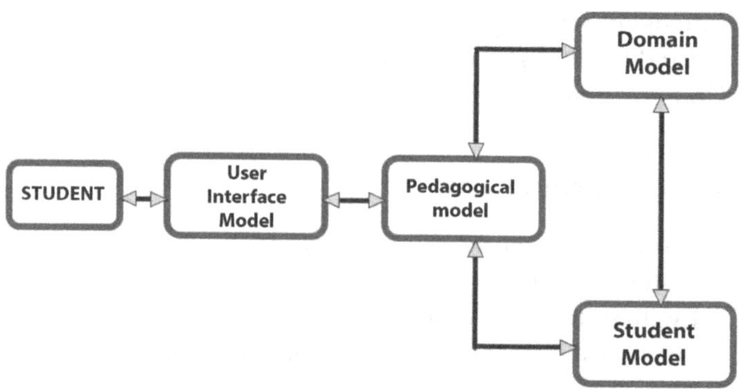

Figure 4.1 Intelligent tutorial system.

variety of learning techniques, helping both educators and students alike. Figure 4.1 shows the model diagram of intelligent tutorial system.

- The student model is in charge of gathering information about the learner and assessing their level of knowledge.
- Using the data gathered to guide the learning process, the tutoring model connects the first two elements.
- The interface component serves as a conduit for communication between the other components and the learner. This is the fundamental way that ITSS functions, albeit some may have additional complications.

4.4.2 Intelligent Tutorial System Future

The future of intelligent tutorial systems holds the promise of transformative advancements in education. As technology and artificial intelligence (AI) continue to evolve, the capabilities and potential of intelligent tutorial systems are set to redefine the learning experience in profound ways:

a) **Hyper-Personalization:** Future intelligent tutorial systems will be able to create even more finely tuned personalized learning pathways for individual students. These systems will use advanced data analysis and machine learning to not only adapt to a student's learning style but also factor in real-time feedback, emotions, and cognitive states, ensuring a truly tailored and effective learning journey.
b) **Emotional Intelligence:** Intelligent tutorial systems of the future might incorporate emotional intelligence capabilities. They could gauge a student's emotional state through facial recognition, tone analysis, or biometric sensors, and adjust their interactions accordingly. If a student shows signs of frustration, the system could offer encouragement or suggest a break, enhancing the emotional well-being of learners.
c) **Augmented Reality (AR) and Virtual Reality (VR):** Integrating AR and VR technologies into intelligent tutorial systems could provide immersive and interactive learning experiences. Students could engage in virtual labs, historical reconstructions, or explore complex 3D models, enhancing their understanding through hands-on exploration.
d) **Collaborative Learning:** Future systems might facilitate collaborative learning experiences through AI-driven

group interactions. These systems could analyze individual strengths and weaknesses within a group, assign roles, and generate collaborative projects that encourage peer learning and cooperation.

e) **Continuous Learning and Lifelong Education:** Intelligent tutorial systems could evolve beyond formal education settings. They might become integral parts of individuals' lifelong learning journeys, offering personalized skill development, career guidance, and upskilling recommendations throughout various stages of life.

f) **Ethical and Responsible AI:** As intelligent tutorial systems become more advanced, addressing ethical considerations will be crucial. Future systems should prioritize data privacy, transparency, and unbiased content delivery, ensuring that AI technologies contribute positively to education without perpetuating bias or discrimination.

g) **Human–AI Symbiosis:** The future might see a seamless integration of AI and human educators, where AI acts as a supportive partner. AI could handle administrative tasks, provide real-time data analytics, and offer insights, allowing educators to focus on building strong mentorship relationships, creativity, and fostering critical thinking.

4.4.3 Virtual Facilitators and Learning Environment

AI-powered virtual facilitators enhance the learning experience by offering interactive and immersive environments. These virtual entities can simulate real-world scenarios, conduct simulations, and facilitate group discussions. They engage students in active learning and problem-solving, fostering critical thinking and collaboration skills. Moreover, AI can create virtual classrooms that enable remote and flexible learning, ensuring accessibility and inclusivity for students from various backgrounds and locations [10].

The key lies in the integration of "touchless technology" or "gesture recognition technology," an innovative development that empowers virtual facilitators to respond naturally to both verbal and nonverbal cues. By interpreting gestures, expressions, and voice tones, these virtual entities can react intuitively, simulating genuine human interaction. Leveraging the prowess of AI, along with 3D gaming and computer animation, smart learning environments harness these technologies to imbue virtual characters with lifelike qualities, facilitating authentic social interactions.

4.4.4 Content Analytics

AI-driven content analytics represents a transformative tool that empowers educators with nuanced insights into the intricate dynamics of student engagement and performance within the realm of education. This advanced technological application hinges on the analysis of multifaceted data streams, encompassing how students interact with diverse learning materials, digital platforms, and instructional resources. By delving into this rich trove of information, educators can embark on a profound journey of discovery, deciphering the effectiveness of their pedagogical content and teaching methodologies.

The process is underpinned by the sophisticated capabilities of artificial intelligence, a realm where algorithms discern patterns, detect trends, and unveil latent correlations that might otherwise remain obscured to the human eye. This intricate web of data points and behavioral cues unfurls a comprehensive portrait of student learning experiences. AI's discerning eye is capable of deciphering not only the surface-level interactions but also the more subtle nuances embedded within each learning engagement [11].

Through the vigilant scrutiny of this data tapestry, educators gain the ability to gauge the efficacy of their pedagogical choices. They can ascertain which aspects of the curriculum resonate most profoundly with students, pinpoint the junctures where engagement wanes, and identify areas where learning flourishes. The revelations extend beyond mere quantitative metrics, encapsulating qualitative facets that encapsulate the essence of the educational journey.

The discernment of patterns and trends within this data mosaic serves as the bedrock upon which informed decisions are forged. Educators, armed with a panoramic view of learning dynamics, can deftly steer the trajectory of instructional design. Insights gleaned from AI-driven content analytics lay the groundwork for a data-informed approach to curriculum enhancement and instructional refinement.

This manifests in a dynamic cycle where data insights drive adjustments, leading to iterative improvements that foster enhanced learning outcomes. By harnessing this data-driven approach, educators orchestrate a symphony of teaching strategies harmonized with the evolving cadence of student needs and preferences. Learning pathways are optimized, and pedagogical content is tailored with precision, ensuring that the educational journey is not a static monologue but a dynamic dialogue between teacher, student, and technology. Ultimately, the amalgamation of AI-driven content analytics with educational endeavors propels the teaching profession into an era of adaptive, effective, and finely tuned instruction, where data insights guide the orchestration of enriched learning experiences.

4.5 Data Processing and AI in Human-Centered Manufacturing

Data processing and artificial intelligence (AI) are within the context of human-centered manufacturing. We explore how these technologies are reshaping manufacturing processes to prioritize human needs, enhance efficiency, and optimize production outcomes. At the heart of this transformation is the utilization of data processing techniques to gather, analyze, and interpret vast amounts of manufacturing data. Through real-time monitoring and analysis, manufacturers can gain insights into production workflows, identify bottlenecks, and make informed decisions to improve overall efficiency and quality [12]. AI plays a pivotal role by employing advanced algorithms to uncover patterns, trends, and anomalies in the data, enabling predictive maintenance, quality control, and resource allocation.

Figure 4.2 shows the evidence of Human-centered manufacturing emphasizes the well-being and capabilities of workers. AI-driven solutions can augment human capabilities by automating repetitive and mundane tasks, freeing up skilled workers to focus on more creative and complex aspects of production. Collaborative robots (cobots) equipped with AI can work alongside human operators, enhancing productivity and safety in a harmonious partnership. Moreover, AI-driven analytics can enhance the customization of products according to individual customer preferences,

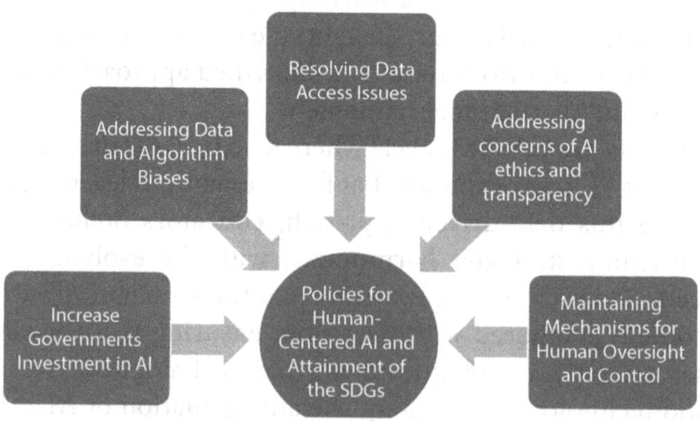

Figure 4.2 AI in human-centered manufacturing.

resulting in more personalized and satisfying experiences. The integration of AI can also facilitate rapid design iterations and simulations, accelerating the product development life cycle and reducing time to market. This synergistic approach aligns technological advancements with human-centric principles, ensuring that manufacturing processes are adaptable, sustainable, and responsive to changing demands. The content highlights the profound impact of data processing and AI on transforming traditional manufacturing into a dynamic, efficient, and human-centric ecosystem.

4.6 Information Learning

4.6.1 Information Learning Through AI—Chatbots

Chatbots are AI-powered conversational agents that interact with users through text or speech, simulating human-like conversations. They have become increasingly prevalent across various industries, transforming customer service, user engagement, and information retrieval. Chatbots utilize natural language processing (NLP) and machine learning algorithms to understand user queries, provide relevant responses, and even perform tasks [13].

These digital assistants can be deployed on websites, messaging platforms, mobile apps, and other interfaces, offering immediate and personalized support around the clock. Chatbots excel in a range of applications:

a) **Customer Service:** Chatbots provide efficient and consistent customer support by answering frequently asked questions, guiding users through troubleshooting processes, and offering assistance in real time. They enhance user experience by reducing wait times and ensuring 24/7 availability.
b) **E-Commerce:** Chatbots enhance online shopping experiences by helping users find products, comparing prices, and making purchase recommendations. They can also handle order tracking, returns, and refunds, streamlining the entire shopping journey.
c) **Lead Generation:** Chatbots engage website visitors and collect information from potential leads. By initiating conversations and qualifying prospects, chatbots help businesses identify potential customers and nurture them through the sales funnel.

d) **Appointment Scheduling:** Chatbots simplify appointment booking processes by allowing users to check availability, choose suitable time slots, and receive confirmation—all without human intervention.
e) **Information Retrieval**: Chatbots serve as instant information sources, answering queries about weather, news, facts, and more. They provide quick access to data and streamline the process of obtaining information.
f) **Language Learning:** Chatbots can aid language learners by engaging in conversations, correcting grammar, and offering vocabulary suggestions in real time.
g) **Healthcare:** Chatbots assist in triaging medical concerns, providing symptom assessments, and offering general health advice. They can also facilitate prescription refills and appointment scheduling.
h) **Banking and Finance:** Chatbots handle banking inquiries, balance checks, fund transfers, and help users manage their accounts securely.
i) **Entertainment:** Chatbots can engage users in interactive storytelling, games, and other forms of entertainment, offering a unique and engaging experience.
j) **Internal Processes:** Chatbots can automate internal processes within organizations, such as IT support, HR inquiries, and knowledge base access for employees.

4.6.2 Information Learning Through AI—Virtual Reality (VR)

In Figure 4.3 shows the evidence of Virtual reality (VR) is an immersive technology that transports users into a computer-generated, interactive 3D environment, creating a sense of presence and engagement. By simulating real-world experiences, VR enables users to interact with digital surroundings as if they were physically present, opening up a wide range of applications across various fields [14]:

a) **Entertainment and Gaming:** VR is widely known for its applications in entertainment, offering immersive gaming experiences where players can explore virtual worlds, interact with objects, and engage in thrilling adventures.
b) **Education and Training:** VR provides a powerful tool for education and training by allowing users to virtually experience complex concepts. It enables hands-on learning in

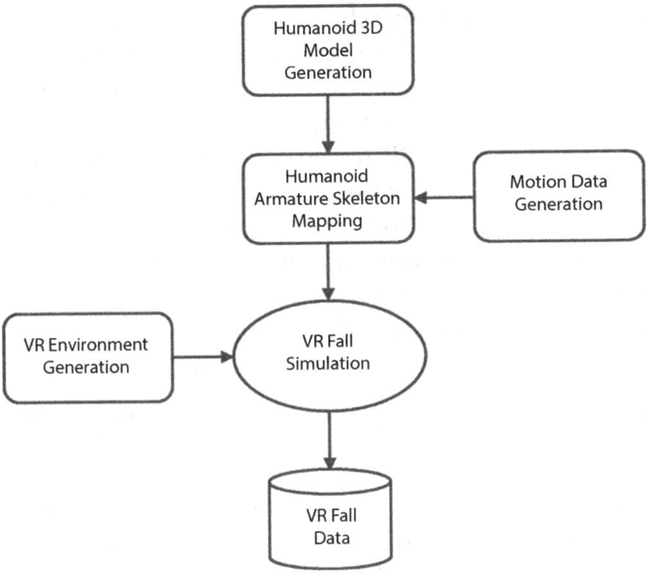

Figure 4.3 Virtual reality (VR).

fields like medical training, pilot simulation, architectural design, and more.

c) **Healthcare:** VR is used for pain management, therapy, and rehabilitation. Patients can be immersed in relaxing environments to reduce stress or engage in therapeutic exercises within a virtual space.

d) **Real Estate and Architecture:** VR allows potential buyers or tenants to virtually tour properties before making decisions. Architects and designers can also visualize and modify designs in an immersive environment.

e) **Tourism and Exploration:** VR offers virtual tours of destinations, historical sites, and cultural landmarks, giving users a sense of travel and exploration from their own homes.

f) **Social Interaction:** VR platforms enable users to interact with others in virtual spaces, attending events, meetings, or social gatherings as avatars, fostering a sense of presence and connection.

g) **Manufacturing and Design:** VR aids in product design, prototyping, and collaborative decision-making by providing a 3D visualization of concepts and allowing stakeholders to interact with virtual prototypes.

h) **Simulations and Research:** VR is used for simulations and research in fields such as science, engineering, and psychology. It enables researchers to replicate and study real-world scenarios in controlled environments.
i) **Art and Creativity:** VR serves as a canvas for artists to create immersive digital artworks, sculptures, and experiences that can be explored from different angles.
j) **Therapy and Exposure:** VR is utilized for exposure therapy, helping individuals confront and manage fears and phobias in a controlled and safe environment.

4.6.3 Information Learning Through AI—Management of Learning (LMS)

Learning management systems (LMS) are software applications designed to facilitate the administration, delivery, and management of educational courses, training programs, and learning content. LMS platforms provide a centralized hub for educators, trainers, and learners to interact, collaborate, and engage in various learning activities [15]. They play a pivotal role in modern education and training environments, offering a wide range of functionalities and benefits:

a) **Course Delivery and Content Management:** LMS platforms enable instructors to create and organize course materials, such as lectures, quizzes, assignments, and multimedia content, in a structured manner. These resources are available to learners at their own convenience and speed.
b) **Accessibility and Flexibility:** LMS platforms provide learners with the flexibility to access learning materials and complete assignments from any location and device with an internet connection. This accessibility enhances the reach of education and accommodates diverse learning styles.
c) **Tracking and Assessment:** LMS platforms offer tools to track learners' progress, performance, and engagement. Instructors can monitor participation, quiz scores, and assignment submissions, facilitating data-driven decision-making to improve instructional strategies.
d) **Collaboration and Interaction:** LMS platforms support communication and collaboration among learners and instructors through discussion forums, chat functionalities,

and virtual classrooms. These features foster engagement, peer learning, and a sense of community.

e) **Personalization and Adaptive Learning:** Some LMS platforms leverage AI and data analytics to deliver personalized learning experiences. They analyze learners' behaviors and preferences to recommend relevant content and adapt learning pathways based on individual progress.
f) **Assessment and Feedback:** LMS platforms facilitate online assessments, quizzes, and exams, offering automated grading and instant feedback to learners. This speeds up the assessment process and provides timely insights into learners' understanding.
g) **Administrative Efficiency:** LMS platforms streamline administrative tasks such as enrollment, user management, and reporting. They offer insights into learner demographics, engagement metrics, and course completion rates.
h) **Certification and Compliance:** LMS platforms can automate the issuance of certificates and badges upon course completion. They also assist in compliance training by tracking mandatory training requirements and certifications.
i) **Blended and Flipped Learning:** LMS platforms support blended learning approaches, combining in-person instruction with online resources. They also facilitate flipped classrooms, where learners engage with content online before attending interactive sessions.
j) **Professional Development:** LMS platforms are used for employee training and professional development within organizations. They provide a structured framework for onboarding, skill enhancement, and continuous learning.

4.6.4 Information Learning Through AI—Robotics

Robotics in AI represents a dynamic fusion of artificial intelligence and robotic systems, resulting in intelligent, autonomous machines that can interact with and adapt to their environment. This convergence leads to a new generation of robots with enhanced capabilities, reshaping industries and advancing technological frontiers [16].

At the core of robotics in AI lies the concept of perception and sensing. AI-powered robots are equipped with an array of sophisticated sensors, including cameras, LiDAR, GPS, and microphones. These sensors enable robots to perceive and comprehend their surroundings, capturing crucial data for analysis and decision-making. Through AI algorithms, sensory input is processed to create real-time maps, detect obstacles, and interpret spatial relationships, empowering robots with the ability to navigate and interact seamlessly within their surroundings.

Cognition and decision-making are pivotal aspects of AI-driven robotics. By integrating AI algorithms, robots gain cognitive abilities that enable them to process complex information and make informed choices. Machine learning, a subset of AI, empowers robots to learn from past experiences, recognize patterns, and continually improve their performance. This adaptive learning is particularly valuable in scenarios where robots must dynamically respond to changing conditions, such as autonomous vehicles maneuvering through traffic or robotic systems adapting to variations in manufacturing processes.

Autonomous navigation is a prime application where the marriage of robotics and AI truly shines. Through AI-driven algorithms, robots achieve the capability to autonomously operate and navigate without direct human intervention. These algorithms analyze sensory data to devise optimal paths, avoid obstacles, and ensure safe traversal.

A notable example is the emergence of self-driving cars, where AI-powered robots navigate complex roadways, make split-second decisions, and prioritize passenger safety.

The synergy of robotics and AI extends beyond technical functions, enhancing human–robot interaction. AI enables robots to comprehend and respond to human cues, such as natural language, gestures, and expressions. This breakthrough in communication fosters intuitive and accessible interaction, making robots more user-friendly and adaptable for a wide range of applications.

Task automation, a hallmark of both robotics and AI, reaches new heights when combined. Robots embedded with AI capabilities automate tasks across industries, from manufacturing and healthcare to service sectors. These robots can adapt to variations in production lines, execute precise surgical procedures, or assist with intricate assembly processes. AI-powered robots redefine efficiency and accuracy in various domains.

Collaboration and safety are paramount considerations in robotics, and AI contributes to making human–robot partnerships harmonious and secure. Advanced algorithms enable robots to recognize human presence, predict movements, and adjust actions to ensure safe and efficient collaboration. This feature is pivotal in scenarios where robots work alongside humans, enhancing productivity while maintaining a high degree of safety.

Looking ahead, the trajectory of robotics in AI points toward continuous evolution. As AI algorithms advance, robots are poised to attain higher levels of autonomy, decision-making, and adaptability. The future holds the promise of robots capable of handling increasingly complex tasks, contributing to scientific research and exploration endeavors, and providing indispensable support to humans across diverse aspects of life. The integration of robotics and AI transforms the potential of intelligent machines, paving the way for a future where the boundaries of technology are pushed even further.

4.6.5 AI Invoice Processing is Not Fantastical—It is Fantastic

It just transforms images into editable text. Standard OCR invoice recognition software has to be regularly trained with new templates and rules for every new invoice your company receives in order to deliver successful results. You can break free of the never-ending cycle of education by using OCR and AI-powered data extraction. Each data field on the invoice has a written description that can be read and understood by an OCF platform with strong neural networks. The software's deep learning capabilities allow it to recognize new invoice types with little to no human input after regular use; small changes could occasionally be needed. This is a really significant subject. For example, the terms "Total," "Amount Due," and "To Pay in USD," for instance, might all refer to the same thing. None of these distinctions will be recognized by a straightforward OCR software. The danger of erroneous data collection and the ensuing accounting problems increases when regulations are absent. By learning templates and naming conventions on its own with sporadic help from a human operator, AI helps OCR invoice recognition become more intelligent. This deep learning application is what makes AI invoice processing as exciting as a thinking, feeling robot; it has the potential to alter not just businesses but also individuals by allowing AP team members to move from the back office to the front lines.

4.7 Results

The case study emphasizes the transformative potential of AI invoice processing, particularly through deep learning and OCR technology.

Figure 4.4 underscores how AI can overcome the limitations of traditional OCR, reduce manual training efforts, and enhance accuracy in recognizing various invoice types. Ultimately, the adoption of AI-driven invoice processing has the potential to bring about significant efficiency

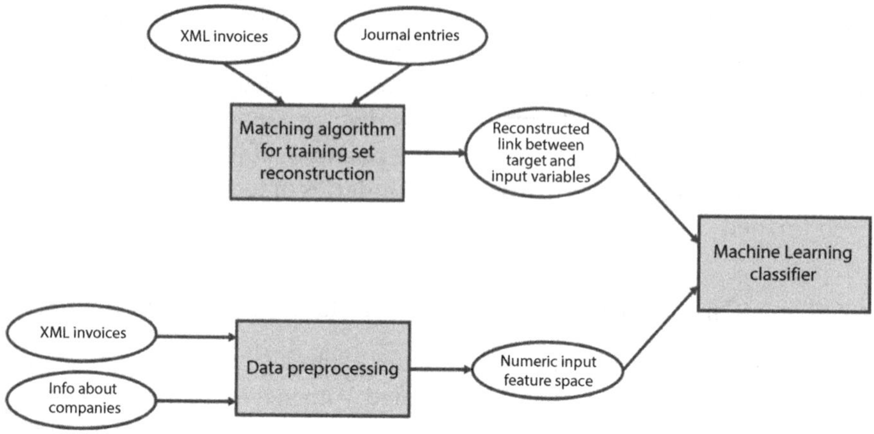

Figure 4.4 Artificial intelligence invoice process.

improvements in businesses and streamline financial operations, making it a promising and exciting development in the field.

4.8 Conclusion

The fusion of artificial intelligence (AI) and robotics is reshaping industries and education alike, ushering in a new era of innovation and efficiency. Across sectors, from healthcare to manufacturing, AI-driven robotics are enhancing processes, boosting precision, and augmenting human capabilities. In education, personalized learning experiences, virtual facilitators, and content analytics are revolutionizing how knowledge is imparted, catering to diverse learning styles and needs. While challenges and considerations accompany this technological journey, the potential for AI and robotics to elevate human potential and transform industries is undeniably promising. As we embrace these advancements, we pave the way for a future where collaboration between humans and intelligent machines creates a more connected, intelligent, and thriving world.

References

1. Burri, Srinivasa Rao, Sachin Ahuja, Abhishek Kumar, and Anupam Baliyan. "Exploring the Effectiveness of Optimized Convolutional Neural Network in Transfer Learning for Image Classification: A Practical Approach." In

2023 International Conference on Advancement in Computation & Computer Technologies (InCACCT), pp. 598-602. IEEE, 2023.

2. Kumar, Abhishek, Swarn Avinash Kumar, Vishal Dutt, S. Shitharth, and Esha Tripathi. "IoT based arrhythmia classification using the enhanced hunt optimization-based deep learning." *Expert Syst.*, (2023): e13298.
3. Akhatov, A., I. Himmatov, Christo Ananth and T. Ananth Kumar. "System of Persons Identification Based on Human Characteristics." In *International Conference on Data Management, Analytics & Innovation*, pp. 1029-1046. Singapore: Springer Nature Singapore, 2023.
4. Benkhaddra, Ilyas, Abhishek Kumar, Mohamed Ali Setitra, and Lei Hang. "Design and Development of Consensus Activation Function Enabled Neural Network-Based Smart Healthcare Using BIoT." *Wirel. Pers. Commun.*, 130, no. 3 (2023): 1549-1574.
5. Henze, Alex. "Augmented Reality Vs Virtual Reality." *TeamViewer*, 12 Apr. 2022, www.teamviewer.com/en/augmented-reality-ar-vs-virtual-reality-vr.
6. "Intelligent Tutoring System." *Intelligent Tutoring System | Encyclopedia MDPI*, encyclopedia.pub/entry/28717.
7. Guo, Lu, *et al.* "Evolution and Trends in Intelligent Tutoring Systems Research: A Multidisciplinary and Scientometric View - *Asia Pacific Educ. Rev.*" SpringerLink, 4 May 2021, https://doi.org/10.1007/s12564-021-09697-7.
8. Srivastav, Arun Lal, Markandeya, Naveen Patel, Mayank Pandey, Ashutosh Kumar Pandey, Ashutosh Kumar Dubey, Abhishek Kumar, Abhishek Kumar Bhardwaj, and Vinod Kumar Chaudhary. "Concepts of circular economy for sustainable management of electronic wastes: challenges and management options." *Environ. Sci. Pollut. Res.*, 30, no. 17 (2023): 48654-48675.
9. Zhu, W., Levinson, S.: Vision-based reinforcement learning for robot navigation. In: *Proceedings of the International Joint Conference on Neural Networks*, Washington DC, vol. 2, pp. 1025–1030 (2001)
10. Dahl, T.S., Matarić, M.J., Sukhatme, G.S.: Multi-robot task allocation through vacancy chain scheduling. *J. Robot. Auton. Syst.*, 57(6), 674–687 (2009)
11. Inamura, T., Inaba, M., Inoue, H.: User adaptation of human-robot interaction model based on Bayesian network and introspection of interaction experience. In: *International Conference on Intelligent Robots and Systems (IROS 2000)*, vol. 3, pp. 2139–2144 (2000)
12. Mohri, M., Pereira, F., and Riley, M. (2002). Weighted finite-state transducers in speech recognition. *Comput. Speech Lang.*, 16(1), 69–88.
    Montague, R. (1970). English as a formal language. In *Linguaggi nella Societ `a e nella Tecnica*, pp. 189– 224. Edizioni di Comunit`a.
13. Riazanov, A. and Voronkov, A. (2002). The design and implementation of VAMPIRE. *AI Commun.*, 15(2–3), 91–110.
14. Kumar, Abhishek, Swarn Avinash Kumar, Vishal Dutt, S. Shitharth, and Esha Tripathi. "IoT based arrhythmia classification using the enhanced hunt optimization-based deep learning." *Expert Syst.*, (2023): e13298.

15. Kumar, T. Ananth, R. Rajmohan, Sunday Adeola Ajagbe, Tarek Gaber, Xiao-Jun Zeng, and Fatma Masmoudi. "A novel CNN gap layer for growth prediction of palm tree plantlings." *PLoS One*, 18, no. 8 (2023): e0289963.
16. Richter, S. and Westphal, M. (2008). The LAMA planner. In *Proc. International Planning Competition* at ICAPS.

5

Computational Intelligence Approach for Exploration of Spatial Co-Location Patterns

S. LourduMarie Sophie[1*], S. Siva Sathya[1], S. Sharmiladevi[1] and J. Dhakshayani[2]

[1]Department of Computer Science, Pondicherry University, Puducherry, India
[2]Department of Computer Science, National Institute of Technology, Karaikal, India

Abstract

A spatial co-location pattern is a collection of spatial occurrences as they tend to appear in contiguous geographic vicinity. Numerous co-location algorithms with the objective of identifying lossless condensed spatial co-location patterns have been presented, but these methods are sequential. Co-location patterns are subgroups of spatial characteristics whose instances are regularly situated in close proximity. The issue is crucial in numerous applications, like the analysis of crime or illness associations with environmental parameters; however, it is computationally difficult given the huge number of occurrences. This work proposes a computational intelligence approach for detecting unique spatial patterns in a clustered neighborhood by employing a Grid Clustered technique. The Top-K co-location technique is also utilized to generate the most highly co-located spatial patterns. The suggested technique is implemented using the MapReduce framework, a parallel processing framework that enables rapid and efficient processing. MapReduce increases the efficiency of spatial pattern mining and works best with big spatial datasets. The experimental assessment offers a summary of the algorithm's efficacy across a spectrum of data sizes.

Keywords: Co-location pattern, grid clustering, map reduce, spatial data mining, spatial pattern mining, top K pattern mining

**Corresponding author*: lourdumariesophie15@pondiuni.ac.in

T. Ananth Kumar, E. Golden Julie, Venkata Raghuveer Burugadda, Abhishek Kumar and Puneet Kumar (eds.) Computational Intelligence: Theory and Applications, (117–144) © 2024 Scrivener Publishing LLC

5.1 Introduction

A vast volume of geographical information includes the establishment of complicated relationships that poses a number of obstacles in the current state of study in data analysis. Geospatial data may be reflected in two ways: as raster images or as vector images. n-dimensional bit mappings or pixel mappings are used to describe raster data, whereas vector relevant data are being expressed as a union or overlaying of fundamental geometric constructions like points, planes, and polygons used to describe vector relevant data. Geographical data mining is the process of extracting information, spatial connections, and other co-occurrences from geospatial data that are not specifically recorded in the information gathering phase. Mining co-located patterns from massive geographic event data presents a number of computational difficulties. To determine the prevalence of a prospective co-location pattern, we must first construct its instances. Checking geographical neighborhood associations between various instances is computationally costly, especially when the instance count is higher and clumsy. The potential co-location patterns count is proportional to the extracted spatial instances. A high quantity of possible patterns might be computationally burdensome to evaluate. Lastly, the unequal distribution of event occurrences in the space might make it difficult to create parallel data structures and algorithms. By considering these challenges, this work tackles the topic of co-location pattern mining for massive geographical event data by employing a clustering approach to detect closely located patterns.

The increase in the geographic data and the usage of spatial databases underline the basic need for spatial expertise. The spatial database stores and queries data points in a geometric space. Spatial data are the occupied data points. These data typically contain distance information and need a special indexing strategy to work well [21]. The complexity of these spatial data along with their inborn spatial connections restrains the employment of traditional data mining techniques for deriving the spatial feature [7]. Spatial data or geospatial data enable the global finding and location of individuals or devices. The process of mining interesting and formerly unknown spatial patterns from spatial datasets is called spatial data mining or knowledge discovery.

Identifying and quantifying similarities is important in data processing, information retrieval, and system integration. Most programs require items to be connected in order to comprehend coordination, connection, dependency, and the common goal. Dissimilarity can be used to describe negative associations or correlations. A set of feature values can predict object behavior [37]. Researchers found that entities with similar object properties may be compared. Intelligent gadgets capture the properties of many data items and the physical positions of entities at a given time. In a spatial domain [10], objects might be dynamic or static. Object attributes, including placement on the globe, may change over time. Identifying a group of people involved in a dispute, customers with similar purchase patterns, people with a common perspective on a social or basic issue, and people with similar ideas on various themes are examples. Euclidean distance, cosine similarity, and others were created to determine the difference between two sample points. These metrics employ numerical data points to compare two items. Current similarity measures are unsuitable for applications that require some qualities to be more essential than others. A geographical data item has a location and a collection of data quantities that correlate to geographic data parameters. Geographic distance or behavioral proximity can tell if two objects are physically related. Two religious venues may be equal in terms of total surface area, daily visits, quarterly revenue, visitor's viewpoint, and religious importance, despite being geographically apart. Inferring information from spatiotemporal datasets is called spatiotemporal data mining [57, 58].

Nowadays, a huge volume of data is produced on a daily basis at an unpredictable rate from heterogeneous sources like health care [10], social networks [25, 26], location services [27, 28, 55], public transportation [23, 11, 24], and so on. The so-called "Big Data" is an evolving field to analyze and manage such extremely large datasets that are too complex to be dealt with available database management tools or with any other traditional data processing software. In short, Big Data is a collection of data that are huge in size yet growing exponentially with time. In Market Research, it is defined by 4V's (Volume, Variety, Velocity, and Veracity) for enhanced decision-making.

Applying Big Data concept to spatial pattern mining gives rise to several challenges: (i) retaining computational efficiency, (ii) storing of these spatial Big Data on cloud leading to unnecessary charges for users even when the server is idle, and (iii) automatic partitioning of input data often leads to incomplete patterns. For instance, when a job is submitted, the MapReduce framework will automatically partition the input into blocks and send it to the DFS (Distributed File System); this explicit partitioning of data may result in incorrect or incomplete mined patterns. In this work, the aforementioned challenges are addressed and a series of MapReduce algorithm that uses Grid clustering and Conditional Neighborhood concept to mine the spatial co-location patterns has been proposed.

The rest of the paper is structured in the following manner. Section 5.2 lays the groundwork on the Spatial Data Mining concept. Section 5.3 deals with the basic preliminaries employed in this work along with the key concepts of co-location pattern mining and the MapReduce framework along with the literature work. Proposed MapReduce algorithms for spatial co-location pattern mining are given in Section 5.4. Experimental setup and performance analysis are furnished in Section 5.5 and Section 5.6 draws the conclusion.

5.2 Spatial Data Mining

It is the way of analyzing spatial information. Spatial data are geographical information in which the Earth's atmosphere serves as the fundamental point of reference [53]. Spatial information may be gathered from a variety of resources, including satellite photos, hospital instruments, recording devices, and other similar devices. Spatial datasets include information about things that are spatially referenced. Entity sets are collections of objects that are similar to one another. Identifying and recommending a set of things that are regularly co-located may be required for some programs. An individual who has recently moved to a metropolis area might like to choose a place that is convenient to his or her current workplace and also has additional amenities including a decent place to live, a clinic for medical treatment, a theater for amusement, a bookstores, a shopping mall, a religious center, etc. Identification of items that are both intriguing and in close vicinity is necessary, with the criterion that no two objects correspond to the very same item set being met as a result of the identification process. Spatial co-location patterns are formed by the arrangement of these items.

Spatial statistics and data mining approaches are the two types of methodologies that have been used to uncover co-location criteria in the research, respectively. Geographical statistics-based techniques quantify the interactions between two forms of visual characteristics by calculating estimates of spatial interactions among the elements. In addition to the cross-K value with the Monte Carlo method [47], the average nearest-neighbor proximity [46], spatial linear regression [46], and other indicators of correlations exist. It is substantially difficult to compute spatial correlation measurements for all potential co-location sequences, owing to the enormous set of candidate subgroups that may be generated from a huge collection of geographical Boolean characteristics.

5.2.1 Spatial Co-Location Pattern Mining

Spatial co-location feature identification is a subset of spatial data mining that seeks to identify items that have spatial properties or occurrences that are commonly co-located in the same geographic place. It has the potential to uncover essential occurrences in a wide variety of uses, which include location-based amenities, global positioning systems, geo-marketing, satellite imagery, online image investigation, diagnostic imaging, route planning, traffic monitoring, and environmental engineering, to name just a few examples. Certain sorts of activities, like discovering the farmland that is closest to a stream bed, might well be sought in a nearby geographic region. Location-based wireless carriers are particularly curious to learn which methods are generally demanded jointly and which are in geographically close proximity. The finding of co-location patterns and the identification of rule sets are both components of the spatial data mining. In general, the distinctions among spatial databases and traditional data mining may be summarized as follows: data intake, statistical basis, pattern outcome, and computing method.

Generally speaking, a co-location pattern is characterized as the inclusion or exclusion of geographic item kinds that are positioned in close proximity to one another [38, 56]. The finding of co-location connections requires the use of geometric properties that are entrenched in continuous domain, which is more difficult than using traditional knowledge, which is frequently discontinuous [39]. The healthcare system, infrastructure, transportation, ecology, and town council are only a few instances of co-location phenomena that may be seen in the many fields mentioned above. Co-location pattern extraction may be accomplished using a variety of strategies, including the Event-centric approach, the Rule-based concept, the Join-less, and the Partial Join framework. Geospatial information system (GIS) data are used in co-location pattern analysis, which includes the Event-centric module that is allowed as well. Typically, geographical data are kept in a database schema format in a geographic information system data center. Co-location patterns in geographical datasets are an intriguing series of things that are distinct yet are positioned in close vicinity to one another. We store items related to one another in an itemset and ensure that neither two objects in a co-location sequence are members of the same item set. The Euclidean distance metric is used to determine closeness between two points. Co-location patterns in commercial databases, on the other hand, are not immediately relevant to geographical data sources for which techniques for extracting trends are developed. In the case of parallel time series, conventional techniques are inapplicable, because many technologies that generate geographical datasets are intrinsically dispersed in origin. In reality, it has been discovered that spatial things are in motion. Anything (living or non-living) that we are engaged in may alter their spatial position, or different innovations may be added to our concerned zone, or prior entities may be removed from our concerned province. Intelligent machines will continually gather information about the items they are monitoring. When recently gathered data are coupled with a timeframe, it is possible that co-location patterns will alter as well.

Co-location rules [52] are methods for inferring the existence of binary spatial objects in the vicinity of occurrences of many other categorical spatial characteristics that are not themselves Boolean spatial characteristics. Identification of co-location patterns is accomplished by the use of huge geographical data including a significant number of logical attributes, which is known as co-location rule generation. Due to the obvious absence of interactions, the spatial co-location rule finding challenge seems to be comparable to, and yet is fundamentally distinct from, the association rule mining issue [48]. In association with rule mining, interactions are established based on the surrounding instances of a specific spatial characteristic, and interactions are created on instances of that characteristic. It makes use of spatial propositions as product variants in its construction. However, breaking down geospatial information into events may cause correlations to shift. As a result, the use of co-location mining enhances the effectiveness with which intriguing patterns may be discovered from very broad spatial datasets. Through the use of neighborhood characterization and spatial connections, co-location patterns may be detected.

As with association rules, spatial co-located patterns could be exploited in a manner comparable to that of frequent patterns. It is possible to extract spatial association principles from geographic datasets by taking into account spatial features and conditional statements. Association rule mining is an essential element of spatial co-location pattern analysis [40, 41], which is used in machine learning [42–45]. Spatial co-location mining techniques is a subset of association rule mining [40, 41]. It was discovered that association rules might be used to uncover recurring patterns among objects in a big relational model.

Spatial co-location pattern analysis is generally equivalent to association rule mining; however, it differs in terms of technological implementation. A co-location pattern is a collection of elements that are regularly seen in close proximity to one another. In fact, a location is indeed not synonymous with a transaction, and two qualities are scarcely seen in the same place at the same time. As a result, a user-specified neighborhood is required as a containment in order to determine which attributes are shared by many neighborhoods [54]. Several algorithms have been suggested to analyze spatial co-location characteristics. Spatial co-location pattern is defined as the process of identifying a set of items or events occurring at multiple locations in a given time period. The difficulty in retrieving such patterns from geographic information is dependent on the complex features of spatial datasets, spatial linkages, and spatial auto-correlation, among other factors. It is important to mine the spatial co-location pattern for information. A civil engineer, for instance, may discover that the popular pattern "university, convenience store, eatery" is not present near the "university," indicating that a new "convenience store" or "eatery" should be constructed in the vicinity of the "university."

Spatial co-location patterns are subgroups of spatial relationships whose occurrences are regularly situated near close geographic vicinity, and spatial co-location data discovery intends to unearth the intriguing and partial correlation spatial information in a variety of disciplines by analyzing spatial co-location patterns. Co-location patterns, for instance, might reveal that the zone wherein insects are prevalent and livestock are maintained routinely has West Nile virus in the neighborhood; alternatively, they may reveal that the proportion of sub-humid evergreen annual and perennial woods flourishing with orchid plants could approach 80% of the total [10, 18]. The frequency metric was used in the classic paradigm for discovering spatial co-location patterns, which was developed in the 1960s. In order to calculate the frequency of a co-location pattern, the number of clique occurrences for each spatial neighbor connections must be counted. The fundamental terms involved in the search for co-located patterns are discussed in further detail in subsequent sections.

5.3 Preliminaries

This section deals with some of the abstract concepts and definitions involved in spatial co-location pattern mining, the MapReduce framework and the literature works.

5.3.1 Basic Concepts

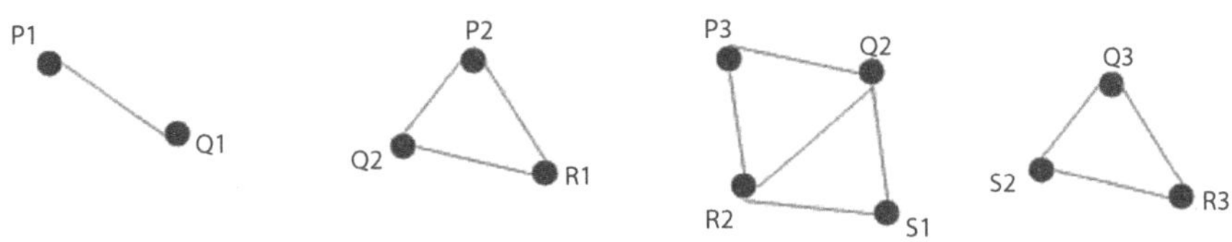

Figure 5.1 Spatial dataset.

(PI – 1)

A	B
P1	Q1
P2	Q2
P3	Q3
PR: 1	2/3

(PI – 1/3)

A	B	C
P2	Q2	R1
P3	Q2	R2
PR: 2/3	1/3	2/3

(PI – 2/3)

A	C	D
Q2	R2	S1
Q3	R3	S2
PR: 2/3	2/3	1

(PI – 1/3)

A	B	C	D
P3	Q2	R2	S1
PR: 1/3	1/3	1/3	1/2

Figure 5.2 PR and PI values with respect to co-location patterns.

5.3.1.1 *Feature Instance*

Let F be the feature having n number of instances provided n >1. As per Figure 5.1, the spatial dataset has four feature types, i.e., F = {P,Q,R,S}, of which feature P has three instances, Q has three instances, R has three instances, and S has two instances.

5.3.1.2 *Participation Ratio (PR)*

For any co-location pattern "p" with reference to its feature "f", its PR is given in Equation 5.1:

$$\mathrm{PR}(p,f)=\frac{\text{number of unique instances of the feature in the pattern}}{\text{Total number of instances}} \tag{5.1}$$

From Figure 5.2, the PR of the features P, Q, R, and S contained in pattern PQRS can be derived as follows:

$$\mathrm{PR}(\mathrm{PQRS},\mathrm{P})=\frac{1}{3}$$

$$\mathrm{PR}(\mathrm{PQRS},\mathrm{Q})=\frac{1}{3}$$

$$\mathrm{PR}(\mathrm{PQRS},\mathrm{R})=\frac{1}{3}$$

$$\mathrm{PR}(\mathrm{PQRS},\mathrm{S})=\frac{1}{2}$$

5.3.1.3 *Participation Index (PI)*

For any co-location pattern "p", its PI is defined as the minimum PR of the pattern with respect to each of its instance; the PI calculation with respect to PR is given in Equation 5.2,

$$PI(p) = \min_{f \in c}\{PR(p, f)\} \tag{5.2}$$

From Figure 5.2, the Participation Index of the patterns {P,Q}, {P,Q,R}, {Q,R,S}, and {P,Q,R,S} is derived as follows:

$$\begin{aligned} PI(PQ) &= \min\{PR(PQ,P), PR(PQ,Q)\} \\ &= \min\left\{1, \frac{2}{3}\right\} \\ &= 1 \\ PI(PQR) &= \min\{PR(PQR,P), PR(PQR,Q), PR(PQR,R)\} \\ &= \min\left\{\frac{2}{3}, \frac{1}{3}, \frac{2}{3}\right\} \\ &= 1/3 \\ PI(QRS) &= \min\{PR(QRS,Q), PR(QRS,R), PR(QRS,S)\} \\ &= \min\left\{\frac{2}{3}, \frac{2}{3}, 1\right\} \\ &= 2/3 \\ PI(PQRS) &= \min\{PR(PQRS,P), PR(PQRS,Q), PR(PQRS,R), PR(PQRS,S)\} \\ &= \min\left\{\frac{1}{3}, \frac{1}{3}, \frac{1}{3}, \frac{1}{2}\right\} \\ &= 1/3 \end{aligned}$$

5.3.1.4 *Neighbor Relation*

Let F be a feature set in a spatial dataset, I be its associated instance, and R be the neighbor relation over I, such that the co-location pattern $C \subseteq F$.

R can either be Euclidean distance or Haversine distance (a great circle distance calculated for a spatial region utilizing grid partitioning technique along with "d" as their base limit). Any two data points in a spatial dataset are said to be neighbors if their distance value $\leq$ threshold (D).

From Figure 5.1, P1 and Q1 are said to be neighbors iff, Distance(P1,Q1) ≤ D.

5.3.1.5 *Conditional Neighborhood*

Let X(T,D) be a graph with neighbor relation, where T is the vertex and D is the edge. For each t ϵ T, the Conditional Neighborhood for the vertex t, CN(t), is termed as the collection of all other vertices (u) that are near to t satisfying the condition, t.type < u.type [8], where type may be distance, priorities, or any other parameter.

CN(t) = set of all vertices adjacent to t, such that

$$\{ t,u \in T, (t,u) \in D, \text{ and } t.type < u.type \} \tag{5.3}$$

From Figure 5.1, the conditional neighborhood records satisfying the conditions are as follows,

P1,	Q1		
P2,	Q2,	R1	
P3,	Q2,	R2,	S1
Q1			
Q2,	R1		
Q2,	R2,	S1	
Q3,	R3,	S2	
R1			
R2,	S1		
R3			
S1			
S2			

5.3.2 Apache Hadoop—MapReduce

Apache Hadoop is a framework for processing a huge amount of data. This framework enables one to store and process huge volumes of data simultaneously in a distributed fashion. The problem of storing huge data in Hadoop is dealt by HDFS (Hadoop Distributed File System), which hands over the data across various machines and these machines are interlinked in a Hadoop cluster. HDFS gives the programmer unlimited storage [5].

MapReduce is a programming unit of Hadoop allowing simultaneous processing of data that are lying across the Hadoop cluster. It is used for performing distributed computations and data processing on massive datasets of commodity servers [22]. While engaging with distributed systems may be complicated, MapReduce makes it easier by extracting out the difficulties of interacting with them. This includes issues like computationally parallel programming, job allocation, and contending with unreliability in equipment and software design.

The MapReduce computational structure is intended for the processing of massive amounts of data quickly and efficiently. This design divides the data into little pieces, allowing for simultaneous data analysis to be accomplished more efficiently. There are two basic components of functionality, the Mapper and the Reducer, that will take regular bits of information and distribute them over several nodes in parallel computing. On the beginning, information will be treated by the Mapper function in various nodes, and the result would be stored into a system called the HDFS (Hadoop Distributed File System). Once all of the mapper processes have been completed, interim data will be created. The Hadoop central server will conduct filtering and scrambling activities on the intermediatory data, and it will split and redistribute this ordered set of data across the reducer processes. Next, the Reducer will retrieve the data block from HDFS and analyze it on many nodes at the same time, according to inference, in order to create the output in the structure that was anticipated. As soon as all of the Mappers have completed their responsibilities, the Reducer part begins. This type of programming could also relate to the implementation mechanism that is used to organize the program execution developed in this specific way. MapReduce divides a task provided by a client into smaller parallel computing processes, which are then combined together. The fact that MapReduce has in-built fault tolerance mechanism is a key

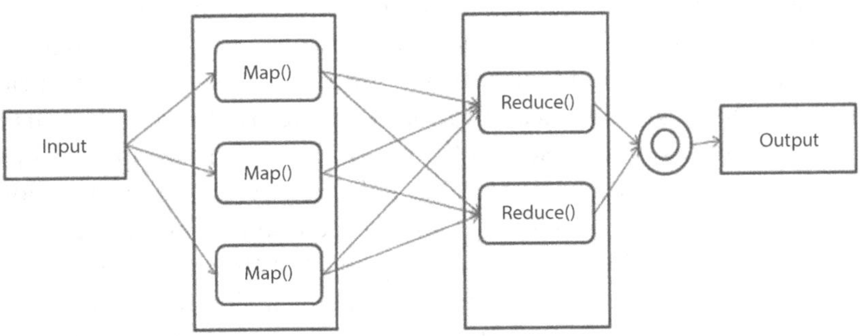

Figure 5.3 MapReduce execution model.

characteristic. Any time a map or reduce job fails, the keys given to that job are redistributed to another accessible cluster node, and the failed task is re-executed without having to redistribute the keys allocated to certain other jobs. MapReduce was first created by Google and has subsequently gained significant use through the use of an open-source version known as Hadoop [34], which is available for free. Since then, MapReduce is regarded to be the most effective option for several business analytics activities when performed across highly distributed clusters [35, 36].

The MapReduce model is depicted in Figure 5.3. In short, a MapReduce job performs two distinct tasks, namely, the map and reduce task. The Map job takes a block of data, reads it, and processes it to produce a key-value pair as an intermediate output that is fed as an input to the reducer. The Reduce job takes input from various map jobs and consolidates them to give a single final key-value pair. In case of large spatial data [1], when a client submits a job, the input data are divided into independent chunks and processed in a parallel way. The respective input and output are put in a DFS (Distributed File System), which is taken care by the framework [4].

5.3.3 Related Work

This section throws light on the recent literature pertaining to co-location pattern mining.

Reference [9] offers a partial join-based strategy to mine spatial co-location patterns using a transaction-based Apriori algorithm to produce co-location instances not recognized by the transaction. The suggested method reduces execution time compared to join-based techniques, where a substantial part of the algorithm focuses on calculating joins to discover co-location pattern occurrences. Reference [20] presents a join-based strategy to construct the candidate's co-location pattern. The solution employs an efficient feature selection mechanism employing indexing to decrease join time. Wang *et al.* [31] suggest using a join-based method for spatial co-location analysis, which combines geometrical and computational techniques for neighborhood identification. The authors use modified Apriori to detect probable geographically co-located patterns, then cut them using a predominant threshold based on the apriori feature. This approach's join phase is computationally expensive. In Ref. [32], Watson presents a join-less solution using an individual look-up technique. The emergence of star occurrences eliminates the need for joins, but the production of final spatial co-located patterns from people remains a significant bottleneck. In the worst-case scenario, all-star occurrences of all dimensions must be inspected for plausible spatial pattern instances before any subsequent spatial co-located pattern instances can be generated. In the works referenced, neighborhood restrictions are given by a predetermined distance, which may be the maximum distance between two instances before they are neighbors. Liu and Shi [33] present a greedy technique for spatial pattern analysis with dynamic neighborhood restrictions.

Associative rule-based approaches are transactional and distance-based. Transaction-based algorithms detect space-based interactions to allow Apriori-like methods [48]. A reference-feature-centered paradigm [49] can define global transactions. This paradigm forms transactions around user-defined geographical characteristics. In this scenario, Apriori [48] generates common patterns. All detected rules relate to the reference feature. This approach is not easily extended to models without explicit reference features. Several potential relationships may have duplicate counts if interactions are built around all aspect positions. Huang *et al.* [10] present a transaction-free method for generating co-location patterns using user-specified proximity neighborhoods. Proximity neighborhood idea employs participation index, which is connected to cross-K, a statistical number that indicates the level of interaction between geographical elements [3]. The approach uses multi-resolution pruning to reduce search space by auto-correlating spatial data. The user must define the closeness range each time, which is impossible without precise dataset knowledge. Morimoto [50] and Shekhar and Wang [51] provide a distance-based method. Distance-based designs are k-neighboring category sets, where the amount of occurrences for each pattern is used as a predominant indication, and do not have an anti-monotone quality by origin. The authors got this measure's anti-monotone feature by utilizing a non-overlapping instance condition.

Most spatial co-location mining algorithms require some threshold values in order to generate the co-location patterns, but it is difficult for the user to specify the prevalence threshold without having a clear understanding of the spatial dataset. To remediate this problem, Ref. [13] suggested a top K mining algorithm to find the topmost compact patterns in spatial dataset without specifying the threshold. Similarly, Ref. [14] extended and implemented the Top K algorithm for transactional dataset to mine the sequential co-occurring items along with an index for saving co-occurrence information. This increased the scalability feature of the mined patterns. Reference [15] proposed a series of algorithm for mining co-location patterns using threshold values. Experiments were carried out on dynamic spatial datasets for a time span and the mined patterns had a strong symbiotic relationship among their instances that improved the efficiency of the algorithm.

Reference [16] proposes an Adaptive Maximal Co-location Mining algorithm that aims in obviating the use of setting the proximity measure to generate the neighborhood instances. In the first stage, the proposed algorithm makes use of a Voronoi diagram [19] to generate the nearby pairs of instances in a spatial plane along with their distance. Later in Ref. [17], the algorithm was modified to use a reward-based verification model by which each generated pattern is associated with a reward value to get the most prevalent pattern. Based on real-time evaluation, the proposed algorithm proved to have efficient results than the Order-clique [18] and Delaunay triangulation [2, 12] approach.

5.4 Proposed Grid-Conditional Neighborhood Algorithm

The ultimate aim of the developed algorithm is to discover spatial patterns using a grid-based structure associated with a conditional neighborhood algorithm in the least possible time. Since most of the datasets are very large, a Hadoop framework is used to derive the spatial patterns in a clustered co-location neighborhood. The Hadoop-MapReduce structure breaches the input records into blocks and sends them to the Map function, which in turn processes the data and generate key value pairs as output that is fed to the Reducer. The Reducer function gives cumulative result as output in the form of key value pair. The proposed work uses four MapReduce jobs. The computation time is reduced drastically as the entire process is carried out in parallel. Figure 5.4 represents the generic view of the presented system.

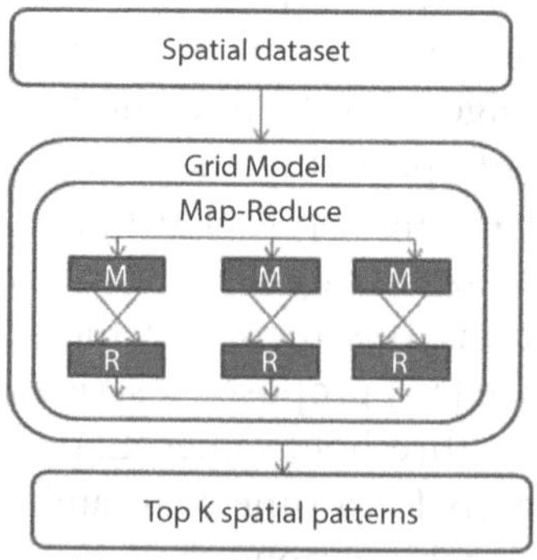

Figure 5.4 Block diagram of the proposed system.

5.4.1 Module Description

The proposed work consists of four modules:

i. Search Neighbor
ii. Group Neighbors
iii. Pattern Search
iv. Top K Pattern generation

The output key value pair of each module is fed as input for the subsequent modules. Each module and their corresponding algorithm are explained in the subsequent sections. The generic flow of the proposed work is depicted in Figure 5.5.

5.4.1.1 Search Neighbor

The first MapReduce job is to find the spatial neighborhood objects using a grid-based partition approach [6]. The mapper takes all data objects as input and maps them to a gridId based on their geographic attributes like district, ward, and so on. All objects having the same gridId are assigned with a gridNum, i.e., crimes that occurred in a district are assigned to a common grid number. The output of the mapper will be a key value pair (key = gridNum, value = [o]) where o ϵ Sd is a spatial data object. Once all mapper instances are completed, the framework will collect their respective values (in this case, an array of "o") and feeds them to the reducer. The function of the reducer is to load the distance threshold and calculate Euclidean or Haversine distance. The distance calculation depends on the coordinate format of the spatial dataset and finds all neighbor pairs based

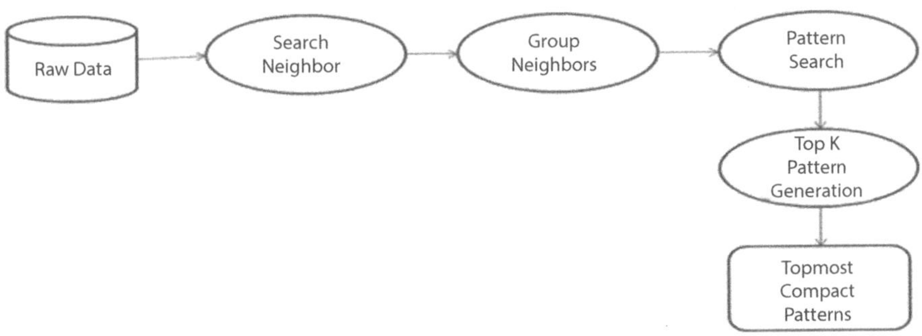

Figure 5.5 Flow diagram of proposed system.

```
Proc Mapper (key, value=o)
    gridId ← findRegion (o)
    gridNum ← same(gridId)
    emit(gridNum, o)
end Proc
Proc Reducer (key=gridNum, value=[o])
    distThreshold ← load(' distance measure threshold ')
    Dist ← calculate_distance(x,y)
    for all o_i ϵ O do
      if (( Dist) ≤ distThreshold) then
      emit(o_i, o_j ) as neighbors
      end if
    end for
end Proc
```

Figure 5.6 Search neighbor algorithm.

on the condition, distance < threshold. Figure 5.6 depicts the functions of the Neighbor Search module.

5.4.1.2 Group Neighbors

The next job is to group the neighbor records based on the conditional neighborhood concept (refer 2.1.5). As depicted in Figure 5.5, the output of previous module is fed as input to the map function. The map function checks for the neighborhood condition, and all objects satisfying the condition are termed conditional neighborhood pairs and the mapper outputs value as (key=o_i, value=CN[o_i]). The reducer function sorts the value list and outputs (key=o_i, value=nRecord), where nRecord ϵ neighborhood

```
Proc Mapper (key=o_i, value=o_j)
    for all o_i
        if (o_i == o_j || o_i.type < o_j.type)
            generate_conditional_neighborhood (CN[o_i])
        end if
    end for
end Proc
Proc Reducer (key=o_i, value=CN[o_i])
    nRecord ← sort (CN[o_i])
    emit(o_i, nRecord)
end Proc
```

Figure 5.7 Group neighbor algorithm.

pairs. Figure 5.7 represents the pseudocode of the Group Neighbors module.

5.4.1.3 *Pattern Search*

The third MapReduce job is to generate the spatial patterns. The map function takes the output of the previous job as input and checks whether the co-location pattern of size n (here, n takes the value of 2 and 3) is present in the neighborhood pair, and if not, it saves the pattern provided the pattern is identified in a different grid. That is, if size n patterns are found in a different grid location, they are considered as unique neighborhood patterns and they are saved in the pattern list. This ensures that the size n patterns that are super patterns are only generated in the patternSet; this redundancy in the derived spatial pattern is reduced as a similar pattern contained in the super pattern is omitted. As in Figure 5.8, the reducer function generates the prevalence score for each of the object instance in the typeset and emits the key value pair containing the pattern with their prevalence score (key=event, value=prevalencescore).

5.4.1.4 *Top K Pattern Generation*

The last MapReduce job is to generate the topmost K compact patterns utilizing Top-K algorithm. The map function takes the pattern list as input along with their prevalence score from past job; it then sorts the patterns in the key list by their score value and sends the sorted list to the reducer (key=kRecord, value=eventSet). The reducer function produces K patterns

```
Proc Mapper (key=event, value=prescore)
    scanNTransaction(event)
    kRecord ← sort(event, prescore)
    save(kRecord)
    eventSet ← count.TypeOf(eventInstance)
    emit(kRecord, eventSet)
end Proc
Proc Reducer (key=kRecord, value=eventSet)
    Truncate(eventSet >K)
    for all kRecord ϵ nRecord
        emit(kRecord, prevalencescore)
    end for
end Proc
```

Figure 5.8 Pattern search algorithm.

```
Proc Mapper (key=oi, value=CN[o])
    if (oi.type.instanceSet != CN[oi])
        save(oi)
    end if
    emit(oi, typeSet)
end Proc
Proc Reducer (key=oi, value=patternSet[])
    for each oi ϵ O do
        generate_prevalenceScore()
    end for
    save(event, prevalencescore)
    emit(event, prevalencescore)
end Proc
```

Figure 5.9 Top-K algorithm.

with their prevalence score as output (key=kRecord, value= prevalence-score). The pseudo code of Top K module is given in Figure 5.9.

5.5 Experimental Setup and Analysis

The developed framework was actualized in Java, MapReduce, and HBase library capacities. HBase [29] is a section arranged database; it has an executive framework that runs over the HDFS. HBase was utilized to save the middle outcome, for example, prevalence score of the co-located pattern types and co-area event types. The execution assessment of the proposed MapReduce algorithm was led on Oracle VM Virtual Box version 5.2 with Linux-CentOS7. Additionally, Apache Hadoop variant 2.6-cdh5.5 and Hbase variant 0.98.6-cdh5.3.1 was utilized for mining the spatial co-located patterns.

5.5.1 Dataset Used

For the exploratory investigation, real-time crime dataset with latitude, longitude, and crime description recorded for the city of Chicago during January 2018–January 2019 was used [30]. The dataset has 22 attribute types and 14 crime categories. Table 5.1 shows the 14 crime types and Table 5.2 depicts the attributes used in the Chicago crime dataset.

Table 5.1 Different crime categories in dataset.

Crime type	Instance count
Criminal damage (CD)	99
Other offenses	24
Battery	207
Theft	156
Burglary	10
Weapons violation (WV)	24
Assault	50
Narcotics	108
Criminal trespass (CT)	18
Motor vehicle theft (MVT)	50
Offense involving children	12
Deceptive practice (DP)	18
Robbery	12
Public peace violation	6

Table 5.2 Attribute type in dataset.

ID	District
Case number	Ward
Date	Community area
Block	FBI code
IUCR	X coordinate
Primary type	Y Coordinate
Description	Year
Location description	Updated on
Arrest	Latitude
Domestic	Longitude
Beat	Location

5.5.2 Performance Analysis

To evaluate the performance of the proposed algorithm, the dataset was divided into 4 categories based on the number of months: 3 months (1 MB), 6 months (900 MB), 9 months (1.5 GB), and 12 months (2 GB) data. In addition, the number of nodes in the Hadoop was varied to check the execution time of the developed algorithm with respect to the data size. It is observed that an increase in the cluster nodes drastically reduced the runtime of the algorithm. Figure 5.10 shows the runtime of the proposed algorithm with respect to the varied cluster nodes.

Figure 5.11 depicts the observed pattern count for each of the data size. For example, 36 effective spatial patterns were determined for 3 months' data (1MB). Table 5.3 shows the outcome of the spatial patterns obtained. These patterns denote that they have occurred in a close proximity and the count denotes their likeness to occur in the future.

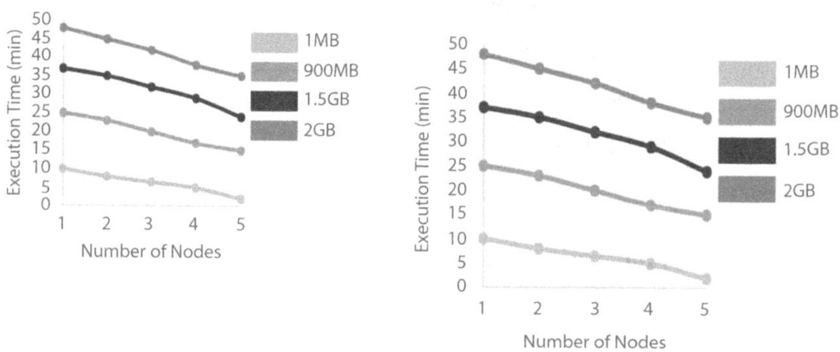

Figure 5.10 Execution time for different data sizes.

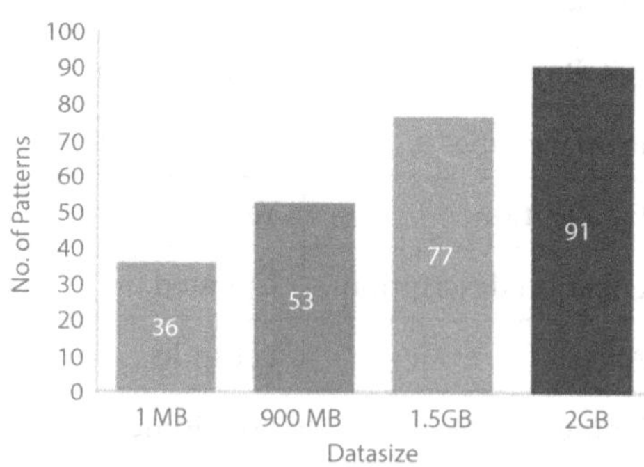

Figure 5.11 Spatial pattern count for different data sizes.

Table 5.3 Derived spatial pattern for 1 MB data.

Patterns	**Occurrence**
Assault _ Narcotics	7
Assault _ Weapons Violation _ Robbery	11
Battery _ Battery	10
Battery _ Theft	7
Burglary _ Burglary	2
Burglary _ Weapons Violation	14
Criminal Damage _ Battery _ Theft	21
Criminal Damage _ Battery _ Theft _ Motor Vehicle Theft	3
Criminal Damage _ Criminal Trespass	7
Criminal Damage _ Criminal Trespass _ Theft	19
Criminal Damage _ Public Peace Violation _ Robbery	2
Criminal Damage _ Theft	1
Criminal Trespass _ Burglary _ Assault	15
Criminal Trespass _ Deceptive Practice	2
Criminal Trespass _ Public Peace Violation	4
Criminal Trespass _ Robbery	2
Motor Vehicle Theft _ Battery	14
Motor Vehicle Theft _ Burglary	2
Narcotics _ Criminal Damage _ Burglary	18
Narcotics _Narcotics	5
Offense Involving Children _ Deceptive Practice	3
Offense Involving Children _ Deceptive Practice_ Criminal Damage	8
Offense Involving Children _ Narcotics	5
Other Offense _ Assault	1

(Continued)

Table 5.3 Derived spatial pattern for 1 MB data. (*Continued*)

Patterns	Occurrence
Other Offense _ Battery	6
Other Offense _ Criminal Trespass	1
Other Offense _ Weapons Violation	8
Public Peace Violation _ Narcotics	4
Robbery _ Assault	7
Robbery _ Assault _ Narcotics	17
Robbery _ Narcotics	4
Theft _ Assault	2
Theft _ Motor Vehicle Theft _ Robbery	4
Theft _ Robbery _ Assault	1
Theft _ Theft	1
Weapons Violation _ Theft _ Burglary	7

For instance, the pattern "Assault _ Narcotics" implies that they both have occurred in a close geographic proximity 7 times, leading to the inference that whenever Assault occurs, there is a chance that Narcotic crime may also occur.

The trial outcome demonstrates that the proposed MapReduce co-location algorithm is generally parallelized, avoids redundancy in the derived neighbor pairs, and pursues a critical increment in speed with increased number of nodes.

5.6 Discussion and Conclusion

Due to substantial advances and widespread usage of the Global Positioning System (GPS), it is now possible to incorporate the geolocation of any occurrences, entities, or other things into a database, together with their geographical place and time information. Numerous autonomous systems are analyzing information, such as the locations of educational institutions, pharmacies, retail complexes, and federal buildings, among other things, and storing it in databases. Certain individuals are fascinated by the wildlife and their motions, which are sometimes documented along with their places by the biologists. The locations of structures such as healthcare and education do not change on a routine basis; however, the locations of wildlife change on a relatively frequent basis. This sort of geospatial information is typically quite large in terms of file size. It is critical to analyze this large volume of data as effectively as possible. Big Data is defined as a large volume of data with a complicated structure and an increased number of information created by several independent sources. These independent sources are also responsible for the generation of spatial data. The relationships that exist among the objects are shifting throughout time. Because certain spatial entities are changing in origin and the information related with such movements is being captured over time, we are curious to learn the changing relationships that exist between different objects. The Big Data framework defines an infrastructure for preserving large amounts of data in a decentralized way, retrieving the stored information when needed, and finally processing the data for extracting useful information and discovery. Distributed data processing is made possible through the use of the Hadoop MapReduce computing platform.

Employing MapReduce architecture to spatial co-location mining possesses a number of difficulties that needs to be overcome to retrieve the optimal co-located patterns from the given search space. The restricted connectivity between clusters necessitates the parallelization of all co-location mining processes in an inter-dependent manner. Nevertheless, it is not straightforward to partition the search area of co-location occurrences, in other words, a collection of geographic objects that have neighbor connections with one another, in order to allow for parallelization to occur. It is possible that intentional random search segmentation will cause co-location entities to be lost between multiple partitions, resulting in incorrect or misleading mining results. The MapReduce framework separates the model parameters input into logical chunks and transmits all the logical chunks to the distributed systems on the fly whenever a client uploads a work tasks. Nevertheless, since spatial objects are immersed in continuous multidimensional space and have a variety of interactions with one another, this intentional data partitioning and dissemination may result in the loss of certain spatial linkages between objects in space. Aside from that, distributing appropriate workloads across nodes is a challenging issue to solve.

In this work, a new parallelized approach to find the topmost compact spatial patterns that occur in a geographic proximity has been proposed. The existing works pose numerous challenges like generating a large number of potential patterns, making the system computationally intensive and resulting in the uneven distribution of event occurrences. The proposed approach overcomes these constraints by constructing a grid-constrained neighborhood search while performing clustering operation utilizing the Hadoop MapReduce framework. At first, the spatial objects are clustered based on the grid partitioning technique and then neighborhood concepts are applied to find the compact patterns without any missing and duplicate spatial patterns. As the proposed work utilizes a parallel technique, it drastically reduces the runtime of spatial data mining. In addition, it is capable of managing a massive dataset and yields productive outcomes. Later on, focus will be given on improvising the algorithm for temporal attributes so that patterns for different time spans can be derived. Moreover, validation of the proposed technique with various kinds of dataset is planned.

References

1. Ridge, O., Stefanidis, A., & Ber, D. O. E. (2012). *Spatiotemporal Data Mining in the Era of Big Spatial Data* :, 1–10.
2. Sundaram, V. M., Thnagavelu, A., & Paneer, P. (2012). Discovering co-location patterns from spatial domain using a delaunay approach. *Proc. Eng.*, *38*, 2832–2845. https://doi.org/10.1016/j.proeng.2012.06.332
3. Wang, L., Bao, X., Chen, H., & Cao, L. (2018). Effective lossless condensed representation and discovery of spatial co-location patterns. *Inf. Sci.*, *436–437*, 197–213. https://doi.org/10.1016/j.ins.2018.01.011
4. Sheshikala, M., Rao, D. R., & Prakash, R. V. (2016). Parallel Approach for Finding Co-location Pattern - A Map Reduce Framework. *Proc. Comput. Sci.*, *89*, 341–348. https://doi.org/10.1016/j.procs.2016.06.081
5. Refaye, E. M., & Hegazy, O. (2016). Parallel co-location pattern mining discovery: Constraint neighborhood approach. *Int. J. Appl. Eng. Res.*, *11*(1), 586–591.
6. Mann, A., & Kaur, N. (2013). Grid Density BasedClustering Algorithm. *Int. J. Adv. Res. Comput. Eng. Technol. (IJARCET)*, *2*(6), 2143–2147. Retrieved from www.ijarcet.org
7. Mining, S. D. (n.d.). *Spatial Data Mining.*
8. Yoo, J. S., Boulware, D., & Kimmey, D. (2014). *2014 IEEE International Congress on Big Data A Parallel Spatial Co-location Mining Algorithm Based on MapReduce*, 25–31. https://doi.org/10.1109/BigData.Congress.2014.14
9. Yoo, J. S., Shekhar, S., Smith, J., & Kumquat, J. P. (2004). A partial join approach for mining co-location patterns. *Proceedings of the 12th Annual ACM International Workshop on Geographic Information Systems - GIS '04*, 241. https://doi.org/10.1145/1032222.1032258

10. Huang, Y., Shekhar, S., & Xiong, H. (2004). Discovering Co-location Patterns from Spatial Datasets : A General Approach, 612–626.
11. Yu, W. (2016). Spatial co-location pattern mining for location-based services in road networks. *Expert Syst. Appl.*, *46*, 324–335. https://doi.org/10.1016/j.eswa.2015.10.010
12. Jiang, Y., Liu, Y., & Zhang, F. (2010). An efficient algorithm for constructing Delaunay triangulation. *2010 2nd IEEE International Conference on Information Management and Engineering*, *7*(6), 600–663. https://doi.org/10.1109/ICIME.2010.5478228
13. Yoo, Jin Soung, and Mark Bow. 2011. "*Mining Top k Closed Co-Location Pattern.*"
14. Kieu, T., Vo, B., Le, T., Deng, Z., & Le, B. (2017). Mining top- k co-occurrence items with sequential pattern, 85, 123–133. https://doi.org/10.1016/j.eswa.2017.05.021
15. S. R. Burri, A. Kumar, A. Baliyan and T. A. Kumar, "Predictive Intelligence for Healthcare Outcomes: An AI Architecture Overview," *2023 2nd International Conference on Smart Technologies and Systems for Next Generation Computing (ICSTSN)*,Villupuram, India, 2023, pp.1-6, doi: 10.1109/ICSTSN57873.2023.10151477.
16. Sriram, S., J. Manikandan, P. Hemalatha and G. Leema Roselin. "A Chatbot Mobile Quarantine App for Stress Relief." In *2021 International Conference on System, Computation, Automation and Networking (ICSCAN)*, pp. 1-5. IEEE, 2021.
17. Burri, Srinivasa Rao, Sachin Ahuja, Abhishek Kumar, and Anupam Baliyan. "Exploring the Effectiveness of Optimized Convolutional Neural Network in Transfer Learning for Image Classification: A Practical Approach." In *2023 International Conference on Advancement in Computation & Computer Technologies (InCACCT)*, pp. 598-602. IEEE, 2023.
18. Hemalatha, P., J. Manikandan, G. Leemarosilin and P. Kanimozhi. "SEA FOOD PROCESSING USING INTERNET OF THINGS AND CLOUD TECHNOLOGIES." *PalArch's J. Archaeology Egypt/Egyptology* 17, no. 9 (2020): 5877-5885.
19. Manikandan, J., Brahmadesam Viswanathan Krishna *and* K. Surendar. "Sign Language Recognition using Machine Learning." In *2022 International Conference on Innovative Computing, Intelligent Communication and Smart Electrical Systems (ICSES)*, pp. 1-5. IEEE, 2022.
20. Subbulakshmi, N., R. Manimegalai, G. Rajakumar, T. Ananth Kumar, and Umadevi Kosuri. "A novel design of low-cost hearing aid devices using an efficient lifting filter bank with a modified variable filter." *Expert Rev. Med. Devices* 19, no. 12 (2022): 991-999.
21. Vijay, K., J. Manikandan, Babu Rajendiran, K. R. Sowmia, and Eugene I. Berna. "Deep Dive on Oversampling and Under Sampling Techniques in Machine Learning." In Recent Trends in Computational Intelligence and Its Application: *Proceedings of the 1st International Conference on Recent Trends*

in Information Technology and its Application (ICRTITA, 22), p. 423. CRC Press, 2023.

22. Akhatov, A., I. Himmatov, Christo Ananth and T. Ananth Kumar. "System of Persons Identification Based on Human Characteristics." In *International Conference on Data Management, Analytics & Innovation*, pp. 1029-1046. Singapore: Springer Nature Singapore, 2023.
23. Manikandan, J. and R. Yogeshkumar. "Glaucoma Disease Detection Using Hybrid Deep Learning Model." In *2023 Eighth International Conference on Science Technology Engineering and Mathematics (ICONSTEM)*, pp. 1-7. IEEE, 2023.
24. Kumar, Abhishek, Swarn Avinash Kumar, Vishal Dutt, S. Shitharth, and Esha Tripathi. "IoT based arrhythmia classification using the enhanced hunt optimization-based deep learning." *Expert Syst.* (2023): e13298.
25. Manikandan, J., S. Adolphine Shyni, R. Dhanalakshmi, S. V. Akshaya and S. Dharshini. "Segmentation and Detection of Pneumothorax using Deep Learning." In *2023 7th International Conference on Intelligent Computing and Control Systems (ICICCS)*, pp. 468-473. IEEE, 2023.
26. Srivastav, Arun Lal, Markandeya, Naveen Patel, Mayank Pandey, Ashutosh Kumar Pandey, Ashutosh Kumar Dubey, Abhishek Kumar, Abhishek Kumar Bhardwaj, and Vinod Kumar Chaudhary. "Concepts of circular economy for sustainable management of electronic wastes: challenges and management options." *Environ. Sci. Pollut. Res.* 30, no. 17 (2023): 48654-48675.
27. Manikandan, J., Brahmadesam Viswanathan Krishna, C. Sasivarma, R. Yogesh Kumar and M. Sidharth Raj. "Cataract Fundus Image Detection Using Hybrid Deep Learning Model." In *International Conference on Computational Intelligence in Data Science*, pp. 300-313. Cham: Springer Nature Switzerland, 2023.
28. Lu, J., Wang, L., Fang, Y., & Zhao, J. (2018). Knowledge-Based Systems co-location patterns,Mining strong symbiotic patterns hidden in spatial prevalent co-location patterns, 0, 1–13. https://doi.org/10.1016/j.knosys.2018.02.006
29. Yao, X., Wang, D., Peng, L., & Chi, T. (2017). *An Adaptive Maximal Co-Location Mining Algorithm Lab of Spatial Information Integration* , Institute of Remote Sensing and Digital Earth , Chinese, 5551–5554.
30. Yao, X., Chen, L., Wen, C., Peng, L., Yang, L., Chi, T., ... Yu, W. (2018). A spatial co-location mining algorithm that includes adaptive proximity improvements and distant instance references. *Int. J. Geogr. Inf. Sci.*, 32(5), 980–1005. https://doi.org/10.1080/13658816.2018.1431839
31. Wang, L., Zhou, L., Lu, J., & Yip, J. (2009). An order-clique-based approach for mining maximal co-locations. *Inf. Sci.*, *179*(19), 3370–3382. https://doi.org/10.1016/j.ins.2009.05.023
32. Watson, D. (1993). Spatial tessellations: concepts and applications of voronoi diagrams. *Comput. Geosci.*, *19*(8), 1209–1210. https://doi.org/10.1016/0098-3004(93)90024-Y

33. Liu, R., & Shi, Y. (2013). Engineering Applications of Arti fi cial Intelligence. *Eng. Appl. Artif. Intell.*, Spatial Distance Join Based Feature Selection, *26*(10), 2597–2607. https://doi.org/10.1016/j.engappai.2013.08.016
34. Sophie, S Lourdumarie, S Sivasathya, S Sharmiladevi, and J Dhakshayani. 2018. "A Survey On Spatial Co-Location Pattern Mining Using Point Dataset" 5 (4): 764–69.
35. N. Mahsuda, C. Ananth, N. Isok-Jon, Y. Rayimjon and T. A. Kumar, "Virtual Science is a New Scientific Paradigm," *2023 IEEE Renewable Energy and Sustainable E-Mobility Conference (RESEM)*, Bhopal, India, 2023, pp. 1-5, doi: 10.1109/RESEM57584.2023.10236372.
36. S. An , H. Yang , J. Wang, *et al.*, Mining urban recurrent congestion evolution *patterns* from GPS-equipped vehicle mobility data, *Inf. Sci.* 373 (10) (2016) 515–526 .
37. W. Yu , T. Ai , S. Shao , The visualization and analysis of POI features under network space supported by kernel density estimation, *J. Transp. Geogr.* 45 (2015) 32–47 .
38. X. Song , L. Nie , L. Zhang, *et al.*, Interest inference via structure-constrained multi-source multi-task learning, in: *Proc. IJCAI*, 2015, *pp* 2371–2377 .
39. J. Zhang , L. Nie , X. Wang, *et al.*, Shorter-is-better: venue category estimation from micro-video,in: *Proc. ACM*
40. X. Chang , Z. Ma , M. Lin, *et al.*, Feature interaction augmented sparse learning for fast kinect motion detection, *IEEE Trans. Image Proc.* 26 (8) (2017) 3911–3920 .
41. A. Ene, S. Im and B. Moseley, "Fast Clustering using MapReduce," in *ACM SIGKDD International Conference on Knowledge Discovery and Data Mining*, 2011, pp. 681–689.
42. Reza Rawassizadeh, Elaheh Momeni, Chelsea Dobbins, Joobin Gharibshah, Michael Pazzani, Scalable daily human behavioural pattern mining from multivariate temporal data, *IEEE Trans. Knowl. Data Eng.* 28 (11) (2016) 3098–3112.
43. Y. Jiang, F. L. Chung, S. Wang, *et al.*, "Collaborative fuzzy clustering from multiple weighted views," *IEEE T. Cybern.*, vol.45, no.4, pp. 688-701, 2014.
44. M. White, X. Zhang, D. Schuurmans, *et al.*, "Convex multi-view subspace learning," in *Proc. NIPS*, 2012, pp. 1673-1681.
45. Y. Jiang, F. L. Chung, H. Ishibuchi, *et al.*, "Multitask TSK fuzzy system modeling by mining intertask common hidden structure," *IEEE T. Cybern.*, vol. 45, no. 3, pp. 534-547, 2014
46. Y. Chou. *Exploring Spatial Analysis in Geographic Information System.* Onward Press, ISBN: 1566901197, 1997.
47. N.A.C. Cressie. *Statistics for Spatial Data.* Wiley and Sons, ISBN:0471843369, 1991.
48. R. Agarwal and R. Srikant. Fast Algorithms for Mining Association Rules. In *Proc. of the 20th Int'l Conference on Very Large Data Bases*, 1994

49. K. Koperski and J. Han. Discovery of Spatial Association Rules in Geographic Information Databases. In *Proc. of the 4th International Symposium on Spatial Databases*, 1995
50. Y. Morimoto. Mining Frequent Neighboring Class Sets in Spatial Databases. In *Proc. ACM SIGKDD International Conference on Knowledge Discovery and Data Mining*, 2001
51. S. Shekhar and Y. Huang. Co-location Rules Mining: A Summary of Results. In *Proc. 7th Intl. Symposium on Spatio-temporal Databases*, 2001.
52. kumar Mohan, Senthil, A. John, and Ananth kumar Tamilarasan. "Evolutionary Computing and Swarm Intelligence for Hyper Parameters Optimization Problem in Convolutional Neural Networks." In *Soft Computing Approach for Mathematical Modeling of Engineering Problems*, pp. 157-169. CRC Press, 2021.
53. Shashi Shekhar, Siva Revada, Xuan Liu, "Spatial Databases – Accomplishments and Reasearch Needs",*IEEE Trans. Knowl. Data Eng.*, Vol.11, 1999.
54. Diansheng Guo, Jeremy Mennis, "Spatial Data Mininig and Geographic Knowledge Discovery- An Introduction", *Comput Environ. Urban Syst.* 33 (2009) 403-408.
55. Kumar, T. Deva, TS Arun Samuel and T. Ananth Kumar. "Transforming Green Cities with IoT: A Design Perspective." In *Handbook of Green Engineering Technologies for Sustainable Smart Cities*, pp. 17-35. CRC Press, 2021.
56. J. Dhakshayani, S.Sivasathya, S.Sharmiladevi, S.LourduMarie Sophie, "A Survey On Incremental Pattern Mining And Their Techniques", *J. Emerg. Technol. Innov. Res. (JETIR)* Volume 5, Issue 10, October 2018, 284-290
57. S. Sharmiladevi, S. Siva Sathya, "Evaluation Metrics of Spatial and Spatiotemporal Data Mining Techniques", in *Emerging Technologies in Data Mining and Information Security*, Springer International Publishing, 2021, pp. 449–463.
58. S. Sharmiladevi, S. Siva Sathya and N. Ramesh, "A Survey on Spatiotemporal Co-occurrence Pattern Mining Techniques", in *Applications of Artificial Intelligence in Engineering*, Springer International Publishing, 2021, pp. 225–238. doi: 10.1007/978-981-33-4604-8_18.

6

Computational Intelligence-Based Optimal Feature Selection Techniques for Detecting Plant Diseases

Karthickmanoj R.[1]*, S. Aasha Nandhini[2] and T. Sasilatha[1]

[1]*Department of Electrical and Electronics Engineering, Academy of Maritime Education and Training, Chennai, Tamil Nadu, India*
[2]*Department of Electronics and Communication Engineering, SSN College of Engineering, Chennai, India*

Abstract
Plant disease detection is critical in agricultural applications to increase profitability. To prevent yield loss, illness in leaves must be found early. Early disease diagnosis using machine learning algorithms allows agriculture to take preventive measures to avoid damage to crops in the future. The key contribution of this chapter is the invention of an efficient approach for tracking plants in order to early detect and classify illnesses. The gadget will take pictures of the field's leaves using the camera sensor. The extraction of crucial features for classification is suggested using a segmentation and feature extraction technique. The SVM algorithm is used to categorize the disease at the monitoring station. The efficiency of the system is assessed with regard to both detection and classification.

***Keywords*:** Machine learning, feature vector, edge detection, classification

6.1 Introduction

In the modern context, computational intelligent agriculture—which uses the Internet of Things and artificial intelligence—is essential for increasing crop yields and farmer income. Diseases have a significant impact on crop yield because they affect both quantity and quality. It is indeed essential to

**Corresponding author*: karthickmanoj.r@gmail.com

T. Ananth Kumar, E. Golden Julie, Venkata Raghuveer Burugadda, Abhishek Kumar and Puneet Kumar (eds.) Computational Intelligence: Theory and Applications, (145–158) © 2024 Scrivener Publishing LLC

detect the disease early on and protect the spread of the virus by continuing to develop automatic plant monitoring systems. This automation process will provide a precise option to farm owners manually tracking farms.

As an outcome, this chapter focuses on creating a novel color scheme segmentation and characteristic extraction framework for spotting illness organisms in plant leaves before symptoms appear. Using the color transformation model, the gathered image is turned into the color domain, and all color elements are segmented and feature extracted. It is done using statistical formula to determine segmentation and multi-feature extraction.

The chapter was partitioned into a few sections: Section 6.2, which presents the need of identifying leaf illnesses utilizing ML techniques; Section 6.3, which considers past investigations depending on illness, providing proof as well as classification, particularly a writing survey; Section 6.4, which talks about the different techniques required for the location and classification of plant; and Section 6.5, which clarifies the produced outcomes based on the proposed strategy.

6.2 Literature Survey

Lv *et al.* [1] described a Corn leaf function optimal control framework for improving maize qualities in a complex setting. Robust Alexnet was employed during this research for precise extracting features. Increased usability and accuracy are among the benefits. The job lacks real-time diagnostics and difficulty assessment.

Zhou *et al.* [2] suggested sensing difficulties in rice images such as noise, blurring picture edges, low high detection, and higher noise interference. The results showed that precision had increased while time complexity had decreased. One limitation was that the identification of illness and dynamic scanners of huge paddy cultivation was not carried out.

Kumar *et al.* [3] presented an illness detection approach that is web-enabled designed for effective disease detection via compressed sensing. The research proposal was endorsed by the researchers to use both modeling and novel analyses for a wide range of plants. SVM was used for categorization, yielding an overall accuracy of 98.5. A classification algorithm that is dependent on an evolutionary algorithm and a support vector machine was proposed by Srivastav *et al.* [4]. The proposed task offers a detection rate of 95.71% and an accuracy in classification of 97.6%, according to the results.

For farmer convenience, Kannan *et al.* proposed [5] an efficient plant strain detection mechanism that is automated. The author developed a web-based tool to identify pomegranate diseases based on color and morphology. With an accuracy of 82%, the K-Means method is used for classification and segmentation using SVM. A structure employs a smartphone and a camera to record images of crop leaf images in the field, as well as a gadget that must learn to classify the leaf as healthy or unhealthy. Reference [6] concentrated on leaf crop diseases. The authors created a method to identify plant illnesses in fresh leaves using transfer learning methods like deep learning, using CNN as a trait representation and SVM as a classification engine.

Varshney *et al.* [7] focused on developing a scheme for smart agriculture, specifically for the initial detection of illnesses in leaf tissue, and provided farm owners with solutions. The primary contributions are the innovative pixel replacement fragmentation and the extraction of characteristic methods to improve classification. Karthickmanoj *et al.* [8] illustrate the effectiveness of the structure by evaluating variables such as memory space and safety handling overhead in real time using a WMSN testbed.

A purpose of this research [9] is to inform farmers about cutting-edge innovations for reducing plant leaf illnesses. Because tomato is a common vegetable, methods utilizing machine learning and image analysis with a precise automated system have been recognized for identifying crop disease in tomato plants. The suggested system [10] processes leaf images and extracts texture information using imaging techniques and IoT. Located somewhere at the station, the GLCM features are classified using the RFC method and analyzed by agriculture experts who provide solutions.

Devi *et al.* [11] describes a novel Internet of Things-based full face screening test for public transit, specifically public transport. One such scheme will indeed gather data on a real-time basis by using facial recognition. The primary purpose of this project is to detect facial masks in actual streaming video using convolutional neural networks with deep learning, artificial intelligence, and image processing approaches. In this approach, a complete study of the different methods used in identifying plant illness using AI-based machine learning algorithms techniques has been conducted [12]. Deep learning, on the other hand, has grown in importance in the computer vision field for providing better results for sensing crop diseases.

This research by Jackulin and Murugavalli [13] explores the literature on agricultural machine learning approaches, with a particular emphasis on illness and insect categorization, identification, and forecasting, with a concentration on tomato cultivation. By supporting the creation of strategies that will allow the company to use organic practices and chemical goods while preserving and improving harvest production and quality, this survey intends to enhance smart agriculture and precision agriculture. Domingues *et al.* [14] suggested an automated approach for diagnosing diseases that provides farmers with quick and accurate diagnostic tests for agricultural diseases. Technology of leaf disease in plant sensing systems is essential for speeding up crop diagnostic test. Using computer training and image handling, the above article discusses a method for detecting leaf illness. This framework can accept a leaf image as input.

Shantkumari and Uma [15] use machine learning algorithms to distinguish between diverse disease categories and diagnose grape leaf disease early. For the classification of leaf diseases, an improved K-nearest neighbor model and a neural network-based classification model are also presented. High-quality histogram and expanded histogram attributes are developed to provide fundamental, structure, limit, and discriminative data. The high-quality gradient-based features that arise are subsequently employed in the classification step. The suggested approaches significantly enhance classification precision. The recommended models are tested using the Plant-Village Dataset, a publicly accessible dataset. The recommended models outperform several popular classification methods in terms of classification accuracy.

Reddy *et al.* [16] further explain how to use the Internet of Things to monitor the power efficiency of an electric vehicle. An electric vehicle is obviously entirely reliant on the energy source provided by a power supply. The energy delivered to the vehicle, on the other hand, is progressively lowering, resulting in frame rate drops. The system is capable of recognizing the degraded performance of the battery and sending alert notification to the user for further action, according to the findings of the tests. This method is advantageous in public transport and V2G systems. The suggested technique will facilitate city living while enhancing urban planning. A method for sensing diseases in plants is described in Ref. [17]. Illness is detected on the different yields. The detection of the plant disease system presented here is simple as well as computationally efficient, requiring less time for forecast than other methods having to learn strategies. The accuracy of various leaf and plant diseases is calculated and presented in this paper.

Jumat *et al.* [18] recommend developing a model for low-cost smart farming that can detect plant illnesses early and warn farmers so that preventive actions may be adopted. Additionally, a system that can be accessed online has been created to let farmers keep tabs on the health of the plants in their greenhouses. Farmers will be able to spot illnesses in their plants at an early stage due to the development agricultural leaf disease detection system, reducing production loss due to a full-blown disease outbreak in their greenhouse. One of the system's essential advantages is its ability to categorize the Septoria plant disease, for which defining the stages of disease breakout on the leaf is critical. Furthermore, researchers demonstrated that the Raspberry Pi could conduct categorization using a machine-learning technique without compromising speed. Our study also shows that a random forest classifier combined with a color histogram is the ideal configuration for this prototype to employ for successful plant disease diagnosis.

A farmer can diagnose plant diseases quickly and precisely with automated disease detection systems. Plant leaf disease detection methods must be automated to speed up crop diagnosis. Zamani *et al.* [19] presented a method for identifying leaf disease using computer methods such as picture analysis. This framework may accept a leaf picture as input. First, noise in leaf images is removed during preprocessing. To lower noise levels, use conventional filtering. Histogram equalization improves image quality. The split of a single point of view into several parts or portions is known as segmentation in photography. It helps define image borders. The image is segmented utilizing the K-Means technique. To extract features, significant component analysis is employed.

The authors investigate current improvements in recognizing plant illnesses by examining plant leaves with automated vision and methods of image processing [20]. Edge features are extracted using Canny-edge identification, hue information is obtained using grid chromatic movement, and texture analysis is performed using the Local Binary Pattern. The collected features were then concatenated to form a combined feature vector that was used to train the machine learning optimization techniques. The proposed decision-making support model can distinguish and classify diverse leaf seedlings due to the design of these artificial intelligence algorithms.

The authors originally presented a transfer learning strategy based on fully connected convolutional networks to diagnose plant diseases in this research, which we expect to be implemented on system edge with increasing computing power. Ale *et al.* [21] then developed a light deep neural network technique that IoT devices with minimal resources may use. We alter the convolutional network while decreasing the number of the input sizes to reduce the model's length and computation cost. To select the appropriate size of the source images, the proposed models are trained using various image sizes. The proposed algorithms' efficiency on real-world data is evaluated using simulations; the results show that the proposed approaches may reliably detect plant illness while demanding little technical experience.

Wani *et al.* [22] investigate diseases and infections in various crops. Initially, numerous potential illnesses and diseases on these four types of crops are investigated, as well as their causes and possible identification signals. The multiple stages are involved in plant disease identification and categorization. The fields of machine learning and deep learning are thoroughly investigated. A variety of online resources for detecting plant diseases are also made accessible. A comprehensive examination of existing machine learning including deep neural-based models for classification for four different crops presented by different investigators across the world is additionally addressed, encompassing performance assessments, datasets used, and feature extraction approaches.

Akhatov *et al.* [23] concentrated on three grape diseases. Several ways for identifying illnesses in plants have been described, with the use of deep learning emerging as the method of choice due to its excellent performance. U 2-Net was utilized in this work to eliminate an undesired backdrop from an input picture by choosing multiscale attributes. The EfficientNetV2 model is used in this study to identify cardamom plant illness. A significant number of experiments were run to evaluate the suggested technique's efficacy in comparison to existing systems, such as the one used for deep learning.

Hessane *et al.* [24] offer a framework based on feature extraction and modeling prediction techniques for examining leaf images to diagnose the stages of infection caused by white scaling plague in palm crops. The used dataset's grayscale and color images are used for obtaining gray-level co-occurrence matrices texture features. ML and Ensemble algorithms were explored to classify the WSD. For the training and assessment of the ML models, two datasets were used. The SVM classifier was performed on combining GLCM and HSV data, with an accuracy of 98.29%. The suggested technique might help the oasis agricultural community diagnose date palm white scale disease early and adopt preventive actions to safeguard both date palm plants and crop yield.

This research [25] describes how to construct a single stream CNN for identifying citrus crop diseases. In the first stage, four contrast enhancement methods are utilized to supplement data. Using the transfer learning technique, the revised Mobile Net deep learning network undergoes training on the improved citrus dataset. Even if the newly built model is utilized to extract deep features, a closer look shows that the recovered deep features only include a small amount of redundant data. As a consequence, an upgraded version of the Whale Optimization Algorithm is applied in the third stage. Using machine learning classifiers, the top characteristics are identified in the final step.

6.3 Proposed Framework

For smart agriculture applications, an efficient algorithm for detecting plant leaf disease has been developed. The algorithm prioritizes precise feature selection and feature extraction. A novel color element segmentation method and feature extraction is performed in this framework. The numerical measure-based threshold for each color component is computed separately for segmentation. Figures 6.1 and 6.2 illustrate the proposed algorithms and process flow for a monitoring site.

Each module in the transmission and tracking sections is explained in detail below.

i. **Step of image capture and pre-processing**
A high-resolution camera was used to photograph plant leaves in an agricultural area. The image data are contrast enhanced to improve image quality, and then a color transformation model is used. This work employs the RGB TO HSV color model transformation.

ii. **Image segmentation**
The segments for every color are distinct. Initial computations of the variance as well as the means of the S, V, and H components yield Hu, Hv,

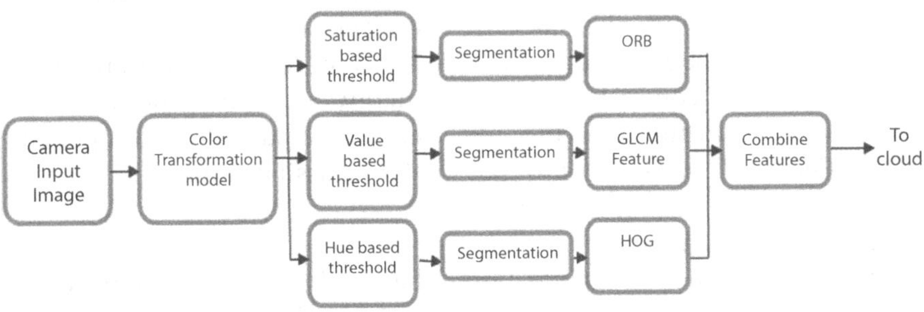

Figure 6.1 Proposed framework.

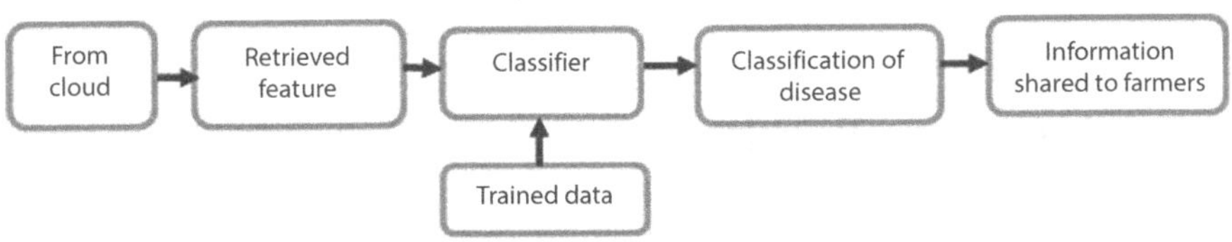

Figure 6.2 Process flow at monitoring site.

Su, Sv, Vu, and Vv, respectively. Equations 6.1 to 6.3 show how adding the variance and the mean of each component yields the color component segmentation threshold (3).

$$T_V = V_v + V_u \tag{6.1}$$

$$T_S = S_v + S_u \tag{6.2}$$

$$T_H = H_v + H_u \tag{6.3}$$

The disease-ridden part is segmented for the color components by trying to compare the pixels to the corresponding threshold values.

iii. **Extraction of color component-based features**
An ORB feature extraction method is used to extract ORB features from segmentation results of the H, S, and V elements. Each element has N features that are derived, and the 3 N features are created by combining the N characteristics. A set of local histograms describes an image in the Histogram of Oriented Gradients (HOG) method. The occurrences of gradient orientation are then accumulated in a small spatially localized portion of the image known as a cell. The features vector is created by concatenating 1D histograms. When using GLCM methods to analyze texture features, grouping images are typically grayscale images. An ideal tool for evaluation is achieved by plotting two pixel values in a matrix, which advances the investigation to the next level. Gray co-matrix features were extracted such as contrast, correlation, energy, and homogeneity. Before being delivered to the receiving unit, this combined feature component GLCM ORB and HOG is sent to the cloud for classification.

iv. **Section of monitoring**
The feature component is retrieved from the cloud platform and supplied to the classifier. The SVM algorithm is used to train the classifier, which is initially trained using a dataset. Farmers are given information on disease classification and treatment alternatives by experts. The proposed algorithm considerably improves accuracy and is employed in the plant disease detection system.

6.4 Simulation Results

The technique was developed in Python software and validated while being tested on the Raspberry Pi board. The Python programming language was utilized, and the Raspbian Jessie operating system was installed.

Using database images from [26], the proposed algorithm was assessed. The classification of illness like cercospora leaf spot, anthracnose, and *Alternaria alternata* was done using pictures of pomegranate plant leaves. Images from the database were used for both testing and training purposes. For classification, the SVM classifier is employed. The damaged leaves of a pomegranate plant appear in the input images in Figure 6.3. The new color identity was used to convert the 256 ×256 RGB input image to HSV. The segmentation threshold is determined by taking the mean and variation of each segmented component value.

Following segmentation of the diseased portion using thresholds, combined features are extracted. To create a feature component of size 15 × 1, features are taken from each component and combined together. These features meet the listing for classification. Figures 6.4 to 6.9 present various segmentation images of the H, S, and V components.

(a) (b) (c)

Figure 6.3 Pomegranate plant (a) Alternaria Alternata, (b) Cercospora leaf spot, (c) Anthracnose.

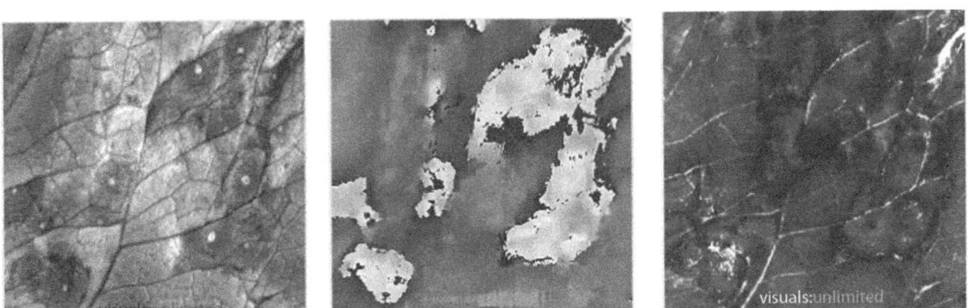

(a) (b) (c)

Figure 6.4 Anthracnose image after HSV transformation: (a) V component image, (b) H component image, and (c) S component image.

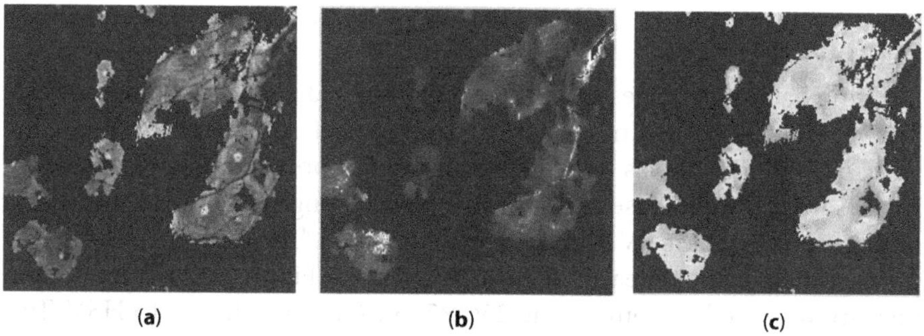

Figure 6.5 Anthracnose segmented image: (a) V component image, (b) H component image, and (c) S component image.

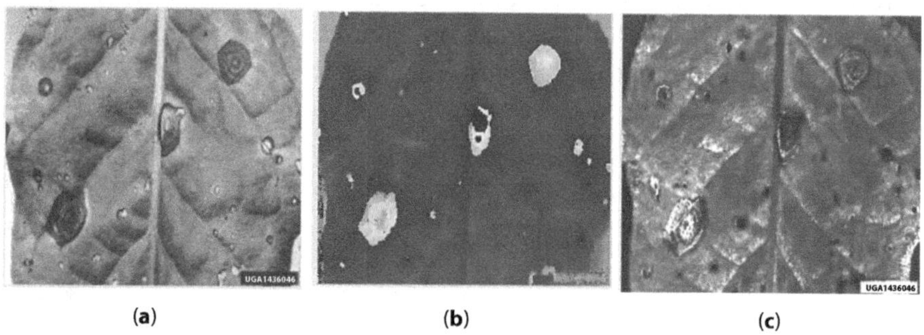

Figure 6.6 *Alternaria alternata* image after HSV transformation: (a) V component image, (b) H component image, (c) S component image.

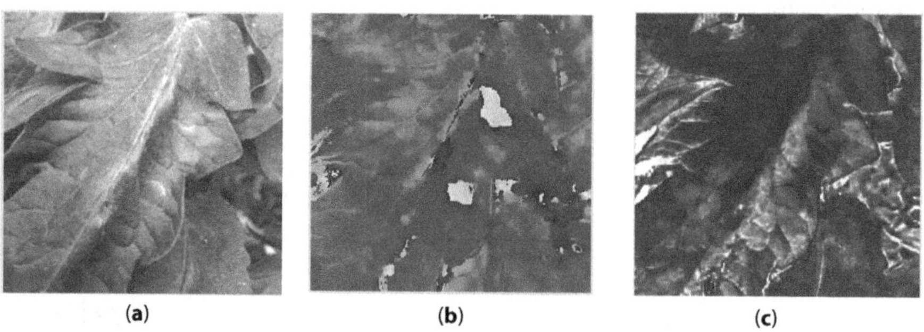

Figure 6.7 HSV transformed image of Cercospora leaf spot. (a) V component image, (b) H component image, and (c) S component image.

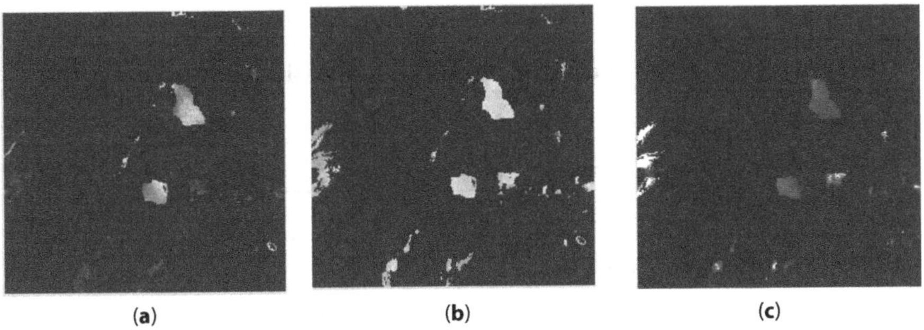

Figure 6.8 Cercospora leaf spot segmented image (a) V component image, (b) H component image, (c) S component image.

Accuracy

Utilizing the detection performance, the effectiveness of the suggested method for disease detection is evaluated.

A bar graph of the prediction performance for pomegranate plant infectious diseases is shown in Figure 6.9. The proposed CSFE framework is estimated to have, as a whole, a recognition rate of 95.3% and an accuracy rate of 92%, 93%, and 94%, respectively, for features of sizes 18, 49, and 95 as shown in Table 6.1.

The proposed CSFE framework is estimated to have, as a whole, a recognition rate of 95.3% and an accuracy rate of 92%, 93%, and 94%, respectively, for features of sizes 18, 49, and 95. The table and chart make it abundantly clear that the proposed framework's accuracy rate exceeds that of the methods described in Refs. [24] and [25].

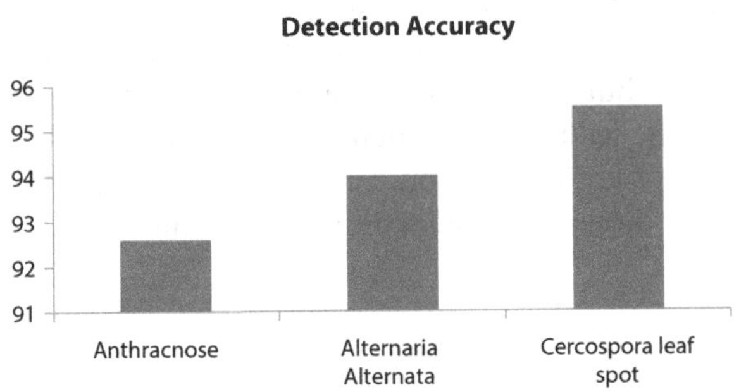

Figure 6.9 Bar chart of the accuracy rate for infectious illnesses of pomegranate plants.

Table 6.1 The proposed CSFE framework's classification accuracy.

Diseases	Features extracted	Classification accuracy (%)
Anthracnose	18	91
	49	91.8
	95	92.6
Alternaria alternata	18	92.1
	49	91.9
	95	93.4
Cercospora leaf spot	18	93.1
	49	96.1
	95	95.8
Overall detection accuracy (%)	18	92
	49	93
	95	94

6.5 Summary

An immediate solution to the significant challenge of plant disease detection must be found in order to improve the economy of the nation. This chapter contributes to the creation of a quick and precise color scheme data processing and feature extraction system for the classification and diagnosis of diseases. The field-captured image is converted from RGB to HSV after segmentation thresholds are established from each modified component. Utilizing categorization threshold values, each sick region is split, and then attributes are recovered and integrated into a single feature element. This same feature component is uploaded to the cloud and then downloaded for SVM classification. Farmers are getting information from experts about the disease's classification and treatment.

References

1. M. Lv, G. Zhou, M. He, A. Chen, W. Zhang and Y. Hu, "Maize Leaf Disease Identification Based on Feature Enhancement and DMS-Robust Alexnet," in *IEEE Access*, vol. 8, pp. 57952-57966, 2020, doi: 10.1109/ACCESS.2020.2982443.

2. G. Zhou, W. Zhang, A. Chen, M. He and X. Ma, "Rapid Detection of Rice Disease Based on FCM-KM and Faster R-CNN Fusion," in *IEEE Access*, vol. 7, pp. 143190-143206, 2019, doi: 10.1109/ACCESS.2019.2943454.
3. Kumar, Abhishek, Swarn Avinash Kumar, Vishal Dutt, S. Shitharth, and Esha Tripathi. "IoT based arrhythmia classification using the enhanced hunt optimization-based deep learning." *Expert Syst.*, (2023): e13298.
4. Srivastav, Arun Lal, Markandeya, Naveen Patel, Mayank Pandey, Ashutosh Kumar Pandey, Ashutosh Kumar Dubey, Abhishek Kumar, Abhishek Kumar Bhardwaj, and Vinod Kumar Chaudhary. "Concepts of circular economy for sustainable management of electronic wastes: challenges and management options." *Environ. Sci. Pollut. Res.*, 30, no. 17 (2023): 48654-48675.
5. Kannan, S., P. Pugazhendiran and N. Rishi Keshav. "Energy optimization mechanism using metastable-smart grid (MSSG)." In *J. Phys. Conf. Ser.*, vol. 2466, no. 1, p. 012024. IOP Publishing, 2023.
6. Karthickmanoj, R., Sasilatha, T. and Padmapriya, J., 2021. Automated machine learning based plant stress detection system. *Mater. Today: Proc.*, 47, pp.1887-1891.
7. Varshney, D., Babukhanwala, B., Khan, J., Saxena, D. and Singh, A.K., 2022, May. Plant Disease Detection Using Machine Learning Techniques. In *2022 3rd International Conference for Emerging Technology* (INCET) (pp. 1-5). IEEE.
8. Karthickmanoj, R., Padmapriya, J. and Sasilatha, T., 2021. A novel pixel replacement-based segmentation and double feature extraction techniques for efficient classification of plant leaf diseases. *Mater. Today Proc.*, 47, pp.2048-2052.
9. Kumar, Abhishek, Pramod Sing Rathore, Ashutosh Kumar Dubey, Rashmi Agrawal, and Kanta Prasad Sharma. "LTE-NBP with holistic UWB-WBAN approach for the energy efficient biomedical application." *Multimedia Tools Appl.*, (2023): 1-15.
10. Harakannanavar, S.S., Rudagi, J.M., Puranikmath, V.I., Siddiqua, A. and Pramodhini, R., 2022. Plant Leaf Disease Detection using Computer Vision and Machine Learning Algorithms. *Global Transitions Proc.*
11. Devi, R.D., Nandhini, S.A., Hemalatha, R. and Radha, S., 2019, March. IoT enabled efficient detection and classification of plant diseases for agricultural applications. In *2019 International Conference on Wireless Communications Signal Processing and Networking (WiSPNET)* (pp. 447-451). IEEE.
12. Kumar, T.A., Rajmohan, R., Pavithra, M., Ajagbe, S.A., Hodhod, R. and Gaber, T., 2022. Automatic face mask detection system in public transportation in smart cities using IoT and deep learning. *Electronics*, 11(6), p.904.
13. Jackulin, C. and Murugavalli, S., 2022. A comprehensive review on detection of plant disease using machine learning and deep learning approaches. *Meas. Sens.*, p.100441.
14. Domingues, T., Brandão, T. and Ferreira, J.C., 2022. Machine Learning for Detection and Prediction of Crop Diseases and Pests: A Comprehensive Survey. *Agriculture*, 12(9), p.1350.

15. Shantkumari, M. and Uma, S.V., 2023. Grape leaf image classification based on machine learning technique for accurate leaf disease detection. *Multimedia Tools Appl.*, 82(1), pp.1477-1487.
16. Reddy, B.A., Krishna, G.S., Saraswathi, K.P., Sadhvika, I., Udutalapally, V. and Das, D., 2022, April. dScout: Unmanned Ground Vehicle for Automatic Disease Detection and Pesticide Atomizer. In *2022 IEEE 7th International conference for Convergence in Technology (I2CT)* (pp. 1-6). IEEE.
17. Themozhi, G., Prabha, A., Radhakrishnan, P. and Manigandan, K., 2021. Battery Monitoring and Smart Charging Using Iot For Electrical Vehicle Applications. *Int. J. Aquat. Sci.*, 12(3), pp.593-601.
18. Jumat, M.H., Nazmudeen, M.S. and Wan, A.T., 2018. *Smart farm prototype for plant disease detection, diagnosis & treatment using IoT device in a greenhouse.*
19. Zamani, A.S., Anand, L., Rane, K.P., Prabhu, P., Buttar, A.M., Pallathadka, H., Raghuvanshi, A. and Dugbakie, B.N., 2022. Performance of Machine Learning and Image Processing in Plant Leaf Disease Detection. *J. Food Qual.*, 2022
20. Waldamichael, F.G., Debelee, T.G., Schwenker, F., Ayano, Y.M. and Kebede, S.R., 2022. Machine Learning in Cereal Crops Disease Detection: A Review. *Algorithms*, 15(3), p.75.
21. Ale, L., Sheta, A., Li, L., Wang, Y. and Zhang, N., 2019, December. Deep learning based plant disease detection for smart agriculture. In *2019 IEEE Globecom Workshops (GC Wkshps)* (pp. 1-6). IEEE.
22. Wani, J.A., Sharma, S., Muzamil, M., Ahmed, S., Sharma, S. and Singh, S., 2022. Machine learning and deep learning based computational techniques in automatic agricultural diseases detection: Methodologies, applications, and challenges. *Arch. Comput. Methods Eng.*, 29(1), pp.641-677.
23. Akhatov, A., I. Himmatov, Christo Ananth and T. Ananth Kumar. "System of Persons Identification Based on Human Characteristics." In *International Conference on Data Management, Analytics & Innovation*, pp. 1029-1046. Singapore: Springer Nature Singapore, 2023.
24. Hessane, A., El Youssefi, A., Farhaoui, Y., Aghoutane, B. and Amounas, F., 2023. A Machine Learning Based Framework for a Stage-Wise Classification of Date Palm White Scale Disease. *Big Data Min. Anal.*, 6(3), pp.263-272.
25. Hassam, M., Khan, M.A., Armghan, A., Althubiti, S.A., Alhaisoni, M., Alqahtani, A., Kadry, S. and Kim, Y., 2022. A single stream modified mobilenet V2 and whale controlled entropy based optimization framework for citrus fruit diseases recognition. *IEEE Access*, 10, pp.91828-91839.
26. https://www.kaggle.com/.

7

Protein Structure Prediction Using Convolutional Neural Networks Augmented with Cellular Automata

Pokkuluri Kiran Sree[1*], Prasun Chakrabarti[2], Martin Margala[3] and SSSN Usha Devi N.[4]

[1]*Department of C.S.E., Shri Vishnu Engineering College for Women(A), Bhimavaram, India*
[2]*ITM SLS Baroda University, Baroda, India*
[3]*School of Computing and Informatics, University of Louisiana at Lafayette, Louisiana, USA*
[4]*Department of C.S.E, UCEK-JNTU Kakinada, Kakinada, India*

Abstract

Protein structure prediction is a challenging task in deep learning. Computational techniques proposed by various researchers are quite impressive, but there is still room for improvement. The primary structure of a protein (sequence of amino acids) can be easily determined from the corresponding gene sequence, but computing the tertiary, secondary, and quaternary structures from the structure of the primary is more complex. Convolutional neural networks are used to model the interactions between subunits based on input features such as amino acid sequences, evolutionary information, or protein–protein interaction data. We have collected the datasets from the Protein Data Bank and applied the same to our work. We have developed CNN network augmented with cellular automata (CA), i.e., CNN-CA-P, for predicting the secondary, ternary, and quaternary structures to build a potential and versatile classifier. We have achieved an accuracy of 96.56%, 91.2%, and 86.32% for predicting the secondary, ternary, and quaternary proteins, respectively. We have used accuracy, AUC, precision, F1 score, and recall as parameters to evaluate our work. CNN-CA-P performance is considerably good compared with the standard baseline methods.

**Corresponding author*: drkiransree.jntuk@gmail.com

T. Ananth Kumar, E. Golden Julie, Venkata Raghuveer Burugadda, Abhishek Kumar and Puneet Kumar (eds.) Computational Intelligence: Theory and Applications, (159–174) © 2024 Scrivener Publishing LLC

***Keywords*:** Deep learning, protein structure prediction, CNN, secondary structure, ternary structure, quaternary structure, cellular automata

7.1 Introduction

Protein structure prediction plays a crucial role in understanding the function and behavior of proteins. Here are some key reasons highlighting the importance of protein structure prediction:

1. **Structure–Function Relationship:** 3D protein structure is defined as a function that has to be identified. By accurately predicting the structure, we can gain insights into how the protein carries out its biological activities, such as enzyme catalysis, molecular recognition, or signal transduction. Understanding the structure–function relationship is vital for advancing fields like drug discovery, bioengineering, and personalized medicine.
2. **Drug Discovery and Design:** Many drugs exert their therapeutic effects by interacting with specific target proteins. Knowing the structure of a protein can aid in rational drug design, as it enables researchers to identify potential binding sites and design molecules that can interact with the protein in a desired manner. Protein structure prediction helps in identifying drug targets [1], understanding protein–drug interactions, and optimizing drug candidates.
3. **Functional Annotation:** With the rapid increase in genomic sequencing, there is a tremendous gap among proteins sequenced and their experimentally determined structures. In the absence of experimental structural data, protein structure prediction can give important insights into the function of proteins. By inferring the structure, we can make informed predictions about their molecular mechanisms, interactions, and potential biological roles [2].
4. **Protein Engineering and Design:** Protein structure prediction can guide protein engineering efforts by providing information about how mutations or modifications might affect protein stability, activity, or specificity. It aids in the design of novel proteins with desired properties, such as enzymes with improved catalytic efficiency, antibodies with

enhanced binding affinity, or proteins with altered functions for biotechnological applications [3, 4].
5. **Understanding Disease Mechanisms:** Many diseases, including genetic disorders and various cancers, are associated with mutations or alterations in protein structure. Protein structure prediction helps in identifying structural changes caused by disease-associated mutations, understanding their impact on protein function, and unravelling the underlying disease mechanisms. This knowledge can guide the development of targeted therapies and personalized medicine approaches [5, 6].
6. **Conservation and Evolutionary Analysis:** Protein family analysis, the detection of conserved structural motifs, and the inference of evolutionary links can all be done using protein structure prediction. By comparing protein structures from different species, we can gain additional insight into the evolution of protein function and identify crucial residues or regions that are crucial for protein stability or activity [7].

Overall, protein structure prediction is crucial for advancing our understanding of protein function, aiding drug discovery, enabling protein engineering efforts, unraveling disease mechanisms, and facilitating personalized medicine. It serves as a valuable tool in various domains of biological and biomedical research, offering insights into the fundamental principles that govern life processes.

Convolutional neural networks (CNNs) are a family of deep learning models that have been effectively used for a number of tasks, including protein structure prediction, picture classification, and natural language processing. Because they can learn to recognize patterns in both the protein's 3D structure and amino acid sequence, CNNs are highly suited for protein structure prediction [8].

There are numerous ways to predict protein structure using CNNs. One such technique is to predict the secondary structure of the protein using a CNN. How efficiently a protein operates is greatly influenced by the secondary structure, or local arrangement of amino acids within a protein.

Another approach to protein structure prediction using CNNs is to identify the protein contact map. The contact map is a representation of the spatial relationships between pairs of amino acids in a protein. CNNs can be trained to predict contact maps by using a dataset of known protein structures and their corresponding contact maps. CNNs have been shown to be effective at predicting both secondary structure and contact maps. Recent advances in protein structure prediction have been made by CNN-based techniques [9].

Methods based on CNN are still under development, but they have the potential to revolutionize protein structure prediction. CNNs are able to learn complex patterns in protein sequences and structures, and they can be used to predict the protein structure, which is tough with other approaches [10]. Cellular automata (CAs) and convolutional neural networks (CNNs) are two potent machine learning methods that have been used to a range of tasks, including the prediction of protein structure. Because they can learn to recognize patterns in both the protein's 3D structure and amino acid sequence, CNNs are highly suited for protein structure prediction [11]. Because CAs may be used to simulate the physical interactions between amino acids, they are also ideal for predicting protein structure. Combining CNNs and CAs has been demonstrated to increase the precision of protein structure prediction in a number of studies [12].

7.2 Methods

We have done an exhaustive literature review on the existing protein structure prediction models, types of CNNs, and several of types of cellular automata that can address this problem.

Here are some examples of CNN-based methods for protein structure prediction:

DeepMind created the protein structure prediction technique called AlphaFold [13]. The deep learning algorithm used by AlphaFold combines a CNN with a recurrent neural network (RNN). Protein structure prediction is carried out using AlphaFold, which has produced state-of-the-art outcomes. RaptorX [14] is a protein structure prediction method developed by the University of Illinois at Urbana-Champaign. RaptorX uses a deep learning model that combines a CNN with a support vector machine (SVM). RaptorX has also attained benchmarked output in the prediction of protein structure.

DeepFRI [15] is a protein structure prediction method developed by the University of California, San Diego. DeepFRI uses a deep learning model that combines a CNN with a graph convolutional network (GCN). DeepFRI [16] has been shown to be effective at predicting the protein structure, which is challenging with other prediction methods [17].

We have examined different CNN formats. DenseNet [22], MobileNet [23], AlexNet [20], and VGGNet [21] are used for prediction. One of the original CNN systems, AlexNet, made substantial strides in the field of large-scale image recognition. The simplicity and consistency of VGGNet are well known. Deep representations are produced by its several layers of 3 × 3 filters and max-pooling layers. The idea of densely connected layers—where each layer is connected to every layer after it—is introduced by DenseNet. The review article [18] discusses the application of deep learning methods in various areas of protein bioinformatics, including protein sequence analysis, structure prediction, function prediction, and protein–protein interaction prediction. It provides an overview of different deep learning architectures and their performance in these tasks.

Ref. [19] describes the Phyre protein structure prediction server, which utilizes advanced algorithms and machine learning techniques for fold recognition and 3D structure prediction. It discusses the challenges in protein structure prediction and the strategies employed by Phyre to address them. This paper provides an overview of recent progress in protein structure prediction methods, including both template-based and *ab initio* approaches. It discusses the challenges, advances, and limitations in the field, highlighting the impact of deep learning techniques.

This architecture promotes feature reuse and alleviates the vanishing gradient problem. MobileNet focuses on efficient CNN architectures for mobile and embedded devices. It employs depth-wise separable convolutions, reducing computational complexity while maintaining reasonable accuracy. We have also reviewed various models of cellular automata [24–27] to augment the same with CNN for a better classifier.

At the end of the literature survey, we understood that cellular automata [28–30] can potentially be used to capture spatial interactions and dynamics within protein structures. By integrating cellular automata with CNNs, we can explore approaches where the CNNs extract local features from protein sequences or structures, while cellular automata capture the long-range interactions and spatial dependencies within the protein, thus becoming a robust model to predict the structure of protein.

Here are some of the advantages of using cellular automata-based CNN for protein prediction:

1. CA images of protein sequences encode information about the entire sequence, not just the local neighborhood.
2. The CNN is able to learn long-range dependencies in protein sequences.

3. The CNN has been shown to achieve benchmarked results on a variety of tasks related to protein structure prediction.

Here are some of the challenges of using cellular automata-based CNN for protein prediction:

1. CA images of protein sequences can be computationally expensive to generate.
2. The CNN can be difficult to train and tune.
3. New protein sequences that are not part of the training dataset may prevent the CNN from generalizing to them.

7.3 Design of the Model

Designing a cellular automata-based CNN (Convolutional Neural Network) CNN-CA-P for protein prediction involves integrating the principles of cellular automata with the architecture and operations of CNNs as shown in Figure 7.2. Here is a high-level outline of the design process:

1. **Dataset Preparation:** Gather a dataset of protein sequences and their corresponding experimentally determined structural features, such as information pertaining to secondary protein structure (e.g., coil, beta-strand, and alpha-helix) or solvent accessibility (e.g., exposed or buried residues). The training data for the CNN model comes from this dataset. The Protein Data Bank (PDB) is used to obtain a dataset of protein sequences.
2. Pre-process the data by encoding the amino acid sequences using techniques like one-hot encoding or embedding. Prepare the target labels, such as secondary structure information (e.g., helix, sheet, and coil) or torsion angles.
3. **Understand Cellular Automata (CA):** Familiarize yourself with the concepts and principles of cellular automata. CA is a discrete computational model where a grid of cells evolves over discrete time steps based on local rules.
4. **Define the CA Grid:** Map the protein sequence onto a grid structure, where each cell represents a specific region or residue in the protein sequence. The grid can be one-dimensional (1D), two-dimensional (2D), or higher-dimensional depending on the protein representation.

5. **Define Cell States:** Assign initial states to the cells on the grid. The states can represent different features or properties of the protein, such as amino acid types, secondary structure labels, or evolutionary information.

   Cellular automata is a combination of cells formed on a large grid, which moves from one state to another with the nature of the rule applied. Figure 7.1 shows the transitions applied on a given rule.
6. **Define Local Rules:** Specify the local rules that govern the evolution of the cellular automaton. These rules determine how the states of cells are updated at each intermediate steps built on the states of their neighboring cells. The rules can capture local interactions and dependencies between residues in the protein sequence.
7. **Encoding Protein Sequences:** Convert the protein sequences into a numerical representation that can be fed into the CNN model. Common encoding schemes include one-hot encoding or embedding.
8. **Integration with CNN Architecture:** Embed the cellular automaton within a CNN architecture. Convolutional layers, pooling layers, and fully linked layers can all be a part of the CNN component. The CNN may use the cellular automaton as a parallel processing module or consider it as a pre-processing stage.
9. **Convolutional Layers:** A convolutional layer extracts the features from the sequences of amino acid. The convolutional layers use a filter to scan the input sequence and identify patterns in the sequence. The filter is a small window

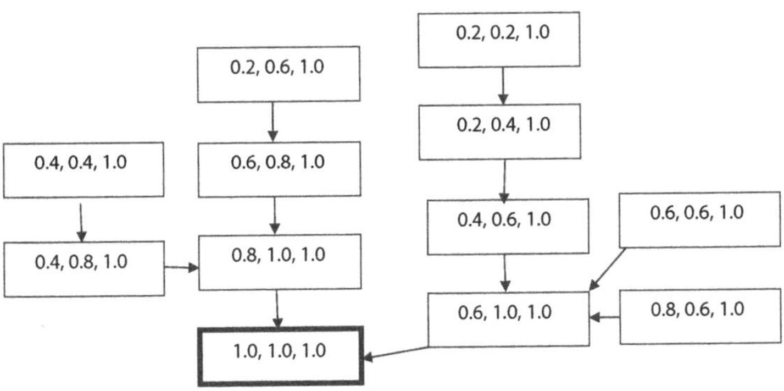

Figure 7.1 Working of cellular automata on a rule <252,18,54>.

of amino acids, and the convolutional layer moves the filter over the input sequence, one amino acid at a time. The convolutional layer outputs a feature map, where each element in the feature map represents a feature that has been extracted from the input sequence.

10. **Pooling Layers:** The pooling layer will reduce the size of the feature maps. The pooling layers use a pooling operation to combine the features in a local region of the feature map. The pooling operation can be pooling maximum, which takes the extreme cost in a local region, or pooling average value, which takes the average cost in a local region as shown in Figure 7.2.
11. **Training and Optimization:** Train the cellular automata-based CNN using a suitable loss function and training data. The training data should consist of protein sequences with known structural annotations. During training, the CNN learns to extract relevant features from the cellular automaton representation and make predictions based on the protein structure.
12. **Evaluation and Validation:** Estimate the performance of the cellular automata-based CNN on validation and test datasets. Measure the accuracy1, precision1, and recall1 to compute the prediction model performance.
13. **Iterative Refinement:** Refine and improve the design iteratively by experimenting with different cellular automaton rules, network architectures, or input representations. Consider incorporating additional information, such as evolutionary profiles or physicochemical properties, to enhance the predictive power of the model.

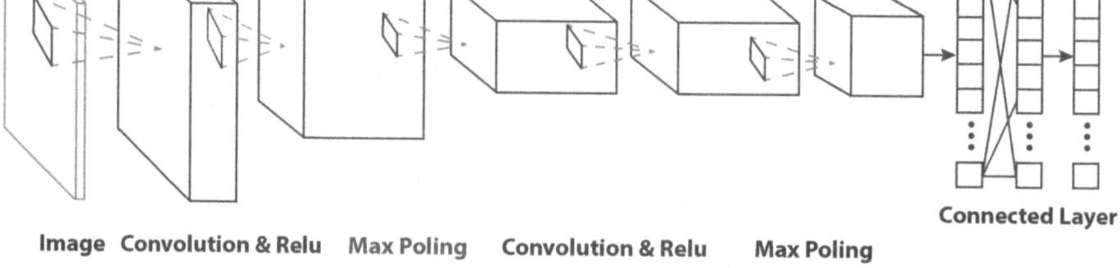

Figure 7.2 Design of CNN-CA-P.

It is important to note that the design and optimization of a cellular automata-based CNN for protein prediction can be a complex and computationally intensive task. Therefore, it requires a deep understanding of cellular automata and deep learning principles, as well as access to appropriate computational resources for training and experimentation.

The cellular automata-based CNN uses a two-layer CNN-CA model. The first layer of the model is a CNN that extracts relevant features from sequence of amino acid. The second layer of the model is a CA that is used to model the physical exchanges among amino acids. The output of the CA layer is used to calculate the secondary protein structure. The cellular automata-based CNN was trained on a dataset of 400,000 proteins. The model was tested with 5,250,890 benchmarked proteins.

7.4 Results and Comparisons

Five Lakh datasets are downloaded from the protein bank to test and train the desired classifier [11]. CNN-CA-P has reported a better training and validation accuracy, i.e., 0.94 and 0.90, as in Figure 7.3 when the numbers of epochs are 8, which are better compared to the existing baseline methods. The developed classifier has reported much lower training value and validation loss, i.e., 0.18 and 0.12, when the numbers of epochs are 8.

Comparing the performance of different methods is challenging, as it depends on various factors, including the specific protein targets, the availability of templates, and the evaluation metrics used. As shown in Figure 7.4, these assessments provide comprehensive comparisons of different methods and their performance on a different sets of proteins.

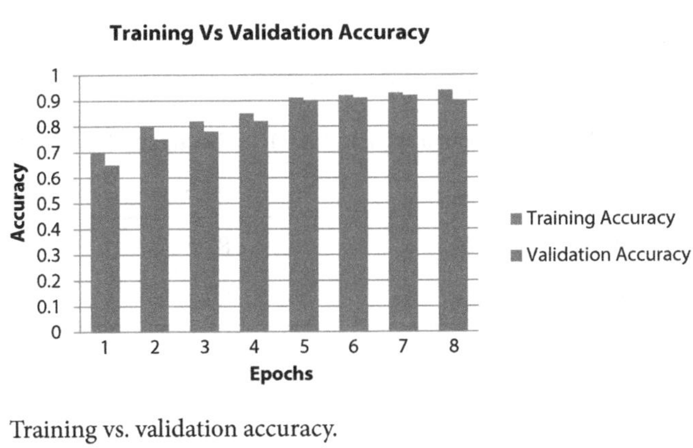

Figure 7.3 Training vs. validation accuracy.

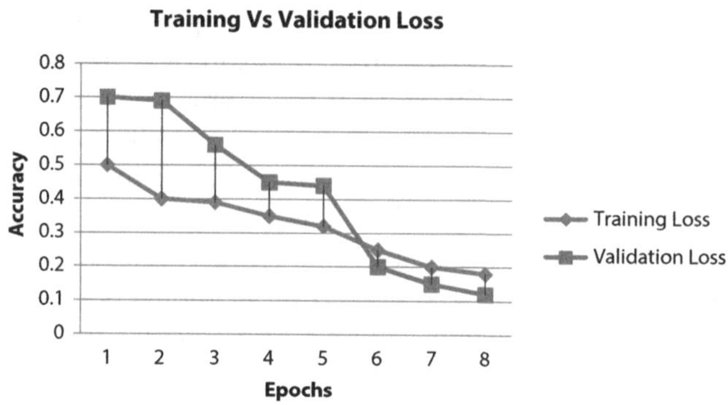

Figure 7.4 Training vs. validation loss.

The PseAAC and CATH accuracies are two different metrics used to measure the accuracy of protein structure prediction methods as shown in Figure 7.7. PseAAC is a measure of the accuracy of the predicted amino acid sequence, while CATH is a measure of the accuracy of the predicted secondary structure. We have compared our work with the existing baseline models, i.e., AlphaFold [1], RaptorX [2], Deep FRI [3], and DeepCNF [4]. Our proposed classifier CNN-CA-P reports a PseAAC accuracy of 92.3 and a CATCH accuracy of 94.5, which outperforms the existing literature. DeepCNF reports the next best PseAAC accuracy of 87.7 where DeepFRI, RaptorX, and AlphaFold report values of 82.3, 81.5, and 85.5, respectively. AlphaFold reports the next best CATH accuracy of 92.5 where DeepCNF, DeepFRI, and RaptorX report values of 87.8, 79.3, and 77.5, respectively, as in Table 7.1 and Figure 7.5.

Table 7.1 Comparison of the performance with existing protein structure prediction systems.

Method	Accuracy (PseAAC)	Accuracy (CATH)
CNN-CA-P	92.2	94.5
DeepCNF	87.7	87.8
DeepFRI	82.3	79.3
RaptorX	81.5	77.5
AlphaFold	85.5	92.5

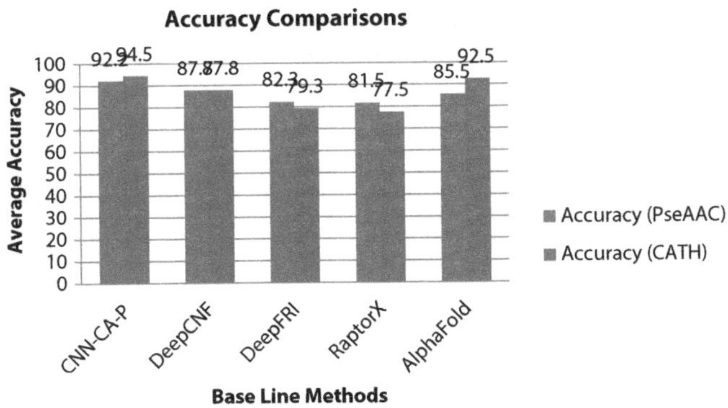

Figure 7.5 PseAAC, CATH accuracy comparisons.

The performance of CNN-CA-P is evaluated using various parameters, AUC, F1 score, precision, and recall, and compared with the existing literature as reported in Table 7.2 and Figure 7.6.

1. **Precision:** Precision is a measure of the quantity of appropriately projected helpful (positive) instances (true positives) out of all occurrences forecasted to be positive. It quantifies the positive prediction accuracy:

$$\text{Precision} = TP / (TP + FP), \text{ TP: True Positives, FP: False Positives}$$

2. **Recall:** It is the measure of the true positive or sensitivity. It measures the proportion of correctly predicted positive instances out of all actual positive instances. It quantifies the capability of the model to classify positive cases.

Table 7.2 Comparison of performance with existing protein structure prediction systems.

Method	F-precision	F-recall	F1 score	F-AUC
CNN-CA-P	0.94	0.95	0.91	0.96
DeepCNF	0.88	0.86	0.90	0.95
DeepFRI	0.92	0.91	0.88	0.89
RaptorX	0.88	0.94	0.92	0.93
AlphaFold	0.92	0.86	0.68	0.96

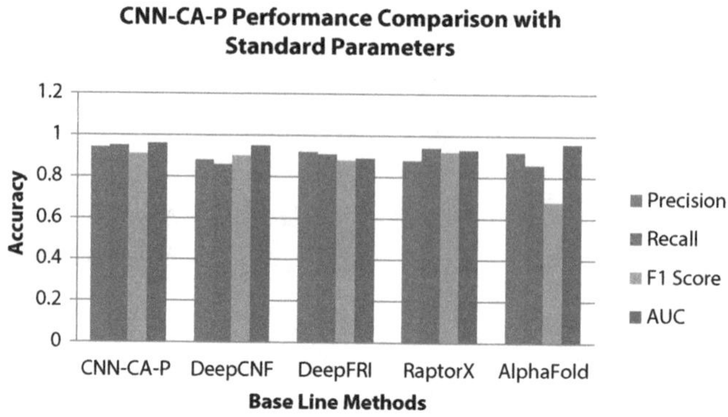

Figure 7.6 Precision, recall, F1 score, and AUC accuracy comparisons.

Recall = TP / (TP + FN), TP: True Positives, FN: False Negatives

3. **F1 score:** The F1 score is the harmonic mean of precision and recall, providing a single metric that will balance the trade-off between precision and recall. It is computed as: F1 score = 2 * (Precision * Recall) / (Precision + Recall)
4. **AUC (Area Under the Curve):** AUC is a common evaluation metric used for binary classification tasks. In the context of protein prediction, it is often used in the analysis of receiver operating characteristic (ROC) curves. The likelihood that a randomly selected positive instance will be given a higher ranking by the prediction model than a randomly selected negative instance is represented by the AUC.

CNN-CA-P reports a precision1, recall1, F1 score1, and AUC1 of 0.94, 0.95, 0.91, and 0.96, respectively. DeepCNF reports a precision2, recall2, F1 score2, and AUC2 of 0.88, 0.86, 0.90, and 0.95, DeepFRI reports a precision3, recall3, F1 score3, and AUC3 of 0.92, 0.91, 0.88, and 0.89, respectively. RaptorX reports a precision4, recall4, F1 score4, and AUC4 of 0.88, 0.94, 0.92, and 0.93, respectively. AlphaFold reports a precision4, recall4, F1 score4, and AUC4 of 0.92, 0.86, 0.68, and 0.96, respectively. CNN-CA-P outperforms all the existing literature in all these parameters. DeepCNF and AlphaFold report a high precision value, i.e., 0.94, after CNN-CA-P. RaptorX reports a high recall value and an F1 score of 0.94 and 0.92 after CNN-CA-P. AlphaFold reports a high AUC value of 0.96 after CNN-CA-P as shown in Table 7.3.

Table 7.3 Secondary, ternary, and quaternary protein prediction comparisons (average accuracy).

Structure	CNN-CA-P	DeepCNF	DeepFRI	RaptorX	AlphaFold
Secondary	96.56	90.3	91.6	90.6	89.3
Ternary	91.2	88.3	85.6	83.2	85.6
Quaternary	86.32	85.6	86.9	89.6	83.6

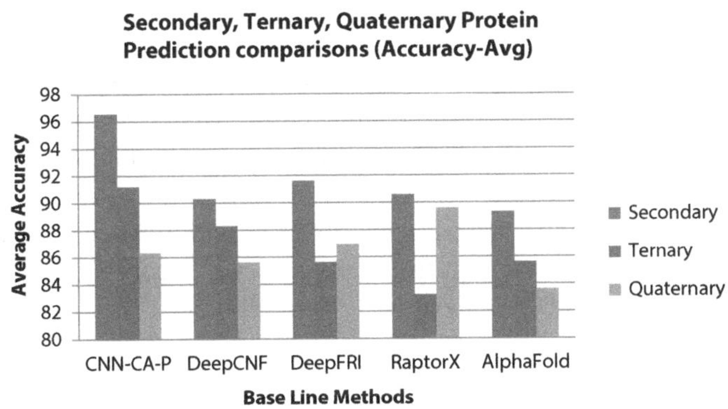

Figure 7.7 Secondary, ternary, and quaternary protein prediction comparisons.

CNN-CA-P has achieved an accuracy of 96.56%, 91.2%, and 86.32% for predicting the secondary, ternary, and quaternary protein, respectively, which outperforms the existing benchmarked baseline methods. The combination of cellular automata and CNNs in protein structure prediction leverages these strengths to enhance efficiency, performance, and accuracy of prediction. The CA component model has added the local interactions and dynamics of amino acids, while the CNN component have learned and extracted the significant feature from the protein sequence.

Runtime and Computational Competence: By considering the computational available resources and runtime essential for running the model. Assess the efficiency of the cellular automata-based CNN compared to other methods in terms of prediction speed and resource utilization. It depends on model complexity, data size, hardware resources, and algorithm optimization. CNN-CA-P reports: Runtime = 1/2 hour, Computational efficiency = 200 proteins/hour for processing a dataset of size 400,000.

7.5 Conclusion

The integration of cellular automata with CNNs has captured local interactions and dependencies in protein sequences, which has enhanced the predictive power of the model with an average accuracy of accuracy of 96.56%, 91.2%, and 86.32% for predicting the secondary, ternary and quaternary proteins, respectively.

By combining the strengths of cellular automata and CNNs, the prediction model potentially benefits from the ability to capture local interactions, learn hierarchical representations, handle noisy data, and parallelize computations. Overall, the cellular automata-based CNN is a promising new approach for protein prediction, which is the first of its kind to process the potential to enhance the accuracy of protein prediction methods, and to make protein prediction more accessible to a wider range of researchers. However, it is worth noting that the success of such a combination relies on the precise implementation, design, and quality, performance, and diversity of training data.

References

1. Jumper, J., Evans, R., Pritzel, A., Green, T., Figurnov, M., Ronneberger, O. & Hassabis, D. Highly accurate protein structure prediction with AlphaFold. *Nature*, 596(7873), 583-589, 2021.
2. Wang, S., Li, W., Liu, S., & Xu, J. RaptorX-Property: a web server for protein structure property prediction. *Nucleic Acids Res.*, 44(W1), W430-W435, 2016.
3. Ben-Sasson, E., Goldberg, L., Kopparty, S., & Saraf, S. DEEP-FRI: sampling outside the box improves soundness. *arXiv preprint* arXiv:1903.12243,2019.
4. Wang, Q., Ni, C. M., Li, Z., Li, X. F., Han, R. M., Zhao, F., ... & Wang, S. Efficient and accurate prediction of transmembrane topology from amino acid sequence only. *BioRxiv*, 627307, 2019.
5. Alley, E. C., Khimulya, G., Biswas, S., AlQuraishi, M., & Church, G. M.. Unified rational protein engineering with sequence-based deep representation learning. *Nat. Methods*, 16(12), 1315-1322, 2019
6. Bala, P. Manju, S. Usharani, R. Rajmohan, T. Ananth Kumar and A. Balachandar. "Bioinspired CNN Approach for Diagnosing COVID-19 Using

Images of Chest X-Ray." In *Smart Computer Vision*, pp. 181-201. Cham: Springer International Publishing, 2023.
7. Kumar, Abhishek, Swarn Avinash Kumar, Vishal Dutt, S. Shitharth, and Esha Tripathi. "IoT based arrhythmia classification using the enhanced hunt optimization-based deep learning." *Expert Syst.*, (2023): e13298.
8. Krizhevsky, A., Sutskever, I., & Hinton, G. E. Imagenet classification with deep convolutional neural networks. *Commun. ACM*, 60(6), 84-90, 2017.
9. Simonyan, K., & Zisserman, A. Very deep convolutional networks for large-scale image recognition. *arXiv preprint* arXiv:1409.1556, 2014.
10. Huang, G., Liu, Z., van der Maaten, L., & Weinberger, K. Q. Densely connected convolutional networks. In *Proceedings of the IEEE conference on computer vision and pattern recognition* (pp. 4700-4708), 2017.
11. Howard, A. G., Zhu, M., Chen, B., Kalenichenko, D., Wang, W., Weyand, T., ... & Adam, H. Mobilenets: Efficient convolutional neural networks for mobile vision applications. *arXiv preprint* arXiv:1704.04861, 2017.
12. Subbulakshmi, N., R. Manimegalai, G. Rajakumar, T. Ananth Kumar, and Umadevi Kosuri. "A novel design of low-cost hearing aid devices using an efficient lifting filter bank with a modified variable filter." *Expert Rev. Med. Devices*, 19, no. 12 (2022): 991-999.
13. Sree, P. K., Babu, I. R., & Devi, N. U. Investigating an Artificial Immune System to strengthen protein structure prediction and protein coding region identification using the Cellular Automata classifier. *Int. J. Bioinf. Res. Appl.*, 5(6), 647-662, 2009.
14. Sree, P. K., & Babu, I. R. Cellular automata and its applications in bioinformatics: a review. *arXiv preprint* arXiv:1404.0453, 2014.
15. Kumar, T. Ananth, R. Rajmohan, M. Pavithra, and Shanmugam Balamurugan. *Evolutionary Intelligence for Healthcare Applications*. CRC Press, 2022.
16. Sree, P. K., & Nedunuri, S. U. D. A novel cellular automata classifier for COVID-19 trend prediction. *J. Health Sci.*, 10(1), 34-38, 2020.
17. S. R. Burri, A. Kumar, A. Baliyan and T. A. Kumar, "Predictive Intelligence for Healthcare Outcomes: An AI Architecture Overview," *2023 2nd International Conference on Smart Technologies and Systems for Next Generation Computing (ICSTSN)*, Villupuram, India, 2023, pp.1-6, doi: 10.1109/ICSTSN57873.2023.10151477.
18. Berman, H. M., Battistuz, T., Bhat, T. N., Bluhm, W. F., Bourne, P. E., Burkhardt, K., ... & Zardecki, C. The protein data bank. *Acta Crystallogr., Sect. D: Biol. Crystallogr.*, 58(6), 899-907, 2002.
19. Srivastav, Arun Lal, Markandeya, Naveen Patel, Mayank Pandey, Ashutosh Kumar Pandey, Ashutosh Kumar Dubey, Abhishek Kumar, Abhishek Kumar Bhardwaj, and Vinod Kumar Chaudhary. "Concepts of circular economy for sustainable management of electronic wastes: challenges and management options." *Environ. Sci. Pollut. Res.*, 30, no. 17 (2023): 48654-48675.
20. Lee, S., Kim, S., Lee, G. R., Kwon, S., Woo, H., Seok, C., & Park, H. (2023). Evaluating GPCR modeling and docking strategies in the era of deep

learning-based protein structure prediction. *Comput. Struct. Biotechnol. J.*, 21, 158-167.

21. Yang, Q., Xia, D., Syed, A. A. S., Wang, Z., & Shi, Y. Highly accurate protein structure prediction and drug screen of monkeypox virus proteome. *J. Inf.*, 86(1), 66-117, 2023
22. Schauperl, Michael, and Rajiah Aldrin Denny. "AI-Based protein structure prediction in drug discovery: Impacts and challenges." *JCIM* 62.13 : 3142-3156.2022.
23. Ilyas, Benkhaddra, Abhishek Kumar, Mohamed Ali Setitra, ZineEl Abidine Bensalem, and Hang Lei. "Prevention of DDoS attacks using an optimized deep learning approach in blockchain technology." *Trans. Emerg. Telecommun. Technol.*, 34, no. 4 (2023): e4729.
24. Hazari, R., & Pal Chaudhuri, P. Analysis of coronavirus envelope protein with cellular automata model. *Int. J. Parallel Emergent Distrib. Syst.*, 37(6), 623-648, 2022.
25. Souza, L. F., Pereira, H. B., Rocha Filho, T. M., Machado, B. A., & Moret, M. A. *Similarity analysis and phylogenetic trees from cellular automata imaging of lysozyme proteins*, 2022
26. Del Amo, I., & Konkoli, Z. On Applications of Cellular Automata Memristor Networks for Reservoir Computing: Classifying Protein Toxicity. *Int. J. Unconv. Comput.*, 17,2022.
27. Kavitha, R., Jothi, D. K., Saravanan, K., Swain, M. P., Gonzáles, J. L. A., Bhardwaj, R. J., & Adomako, E. (2023). Ant Colony Optimization-Enabled CNN Deep Learning Technique for Accurate Detection of Cervical Cancer. *Biomed. Res. Int.*, 2023.
28. N. Mahsuda, C. Ananth, N. Isok-Jon, Y. Rayimjon and T. A. Kumar, "Virtual Science is a New Scientific Paradigm," *2023 IEEE Renewable Energy and Sustainable E-Mobility Conference (RESEM)*, Bhopal, India, 2023, pp. 1-5, doi: 10.1109/RESEM57584.2023.10236372.
29. Macrae, R. M. Mixed-valence realizations of quantum dot cellular automata. *J. Phys. Chem. Solids*, 177, 111303,2023.
30. Li, H., & Reynolds, J. F. Modeling effects of spatial pattern, drought, and grazing on rates of rangeland degradation: A combined Markov and cellular automaton approach. In *Scale in remote sensing and GIS* (pp. 211-230). Routledge, 2023.

8

Modelling and Approximating Renewable Energy Systems Using Computational Intelligence

B. Balaji[1]*, P. Hemalatha[2], T. Rampradesh[1], G. Anbarasi[1] and A. Eswari[1]

[1]Department of EEE, IFET College of Engineering, Villupuram, TN, India
[2]TIFAC-CORE in Cyber Security, Amrita School of Computing, Amrita Vishwa Vidyapeetham, Coimbatore, India

Abstract

Artificial neural networks (ANNs) and expert systems (ES) are the two main subfields that make up artificially intelligent (AI) systems (ANNs). This study's main goal is to show how artificial intelligence techniques could potentially be very useful for modeling and forecasting the effectiveness of renewable energy sources. By providing a number of problems connected to the various subfields that make up renewable energy engineering, this study aims to provide a knowledge of how expert systems and neural networks function. Below is a list of the numerous uses of expert systems and neural networks, organized by topic rather than chronologically or in any other way. The results of this study demonstrate the potential of artificial intelligence as a design tool in a number of subfields of renewable energy source engineering. The primary objective of this research is to prove that neural network can be applied successfully to applications involving renewable energy. This will be accomplished by demonstrating the application of expert systems and artificial neural networks to a variety of renewable energy-related issues.

***Keywords*:** Artificial neural networks, expert system, renewable energy system, computational intelligence, solar energy

**Corresponding author*: balaji.bc91@gmail.com

T. Ananth Kumar, E. Golden Julie, Venkata Raghuveer Burugadda, Abhishek Kumar and Puneet Kumar (eds.) Computational Intelligence: Theory and Applications, (175–188) © 2024 Scrivener Publishing LLC

8.1 Introduction

The thought that humanity would be able to create a machine that could "think" has attracted mankind since the dawn of time. The French philosopher and mathematician Rene Descartes asserted in the year 1637 that it would be impossible to build a machine that thought similarly to humans. However, the British scientist and computer innovator Alan Turing prophesied that a machine would eventually be able to mimic human understanding in every way in 1950. In 1956, Turing's forecast came to pass. Machine learning (AI) is the capacity of a machine or even other devices to perform the kind of tasks that are exclusive to the human brain (AI). In its broadest sense, artificial intelligence (AI) is the capacity of a machine or other things to think like a human. The phrase "artificially intelligent" (AI) has been used to describe computer systems and programs that are capable of actions that are more complex than simple programming but fall far short of true cognition. The two subfields of artificial intelligence are expert systems and artificial neural networks (AI).

Expert systems (ES), a class of logic software that analyzes data and selects one alternative from a range of potential outcomes, allow computers to "make decisions." Expert systems are built using a technique called rule-based inference, which goes beyond simple computer programming. This approach, on which expert systems are based, uses pre-established rule sets to interpret the data. Systems are incredibly clever, but they lack the complexity of truly intelligent cognition by a wide margin. Artificial neural networks, abbreviated as ANNs, are connected groups of numerous tiny single processing units. Information is exchanged along the different links that connect these parts. There are two values that can be used to describe an incoming connection: an input value as well as a weight. These two variables are linked together by the relationship. The performance that the machine produces is affected by the accumulated value. Despite becoming computer-based, ANNs really are not designed to do any particular activities. They are instead educated in regard to data collections until they comprehend the offered pattern and get the desired result. Additional patterns may be presented to them after they have been trained so they can make predictions or classify data.

Estimating the efficiency of renewable energies and the flow of energy across those systems typically involves the use of analytical computer codes. Frequently, the applied approaches involve the resolution of a wide variety of difficult differential equations. In order to make accurate projections, these systems frequently demand a great deal of computer power and time. Renewable energy systems create naturally ambiguous data, making them great challenges for artificial intelligence. Since AI research is based on previous data about just a system, architects are more likely to value and comprehend it than other theoretical and empirical methodologies. AI is capable of providing innovative solutions to design problems and will allow designers to obtain an expert's judgement very quickly on the impacts of a proposed layout change. Categorized challenges will demonstrate the value of methods and artificial neural networks as modeling and per well for renewable energies. However, ANNs are associated with the overwhelming bulk of the investigated applications. The purpose of this study is to evaluate the most advanced artificial intelligence tools and approaches for energy monitoring, maintenance, and control of renewable energy systems, with a specific focus on solar power systems [1]. The topic of this study [2] is the deployment of artificially intelligent (AI) technology, which can directly extract relevant information from vast amounts of data in order to manage complex non-linear circumstances with assuming things or simplifying them. Liu *et al.* [3] focus on the regularly employed AI-related technologies and explores the advantages in terms of functionality that these approaches have when implemented in various renewables sectors. Additionally, it analyzes how such strategies have improved the overall operational effectiveness and optimized the control mechanisms for renewable energy. This study evaluates the effectiveness of these applications using both theoretical justifications and a number of case studies. In addition, actual AI implementations in humongous renewables integration systems are discussed.

Traditional energy sources such as coal, petroleum, and nat gas are being used more frequently now than ever before, which has resulted in an alarming increase in CO_2 emissions [4], thereby contributing to the phenomenon of global warming. Due to global energy and environmental concerns, renewable energy sources must be utilized extensively. Renewable energy production is currently receiving a lot of attention and is being widely used as one of the most common ways to ease energy and environmental difficulties [5]. This is especially true of solar and wind energy. On the other hand, solar and wind power generation technologies struggle to maintain continuity and are prone to service interruptions [6]. Irregular supply of power output has serious consequences for the power grid, including voltage changes, frequency variations, active and reactive, system breakdowns, and frequent changing of electrical devices [7]. Additionally, it has significant effects on load management, forecasting and scheduling, and storage systems. Voltage increases in the system could occur as a result of the generation of substantial amounts of renewable energy, which would be significant in the case of grid-connected solar (PV) power [8]. Furthermore, non-uniform power generation due to the intermittent availability of solar energy may exceed the capacities of the related transformers and have the potential to cause phase imbalances across the entire grid [9]. In Refs. [23, 24], the use of FOPID and sliding mode controllers to preserve system stability is examined.

8.2 Expert System

An "expert system" is a computer program that, in order to solve problems or provide guidance, can incorporate the expertise of a "subject matter expert" [10]. Expert systems are gaining in popularity [11]. Expert system hence refers to a program that can simulate human cognitive abilities such as problem solving, visual perception, and language understanding. A standard application program cannot be compared to an expert system since the former possesses specific qualities that the later does not have. An expert system can be identified by the presence of certain qualities. In this particular case, an expert system [11]:

- ✓ Has the potential to be programmed to solve difficult tasks that would normally require human intelligence.
- ✓ Contains both knowledge and the instruments for rationally inferring it; the first should be maintained in a symbol descriptive language, whereas the latter can include heuristics search and argumentation methods.
- ✓ Can achieve excellent performance in narrowly specified incremental development domains, handle partial or uncertain data, and explain or justify outcomes, only applicable to a given human knowledge subfield.
- ✓ Can be programmed to develop in an evolutionary manner, thus enhancing its "expertise" as it gets older.
- ✓ Is able to express knowledge using facts and rules and is able to employ a variety of knowledge representation techniques to cope with data that cannot be fully stated by rules.

It should also be able to justify the choices taken by briefly summarizing each phase of its thought process. Additionally, it must be able to describe the steps it will undertake in reaction to the responses provided by the user to the questions that the platform is built to elicit [10, 11]. It should be possible to do this in a fashion that is comparable to how an expert would present their findings. A level of expertise, a strategy for finding, as well as a user interface are the standard components of an expert system [11]. In a knowledge base, both static and dynamic databases are usually present. A particular formalism is used to represent the knowledge base that is kept in the stable database. Despite being modifiable while the system is in operation, it is only ever generated once, when the user is setting the system. Each time the program was iterated, the dynamic database might add new data, but after the iteration was complete, the data would be lost. It is used to store all information gathered from the user, as well as interim outcomes (facts) that are deduced during the reasoning process.

The inference engine of the system is the component that contains the control strategies that indicate how the available data should be processed to reach conclusions and solutions to the issue. It is a reflection of the way the system uses the knowledge it has learned to reason, and it is related to how people reason. The user interface explains to the user how the system operates, collects from the user the data that the technology need to function, and displays the conclusions reached during the deductive process. Additionally, the user interface collects from the user the data that the device need to function. There are very few expert system applications in the field of renewable energy systems. Burri [12] demonstrate an expert system developed and applied for solar household hot water system selection and design. Frame and class formalism, as well as both forward backward chaining techniques, were used for knowledge representation. These methods were applied to infer conclusions and take advantage of the data that had been obtained. It was shown that the program operated successfully for 21 distinct solar home hot water system options and designs that are offered on the Greek market. The program that was created helps the facility not only choose and design solar hot water system, but also update its knowledgebase with fresh information so that it may be adjusted to market developments. Along with this, the initiative encourages the choice and development of solar home hot water systems. The application reportedly proved to be highly functional and user-friendly.

8.3 Artificial Neural Networks

Even though the notion of artificial neural analysis has been for over 50 years, software to solve real issues has only been developed in the last two decades. This article will simply give a very high-level summary of how neural networks work and will not go into detail into the theory or history of neural networks. Numerous distinct published books have provided descriptions of the development and theory of neural networks. ANNs perform admirably in some applications but poorly in others. To be more precise, individuals perform exceptionally well in tasks involving incomplete data sets, ambiguous or missing information, as well as extremely complex and poorly defined challenges, which are circumstances in which people often rely their conclusions on intuition. They are able to draw lessons from past mistakes and overcome obstacles that do not present themselves in a straight line. They also have a high pain tolerance for mistakes and are durable. Logic and mathematical activities, which demand a high level of accuracy and precision, cannot be successfully completed by ANNs. The application of ANNs has been successful in numerous fields, notably math, construction, health, economics, and neurology. Notable uses include the study of electromyographs as well as other physiological data; the identification of rhythms, noises, and language; the identifying of military objectives; and the detection of hidden bombs in passenger luggage. Numerous additional purposes, including the control scheme of robotic equipment, the prediction of industry trends and weather systems, the identification of possible places for mineral exploitation, and the prediction of thermal and electrical demand, have also utilized this technology. For systems integration, neural networks are utilized because they are able to construct predictive models of the process utilizing high-dimensional sensor data.

A deep network is indeed a highly distributed and parallel processor that stores and shares experience data [13]. Neural networks have a natural inclination to store and access online experiential knowledge. It is analogous to the human mind in two ways: first, the network learns new information, and second, it stores that information using synaptic weights, or the strength of the connections between neurons. In the realm of engineering, ANN models can be utilized as an alternate tool for analysis and prediction. ANN attempts, in some respects, to imitate how the human mind learns. They work similarly to "black box" models in that no specialized system knowledge is required. Instead, they examine historical data to better understand the link between input variables, controlled variables, and uncontrolled variables. ANN requires no preconceptions about system being represented, unlike multiple regression. Neural networks have been used to solve a number of issues, including non-linear ones. Neural networks frequently succeed where other approaches fail, and they have been used in circumstances when previous approaches have failed. Utilizing ANNs has the added advantage of being able to control vast, intricate systems with a lot of interconnected factors. They seem to just ignore any new information that adds little to the process and concentrate instead on the inputs that are more important. Deep neural networks do not need complex rules and math to understand multidimensional information patterns. Neural networks are noise-resistant and error-tolerant [14].

Figure 8.1 shows a modified convolutional neural network topology. Input, hidden, and output layers are standard network configuration. Variable synaptic weights let a neuron connect with lower-level neurons. Neurons create these connections. Total cases, input variables, and output factors affect network form. The network has an "input" level with one cell per input variable, a "hidden" layer, and a "exit" layer including one neuron per output. Neurons are crucial to neural networks. The output of a neuron, which is also known as a processing element, is determined by the neuron's summarizing and activating processes (see Figure 8.1). It also depends on the overall amount of training samples. Despite the fact that this also depends on the overall volume of training examples, this is valid. By having too many neurons in the buried layer, overtraining, also known as a lack of generalization, and serious verification mistakes can be caused. Significant errors during "training" and "verification" can be caused by a lack of neurons. Typically, the data are recorded as a collection of network parameters. Training modifies and organizes connection weights using an appropriate learning technique. This is "Training." The network enables learning. In this technique, the network is given an input and the intended output, then the parameters are modified.

In order to provide the highest-quality results in the quickest amount of time feasible, it is usual practice to apply a range of different algorithms. Additionally, there are numerous distinct types of neural network infrastructure, each of which can be used in a variety of ways that are particular to themselves, depending just on nature of the issue that has to be solved. One of the most crucial things to think about when attempting to assess whether or not a specific paradigm and method can be used successfully

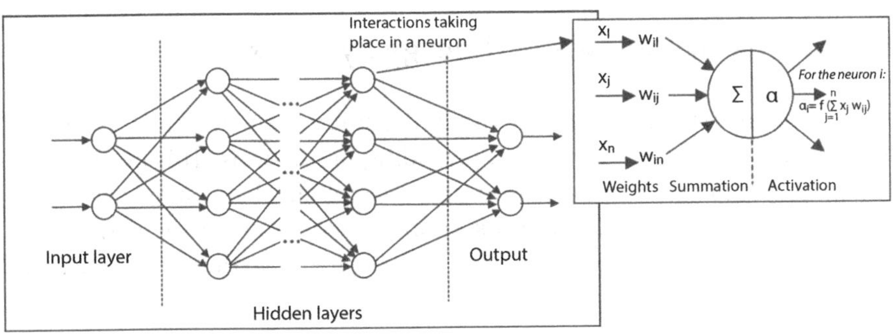

Figure 8.1 Feed-forward multilayer neural network.

is the type of the issue that needs to be solved. Variations of the backpropagation (BP) approach are currently the most extensively used types of machine learning software [14]. The backpropagation algorithm is among the most effective neural network learning methods. This algorithm is commonly known as the "gradient descent approach." By adjusting the weights as individuals decrease the gradient, it is possible to increase the performance of the neural network by minimizing the total amount of error. This URL provides access to the work of Kumar *et al.* [15], which has additional details about the BP algorithm.

The first stage in tackling a particular problem is to collect all relevant data and enter into a sheet in the appropriate columns and rows. It is recommended to utilize distinct sections in the spreadsheet to denote the various input and output attributes. In addition to a file for retraining, you must also have files for testing and validation. The data set consists of these three file classes. Up to 10% of the cases from the training file may be included in the test file, but the initial and second files should contain sample sizes of every case the system must handle. Both of these should demonstrate all of the situations that the network must manage. Both parties should provide specific examples of the myriad issues that the connection is intended to address. The network is verified during the training phase by matching it to the test file. When the average mean error does not change after a specific number of repetitions, the training process should be terminated. This is done to prevent excess, which happens whenever the network learns the training patterns flawlessly but cannot anticipate when given with fresh data sets. This can be prevented by taking the measures listed below. By following the advice suggested in this article, you can avoid this from occurring. ANNs need the best design, learning rate, momentum, hidden neuron count, and activation function. Certain variables can be predicted with adequate expertise, lowering work time.

8.4 ANN in Renewable Energy Systems

Many scholars have employed ANNs in the study of renewable energy systems for the goal of modeling and providing predictions. This essay offers a variety of applications in this vein in a chronological and subject-specific sequence. Due to space constraints, more information is provided on the author's most recent work in the field. In Ref. [15], a further in-depth analysis of the situation is provided.

(i) Solar Generator modeling

A complete model of a photovoltaic steam generator was developed to use an artificial neural network. The system consists of a flash canister, a pressurized water circulating engine, a parabola dish collection, and the piping connecting these components. The phrases that follow describe a portion of the research undertaken on this system. Indeed, the "interception factor" is the ratio of the total energy impinging on the aperture of the concentration to the amount of energy received by the receiver. The interception factor can be employed to evaluate the collector's optical efficiency. This parameter affects solar concentrated collectors' total efficiency. ANNs can forecast interception factor with less than 0.4% inaccuracy compared to the far more advanced Energy Deposition computer algorithm [16]. In this profile, it is possible to see the "bell"-shaped radiation profile displayed on the collector's receiver. Local concentration ratios, which are obtained at ten-minute intervals around the periphery of the receiver, are used to show this.

It is critical to be able to evaluate this pattern because doing so enables the determination of the crucial collectible efficiency level. It is essential for one to be able to evaluate this profile. This evaluation must be conducted at a number of additional incident angle in addition to the standard incidence angle of zero degrees. The breadth of the collections makes this an almost always difficult-to-complete endeavor. Various artificial neural networks (ANNs) have been utilized to acquire the radiation pattern from field observations at angles where testing could be performed and to create projections for other degrees, such as the average incidence angle [17]. These forecasts take into account the typical incidence angle. The results show that there is a maximum disparity between the predictions made by ANN and the experimental test data of 3.2%. For the majority of applications, this level of accuracy is thought to be enough. Additionally, initializing a system has been represented using artificial neural networks (ANNs) [18]. It is crucial for the designer of such systems to have the capacity to precisely anticipate the amount of energy needed during morning start-up because it has a substantial impact on the system's functionality. It is particularly challenging to employ analytical techniques to resolve this problem because the environment in which the system works is always changing. It was found that ANNs could accurately forecast the temperature distributions at different points across the system with an accuracy of 3.9% or better. For design purposes, this degree of accuracy is seen to be sufficient.

The temperature profiles may be simply utilized to estimate the amount of energy that was used during the heating up phase due to how simple they are to interpret. The system's mean average monthly steam output is a critical aspect that must be supplied in order to complete the design of such systems. The network was trained using 3.5 to 2160 m^2 of statistical data and could make predictions within and outside of the training range [19]. The network was trained using 3.5–2160 m^2 of data. Its ANN properly predicted monthly mean average steam output with a 5.1% maximum variance. A comparison of ANN and synthetic data shows this. This precision is satisfactory by most criteria.

(ii) Water heating system using solar energy

An artificial neural system (ANN) has been developed using 30 examples of SWH systems that are well-known. The training was carried out using these values, and the collector areas in these systems ranged in size from 1.81 m^2 to 4.38 m^2. Both closed and open storage technologies, as well as vertical and horizontal storage tanks, have received attention. The network was prepared to accept and successfully deal with a wide of extraordinary scenarios as a result of a determined effort to take into account a varied range of environmental variables. The input data consisted of ten experimental observations of the ordinary noise exposure air temperature, the water temperature in the holding tank at the beginning of each day, and the daily total radiation from the sun, in addition to the hoarder area, the thermal dissipation correlation and quantity of a holding tank, the category of tank, the type of system, and information about the heat loss coefficient and quantity of a storage tank. Additionally, the data included the storage tank's collector area, heat loss coefficient, capacity, tank type, and system type. The sum of the useable energy recovered from the system is referred to as the network's output. The rise of temperature of the water that is stored is also considered to be part of the network's output. The level of forecasting accuracy that could be reached was evaluated utilizing unknowable facts. Forecasting accuracy was found to be 7.1% and 9.7%, correspondingly [20].

These experiments demonstrated that the proposed technique may be utilized to properly assess system energy loss and water temperature rise. Compared to traditional mathematical methods, this approach has many benefits, including increased speed and simplicity as well as the network's ability to learn from past mistakes. The results of training the network with actual weather data have proven to be more accurate than the results of many other consistent shows, which rely on data from a typical meteorological year (TMY), which does not always correspond to the actual environment in which a system operates. This is the case because data from a typical meteorological year is used in other modeling programs. In addition, the network's training process made use of actual weather data. At three different sites in Greece, similar systems were subjected to several tests and scenarios in accordance with the ISO 9459-2 standard to see how they would perform over an extended period of time. This was performed to determine how effectively the technologies will function over time. Information was used for the network's training and testing on 27 systems, whereas data were used for the last three systems' confirmation.

Several ANNs have indeed been formed to use the monthly data supplied by the standard's included modeling tool. Consequently, both ANNs can now pursue higher studies. The next network was taught to estimate both the system's regular monthly hot water output (Vd) and its renewable power output at 35°C and 40°C demand temperatures, respectively. The first network trained to estimate solar and wind energy with a storage tank draw. Both networks went through training to determine how much solar energy the system produced. For these computations, the demand temperature either was set at 30 or 40°C. Similar input data to that utilized by the software that is a part of the standard is used by both networks. These input values are used to calculate the output data. These comprise a range of climate data in addition to the size of each system and the distinctive features of its performance. The desired temperature was also an input for the second network that was used. Jessintha *et al.* [21] discovered that when unknown data were utilized to gauge prediction performance, the first networks had statistical R^2 values equal to 0.9917 and the network had R^2 values between 0.9800 and 0.9955. Its analytical R^2 values for the initial network varied from 0.9800 to 0.9955, whereas they were 0.9917 for the second network.

The importance of data analytics for power and energy systems were highlighted in [18]. Meanwhile [22] focuses the performance analysis of integrated power conversion system, in which the findings of two modalities are compared against traditional systems. In [25], authors suggested energy efficient solutions which incorporates image processing and deep learning approaches to perform landslide detection. Additionally in [26], authors proposes future research orientations and policies for sustainable energy solutions in marine environments.

8.5 Conclusion

Diverse businesses have utilized both expert systems and artificial neural networks for estimating and forecasting in renewable energy systems, in accordance with the problem definitions presented previously. These systems involve the choice of the right inference engine or nn, as well as the collection of data that represents the past performance and behavior of a real system. Unquestionably, the list of examples mentioned in this article is not comprehensive; instead, it is only a selection of examples that show the great potential of AI technologies. Artificial intelligence models have relative advantages and limitations, just like any other approximation technique. There is no set method for determining whether a specific application is a good fit for this particular technology. According to the studies described in this article, AI is thought to provide a different approach, the importance of which should not be overstated.

References

1. N. Mahsuda, C. Ananth, N. Isok-Jon, Y. Rayimjon and T. A. Kumar, "Virtual Science is a New Scientific Paradigm," *2023 IEEE Renewable Energy and Sustainable E-Mobility Conference (RESEM)*, Bhopal, India, 2023, pp. 1-5, doi: 10.1109/RESEM57584.2023.10236372.
2. Weihao Hu, Qiuwei Wu, Amjad Anvari-Moghaddam, Junbo Zhao, Xiao Xu, Sayed Mohamed Abulanwar, Di Cao, Applications of artificial intelligence in renewable energy systems, *IET Renew. Power Gener.*, DOI: 10.1049/rpg2.12479.
3. Zhengxuan Liu, Ying Sun, Chaojie Xing, Jia Liu, Ying dong He, Yuekuan Zhou, Guoqiang Zhang, Artificial intelligence powered large-scale renewable integrations in multi-energy systems for carbon neutrality transition: Challenges and future perspectives, *Energy AI*, August 2022.
4. Pradeep, S., Yogesh Kumar Sharma, Umesh Kumar Lilhore, Sarita Simaiya, Abhishek Kumar, Sachin Ahuja, Martin Margala, Prasun Chakrabarti, and Tulika Chakrabarti. "Developing an SDN security model (EnsureS) based on lightweight service path validation with batch hashing and tag verification." *Sci. Rep.*, 13, no. 1 (2023): 17381.
5. Ahmad T, Zhu H, Zhang D, Tariq R, Bassam A, Ullah F, AlGhamdi AS, Alshamrani SS. Energetics systems and artificial intelligence: applications of industry 4.0. *Energy Rep.*, 2022;8:334–61.
6. Liu Z, Zeng C, Zhou Y, Xing C. 9 - The main utilization forms and current developmental status of geothermal energy for building cooling/heating in developing countries (Eds.). In: Noorollahi Y, Naseer MN, Siddiqi MM, editors. *Utilization of thermal potential of abandoned wells*. Academic Press; 2022. p. 159–90.
7. Ram JP, Rajasekar N, Miyatake M. Design and overview of maximum power point tracking techniques in wind and solar photovoltaic systems: a review. *Renew. Sust. Energ. Rev.*, 2017;73:1138–59.

8. Alanazi M, Mahoor M, Khodaei A. Co-optimization generation and transmission planning for maximizing large-scale solar PV integration. *Int. J. Electr. Power Energy Syst.*, 2020;118:105723.
9. Zhou Y, Cao S. Quantification of energy flexibility of residential net-zero-energy buildings involved with dynamic operations of hybrid energy storages and diversified energy conversion strategies. *Sustain. Energy, Grids Netw.*, 2020;21: 100304.
10. Jackson P. (1990) *Introduction to Expert Systems.* Addison Wesley Publishing Company.
11. Pham D.T. (1988) *Expert Systems in Engineering.* IFS publications, Springler, Berlin.
12. Burri, Srinivasa Rao, Sachin Ahuja, Abhishek Kumar, and Anupam Baliyan. "Exploring the Effectiveness of Optimized Convolutional Neural Network in Transfer Learning for Image Classification: A Practical Approach." In *2023 International Conference on Advancement in Computation & Computer Technologies (InCACCT)*, pp. 598-602. IEEE, 2023.
13. Haykin S. (1994) *Neural Networks: A Comprehensive Foundation*, Macmillan, New York.
14. Rumelhart D.E., Hinton G.E. and Williams R.J. (1986) *In: Parallel Distributed Processing: Explorations in the Microstructure of Cognition*, Cambridge, MA, MIT Press.
15. Kumar, Abhishek, Pramod Sing Rathore, Ashutosh Kumar Dubey, Rashmi Agrawal, and Kanta Prasad Sharma. "LTE-NBP with holistic UWB-WBAN approach for the energy efficient biomedical application." *Multimedia Tools Appl.*, (2023): 1-15.
16. Kalogirou S.A., Neocleous C.C. and Schizas C.N. (1996) *Proc. of Int. Conf. EANN'96*, London, UK, pp. 5-8.
17. Kalogirou S.A. (1996) *Proc. of Eurosun'96, Freinberg*, Germany, pp. 470-475.
18. Malik, H., Ahmad, M.W. and Kothari, D.P. eds, Intelligent data analytics for power and energy systems. Vol. 802, Germany: Springer Nature, 2022.
19. Kalogirou S.A., Neocleous C.C. and Schizas C.N. (1997) *Proc. of Int. Conf. EANN'97*, Stockholm, Sweden, pp. 227-232.
20. Kalogirou S.A., Panteliou S. and Dentsoras A. (1999) *Sol. Energy*, 65, 335.
21. Jessintha, D., Kenjaev Sanjar Sobirovich, Christo Ananth and T. Ananth Kumar. "Design of Optimized low-power GPS-Yagi Antenna using Machine Learning techniques." In *2022 5th International Conference on Contemporary Computing and Informatics (IC3I)*, pp. 619-624. IEEE, 2022.
22. Arunkrishna, P., Asha, C.A. and Preetha, P.K., Performance Analysis of Adaptive Integrated Power Conversion System for Electric Vehicles. *2022 International Virtual Conference on Power Engineering Computing and Control: Developments in Electric Vehicles and Energy Sector for Sustainable Future (PECCON)*, Chennai, India, pp. 1-5, 2022,

23. B. Balaji, S. Ganesan, P. Pugazhendiran & S. Subramanian, Sliding mode controlled DC microgrid system with enhanced response, *J. Control Decis.*, DOI: 10.1080/23307706.2022.2120556, 2022.
24. B. Balaji, S. Ganesan, P. Pugazhendiran & S. Subramanian, Current Mode FOPID Controlled DC Micro-Grid System with Enhanced Response, *J. Harbin Inst. Technol.*, DOI: 10.11720/JHIT.54082022.9, 2022.
25. Y. J. Kumar *et al.*, Developing Sustainable Solutions Using Technological Approaches for Disaster Management and Energy Access in Mountainous Ranges: A Case Study of Sera Village, India, *2024 Fourth International Conference on Advances in Electrical, Computing, Communication and Sustainable Technologies (ICAECT), Bhilai, India*, pp. 1-6, 2024.
26. Rao, G. and Malik, T., Advancements in Offshore Renewable Energy Platforms: Innovations and Challenges in Ocean Engineering. *CINEFORUM*, 64(2), 1-5, 2024.

9

Computational Intelligence and Deep Learning in Health Informatics: An Introductory Perspective

J. Naskath[1]*, R. Rajakumari[1], Hamza Aldabbas[2] and Zaid Mustafa[2]

[1]Department of Computer Science and Engineering, National Engineering College, K.R. Nagar, Kovilpatti, Tamil Nadu, India
[2]Prince Abdullah bin Ghazi Faculty of Information and Communication Technology, Al-Balqa Applied University, Al-Salt, Jordan

Abstract
The past decade has seen a significant increase in the importance of data analytics in the field of health informatics, largely due to the influx of diverse multimodal data. This has led to a growing interest in developing analytical models based on machine learning (ML) specifically tailored for health informatics. In recent years, deep learning (DL), a technique rooted in artificial neural networks, has emerged as a powerful tool in the realm of machine learning, with the potential to bring about transformative changes in the field of artificial intelligence (AI). Its capacity to automatically enhance complex high-level features and perform semantic analysis on input data is complemented by rapid advancements in computational capabilities, efficient data storage, and seamless connectivity, all of which contribute to its rising prominence. This article not only offers a comprehensive assessment of the relative advantages, potential limitations, and future possibilities of this technology but also provides a contemporary and meticulous examination of the integration of deep learning in contexts related to health. The central focus of this investigation predominantly revolves around exploring key applications of deep learning, spanning translational bioinformatics, continuous sensing, medical imaging, and public health domains.

Keywords: Health information, deep learning, machine learning, EEG, wearable devices, computational intelligence, health mobile applications

**Corresponding author*: naskath.neccse@gmail.com

T. Ananth Kumar, E. Golden Julie, Venkata Raghuveer Burugadda, Abhishek Kumar and Puneet Kumar (eds.) Computational Intelligence: Theory and Applications, (189–212) © 2024 Scrivener Publishing LLC

9.1 Introduction

The realm of machine learning has recently witnessed a captivating evolution, driven by the emergence of deep learning [29]. While the theoretical foundations of deep learning have roots in traditional neural networks, it distinguishes itself through the incorporation of multiple hidden neurons and more than two layers of structures, accompanied by innovative training methodologies, a paradigm often referred to as computational intelligence (CI). This intricate design, featuring numerous neurons, facilitates comprehensive coverage of raw data, while a layered process of non-linear fusion of their outputs results in a lower-dimensional projection of the input space. Each of these projections into lower dimensions corresponds to an elevated level of understanding.

The significance of health informatics spans across both developed and developing countries, underlining its crucial contribution. Within this landscape, the utilization of machine and deep learning strategies plays a pivotal and rapidly evolving role. Particularly in health informatics, deep learning assumes a pivotal role, aiding researchers in the analysis of health data for diagnostic and therapeutic purposes [36]. It proves invaluable in early disease detection, including conditions like cancer and Alzheimer's, fostering a proactive approach to healthcare. The focal intent of this chapter is to delve into the avenues of research and potential within deep learning, specifically within the medical sphere, with the aim of enhancing patient quality of life and equipping clinicians with robust predictive capabilities [41].

This chapter delves into the diverse applications of deep learning within health informatics, highlighting its role in streamlining hospital administrative processes, facilitating disease mapping and specialized medical treatment. It stands as a tool for the early identification of ailments, personalizing treatment regimens for optimal outcomes. Moreover, it serves as a means of patient education regarding infectious diseases and their treatment possibilities, subsequently enhancing hospital and healthcare system efficiency while reducing overall healthcare costs [19]. Leveraging deep learning in healthcare enhances medical information management, modernizes workflows, provides access to clinical data, and augments the accuracy of medical records, ultimately fostering a more efficient and transparent information processing framework [41]. Furthermore, this article navigates the real-world challenges that must be surmounted to seamlessly integrate deep learning techniques into the realm of health informatics, emphasizing the need for computational intelligence-driven solutions.

A fascinating new trend in machine learning has recently emerged due to deep learning. Deep learning's theoretical underpinnings are well ingrained in the literature on traditional neural networks. However, unlike more conventional uses of neural networks (NNs), deep learning takes into account the usage of numerous concealed neurons and its more than two layers of structures in combination with novel training procedures. While using a large number of neurons enables thorough coverage of the available raw data, a lower-dimensional projection of the input space is produced via a layer-based pipeline of non-linear mixing of their outputs. Every projection into a lower dimension correlates to a higher level of perception.

The useful elite abstraction of raw data or information is generated when the network is optimally weighted. The contribution of health informatics in developed and developing countries is very important. The use of machine and deep learning knowledge strategies in health informatics is important and is evolving rapidly. Deep learning helps researchers analyze health data to treat illnesses. It also aids in the early detection of diseases such as cancer, Alzheimer's disease, and others. This chapter examines deep learning's research directions and future possibilities in the medical area, intending to assist patients in improving their quality of life. It also makes it easier for clinicians to make solid predictions based on the datasets that have been reviewed [5].

In health informatics, deep learning has a plethora of applications. This chapter will focus on some of the most typical applications. Deep learning aids in the efficiency of hospital administrative processes and facilitates the mapping and treatment of various diseases for specialized medical care. For example, it aids in the earliest detection of diseases and customizes treatment plans to guarantee the best possible outcome. It can be used to educate patients about infectious illnesses and their consequences that follow various treatment options. As a result, it can increase hospital and healthcare system efficiency while lowering healthcare costs. Deep learning can be used in healthcare to improve the management and sharing of medical information to improve and modernize workflows, gain access to clinical data, and improve the accuracy of medical records [41]. Above all, it makes the information process more efficient and transparent. Moreover, this article discusses the real-world obstacles that need to be overcome to make deep learning techniques easier in health informatics.

9.2 Mobile Application in Health Informatics Using Deep Learning

A mobile app, a manifestation of computational intelligence, constitutes software engineered for deployment on mobile devices like smartphones and tablets. These apps often endow users with services akin to those found in personal computers [20]. Typically, an app is a compact, standalone software module with constrained functionalities. Native apps, a category of mobile apps, are tailor-made for specific platforms and are built using languages like Swift, Java, Kotlin, Python, Objective-C, React, and C++. Web-based apps, on the other hand, embrace responsive designs that cater to diverse mobile devices and systems, facilitated through mobile browsers employing embedded HTML5, CSS, JavaScript, Ruby, and IOT components [18]. A hybrid mobile app amalgamates the attributes of a native app and a web app, accessible via icons or downloadable from App Stores. These hybrid apps are constructed utilizing languages such as Objective-C, Swift, and HTML5 [28]. The process of extracting data from Android apps encompasses several stages. In the initial step, rooted emulators or devices enable access to files within the data folder. For non-rooted devices, various adb shell commands facilitate data extraction from data files. Mobile app developers, drawing upon computational intelligence principles, have crafted a spectrum of medical informatics apps, tailored to cater to the needs of healthcare professionals and the general public. These apps encompass communication and consultation web apps, clinic administration tools, health record management and access apps, monitoring utilities, reference and information retrieval tools, and medical education and training applications.

Deep learning models' computer power has made it possible to operate healthcare systems quickly, and effectively [46]. Deep learning networks are fundamentally transforming patient care and assuming a pivotal role in the clinical landscape within health systems. The most often applied deep learning algorithms in healthcare are those for computer vision, natural language processing, and reinforcement learning. Examples include medical imaging, health data analytics, chatbots for mental health, individualized medical care, medication audits, etc. Not only can mobile applications benefit patients, but they also make it easy for doctors to collect and retain patient health information. Mobile apps allow patients to input their insurance cards and other information directly, which reduces administrative errors for medical personnel. Examples include Leafly, MySugr, Teladoc (24/7 access to a doctor), MDacne (custom acne treatment), EyeCare Live, and others. The last decade has witnessed a significant surge in the significance of data analytics in health informatics, primarily due to the substantial influx of multimodal data [47]. This surge in interest towards crafting analytical, data-centric methodologies based on machine learning within the realm of health informatics was precipitated by the work of Imteaj and Hossain [13]. In recent times, artificial neural network-driven deep

Table 9.1 Health info-based mobile apps using deep learning algorithms.

S. no.	Author and year	Domain	Algorithms	Results and applications
1	Daniele Ravì *et al.*, 2020 [12]	Deep learning and machine learning	Auto encoders and deep auto encoders, RNN, RBM, CNN	Health education, monitoring, and training-based mobile apps: various research scientists employed the mobile apps using deep learning in health informatics and public health.
2	Feng Yang *et al.*, 2020 [11]	Deep learning and machine learning	CNN, Iterative Global Minimum Screening (IGMS), OpenCV4 Android SDK library	Communications and consulting mobile apps are designed using DL techniques to measure accuracy, sensitivity specificity, precision and negative predictive values.
3	Ahmed Imteaj *et al.*, 2016 [13]	Deep learning	Android os, bKash system	Information Management, Record Maintenance and Access management mobile apps are used to choose suitable clinical centers and book the doctors during emergencies. Moreover, it monitored everyday activities and provided aids, medication information, pills reminder system, etc.

(Continued)

Table 9.1 Health info-based mobile apps using deep learning algorithms. (*Continued*)

S. no.	Author and year	Domain	Algorithms	Results and applications
4	K. Yazhini; D. Loganathan	Deep learning and machine learning	Stacked Sparse AE, CNN, LSTM, RNN, RBM, Stacked Denoising AE, GRU	Information Management, Record Maintenance and Access management mobile apps using DL techniques are reviewed in terms of ECG, image analysis, EHR maintenance, genomes analysis and wearable devices [22].
5	Sandra Hakiem Afrizal *et al.*, 2019 [14]	Deep learning	SIMORI	Monitoring and consulting mobile apps implemented for designing, examining and indexing mHealth app as SIMORI combined with ANC service, especially in primary health care applications.
6	Budi Wiweko *et al.*, 2016 [15]	Deep learning	Teleradiology Services, Tele-ECG services	Victim Monitoring, medical Record Maintenance and Access based apps proposed telehealth services such as teleECG and teleradiology for Indonesian.

(*Continued*)

Table 9.1 Health info-based mobile apps using deep learning algorithms. (*Continued*)

S. no.	Author and year	Domain	Algorithms	Results and applications
7	Zhang, *et al.*, 2019 [44]	Computational intelligence	CI-based medical image analysis on mobile devices	The application of deep learning models for medical image analysis on mobile devices. It highlights the potential of leveraging computational intelligence techniques for real-time image processing and diagnosis within mobile health apps.
8	Chen, H., *et al.* (2019) [45]	Computational intelligence	User experience (UX) within mobile apps and how computational intelligence can significantly augment this crucial facet	Innovative integration of computational intelligence techniques to enhance app interaction, responsiveness, and overall usability. By infusing computational intelligence, the authors highlight the potential to transform the mobile app landscape and elevate user satisfaction.

(*Continued*)

Table 9.1 Health info-based mobile apps using deep learning algorithms. (*Continued*)

S. no.	Author and year	Domain	Algorithms	Results and applications
9	Jose *et al.*, 2018 [16]	Deep learning	DNN, ANN	Health Education and Training Apps: Developed DL-enabled mobile apps with offline support for educating early symptoms of traumatic brain injuries.
10	Gaurav *et al.*, 2018 [17]	Deep learning and machine learning	Carezone, Tweri Alzheimer Medical App, CURAAP, Alzheimer Assistant	Patient monitoring apps: Apps play the main role in the family unit of the people living with Alzheimer's to denote their routine activities and notifications about them.
11	Gupta, R., *et al.* (2020) [38]	Computational intelligence	Creating cross-platform mobile applications utilizing HTML5 and JavaScript. Enhancing app development across various platforms.	Facilitate seamless user experiences while catering to diverse device ecosystems.

learning has emerged as a formidable machine learning paradigm, showcasing the potential to revolutionize the landscape of artificial intelligence.

Table 9.1 outlines the health information-based mobile apps using deep learning algorithms. Rapid increases in computing power, fast data storage, and serialization have contributed to the technology's rapid adoption, in addition to its forecasting ability and capacity to automatically create optimal features and semantic analysis from the key data [5]. Health information delivery, clinical and behavioral interventions, health monitoring, and the provision of healthcare services are all being changed by mobile phone health applications [20]. Future private and public mental healthcare projects are expected to rely heavily on smartphone technology [11].

9.3 Health Informatics Wearables Using Deep Learning

Wearable devices, imbued with computational intelligence, encompass electrical and software-controlled elements that can be seamlessly integrated into attire or worn as body accessories. Among these, smart jewelry, comprising rings, wristbands, wristwatches, and brooches, forms a notable category [25, 42]. Leveraging the power of computational intelligence, smaller wearables often employ smartphone apps for user interface and data presentation. These devices host sensors that capture and transmit biological data, particularly for medical applications. In the domain of health and fitness, commonplace accessories like wristbands, belts, and headbands incorporate sensors that diligently monitor physical activity and essential physiological markers [1]. These trackers establish wireless connections to designated apps, effectively facilitating data processing, comprehensive reporting, and secure storage through the lens of computational intelligence [6].

Wearable Devices Categories: In common, there are two groups of wearable technology. One is implantable devices; these include cardiac pacemakers and deep brain stimulators, which deliver current to specific organs for five to ten years after being installed inside the body. Additionally, there are wearable contact devices designed to discreetly collect an array of physiological data from the body. These unobtrusive gadgets monitor parameters such as heart rate, physical activity, body temperature, muscular activity, and blood and tissue oxygenation, among other relevant metrics [22, 23]. These devices employ a variety of deep learning algorithms, including CNN [27], RNN, SVM, and others [26]. It extracts the data source from a variety of sources, including smartphones, wearable technology, smart cities, smart buildings, and even personal appliances [2].

Leveraging computational intelligence, Table 9.2 categorizes wearables according to health data using deep learning algorithms. Recent years have witnessed the emergence of artificial neural network-based deep learning, a potent technology with the potential to revolutionize artificial intelligence. The rapid adoption of this technology is attributed to advancements in processing power, expedited data storage, parallelization, predictive capabilities, and its proficiency in deriving optimal high-level features and semantic interpretations from incoming data [5]. Proposing an innovative LSTM-based ECG classification [24] algorithm that surpasses previous efforts, this study not only maintains low computational overhead but also adheres to temporal constraints for seamless execution on wearable devices with limited computational resources [21]. In 2019, a system architecture for wearables and mobile apps powered by deep learning was elucidated, as depicted in Figure 9.1 [9].

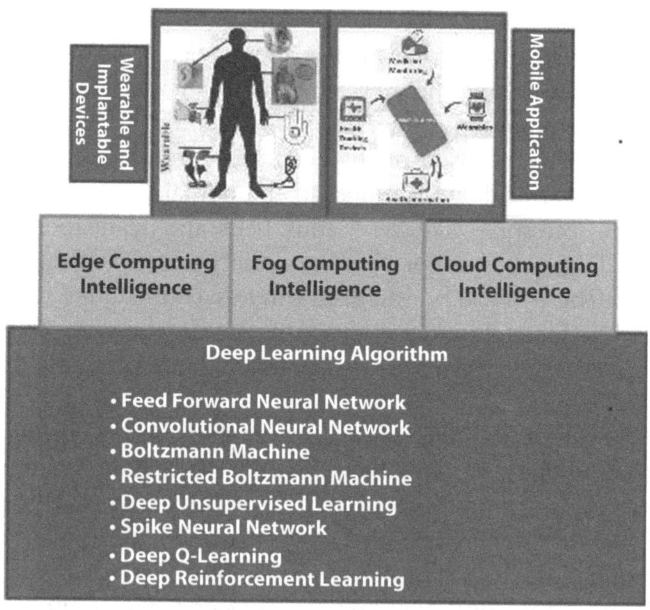

Figure 9.1 System structure of deep learning-based wearable and mobile apps.

Table 9.2 Wearable using deep learning algorithms.

S. no.	Authors and year	Domain/ application	Algorithms/ models	Data usage	Applications/results
1	Supreeth Prajwal Shashikumar, *et al.*, 2017 [1]	Deep Learning	CNN	Multichannel wrist-worn device used to collect the data form Pulsatile Photoplethysmographic and triaxial accelerometry data set.	AUC pooled for leave-one-out cross-validation was 0.95 (accuracy: 91.8%).
2	Aras R. Dargazany, *et al.*, 2018 [2]	Deep learning	IOT, ANN	The data sources are deep brain stimulator, cardiac pacemaker devices from various patients, and insulin pumps for diabetic patients.	IOT-based big data analytical methods are used to analyze a large volume, variety, and data generated at various frequencies to address wearable DL problems.
3	Brett M. Meyer *et al.*, 2020 [3]	Deep learning	RNN	Data from two wearable sensors, affixed to the human body, captured accelerometer readings during a one-minute walking activity.	Utilizing accelerometer data gathered from wearable sensors during a 60-second walking task, a bidirectional long short-term memory (BiLSTM) deep neural network exhibited the ability to identify individuals with multiple sclerosis (PwMS) who may be prone to falling.

(Continued)

Table 9.2 Wearable using deep learning algorithms. (*Continued*)

S. no.	Authors and year	Domain/ application	Algorithms/ models	Data usage	Applications/results
4	Hamidreza Bolhasani *et al.*, 2021 [4]	Deep learning	DNN and IOT	Clinical IoT, digital images, electronic health record (EHR) details, genomic data, and centralized health repositories.	Researchers, engineers, clinical practitioners, and protocol developers involved in the realm of IoT in healthcare find various attributes valuable, encompassing aspects like feature extraction, recognition, cost, latency, computational load, and more.
5	Elena Anca Paraschiv and Catalina-Maria Rotaru, 2020 [6]	Machine learning and deep learning	CNN	Scientific challenge respiratory database.	With a reasonable time of about two hours and accuracy findings of 96.99 percent for training and 90.21 percent for testing, the evaluation was run on the testing dataset.
6	Xiao Zhang *et al.*, 2021 [7]	Deep learning	Multimodality, learning model	HHAR dataset, PAMAP2 dataset	In contrast to conventional learning algorithms, recognizing human activities based on multimodality sensor information in an incremental learning technique forwarded to new relevant activities while maintaining the best storage area during the training process.

(*Continued*)

Table 9.2 Wearable using deep learning algorithms. (*Continued*)

S. no.	**Authors and year**	**Domain/ application**	**Algorithms/ models**	**Data usage**	**Applications/results**
7	Xiyuan Hu *et al.*, 2022 [8]	Artificial intelligence	CNN	Snore recording dataset	Shown how the suggested CNN approach may be used to accurately and reliably identify snore recordings. Additionally, it opens the door for the creation of wearable snore-detection technology.
8	Chongyu Zhou *et al.*, 2018 [10]	Deep learning	Artificial neural network	Vital signs are collected as patient data	Victim information is verified using the feature-based learning block. The assessments are produced by the classification block based on the calculated victim representations.

9.4 Electroencephalogram

The brain's electrical signals can be effectively captured using an electroencephalogram (EEG), a non-intrusive technique. Employing small scalp-affixed sensors, these signals are detected and subsequently recorded by a machine, undergoing careful analysis by medical experts. This process proves invaluable in the diagnosis and treatment of a spectrum of conditions, including brain tumors, traumatic brain injuries, sleep disorders, and various forms of brain dysfunction, each manifesting distinct symptoms [31, 34, 36]. One primary application lies in the identification of seizure activity associated with epilepsy, a common endeavor undertaken by medical practitioners. Furthermore, EEGs serve as a valuable tool to track medical disorders and discern the underlying source of specific symptoms. In scenarios such as brain surgery or monitoring individuals in a coma, EEGs find utility [32]. Notably, EEGs contribute to the identification and assessment of stroke patients, a critical facet acknowledged by the American Stroke Association. It is essential to recognize that severe stroke symptoms can manifest suddenly in individuals, often overnight, encompassing a range of indications that warrant immediate attention [37].

- Arm, leg, or facial numbness or weakness (especially on one side of the body).
- Difficulty comprehending or speaking clearly.
- Issues with one or both eyes' vision.
- Walking difficulties, lightheadedness, lack of balance, or issues with coordination.
- Excruciating headache with no apparent cause.

Epilepsy is a neurological condition that can be diagnosed via encephalography (EEG). Manual assessment of EEG brain waves is a labor- and time-intensive technique that significantly strains neurologists and reduces their productivity. Using traditional procedures, several automatic algorithms were proposed to help neurologists detect binary epilepsy situations, such as seizure and non-seizure. The following figure shows the block diagram of EEG classification. Figure 9.2 depicts the system structure of classification of EEG using deep learning and Table 9.3 samples some EEG signal analysis using deep learning algorithms [38].

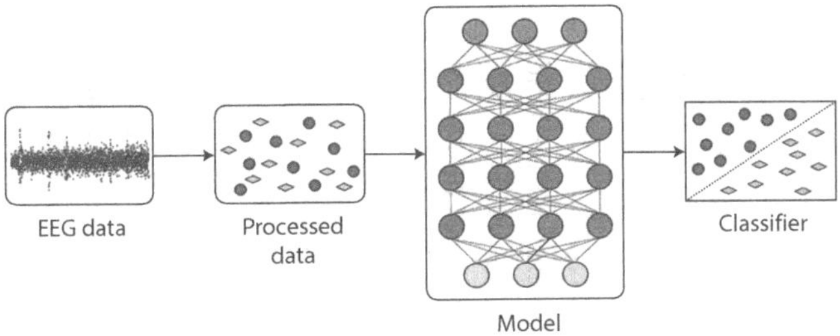

Figure 9.2 System structure of classification of EEG using deep learning.

By allowing automatic feature development and minimizing human interaction, deep learning has enabled the advancement of data-driven clarifications in the field of health informatics [1]. Without human participation, the production of an autonomous feature set provides several benefits in areas like health informatics. For instance, some features in medical imaging may be more complex and challenging to understand, particularly in the prediction of malignancies, various neurological illnesses and their unique properties, DNA & RNA sequences, protein structure, and many other fields [3]. We have mainly covered a range of deep learning techniques in the healthcare industry in this chapter. Additionally, this chapter has covered EEG, wearable, and mobile app application areas in the fields of health informatics and medical imaging.

9.5 Conclusion

The realm of computational intelligence has brought forth remarkable strides in shaping data gleaned from EEG, wearable, and mobile app sources through the lens of deep representation learning. The infusion of deep representation learning stands as a promising avenue to engender robust, resilient, and precise data representations, deriving considerable benefit from the innate capabilities of deep learning models to tackle the intricate challenges posed by diverse datasets. Within this context, patient or victim representation learning represents a deliberate endeavor to surmount the intricacies intertwined with patient data, augmenting scientific exploration by infusing sophisticated learning methodologies alongside meticulous model design. This chapter undertakes an exhaustive exploration of this research domain, delving into the intricacies of patient representation learning and its nuanced integration with complex learning practices. Moreover, the chapter navigates through diverse scenarios that

Table 9.3 Electroencephalography using deep learning algorithms.

Sl. no.	Author and year	Domain	Algorithms	Results and applications
1.	Birjandtalab Javad, *et al.*, 2017 [31]	Deep LEARNING	DNN with multilayer perceptrons	EEG signals are the finest markers for the finding of epileptic seizures. The author extracted frequency-domain metrics from EEG signals. A DL-based multilayer perceptron was applied to improve the accuracy of seizure detection.
2.	Ullah I, Hussain M, Aboalsamh H 2018 [33]	Deep learning	P-1D-CNN	For the classification of EEG signals, a one-dimensional pyramidal CNN is suggested. It is contrasted with the conventional CNN. P-1D-CNN is suggested as a way to reduce the vast number of learnable parameters, and the refinement strategy leads to 60 percent fewer parameters than conventional CNN models.
3.	Shu Lih Oh, V *et al.*, 2020 [34]	Deep learning	CNN	Highlighted the significance of using convolutional neural systems in EEG classification, specifically for detecting schizophrenia, a brain abnormality linked to symptoms such as hallucinations and disorganized speech. Employing an eleven-layered CNN model [30], the signals were automatically processed through convolution and max-pooling stages to extract essential features. Classification was then executed through a fully connected layer.

(Continued)

Table 9.3 Electroencephalography using deep learning algorithms. (*Continued*)

Sl. no.	Author and year	Domain	Algorithms	Results and applications
4.	Lasitha S Vidyaratne, Khan M Iftekharuddin, 2017 [35]	Machine learning	HWPT, SVM	This study showcases a patient-specific, real-time automatic method for detecting epileptic seizure onset using scalp and intracranial electroencephalograms. The approach involves extracting fractal properties through self-similarity and harmonic multi resolution from EEG. Rapid frequency resolutions are achieved through harmonic wavelet packet transform (HWPT), enhancing accuracy without recursive calculations. Additionally, the method estimates fractal dimension (FD) to identify recurrent self-similar patterns in the EEG signal.
5.	Yang Li, *et al.*, 2018 [37]	Machine learning	MRBF-MPSO-SVM	Utilizing multiscale radial basis functions (MRBF) and altered molecule swarm optimization, the creators displayed a versatile and localized time-frequency representation in EEG signals. In addition, it simultaneously progresses the time and recurrence determination. The dimensionality decreases the calculation employment rule component examination. Analysts utilized a back vector machine (SVM) classifier with the spiral premise work to isolate epileptic seizures from seizure-free EEG records.

(*Continued*)

Table 9.3 Electroencephalography using deep learning algorithms. (*Continued*)

Sl. no.	Author and year	Domain	Algorithms	Results and applications
6.	Ramy Hussein *et al.*, 2019 [39]	Machine learning	LSTM	Deep neural network architecture provides temporal correlations in EEG data for reliable seizure detection. First, a deep Long Short-Term Memory (LSTM) network is used to study the high-level demonstrations of distinct EEG patterns. Then, using a Fully Connected (FC) layer, the EEG features that are most reliable and pertinent to epileptic seizures were retrieved. Last, a softmax layer receives these attributes and produces predicted labels.
7.	Mohammadpoory Z, Nasrolahzadeh M, Haddadnia J, 2017 [40, 43]	Machine learning	SVM, KNN, DT, NB	This research introduced an approach based on weighted visibility graph entropy (WVGE) to identify seizures from EEG signals. Single-channel EEG data are mapped to WVGs, then used to calculate WVGEs. The brain signals are classified into three groups: normal, seizure free, and during a seizure using features retrieved from WVGEs. SVM, KNN, Decision Tree, and Naive Bayes are the classifiers used in this study.
8.	H Dhuria, M *et al.*, 2021 [41]	Machine learning	SVM, KNN, DT, NB	The EEG data of epileptic and healthy patients were divided into frequency sub-bands using Discrete Wavelet Transform (DWT). Ten features were recovered from these frequency sub-bands through the feature extraction process. The four different classifiers SVM, kNN, Nave-Bayes, and Decision Tree were then given the obtained attributes.

beckon for future advancements in patient representation learning. The unfolding narrative within this chapter envisions an escalating proliferation of pioneering techniques dedicated to the cultivation of refined patient representations. It is anticipated that these representations will assume an increasingly pivotal role in the healthcare landscape, contributing substantively to the realm of computational intelligence applied to medical and patient-centric domains.

References

1. Supreeth P. Shashikumar, A. J. Shah, Q. Li, G. D. Clifford and S. Nemati, "A deep learning approach to monitoring and detecting atrial fibrillation using wearable technology," *2017 IEEE EMBS International Conference on Biomedical & Health Informatics (BHI)*, Orlando, FL, USA, 2017, pp. 141-144, doi: 10.1109/BHI.2017.7897225.
2. Aras R. Dargazany, Paolo Stegagno, and KunalMankodiya, WearableDL: Wearable Internet-of-Things and Deep Learning for Big Data Analytics—Concept, Literature, and Future, *Hindawi*, Volume 2018, Article ID, 8125126, https://doi.org/10.1155/2018/8125126, 2018.
3. Brett M. Meyer, Lindsey J. Tulipani, Reed D. Gurchiek, Dakota A. Allen, LukasAdamowicz, DaleLarie, Andrew J. Solomon, NickCheney, Ryan S. McGinnis, Wearables and Deep Learning Classify Fall Risk From Gait in Multiple Sclerosis, *IEEE J. Biomed. Health. Inf.*, 2021, Volume: 25, Issue: 5, May 2021.
4. Hamidreza Bolhasani, MaryamMohseni, Amir Masoud Rahmani, Deep learning applications for IoT in health care: A systematic review, 2021 (https://www.sciencedirect.com/science/article/pii/S235291482100040X)
5. Daniele Ravì; Charence Wong; FaniDeligianni; Melissa Berthelot; Javier Andreu-Perez, Deep Learning for Health Informatics, *2017 IEEE Journal of Biomedical and Health Informatics*, 2017, Volume: 21, Issue: 1.
6. Elena Paraschiv and C. -M. Rotaru, "Machine Learning Approaches based on Wearable Devices for Respiratory Diseases Diagnosis," *2020 International Conference on e-Health and Bioengineering (EHB)*, Iasi, Romania, 2020, pp. 1-4, doi: 10.1109/EHB50910.2020.9280098.
7. Xiao Zhang; Hongzheng Yu; Yang Yang; JingjingGu; Yujun Li; Fuzhen Zhuang, Har MI: Human Activity Recognition Via Multi-Modality Incremental Learning, 2022 *IEEE J. Biomed. Health. Inf.*, 2022, Volume: 26, Issue: 3, March 2022.
8. Xiyuan Hu; Jingpeng Sun; Jinping Dong; Xuyun Zhang, Auditory Receptive Field Net based Automatic Snore Detection for Wearable Devices, *2021 IEEE J. Biomed. Health. Inf.*, 2021, DOI: 10.1109/JBHI.2022.3164517.

9. Saeed Saadatnejad; Mohammad hoseinOveisi; MatinHashemi, LSTM-Based ECG Classification for Continuous Monitoring on Personal Wearable Devices, *2020 IEEE J. Biomed. Health. Inf.*, 2020, Volume: 24, Issue: 2.
10. Chongyu Zhou; Yao Jia; Mehul Motani,Optimizing Autoencoders for Learning Deep Representations From Health Data,*2019 IEEE J. Biomed. Health. Inf.*, 2019, Volume: 23, Issue: 1.
11. Feng Yang; Mahdieh Poostchi; Hang Yu; Zhou Zhou; KamolratSilamut; Jian Yu; Richard J. Maude; StefanJaeger; Sameer Antani, Deep Learning for Smartphone-Based Malaria Parasite Detection in Thick Blood Smears, *IEEE J. Biomed. Health. Inf.*, 2020, Volume: 24, Issue: 5.
12. Daniele Ravì; Charence Wong; Benny Lo; Guang-Zhong Yang, "A Deep Learning Approach to on-Node Sensor Data Analytics for Mobile or Wearable Devices", *IEEE J. Biomed. Health. Inf.*, 2020, Volume: 21, Issue: 1.
13. Ahmed Imteaj and M. K. Hossain, "A smartphone based application to improve the health care system of Bangladesh", *2016 International Conference on Medical Engineering, Health Informatics and Technology* (MediTec), Dhaka, Bangladesh, 2016, pp. 1-6, doi: 10.1109/MEDITEC.2016.7835358.
14. Sandra Hakiem Afrizal; Achmad Nizar Hidayanto; Nashrul Hakiem; Arief Sartono; Seno Priyambodo; Tris Eryando, "Design of mHealth Application for Integrating Antenatal Care Service in Primary Health Care: A User-Centered Approach", *2019 Fourth International Conference on Informatics and Computing (ICIC).*
15. Budi Wiweko; AuliaZesario; Prince Gusti Agung Overview the development of tele health and mobile health application in Indonesia *2016 International Conference on Advanced Computer Science and Information Systems (ICACSIS).*
16. Jose, Benedetto, Pablo Sanabria, ORCID, AndresNeyem ORCID, JaimeNavon, "Deep Neural Networks on Mobile Healthcare Applications: Practical Recommendations", *12th International Conference on Ubiquitous Computing and Ambient Intelligence (UCAmI 2018)*
17. Gaurav Gupta, AnkitGupta,VarunJaiswal, Mohd Dilshad Ansari "A Review and Analysis of Mobile Health Applications for Alzheimer Patients and Caregivers", *2018 Fifth International Conference on Parallel, Distributed and Grid Computing (PDGC)* .
18. M., Harini Vasaki, R., KamalaHarini, V., Ganthimathi, J., Naskath, "An IoT based college bus trailing and surveiling system", *AIP Conference Proceedings*,Volume 2444, Issue 1, Pages 070001, AIP Publishing LLC, 2022.
19. S Muthukaviya, MR Shree, SRVS Vardhini, J Naskath , "IoT based trolley for isolated patients", *AIP Conf. Proc.*, vol. 2444, issue 1, 2022.
20. Janofer Ibrahima, J., Naskath, J., Lakshmi Prabha, S., Paramasivan, B., "Phone directory using mobile application", *Int. J. Sci. Technol. Res.*, 2020, 9(3), pp. 6495–6498.

21. Sandra Smigiel, Krzysztof Pałczynski and Damian Ledzinski, "Deep Learning Techniques in the Classification of ECG Signals Using R-Peak Detection Based on the PTB-XL Dataset", *Sensors*, vol.21, 8174, page no.1-18, 2021.
22. Zahra Ebrahimi, Mohammad Loni, Masoud Daneshtalab, Arash Gharehbaghi, "A Review on Deep Learning Methods for ECG Arrhythmia Classification, *Expert Syst. Appl.: X*", vol.7 , page no.10 - 33, 2020.
23. Antonio H. Ribeiro *et al.*, "Automatic diagnosis of the 12-lead ECG using a deep neural network", 2020, https://doi.org/10.1038/s41467-020-15432-4.
24. Miquel Alfaras, Miguel C. *Soriano and Silvia Ortín, "A Fast Machine Learning Model for ECG-Based Heartbeat Classification and Arrhythmia Detection", Front. Physics*, 2019, Volume 7 - 2019 | https://doi.org/10.3389/fphy.2019.00103.
25. Ping Xiong, Simon Ming-Yuen Lee and Ging Chan, "Deep Learning for Detecting and Locating Myocardial Infarction by Electrocardiogram: A Literature Review", *Front. Cardiovasc. Med.*, 2022, Volume 9 - 2022 | https://doi.org/10.3389/fcvm.2022.860032.
26. Kumar, T. Ananth, R. Rajmohan, Sunday Adeola Ajagbe, Tarek Gaber, Xiao-Jun Zeng, and Fatma Masmoudi. "A novel CNN gap layer for growth prediction of palm tree plantlings." *PLos One,* 18, no. 8 (2023): e0289963.
27. Jonas L Isaksen, *et al.*, "Artificial intelligence for the detection, prediction, and management of atrial fibrillation", *Herzschr Elektrophys*, 2022, vol. 33, page no. 34–41.
28. Pradeep, S., Yogesh Kumar Sharma, Umesh Kumar Lilhore, Sarita Simaiya, Abhishek Kumar, Sachin Ahuja, Martin Margala, Prasun Chakrabarti, and Tulika Chakrabarti. "Developing an SDN security model (EnsureS) based on lightweight service path validation with batch hashing and tag verification." *Sci. Rep.,* 13, no. 1 (2023): 17381.
29. Rasmus S. Andersen, AbdolrahmanPeimankar, Sadasivan Puthusserypady, "A deep learning approach for real-time detection of atrial fibrillation", *Expert Syst. Appl.*, 2019, vol.115, page no. 465–473.
30. U. Rajendra Acharya, Hamido Fujita, Shu Lih Oh, U. Raghavendra, Jen Hong Tan, Muhammad Adam, Arkadiusz Gertych, Yuki Hagiwara, "Automated identification of shockable and non-shockable life-threatening ventricular arrhythmias using convolutional neural Network", *Future Gener. Comput. Syst.*, 2018, vol. 79, page no. 952–959.
31. Birjandtalab Javad, Mehrdad Heydarzadeh, and Mehrdad Nourani, "Automated EEG-based epileptic seizure detection using deep neural networks", *IEEE international conference on healthcare informatics (ICHI).* IEEE, 2017, DOI: 10.1109/ICHI.2017.55
32. Ashwani Kumar Tiwari, Ram Bilas Pachori, Vivek Kanhangad, Bijaya Ketan Panigrahi, "Automated diagnosis of epilepsy using key-point based local binary pattern of EEG signals", *IEEE J. Biomed. Health Inform.*, vol. 21(4), 2017, page no.888–896.

33. Ullah I, Hussain M, Aboalsamh H, "An automated system for epilepsy detection using EEG brain signals based on deep learning approach. *Expert Syst. Appl.*", 2018,vol. 107, page no. 61–71.
34. Shu Lih Oh, V Jahmunah, Edward J Ciaccio, Rajamanickam Yuvaraj and U Rajendra, Acharya, "Deep convolutional neural network for the automated detection and diagnosis of seizure using EEG signals", *Comput. Biol. Med.* vol. 100, page no.270–278, 2020.
35. Lasitha S Vidyaratne, Khan M Iftekharuddin, "Real-time epileptic seizure detection using EEG", *IEEE Trans. Neural Syst. Rehabil. Eng.*, vol. 25(11), page no.2146–2156, 2017.
36. Naskath, J., Sivakamasundari, G. & Begum, A.A.S. "A Study on Different Deep Learning Algorithms Used in Deep Neural Nets: MLP SOM and DBN". *Wirel. Pers. Commun.*, 2022, https://doi.org/10.1007/s11277-022-10079-4 .
37. Yang Li, Xu-Dong Wang, Mei-Lin Luo, Ke Li, Xiao-Feng Yang, Qi Guo, "Epileptic seizure classification of EEGs using time–frequency analysis based multiscale radial basis functions", *IEEE J. Biomed. Health Inform.*, vol. 22(2), page no.386–397, 2018
38. Gupta, R., *et al.*, "Building Cross-Platform Mobile Apps with HTML5 and JavaScript", *J. Comput. Intell. Mobile Comput.*, 2020, 6(3), 112-122.
39. Ramy Hussein, Hamid Palangi, Rabab K Ward, Z Jane Wang, Optimized deep neural network architecture for robust detection of epileptic seizures using EEG signals. *Clin. Neurophysiol.*, vol. 130(1), page no. 25–37, 2019
40. Mohammadpoory Z, Nasrolahzadeh M, Haddadnia J, "Epileptic seizure detection in EEGs signals based on the weighted visibility graph entropy *Seizure*", vol. 50, page.no. 202–208, 2017.
41. H Dhuria, M Priyadarsini, R Pandit, B Dhar, GK Rajini, A Jabeena, "Epileptic Seizure Detection of EEG Signal Using Wavelet Based Feature Extraction and Machine Learning Algorithms", *Advances in Automation, Signal Processing, Instrumentation, and Control Systems*, 2021, DOI:10.1007/978-981-15-8221-9_129.
42. Alif, R.Raja Kumari, J.Naskath, "Deep learning based clinical images and Electrocardiogram: a survey", *Recent Trends In Multidisciplinary Subjects*, Volume – 3, Red'shine publication pvt. Ltd., Lunawada, 2022.
43. Atefeh Shariat, Asghar Zarei, Sanaz Ahmadi Karvigh, Babak Mohammadzadeh Asl, "Automatic detection of epileptic seizures using Riemannian geometry from scalp EEG recordings", *International Federation for Medical and Biological Engineering (IFMBE)*, vol.59(7-8) page.no.1431-1445, 2021.
44. Zhang, J., Xie, Y., Xia, Y., & Hu, F ,"Deep Learning for Medical Image Analysis on Mobile Devices: A Review", *J. Imaging*, 2019, 5(5), 61.
45. Chen, H., *et al.* "Enhancing User Experience in Mobile Apps through Computational Intelligence", *J. Hum. Comput. Interact.*, 35(4), 287-300, 2019.

46. R. Rajakumari & L. Kalaivani, "Breast Cancer Detection and Classification Using Deep CNN Techniques", *Intell. Autom. Soft Comput.*, 2020, vol. 32, no. 2, pp.1089-1107.
47. R. Rajakumari & L. Kalaivani, "Abnormality Detection And Classification Using Artificial Neural Network", *Int. J. Sci. Technol. Res.*, 2020, vol. 9, issue 03, pp. 1234-1237.

10

Computational Intelligence for Human Activity Recognition (HAR)

Thangapriya* and Nancy Jasmine Goldena

Department of Computer Applications and Research Centre, Sarah Tucker College (Autonomous), Affiliated to Manonmaniam Sundaranar University, Abishekapatti, Tirunelveli, Tamil Nadu, India

Abstract
Computational Intelligence (CI) is a set of computational approaches that address real-world problems. Usually, it involves solving complex problems in terms of natural processes. Although many of the issues are similar to those that can be solved using formal models, CI generally uses a unique, nature-inspired methodology to learn a specific task from experimental observation. With the rising involvement of CI in our day-to-day applications, the need for Human Activity Recognition (HAR) has made its presence known to the concerned research community. Typically, a sensor or another device can physically capture activity, which can then be processed by another mechanism to provide human activity. HAR is important in interpersonal relationships and human-to-human interaction, because it contains information on a person's identity, personality, physiological state, gestures, atomic actions, group actions, behaviors, and events. The main purpose of this chapter is to provide a detailed examination of CI paradigms for HAR, such as Fuzzy Logic (FL), Artificial Neural Network (ANN), Swarm Intelligence (SI), Evolutionary Computing (EC), and Artificial Immune System (AIS). The majority of researchers are working on HAR and developing it with CI algorithms. CI is an excellent platform for a variety of applications. This chapter discusses each CI technique and how it supports HAR as well as its merits and downsides from diverse research perspectives.

***Keywords*:** Action recognition, algorithms, biologically inspired system, computational intelligence

**Corresponding author*: priyasaravananrex@gmail.com

T. Ananth Kumar, E. Golden Julie, Venkata Raghuveer Burugadda, Abhishek Kumar and Puneet Kumar (eds.) Computational Intelligence: Theory and Applications, (213–234) © 2024 Scrivener Publishing LLC

10.1 Introduction

The word "computational" describes how computers work, and the ability to learn and use information and skills is termed "intelligence". When traditional modeling is ineffective for a variety of reasons, Computational Intelligence (CI) is a set of scientific nature-inspired, statistical, and especially computational strategies for solving challenging real-world problems. The primary reasons are as follows:

- The processes may be too complicated for mathematical modeling.
- The process may be stochastic.

Human Action Recognition (HAR) is an attractive prospect with the potential to serve humanity by developing assistive technologies especially in healthcare. The HAR is divided into two categories: unimodal and multimodal. Unimodal approaches are further classified as space–time, stochastic, rule-based, and shape-based, while multimodal approaches are classified as affective, behavioral, and social networking as shown in Figure 10.1.

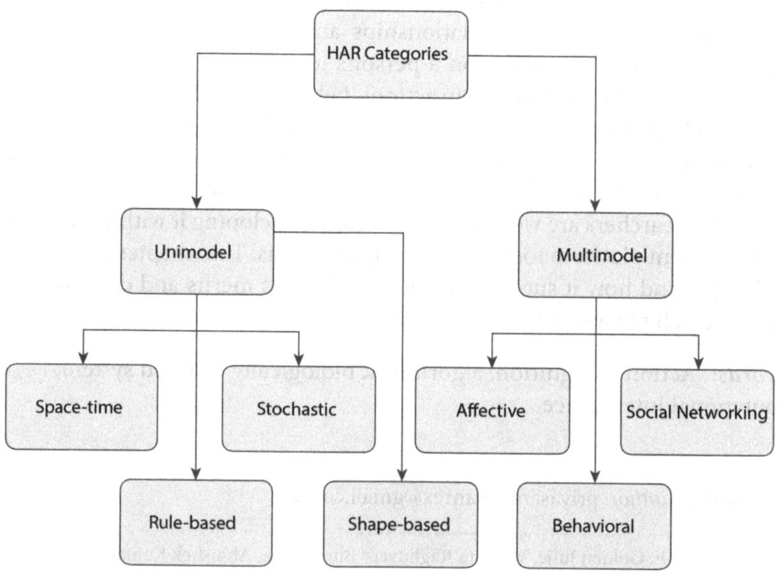

Figure 10.1 HAR categories.

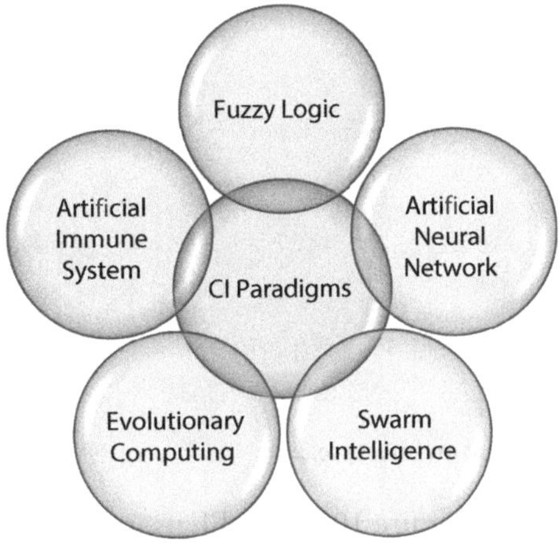

Figure 10.2 Five paradigms of computational intelligence.

The goal of space–time techniques is to recognize activities based on their spatial characteristics. Stochastic methods are used to identify the pattern of behavior states. Rule-based methods utilize a set of rules to predict events. Shape-based approaches are used to identify human activities in different types of spaces such as 2D, 3D, and so on. An affective approach is utilized in emotional intelligence to model a person's ability to express, understand, and control affective states. The behavioral technique is used to identify human behaviors such as gestures, facial expressions, and so on. The social networking method is used to detect social interaction in daily life, such as on YouTube, Twitter, Facebook, Instagram, and other social media platforms.

CI paradigms such as Fuzzy Logic (FL), Artificial Neural Network (ANN), Swarm Intelligence (SI), Evolutionary Computing (EC), and Artificial Immune System (AIS) are shown in Figure 10.2. The primary contribution is to demonstrate how to implement HAR in CI models. Let us take a closer look at each of them individually.

10.2 Fuzzy Logic in Human Judgment and Decision-Making

FL was established by "Lotfi Zadeh". FL is a logical problem-solving method that is relevant to human judgments. The FL approach simulates decision-making and includes all realistic intermediate digital values such as yes, no, maybe, may not, or sometimes assumption-based. Basic FL

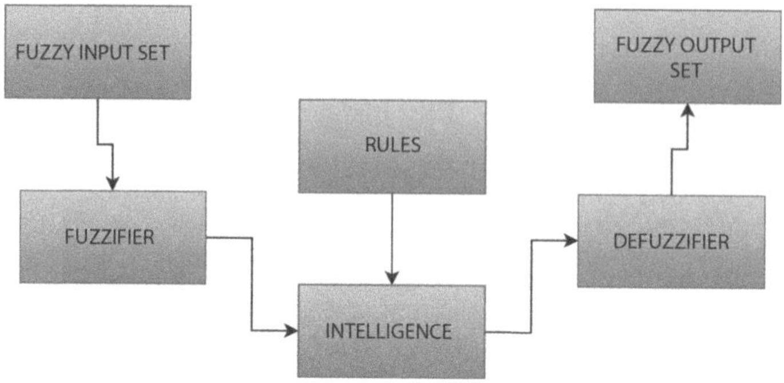

Figure 10.3 Basic fuzzy logic architecture.

architecture is shown in Figure 10.3. The FL uses a variety of possible input values to achieve extremely good results, giving it the most accurate methodology. FL is a technology that can be implemented in both hardware and software. FL is suitable for a variety of applications, including small microcontrollers, networked, and workstation-based control systems.

FL is broken down into four modules: Fuzzification, Knowledge Base, Inference Engine, and Defuzzification.

Fuzzification Module: The input signal is divided into five components (small, medium positive, medium negative, largely positive, and largely negative) and the system's crisp numeric inputs are transformed into fuzzy sets by using fuzzification module.
Knowledge Base Module: The Knowledge Base Module keeps track of looping statements like IF, IF-THEN, IF-THEN ELSE, and so on.
Inference Engine Module: This module simulates human cognition by generating fuzzy inference on inputs as well as using IF-THEN rules.
Defuzzification Module: This module converts the inference engine's fuzzy set into a numerical value.

10.2.1 FL Algorithm

The FL algorithm is used to solve a wide variety of problems in a range of domains. FL provides the best results in decision-making scenarios. The FL algorithm is illustrated below:

Algorithm

Step 1	*Define the variables for input and output.*
Step 2	*Build the membership function.*

Step 3	*Create knowledge-based rules (create a matrix for actual vs. target values), most likely IF-THEN-ELSE rules.*
Step 4	*To generate a final result, combine all of the evaluation results called as a fuzzy value. Obtain the fuzzy value to evaluate the execution of the rules.*
Step 5	*To perform the membership function for the output variable, implement Defuzzification.*

10.2.2 Applications of FL

FL has a wide range of applications in industries. In general, FL is used in the following:

- Used to control the altitude of spacecraft and satellites in the aerospace industry.
- Used to control the speed and acceleration in the automobile industry.
- Suitable for employee personal evaluation and decision-support systems in large organizations predominantly in human resources.
- In the chemical industry to control pH, evaporation, and chemical distillation.
- Used in a variety of AI applications, including as natural language processing.
- Used in most of the intelligent systems.
- Used in car engines to select the best gear for the engine load, driving style, and road circumstances.
- Recognizes handwritten Kanji characters on a Palmtop computer.

10.2.3 Advantages of FL

- Widely utilized in industrial and optimal solutions.
- Controls robots and consumer products in AI.
- It is not the most accurate logic, but it is the only one that can be accepted.
- The most efficient way to deal with complicated problems.
- In data mining (DM), FL assists in dealing with engineering uncertainty.

- ❖ The structure of FLS is simple and straightforward.
- ❖ FLS can handle inaccurate, corrupted, and messy input data.

10.2.4 Disadvantages of FL

- ❖ Sometimes unreliable, so the results are evaluated according to expectations, which may not be commonly accepted.
- ❖ Probability theory is messed up by some fuzzy logic that produces incorrect results.
- ❖ FLS design does not have a systematic methodology and needs simplicity.
- ❖ Extensive hardware testing is required for the validation and verification of a fuzzy knowledge-based system.
- ❖ FLS makes it difficult to create precise and imprecise rules and membership functions [1].

10.2.5 Utilizing FLS and FIS in HAR Research and Health Monitoring

Fuzzy Logic System (FLS) and Fuzzy Inference System (FIS) are used in the majority of FL research.

A. Fuzzy Logic System

FL works on the "Degree of Truth" principle, which is commonly used in reasoning and resembles human logic. Instead of using traditional methods to monitor elderly people's health, FL methods can be used [9]. In HAR research, the FLS model is used to represent, recognize, manage, and analyze human behaviors in different perspectives. For example, in IoT, a sensor device is used to detect human activities [13]. Using a cloud monitoring system, the sensor collects information from the patient and sends a notification to the concerned person, if the patient experiences any difficulties. Using FL, all information is computed and communicated through a device such as a laptop, smartphone, and so on. Finally, FLS generates correct yet definite responses to insufficient, contradictory, damaged, or imprecise (fuzzy) information [7].

B. Fuzzy Inference System

FIS uses the "IF-THEN-ELSE" rules along with connectors "OR" or "AND" for making essential decision rules. The fuzzy input is mapped to the output using fuzzy-set theory. The most popular FIS are Mamdani Fuzzy Models (MFMs) and Sugeno Fuzzy Models (SFMs). MFMs are utilized to capture information for interpolating multiple linear models to model nonlinear systems. SFMs are used for mathematical analysis and particularly suited for optimization problems since they assure output surface continuity [17]. In HAR research, a FIS system is used for classifying physical activities like walking, running, climbing, exercising, and so on [10]. Many HAR research areas use FL to produce the best results based on decision-making. It has several limitations; however, it is often used to detect human activities.

10.3 Artificial Neural Networks: From Perceptrons to Modern Applications

The first Artificial Neural Network (ANN), known as a "perceptron," was developed in 1958 by psychologist Frank Rosenblatt to model how the human brain absorbs visual information.

The normal neural network of the human nervous system is the inspiration for neural networks. Many computer-related solutions have been developed and are still being developed based on human biological systems, for example, artificial eyes and artificial organs [2]. ANNs are made up of several nodes that imitate the neurons present in the human brain.

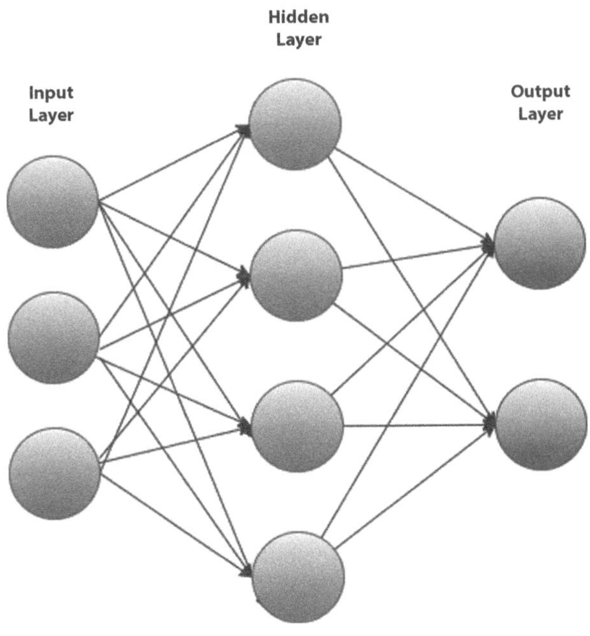

Figure 10.4 Simple ANN.

The neurons are linked together and engaged in intercellular communication. The nodes are capable of receiving information as input and processing it using fundamental operations. The outcomes of these operations have an impact on other neurons. Each connection has a weight, and each node's output is known as its activation or node value. ANN can learn the specific task by changing the values of their weights.

The ANN has three layers: input, output, and hidden. The input layer obtains the data from the network. The hidden layer receives and processes the raw data from the input layer. The calculated value is finally sent to the output layer, which automatically evaluates and transmits information from the hidden layer as shown in Figure 10.4. Two types of neural networks are feed forward ANN and feed backward ANN.

A. Feed forward ANN

The information flow from the input layer to the output layer in the feed forward ANN is only one way, which is referred to as unidirectional shown in Figure 10.5 and explains how to evaluate and analyze input patterns [6].

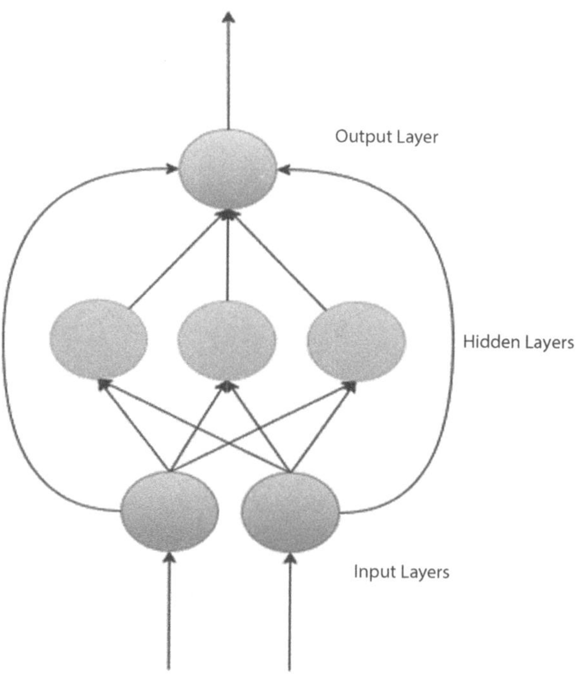

Figure 10.5 Feed forward.

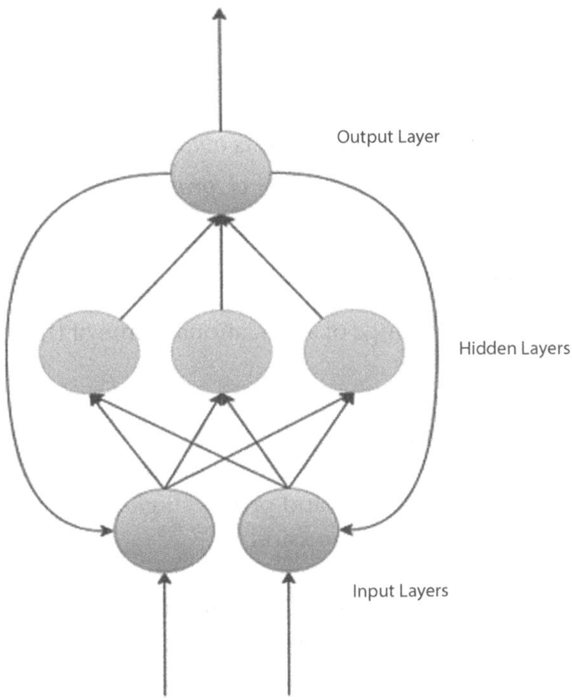

Figure 10.6 Feed backward.

B. Feed backward ANN

The feed backward ANN [2], on the other hand, has some information moving in the opposite direction mostly used in optimization issues as shown in Figure 10.6.

10.3.1 ANN Algorithm

ANN is simple to use. Many studies have utilized ANN for classification. The steps for implementing ANN are listed below:

Algorithm

Step 1	*An external source sends an input signal in the form of a pattern and an image in the form of a vector to hidden layers.*
Step 2	*After passing the input, each value is multiplied by its weights (coefficient of each variable).*

Step 3	*Weighted inputs are calculated and the activation function receives total weighted inputs.*
Step 4	*The difference between the actual and expected results is evaluated and the output is obtained.*
Step 5	*If the error rate is high, back propagation can be performed.*

10.3.2 Applications of ANN

ANN is utilized in a wide range of applications. Some of the primary applications are given below:

- Plays a significant role in image and character recognition.
- Time series forecasting is achieved using ANN.
- Neural networks receive and process big data [3].
- Suitable for image compression.
- Utilized in financial operations, workforce planning, marketing, business intelligence, and product management.
- Utilized in commercial applications like risk analysis, criminal identification, and consumer research solutions.

10.3.3 Advantages of ANN

- In ANN, problems are represented as attribute-value sequences.
- Utilized to solve problems where the target value is discrete, real, or a vector.
- In smart homes, voice-activated functionality, automation, surveillance and event tracking are all common features in smart homes.
- ANN learning algorithms do not have difficulties with noise in the training set. Even if the training samples contain errors, the result will not be affected.

10.3.4 Disadvantages of ANN

- Initialization of the problem in ANN is difficult [4].
- Dependent on hardware.
- The most serious issue with ANN is its unexplained functionality. When ANN provides a solution, there is no

explanation for why or how it provides the solution, which may reduce trust in ANN.

- There is no formal rule for establishing the structure of ANN. Experience, as well as trial and error, should be used to develop an effective network structure. The assurance of proper network structure will be properly considered more extensively.

10.3.5 Artificial Neural Networks in HAR Research

ANN can be trained by supervised, unsupervised, and reinforcement learning techniques. In supervised learning, an ANN can be trained using labeled data, which is primarily used for prediction [14]. Unsupervised learning allows ANNs to be trained on unlabeled data, which is usually used for clustering. In reinforcement learning, ANN can be used for observation. The majority of HAR studies are based on ANN classification [18], for example, predicting the physiological conditions of humans. Sensor signals are used as input, and data acquisition techniques are used to convert sensor data to numerical values. The features are calculated using feature selection techniques. For classification, four target classes are assigned: physical, emotional, mental, and neutral. The target classes can be classified using the ANN classifier [11].

Many study areas can benefit from the usage of ANN as a classifier. It is hardware-dependent and expensive, yet it can still function effectively.

10.4 Swarm Intelligence

Gerardo Beni and Jing Wang introduced the term "cellular robotic systems" in 1989. Swarm intelligence (SI) describes the collective behavior

Figure 10.7 Graphical illustration of a basic swarm intelligence.

of distributed, self-organizing systems, whether they are artificial or natural. Most probably, AI research uses the SI concept. Naturally, the biological system is a frequent source of inspiration. Examples of SI in natural systems include ant colonies, bee colonies, bird flocking, hawk hunting, animal herding, growth of bacteria, and fish schooling. A graphical illustration of fundamental SI is shown in Figure 10.7.

10.4.1 SI Algorithm [10]

Most of the researchers have started to explore the intelligence of the swarm to generate new ideas. The following steps can be used to implement SI based on the Ant Colony Optimization (ACO) algorithm:

Algorithm

Step 1	*The swarm and the food source serve as vertices or nodes, the connections as edges, and the pheromone values as weights for the edges.*
Step 2	*Set up the appropriate parameters and pheromone samples.*
Step 3	*Create the IF-THEN-ELSE logic for the problem and generate the code. At each iteration, all ants are placed at the source vertex, i.e., the ant colony. Values for pheromone trials should be updated.*
Step 4	*Compute the fitness values associated with each ant. The more pheromone added, the shorter the path.*
Step 5	*Using selection methods, find the optimal solution.*
Step 6	*Now, have the assumption result for the desired problem.*

10.4.2 Applications of SI

SI has a wide range of applications. Some of the applications are given below:

- In military operations, tiny, drone-like cameras are created to function as a single entity to conduct extremely sensitive worldwide duties such as searching for survivors in dangerous regions during rescue missions in affected regions.
- In the telecommunications industry, each call traverses through a network of intermediate nodes before receiving at its final destination, which leads to traffic. Telecom center

agents can redirect traffic and minimize delays by using "digital ants" that can be sent across uncongested networks [11].

- In HR and recruitment, SI is used. When competition is minimal and the labor market is small, group recruiting is effective.
- Helps in the logistics and transportation industry, telecommunications industry, factory operations optimization, and better consumer feedback.

10.4.3 Advantages of SI

- Durable, adaptable, and versatile.
- Has a high performance to design complex scenarios.
- Needs low memory requirements because they use simple reactive agents that do not require a lot of prior data.

10.4.4 Disadvantages of SI

- Sometimes poor in local search.
- Difficult to perform theoretical analysis.
- Difficult to implement because the cost of maintaining the AI system on each node is expensive.
- Gives approximate results; hence, it cannot be used to solve problems that require a proper solution.

10.4.5 Swarm Intelligence Techniques in HAR Research

An important area of research in the human–computer interface (HCI) is automatic human activity recognition (AHAR). Getting categorized data is the most challenging task in HAR. The goal of HAR is to provide information on a person's perceptions so that computing systems can assist them in their work more successfully.

Stochastic diffusion search (SDS): SDS is a strategy for probability-based global search and optimization based on agents that are suitable for problems where the objective function may be broken down into multiple different partial functions. SDS can be used to predict human behaviors in social media (also known as rumors in social media) [16].

Particle swarm optimization (PSO): PSO is a bio-inspired technique having a powerful local search function to quickly identify the optimal solution in the computational complexity. PSO is useful for determining the maximum or minimum of a function specified on a multidimensional vector space. The PSO algorithm can be used to solve the optimization problem in terms of human activity prediction [12].

The **ACO** algorithm is based on an ant's foraging behavior in order to find a route leading from their colony to a food source. ACO is a statistical method for problem-solving that produces better solutions using graphs. Virtual "ants" search a parameter space that contains all feasible solutions as a simulation agent to determine the best solution [12].

SI is a new field of study. As a result, the SI needs to do additional data analysis. In this SI, a theoretical survey is necessary. SI can be used to implement various prediction models.

10.5 Evolutionary Computing

Evolutionary computation (EC) is a subfield of artificial intelligence (AI) and soft computing, as well as many other important research fields, that addresses various techniques for global optimization influenced by biological evolution [5]. EC is a population-based trial-and-error problem solver having stochastic optimization properties.

10.5.1 EC Algorithm

EC is really difficult to implement, but once implemented, it produces the best results. The following steps can be used to implement the EC algorithm [15].

Algorithm	
Step 1	*Generate the first population of solutions (there will be an infinite range of approaches to the issue in the population, which are known to as members).*
Step 2	*After a population has been created, its members must be assessed using a fitness function (a fitness function is a function that accepts a member's characteristics and returns a numerical representation solution to determine the viability of a particular solution).*
Step 3	*Calculate each member's fitness and choose a subset of the highest-scoring members.*

Step 4	*Find a single optimum point from each fitness.*
Step 5	*The Pareto frontier is the collection of the best possible solutions, and it includes components that are all equally desirable solutions.*
Step 6	*The set of possible solutions is then refined by using a decider based on the circumstances of the problem.*
Step 7	*The top members are now employed to generate the algorithm's next generation. New children are created by adding the attributes of the chosen parents.*
Step 8	*Depending on the type of data, this could be challenging, but for the majority of combinatorial optimization problems, it is simple to mix possibilities and create combinations that are genuine. If we neglect this crucial step, we will quickly get caught in local extrema and will not get the best results.*
Step 9	*A mutation is simply created when a small portion of the children's genes are changed such that they no longer exactly match the parent's genetic code.*
Step 10	*Most mutations are probabilistic, which means that a probability distribution regulates both the possibility that a newborn can inherit a mutation and its frequency.*
Step 11	*The algorithm is terminated when it achieves its maximum runtime or a certain level of performance* [6].

10.5.2 Applications of EC

There is a need for evolution everywhere. Traditional approaches are not always effective in dealing with current issues. Many evolutionary applications can benefit from EC. A list of EC applications are given below:

- EC is broadly used in image and character assessment, fraud detection, image recognition, facial recognition in social media, and so on.
- EC can help in healthcare, life science, insurance and commercial problems.
- In agriculture and defense, EC plays a significant role.
- EC gives good results in financial optimization problems.

10.5.3 Advantages of EC

- EC is conceptually simple.
- Almost any problem that can be described as a function optimization job can be solved using EC algorithms. It necessitates the use of a data structure to describe solutions, a performance index to evaluate them, and variation operators to create new solutions from existing ones [8].
- EC is a multi-step process. With the help of EC algorithms, real-time problems can be solved efficiently.
- Traditional optimization techniques are sensitive to dynamic environmental changes and finding a solution usually requires a fresh startup.

10.5.4 Disadvantages of EC

- Unable to guarantee that the results are optimal.
- For a good result, there should be a solid solution representation and a function evaluation.

10.5.5 Harnessing Evolutionary Computation for HAR Research

For HAR research, a basic collection of probable solutions is established and continuously updated in EC. The most common uses of EC include data compression and pattern identification, for example, facial recognition. EC can improve overall generalization during the training and testing phases. Normally, to identify human facial behaviors, genetic algorithm (GA) is used. EC can give a better result when compared with GA, because the fitness function is used to accomplish this. The fitness function determines both performance and classification accuracy. Finally, accuracy reveals how well learning has performed [16]. The evolutionary-based methodology revealed quite accurate results than random search purely based on evolution, proving that it is a reliable method for HAR using various data sets from sensing devices. *EC is a straightforward, multi-step procedure and real-time problems can be efficiently solved.*

10.6 Artificial Immune System

Artificial immune systems (AIS) are adaptable problem-solving platforms that gain their inspiration from theoretical immunology as well as from

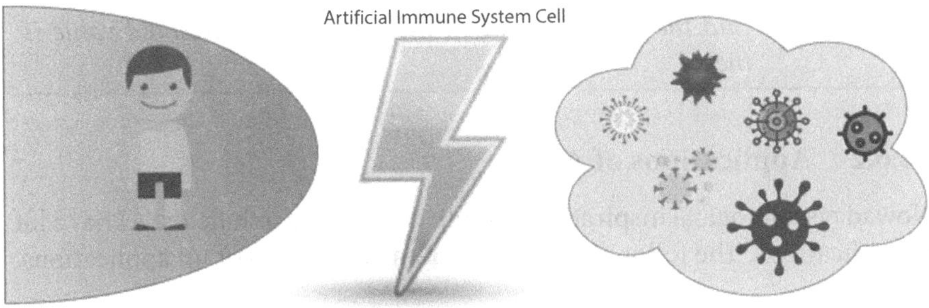

Figure 10.8 Graphical illustration of basic AIS.

ideas, theories, and simulations of actual immune function. AIS is unique from computational immunology and theoretical science, which focus on imitating immunology using a computer and mathematical models in order to better understand the immune system. However, such models acted as the fuel for the field of AIS and continue to serve as a rich source of ideas. AIS cells function as antibodies as well as computational intelligence. The principles and operations of the immune system of vertebrates are the foundation for rule-based machine learning systems. Figure 10.8 shows the graphical representation of basic AIS.

10.6.1 AIS Algorithm

In the current pandemic situation, AIS can be utilized as a creative solution. The AIS algorithm is implemented in the steps below:

Algorithm

Step 1	*Define and analyze the problem.*
Step 2	*Perform negative selection. In negative selection, random recombination of gene libraries produces inactive elements. Thus, tolerization should be performed. Tolerization is the elimination of auto-reactive elements by negative selection and the reduction of the lifespan of non-reactive elements. Negative selection is used to eliminate receptors that match autoantigens.*
Step 3	*Perform the positive selection for the finest non-auto reactive element. Immune components are activated based on a context principle.*

Step 4 *End the procedure, when the criterion or threshold value is met.*

10.6.2 Applications of AIS

Nowadays, biological inspiration is applied in CI research fields. AI has a lot of applications. The following are some of the most important applications.

- Single symbol identification, symbolic regression, and autonomous system management can all benefit from AIS.
- Used to classify remote sensing imagery.
- Used in computer security, virus detection, and robotics.
- Immunotronics is a technique for detecting and recovering errors in digital electronic systems using AIS ideas.

10.6.3 Advantages of AIS

- The immune system is widely dispersed, is extremely adaptive, is self-organizing in nature, and has a memory of previous interactions and also can learn about new encounters on a continuous basis.
- In the current pandemic situation in healthcare, AIS is used as natural immune systems; diversity, distributed computation, error tolerance, dynamic learning, adaptation, and self-monitoring can be included in AIS.
- Researchers have been inspired by the human immune system to develop sophisticated information processing algorithms that have addressed complicated technical challenges.
- Classification problems, optimization challenges, and other disciplines can all benefit from the AIS.

10.6.4 Disadvantages of AIS

- In combination with immune and other systems, AIS machine embedding is a difficult task. As a result, the best way to understand how the immune system works is to use trimming hybrid algorithms.
- In theoretical foundations for AIS, although the AIS technique has been expanded to a variety of problem domains, more work is required to grasp the essence of AISs and

where they are most effective. As a result, diverse AIS implementations are constrained.

10.6.5 Harnessing AIS for Preventive Measures

In the face of a pandemic, intensive research in the health sector is necessary. COVID-19 is the most critical concern in the healthcare industry. Researchers are working on a variety of methods to deal with the epidemic. Currently, computer vision and thermal technology are the most often used preventive methods, for example, the COVID-19 preventive system. The normal body temperature is between 37 and 38°C. The preventive system should be programmed so that if a person's temperature rises beyond 38°C, the system should send a warning message or display a color differentiation, indicating that the individual is experiencing COVID-19 symptoms. The data for the input can be gathered from public surveillance cameras and translated into frames. To convert from RGB to thermal colors, a variety of image processing approaches can be applied. This color variation is adjusted to reflect variations in people's body temperatures, and the data are then shown. Finally, we can personally instruct individuals who are suffering from symptoms on how to isolate themselves in order to avoid further complications. AIS can be used innovatively in pandemic scenarios.

10.7 Conclusion

In CI, there are numerous algorithms and perspectives to be considered. The availability and affordability of CI have driven rapid growth. In general, HAR is formulated as a classification issue. Human actions are recognized using pattern recognition, pervasive computing research, and recently deep learning technology. Researchers have been paying close attention to data analysis in surveillance, anti-terrorism, anti-crime security, fall risk management, fall detection, smart home monitoring, smart city, daily living activities, and also assisted living in the healthcare industry. CI based on HAR is a growing research field with a wide range of opportunities. The majority of research recently have focused on simple activities like walking, running, and sitting. In the future, new activities such as human behavior, events, and physiological conditions need to be focused on. In HAR study, feature selection and extraction techniques need to be utilized as researchers may find it more challenging to identify and extract features.

Because wearing a gadget for an extended period of time is tedious, the gadgets should be compact.

References

1. Reference available from: https://www.guru99.com/what-is-fuzzy-logic.html
2. Kumar, Abhishek, Swarn Avinash Kumar, Vishal Dutt, S. Shitharth, and Esha Tripathi. "IoT based arrhythmia classification using the enhanced hunt optimization-based deep learning." *Expert Syst.*, (2023): e13298.
3. Benkhaddra, I., Kumar, A., Setitra, M.A. *et al.* Design and Development of Consensus Activation Function Enabled Neural Network-Based Smart Healthcare Using BIoT. *Wirel. Pers Commun.*, 130, 1549–1574 (2023).
4. Ajagbe, Sunday Adeola, Yetunde J. Oguns, T. Ananth Kumar, Olukayode A. Okı, Oluwakemi Abosede Adeola-Ajagbe, Abolaji Okikiade Ilori, and Oyetunde Adeoye Adeaga. "Investigating Two-Stage Detection Methods Using Traffic Light Detection Dataset." In *Object Tracking Technology: Trends, Challenges and Applications*, pp. 249-274. Singapore: Springer Nature Singapore, 2023.
5. Reference available from:https://en.wikipedia.org/wiki/Evolutionary_computation
6. Reference available from: Introduction to Evolutionary Algorithms | by Devin Soni | Towards Data Science
7. Devadharshini, S., R. Kalaipriya, R. Rajmohan, M. Pavithra and T. Ananthkumar. "Performance investigation of hybrid Yolo-vgg16 based ship detection framework using SAR images." In *2020 International Conference on System, Computation, Automation and Networking (ICSCAN)*, pp. 1-6. IEEE, 2020.
8. Thiruvikraman, P., T. Ananth Kumar, R. Rajmohan and M. Pavithra. "A survey on haze removal techniques in satellite images." *Ir. Interdiscip. J. Sci. Res. (IIJSR)*, 5, no. 2 (2021): 01-06.
9. J.Susmitha, Kirupa Ganapathy,"*Fuzzy logic system to detect HAR*" Published by Blue Eyes Intelligence Engineering & Sciences Publications. Publication Details:ISSN: 2278-3075, Volume-8 Issue-12, October, 2019.
10. Tongbi Kang, Lian Ying, JiankangWu,Yi Sun and Xiaoli Meng," *Fuzzy Inference System for Physical Activity Recognition based on General Features* and PCA" Published by Atlantis press. Published on April 2013.
11. Min-Cheol Kwon and SunwoongChoi,"Recognition of Daily Human Activity using an Artificial Neural Network and Smartwatch" Published by Hindawi, *Wirel. Commun. Mob. Comput.*, Article Details: Volume 2018, Article ID 2618045, 9 pages, https://doi.org/10.1155/2018/2618045

12. Pugazhendiran, P., K. Suresh Kumar, T. Ananth Kumar and S. Sundaresan. "An Advanced Revealing and Classification System for Plant Illnesses Using Unsupervised Bayesian-based SVM Classifier and Modified HOG-ROI Algorithm." In *Contemporary Issues in Communication, Cloud and Big Data Analytics*, pp. 259-269. Springer, Singapore, 2022.
13. R.Karthigasri, M.Sornam, "Evaluating Performance Measures Using HybridModels With Fuzzy Finite State Machine ForHuman Activity Recognition". Publication Details: *Int. J. Sci. Technol. Res.*, VOLUME 9, ISSUE 04, APRIL 2020 ISSN2277-8616.
14. Prasanalakshmi, B. "Deep Regression hybridized Neural Network in human stress detection." In *2022 International Conference on Smart Technologies and Systems for Next Generation Computing (ICSTSN)*, pp. 1-5. IEEE, 2022.
15. Christine Dewiand Rung-Ching Chen, "*Human Activity Recognition Based on Evolution of FeaturesSelection and Random Forest*". Publication Details: Conference Paper · October 2019, DOI: 10.1109/SMC.2019.8913868
16. Stefan Tsokov, Milena Lazarova, Adelina Aleksieva,"*AN EVOLUTIONARY APPROACH TO THE DESIGN OF CONVOLUTIONAL NEURAL NETWORKS FOR HUMAN ACTIVITY RECOGNITION*". Published on: April 2021.
17. S. R. Burri, A. Kumar, A. Baliyan and T. A. Kumar, "Transforming Payment Processes: A Discussion of AI-Enabled Routing Optimization," *2023 2nd International Conference on Smart Technologies and Systems for Next Generation Computing (ICSTSN)*, Villupuram, India, 2023, pp. 1-7, doi: 10.1109/ICSTSN57873.2023.10151455.
18. Thangapriya and Nancy Jasmine Goldena, "A REVIEW ON HUMAN ACTIVITY RECOGNITION USING DATA MINING TECHNIQUES" Published by *Sarah Res. J.*, with ISSN No: 2319 5134, Volume : 9, ISSUE:1.

11

Computational Intelligence for Multimodal Analysis of High-Dimensional Image Processing in Clinical Settings

B. Balaji*, P. Pugazhendiran, N. Sivanantham, N. Velammal and P. Vimala

Department of EEE, IFET College of Engineering, Villupuram, TN, India

Abstract

Artificial intelligence (AI) has contributed significantly to health research and imaging technology advancements. Biomedical image processing leverages techniques such as image processing, machine learning, computer vision, supervised learning, big data analytics, and cloud technology. The medical industry utilizes fuzzy logic, Bayesian inference frameworks, statistics parts-based models, and reinforcement learning-based multistage picture segmentation methods. These technologies play a crucial role in computer-assisted medical disease detection and enable biomedical data analysts to interpret complex medical data, thus enhancing patient care. Biological data processing faces challenges such as high dimensionality, class imbalance, and limited database capacity. While traditional data collection methods are effective, modern technology offers superior solutions. Accurate diagnosis of interconnected diseases requires high-dimensional biological data and exceptional images. Cloud computing's storage and processing power are utilized to analyze biological data and construct globally accessible systems. DICOM-compliant cloud computing systems store and translate images into high-quality data, enabling the analysis of complexity-rich biomedical data models through multimodal techniques. Artificial intelligence strives to provide high-quality data, accurate models, and straightforward solutions to complex challenges in biomedical processing.

***Keywords*:** Machine learning, artificial neural network, multimodal analysis, image processing, multimodal analysis

**Corresponding author*: balaji.bc91@gmail.com

T. Ananth Kumar, E. Golden Julie, Venkata Raghuveer Burugadda, Abhishek Kumar and Puneet Kumar (eds.) Computational Intelligence: Theory and Applications, (235–262) © 2024 Scrivener Publishing LLC

11.1 Basics of Machine Learning

Machine learning has emerged as a widely embraced approach for tackling complex computational tasks, reflecting human learning methods. This represents a departure from the earlier paradigm prevalent in early AI systems, which heavily relied on rule-based creation and application. The significance of machine learning lies in its ability to effectively learn from examples, which requires both data availability and processing prowess. The early failures of so-called expert systems, partly attributed to their rigid rule-based structure that could not accommodate numerous exceptions, cast doubts on AI's potential. Understanding the mechanics of machine learning involves drawing parallels with human learning and task execution. Consider the process of identifying a specific plant in a collection.

Similarly, a person would examine diverse plant specimens, potentially referring to literature for differentiation cues. Various attributes such as stem length, leaf size, color, and vein orientation become focal points. Implicitly, these steps involve fundamental cognitive actions [1–3].

The human eye initially processes images or instances, akin to image acquisition in medical imaging. Subsequently, distinguishing between stem and leaf corresponds to image segmentation, which is crucial in tasks like discerning muscle areas in mammograms or differentiating brain matter in MRI scans. Beyond aiding feature extraction, segmentation holds independent utility. Returning to our initial example, stem length, and leaf color characteristics assume prominence as distinguishing features. Notably, an array of traits exists in plant anatomy, encompassing intricate aspects such as primary and secondary vein lengths. Selecting discriminative traits constitutes feature selection and extraction [4–8].

Eventually, determining whether the plant is an eggplant or tomato entails aggregating and evaluating data gleaned from these features. This stage is classification, illustrated as a fundamental step in traditional machine learning algorithms (Figure 11.1). Responding to the surge of deep learning's popularity—a subset showcasing prowess in feature learning —the nomenclature "classical machine learning" has recently gained traction. This chapter aims to give newcomers essential insights, facilitating their journey through forthcoming topics in diverse applications. The objective is to provide a concise classical machine learning overview accompanied by illustrative examples rather than an exhaustive introduction. For comprehensive understanding, supplementary references are available [9–11].

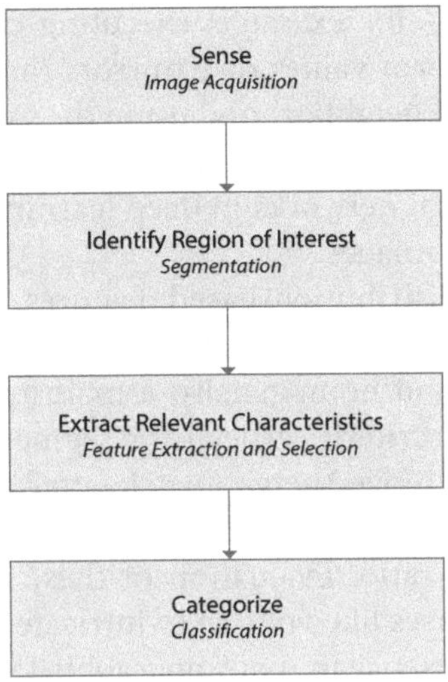

Figure 11.1 Process of classification.

11.2 Feature Extraction

In machine learning applied to imaging, feature extraction plays a pivotal role in extracting pertinent information from images before presenting it to a classifier. For the present discussion, the focus rests on feature selection in image processing applications. Categorization pertinent to medical images, and by extension, images in a broader context, encompasses three primary types: first-order features, second-order features, and higher-order features [12–15].

- Characteristics, in general, are used to extract information that describes the image's content, such as form, texture, color, and so on.
- Application-specific traits like a person's face, iris, or fingerprint exemplify domain-specific qualities. Gabor filters are commonly employed for extracting such features.

Statistical summaries that effectively portray the dynamic changes in intensity within a region of interest encompass essential metrics such as mean, median, and standard deviation alongside more intricate indicators, including skewness and kurtosis. Streamlining this process, there are instances where the convolution of an N × N kernel with an image, followed by a sliding window approach, utilizes matrix multiplication to expedite the operation—for example, executing convolution with a 3 × 3 kernel featuring uniform values of 1 mirrors the outcome of averaging each pixel within a 3 × 3 neighborhood using the same 3 × 3 kernel configuration of all 1s. These kernels and neighborhood determinations, adeptly handled by convolutional networks in deep learning, underpin the salient features extracted from images.

In pixel intensity distribution-based features, two prominent attributes stand out: entropy, which gauges the unpredictability of pixel intensity distribution, and homogeneity, a mainstay in radionics studies. Regarding shape-based criteria, crucial for segmenting suspicious lesion candidates, they characterize the geometric attributes of the target area. Measurements include volume, height, curvature, shape index, diameter, and surface-to-volume ratio. Evaluation of these attributes might range from straightforward cases like volume to intricate scenarios such as indices assessing spicule presence in mammographic lesions, often requiring a preliminary segmentation phase.

Intertwining pixel intensity and spatial relationships, texture features—also known as second-order radiomics features in specific contexts—define the nature of intensity fluctuations within areas of interest. Texture attributes are built through descriptive matrices. Key among these is the gray-level co-occurrence matrix (GLCM), quantifying the lengths of consecutive pixels with identical intensity, and the gray-level run-length (GLRL) matrix, outlining instances of dual intensity levels spanning two pixels at a defined distance and angle. Furthermore, higher-order characteristics can be harnessed for capturing intricate visual patterns by incorporating filters like the Fourier transform, space-frequency analysis through wavelets, or fractal analysis.

11.3 Selection of Features

Feature selection aims to enhance data manageability by eliminating less informative attributes. This can be conceptualized in one of two ways: identifying features that effectively capture the underlying causes of a particular issue or selecting features that yield optimal classification results. Regardless, the feature selection process must withstand data transformations like pre-processing, prioritize features that offer more pertinent data for classification, and discard redundant features. As the classification step is omitted and class labels' information is not utilized, the initial phase primarily focuses on reducing dimensionality based on the inherent feature distribution.

A prominent example of this approach is principal component analysis (PCA), which aims to transform original variables into orthogonal components with maximal variance at each stage. Another method, independent component analysis (ICA), transforms variables, assuming that including independent non-Gaussian distributed sources leads to the observed data. Supervised methods are commonly employed for feature selection in medical imaging processing, particularly in classification tasks. A comprehensive categorization of supervised feature selection techniques is detailed in [4]. This taxonomy is initially divided into two main branches: statistical pattern recognition methods and neural network systems employing node pruning.

The latter branch is further divided into optimal techniques, which assess classification performance across all possible feature combinations, and suboptimal strategies, which refine specific outcomes. For instance, in feedforward selection methodologies, the solution iteratively expands by selecting the feature that maximally enhances classification accuracy at each step. Conversely, evolutionary methods like genetic algorithms can simultaneously evaluate numerous potential solutions. In classification, wrapper techniques are often denoted as multivariate supervised feature selection methods. Given the retrieval of numerous features in radionics applications, feature selection is pivotal, but it holds significance across various applications. It is important to note that simpler, univariate strategies may serve as a helpful starting point for quickly grasping data distribution. Ref. [5] serves as a classic reference, providing a general framework of feature extraction principles, while Ref. [6–8] outlines various techniques utilized in image processing applications. Readers seeking further insights can explore the extensive literature detailing diverse feature extraction techniques.

11.4 Statistical Classifiers

Machine learning encompasses three primary categories: supervised, unsupervised, and semi-supervised learning, each addressing distinct problem types. In supervised learning, a dataset containing input–output pairs (training data) is provided to uncover the relationship between inputs and their corresponding outputs. Once established, this connection enables predicting the associated output for new inputs. An exemplary case of supervised learning is classification, where a supervised approach establishes the connection between features and classes (forming a classification model) based on examples featuring object attributes (features) and their corresponding types (classes), enabling the prediction of an object's class based on its features. In contrast, unsupervised learning operates solely with inputs, lacking corresponding outputs. Its objective is to elucidate the underlying structure inherent in the input data, precious when discerning potential groups or clusters within the data, a process known as clustering. Straddling a middle ground between supervised and unsupervised learning, semi-supervised learning employs a partially complete training dataset containing only some desired outputs [9–12].

Each of these learning challenges can be addressed using various machine-learning techniques. The fundamental concepts, formalisms, and notations in the context of classification involve a set of N instances serving as input data, represented as tuples (x, y), where x = (x1, x2,..., xn) denotes a collection of n attributes, and y signifies the class to which the instance belongs. While feature vectors can include discrete values, most machine learning methods require real-valued features, with the class label denoted as y = y1, y2, yM, encompassing all such labels, where M represents the number of classes. Classification involves learning a target function f that maps each feature vector x to a corresponding class label y, also known as the classification model or classifier. A classifier, represented as a function f with values within y1, yM and defined in X, where X is a subset of Rn, must generalize well beyond the training data to new instances. This entails minimizing the risk of incorrect classification, typically measured by a specific loss function L(y, f(x)) that quantifies the error incurred when predicting f(x) instead of y.

Classifiers can be categorized into statistical classifiers (Bayesian, logistic regression, and SVMs) and non-statistical classifiers (e.g., rule-based expert systems). They can be linear or nonlinear, employing parametric or non-parametric mapping functions. The subsequent discussion will cover the most popular classifiers.

(i) Bayesian Classifiers

A commonly employed method for accurately determining the class of instance x involves treating both the feature vector x and the class label y as stochastic variables. This framework calculates the posterior class probabilities P(y|x) for the specific instance x. Subsequently, instance x is assigned to class i, where P(yi|x) reaches its maximum value [13, 15].

$$x \in yi, \text{ if } P(yi|x) > P(yj|x)\ \forall\ i \neq j \tag{11.1}$$

Although simple in concept, the challenge arises when dealing with the unknown structure of P(y|x) while presented with a collection of N instances {(xi, yi)} Ni = 1. The objective is to estimate P(y|x) based on these prototype instances, a process that follows fundamental principles of probability theory [16–18].

$$P(yi|x)P(x) = P(yi, x) = P(x|yi)P(yi) \tag{11.2}$$

These rules allow us to estimate P(yj|x) in terms of P(x|yj) and P(yj):

$$p(y_i|x) = \frac{p(x|y_i)p(y_i)}{p(x)} \tag{11.3}$$

When aiming to predict, it is often more probable to work with P(x|y) and P(y) instead of directly guessing P(y|x). Here, P(x) is determined as the normalization constant within the denominator, guaranteeing that the posterior probabilities sum up to one. Meanwhile, $P(y_i)$ signifies the class prior probability within the Bayesian statistics framework—the likelihood of an occurrence belonging to class y_i. This parameter can be estimated utilizing the fraction of instances attributed to class y_i within the training set [19, 20]. Within this context, the class-conditional probability density function, denoted as $P(x|y_i)$, represents the likelihood of observing instance x under the condition that it belongs to class y_i. On the other hand, accurately estimating P(x|y) poses challenges as it entails calculating many joint probabilities involving features. For instance, if y is a Boolean and x is an n-dimensional vector of Boolean attributes, estimating the subsequent parameters becomes necessary:

$$\theta_{ki} = P(x_k|y_j) \tag{11.4}$$

Index k encompasses n potential values corresponding to the various possible vector values of xk. Simultaneously, the index I can take on two feasible values. Describing P(x|y) necessitates estimating 2(2n - 1) parameters. The complexity is compounded by the requirement to observe each distinct case to obtain reliable parameter estimates frequently. In practical learning scenarios, this approach becomes profoundly unfeasible. To alleviate the intricacy of estimating P(x|y) and enhance sample efficiency, a straightforward strategy assumes that each feature operates independently of the values of other features given y. This assumption reduces the number of required samples. The following equation captures this assumption of independence:

$$p(x|y_i) = \prod_{j=1}^{n} p(x_j\, |y_i) \tag{11.5}$$

Naive Bayes classifiers [14] are probabilistic classifiers that embrace this assumption. Although the assumption of feature independence often does not hold in real-world scenarios, Naive Bayes classifiers can often outperform more intricate classifiers across diverse datasets [21].

11.5 Neural Networks

The brain's parallel architecture has provided a blueprint for crafting artificial neural networks (ANNs) modeled after biological neural networks. ANNs encompass a set of mathematical formulations tailored to replicate biological functions such as memory and learning [22]. Although grounded in biology, ANNs can be analyzed through statistical methods [10, 23]. ANNs are statistical algorithms that illustrate complex, nonlinear associations between variables. In situations where a sample originates from an unknown function f(x) (coupled with a stochastic element), denoted as $T = (x_i, y_i)\ N_i = 1$,

$$y_i = f(x_i) + €_I \tag{11.6}$$

The network's objective, termed "connection weights," involves constructing an estimator g(x, w) for f(x), where w = (w1...,w) represents a set of independent parameters. From this perspective, an artificial neural network (ANN) essentially functions as g(x, w), an entity that outlines an approximate transformation from input to output. The ANN's composition comprises three pivotal elements: (1) fundamental processing units, referred to as neurons or nodes; (2) network architecture, specifying interconnections among nodes; and (3) the training technique, which identifies parameter values to enable the network's performance in a specific task. This discourse focuses exclusively on supervised neural networks, implying scenarios where models are developed with predefined objective or outcome variables [23].

Nodes within the network are organized in layers, a configuration evident in Figure 11.2. Positioned between the input and output layers are the so-called "hidden" layers. The application's requirements predetermine the

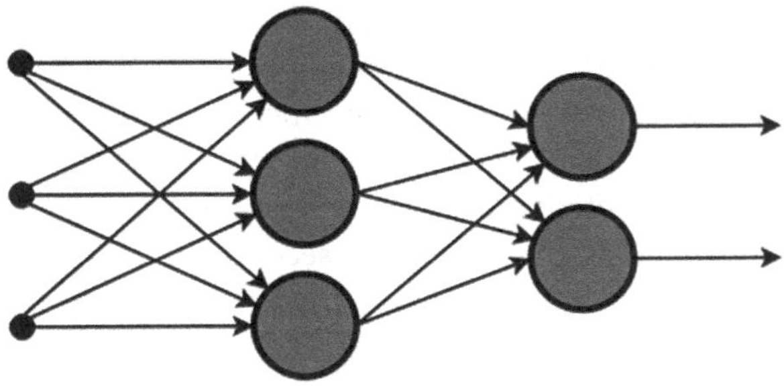

Figure 11.2 Neural network with multilayer.

count of input units. The lines linking nodes illustrate the progression of information from one node to the next. Notably, the network lacks internal loops; no pathways exist within the network that would allow the output of a unit to impact its input. Figure 11.2 showcases this feature, where information strictly flows from the input towards the output in a conventional feedforward network [24].

If the network has loops, it is a recurrent or feedback network rather than a feedforward network. Here, the feedforward network model is mentioned. The nodes in the input layer are passive, meaning they do not alter the data. They replicate a single value from their input over several different outputs. The nodes in the upper layers are semi-linear units that balance the total of their input signals before applying a nonlinear function known as the activation function to the outcome to produce the unit's output or activation. Various activation functions are used, but the majority are sigmoidal functions like the logistic function (x) = 1/ (1+ex) or hyperbolic tangent functions. The rectified linear function f(x) = max is another popular choice (0, x). In a feedforward ANN, each output node's activation is a nonlinear function of the network's input units' activation patterns. The network's weights determine these output values. Each output node provides the output value y_i of belonging to this class by multiplying the input vector by the output set given an unknown input vector $x = (x_1, x_2, \ldots, xn)$ and an output set $y = y_1, y_2, \ldots, y_M$.

$$\hat{y}_i = \Phi\{\sum_k w^{om}{}_{ik}(\sum_k w^{mj}{}_{ki} x_j)\}$$

In this context, the weight linking the kth hidden unit to the ith class output is significant and analogous to a perceptron. The node with the highest value is paired accordingly. The utilization of stochastic gradient training is prevalent in ANN techniques. Refining network weights is instrumental in enhancing its overall performance, a metric often gauged through minimizing or maximizing an objective function. In supervised learning, this objective function translates to the anticipated loss observed across labeled training data. Anticipating the impact of weight adjustments on the network's performance or calculating the second derivative of the objective function concerning each weight using the network's current weights for all connections becomes crucial. A widely employed strategy is backpropagation [23–25], encompassing two distinct phases: forward and backward.

In the forward phase, input signals progress through layers sequentially. Once output layer neurons emit output signals, error signals are generated by contrasting the actual output response with the predicted counterpart. In the subsequent backward phase, the weights of individual neurons are adjusted proportionally to diminish the observed inaccuracies. Comprehensive insights into backpropagation can be found in Refs. [7, 25].

11.6 Biometric Analysis

Image processing plays a crucial role in identifying individuals through biometric images. Biometric systems, whether focusing on faces, fingerprints, or irises, rely on image processing and pattern recognition techniques. An image-based biometric system requires clear, unaltered samples to operate effectively. These systems analyze and interpret biometric images to authenticate and verify individuals' identities accurately.

(i) Biometrics image processing

The user's biometric data are received and processed in a biometric system. The technology applies equations to alter the image, saving the calculation for each pixel. Through digital processing, the data undergo selective enhancement to highlight fine details while eliminating noise. Image processing in this context typically falls into three functional categories: image restoration, smoothing, and enhancement.

(ii) Biometric technologies

Biometric technology has undergone rapid advancement over the past two decades. The term "biometric" is derived from "bio" and "metric," referring to the measurement of biological data. "Biometrics" specifically pertains to bodily traits that serve as unique identifiers for individuals.

1. Biometrics is the measuring of biological signals in broad terms.
2. Biometrics may be classified in various ways, including "strong," "weak," and "soft" identifiers.

Strong identifiers like fingerprints, iris, and retina allow for precise identification or verification of a real person. Soft biometrics refer to traits not explicitly linked to an individual, such as gender or age. Weak biometrics, including bodily form, behavioral patterns, voice, and body noises, are less distinctive or stable. Modern biometric technologies enable automated processing and conversion of biometric identifiers from analog to digital, distinguishing them from analog, human-performed biometrics. Fully automated identification is now possible, thanks to the ability to gather, process, and compare biometric identifiers without human agents. The introduction of potent scanners for biometric identification has led to a large and rapidly developing field of biometric methods. First- and second-generation biometric technology are commonly distinguished in this field.

(iii) Identification, categorization, and detection

Biometric techniques can be categorized into authentication, identification, categorization, and detection as shown in Figure 11.3. Biometric identity involves identifying or verifying a person based on physical, biological, or behavioral features. In this study, "identification" and "authentication" are distinguished in a narrower sense. Authentication is a "one-to-one" comparison that compares a claimant's live template with the saved templates in a template database. In contrast, identification, in this narrower sense, is a "one-to-many" evaluation in which individuals being identified do not assert a specific identity. However, that identity is established—often without their knowledge or consent—by matching live templates with templates saved in a database.

"Biometric classification" is less common than "biometric identity" since "soft" or "weak" biometrics are used. Data not fitting for a herbal character's identity can be used to categorize them according to gender, ethnicity, or health. Depending on the number and level of subcategories, the cumulative mission may also allow or authenticate a herbal character's identification. Last, "biometric detection" can also refer to biometric methodologies used to identify human moods like anger, fear, a specific intent (even to commit a crime), or a particular sickness. Emotional identity structures—structures that recognize or infer feelings, beliefs, or intentions of real persons based on bio-indicators—have drawn much interest [26–29]. Due to the increasing usage of "soft" or "weak" biometrics,

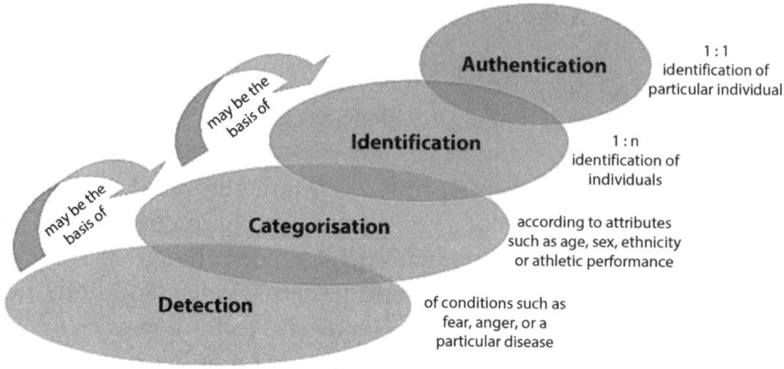

Figure 11.3 Identification, categorization, and detection.

bio-indicators, and behavioral characteristics that computers can detect and process, it is harder to differentiate biometric techniques from herbal character profiling. The term "biometric" generally signifies immutability, i.e., that the character has little to no chance of changing the traits or indications under investigation, such as a face or dactyloscopic pattern. Biometric techniques include evaluating keyboard and mouse dynamics, gesture, signature, speech, and gait attributes. The word no longer refers to behaviors that humans can more easily control, such as purchase preferences, web browsing history, or letter content.

(iv) Biometrics steps

Biometric identification involves multiple techniques, each with its ethical considerations as shown in Figure 11.4. First, pre-market, the technology's development must be legally and ethically justified using biometric sample data. This stage brings comparable legal and ethical issues as data-driven technology grows. Given the sensitivity of biometric ID systems, discriminatory effects must be avoided. The enrollment process involves the collection of biometric data, the extraction of specific features, the input of these features into templates, and the storage of the templates in a reference database. The next step entails gathering and examining real-time templates, which comprise biometric input data obtained from individuals on the street, after the system has become operational. Again, biometric input data require special processing, including trait extraction. After comparing live and saved templates, a matching score is calculated. Based on the system's judgment policies, different match scores will prompt reactions, such as giving or denying building access, requesting additional identity

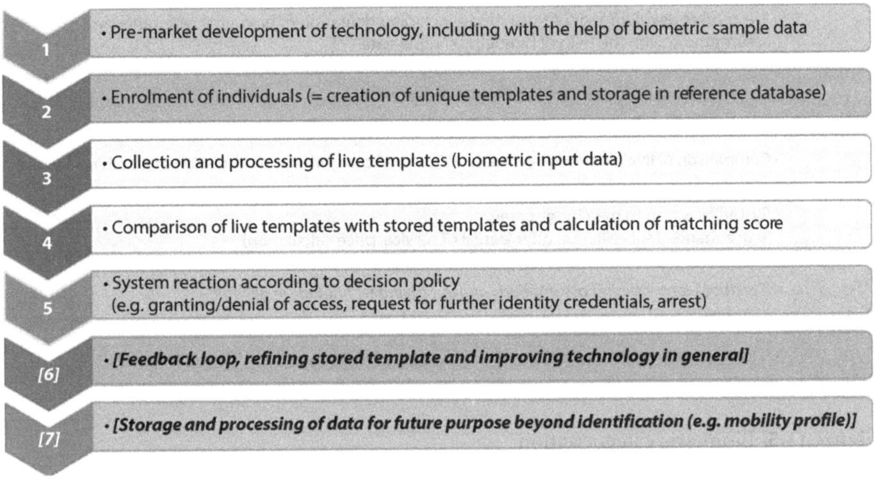

Figure 11.4 Biometric identification.

information, or increasing monitoring. Depending on the responses triggered by algorithms, ethical issues may arise.

(v) Biometric classification steps

While biometric identity structures commonly use "strong" biometric systems to distinctively pick out individuals, biometric categorization structures may also utilize "soft" biometrics. These soft biometrics do not, at least not explicitly, establish unique identity but instead allow for the assignment of individuals to a particular group or class. Such classes may be based on factors like ethnicity, religion, (dis-)ability, or age, with more complex categories including geography, chance, or character. Biometric categorization and identity require different methodologies.

The pre-market development period of biometric categorization systems poses moral challenges. Defining biometric classes and hypotheses, which can be complex, is crucial during development to ensure the technology is not discriminatory or stigmatizing when used. Steps involve collecting and processing live biometric input data, comparing it with preserved statistical classes, and computing matching scores. Decision-making processes, such as responding to a matching score, may include presenting or rejecting a contractual offer or calculating a price. These challenges are not unique to algorithmic decision-making and technology.

Verified classes can contribute to improved device training in the case of biometric categorization as in Figure 11.5. However, collecting and

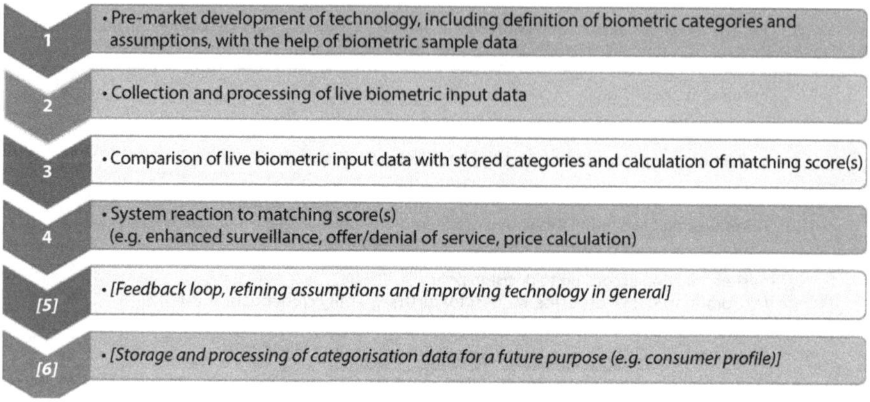

Figure 11.5 Biometric categorization.

processing categorization data for future use, such as creating a customer profile, raises ethical concerns that must be addressed.

(vi) Biometric steps

The steps required for biometric detection are pretty comparable to those for biometric classification, as depicted in Figure 11.6. This is not surprising, given the close relationship between biometric categorization and detection and the frequent use of biometric detection to classify individuals based on certain conditions (such as a specific health condition, e.g., persons with disabilities). Determining which bio-signals lead to which assumptions is crucial, similar to biometric classification systems. The system's responses are equally critical from an ethical perspective.

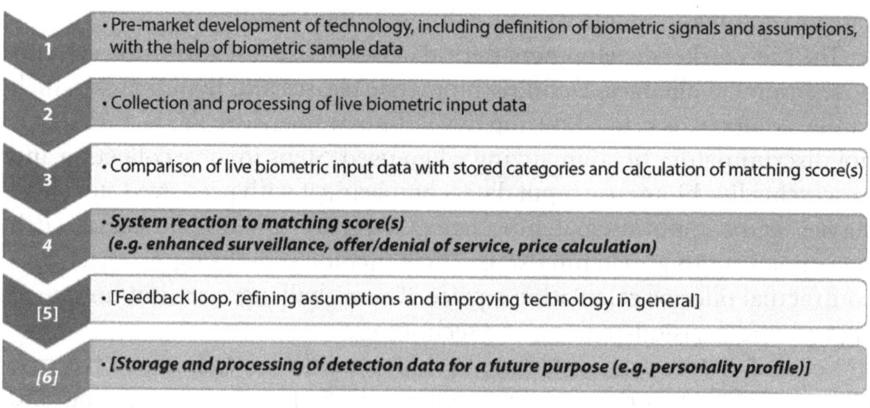

Figure 11.6 Biometric detection.

The collection and processing of live biometric input data in biometric detection are often significantly more ethically sensitive than biometric classification. This is because biometric detection frequently involves extremely personal circumstances, including a person's emotions, thoughts, and intentions. Acquiring this kind of input data may raise privacy, self-integrity, and human dignity issues. However, making general statements regarding different levels of ethical sensitivity in biometric classification and detection is challenging, as the context and objectives of each may differ significantly.

(vii) Risk-based biometrics

The AIA Proposal shown in Figure 11.7, recommends the implementation of a risk-based approach, classifying AI systems into four different risk tiers: unacceptable risk, high risk, transparent risk, and other AI systems that, because of their low risk profile, do not require specific regulations. Biometric procedures can be categorized into one of four risk categories based on their composition and the context in which they are used. Article 5(1)(d) and (2) through (4) of the AIA Proposal delineates the list of "prohibited AI operations," which includes remote, real-time, publicly accessible biometric identification conducted for law enforcement purposes. However, upon closer examination, it becomes apparent that the suggested constraints do not explicitly prohibit these operations; they are permitted only under specific circumstances. The AIA Proposal primarily focuses on "high-risk" AI systems. These systems are subject to the requirement of an ex-ante conformity examination and the legislative requirements outlined in Title III. Article 6(1) identifies the AI systems meeting the criteria for high-risk systems in conjunction with specific product safety standards.

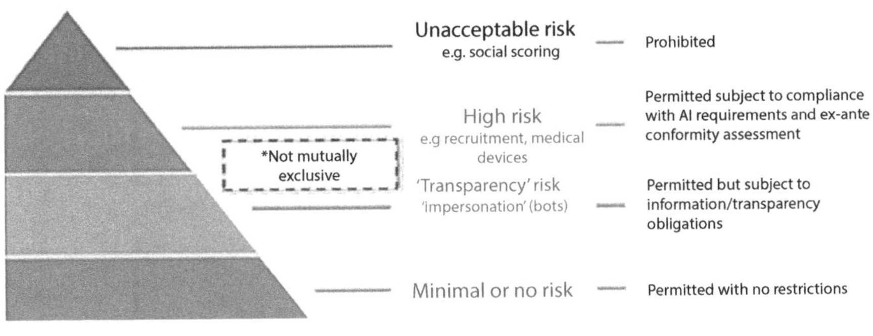

Figure 11.7 AIA Proposal risk-based.

According to Article 52(2) of the AIA Proposal, emotion recognition and biometric categorization systems must have specific transparency measures. This means that users of these systems need to inform people who are being exposed to them about how they work. Biometric procedures are included within the scope of Title IV, which specifically deals with AI systems that present a "transparency risk" and those that are classified as "high-risk" under Title III. Importantly, the levels of hazard are not mutually exclusive. Hence, any biometric identification system that operates remotely in real time and falls under the scope of Title II (unless explicitly prohibited by that Title) must also adhere to all the stipulations outlined in Title III. Emotion recognition systems, similar to biometric categorization systems, may occasionally fulfill the requirements for high-risk systems according to Title IV, owing to their specific uses. This underscores the importance of transparency measures and compliance with regulatory standards across various levels of risk within the AIA Proposal.

Title III of the AIA Proposal includes sections specifically addressing biometrics. According to Article 12(4), biometric identification and classification systems are mandated to record various details, such as the timestamp of each usage, the specific reference dataset used for comparison, the input data leading to a match, and the individuals involved in verifying outcomes. Additionally, Article 14(5) requires that human supervision mechanisms for such systems ensure that users refrain from acting or making decisions based on the system's identification until at least two real people have verified it. Distant biometric identification systems typically undergo third-party conformity assessments, unlike stand-alone high-risk AI systems, which providers often evaluate through internal management

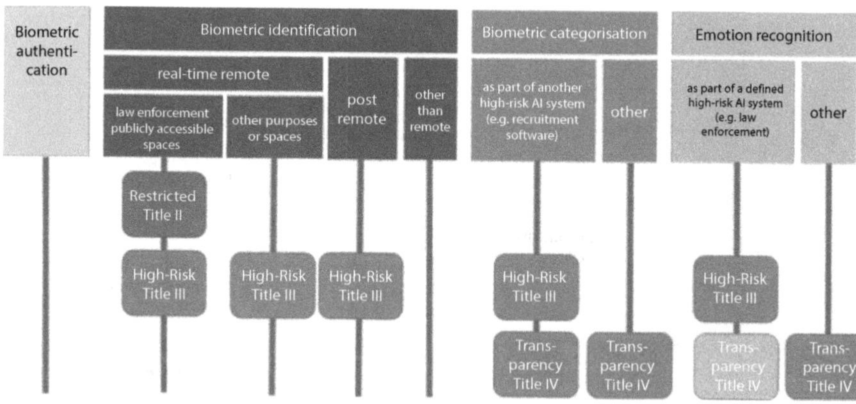

Figure 11.8 Biometric techniques.

checks. This underscores the stringent oversight and accountability measures applied to biometric technologies under the AIA Proposal's regulatory framework. The Biometric techniques is shown in Figure 11.8.

11.7 Data from High-Resolution Medical Imaging

Significant progress has been made in the development of deep learning architectures, computing power, and expert-labeled datasets for medical imaging artificial intelligence (AI) systems. This has allowed these systems to compete with medical professionals. However, the integration of AI systems to assist with basic medical tasks continues to present significant challenges. The introduction of machine learning algorithms into healthcare facilities with the intention of improving the speed at which results can be applied clinically has led to an escalation in patient wait times. End users of AI systems need to learn how to integrate these systems into established medical practices and address issues such as input quality control and network latency outside of controlled laboratory settings.

The initial attempts to apply medical machine learning in practical settings have highlighted the significance of conducting thorough integrative efforts during algorithm development. This is because there are limited opportunities for making modifications once the algorithms are deployed. The advancement of computer performance and the availability of extensive open-source machine learning software libraries have enabled the creation of more complex artificial intelligence systems tailored to address specific medical issues.

Furthermore, it is crucial for future AI systems to consider the systemic biases found in training data, inform end users about the inherent uncertainty in predictions, and provide ways for them to explore and understand the underlying mechanisms behind these predictions. This perspective elaborates on three crucial priority areas for expediting essential AI research in medicine:

1. We are investigating explainability, uncertainty, bias, dataset curation nuances, and architecture challenges associated with machine learning for high-dimensional medical imaging in these systems.
2. We provide a roadmap for academics addressing the concerns and challenges of creating clinically relevant AI systems.

3. We are promoting collaboration between academia, industry, and healthcare providers to foster the development and deployment of AI technologies in medicine.

There is an anticipated shortage in the supply of advanced "AI-ready" annotated medical datasets shortly. Creating retrospective medical ground truth label projects requires significant effort from medical professionals, and aggregating data from multiple institutions for public use presents significant challenges. In addition to "diagnostic AI," which is trained using complex radiological ground truth labels, there is a need for "disease prediction AI" that relies on potentially less accurate composite medical outcome goals.

Collecting prospective data using specific methodologies for capturing and evaluating accurate medical information is essential for creating large-scale imaging datasets across multiple medical centers, which can be correlated with clinical outcomes. However, the existence of sensitive data in extensive multicenter imaging datasets gives rise to several concerns regarding privacy and liability.

The Digital Imaging and Communication in Medicine (DICOM) standard was developed as a solution to address these concerns, and it has since become widely adopted for the collection, storage, and management of medical images. DICOM files store both pixel data and associated metadata. DICOM data can be de-identified using a range of commercial and

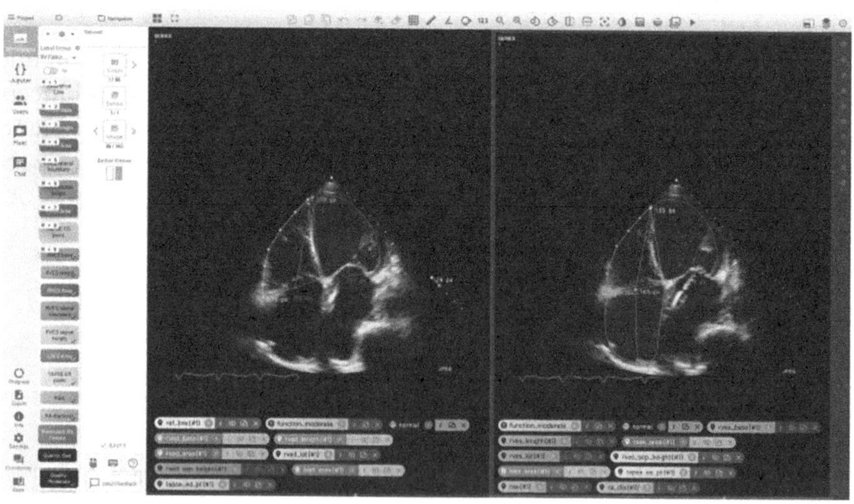

Figure 11.9 Cloud-based tools such as MD.

open-source techniques. Backend clinical informatics frameworks such as the Google Healthcare API enable the implementation of secure de-identification procedures, which involve removing metadata fields that may contain sensitive information.

Despite being widely used, the MIRC Clinical Trials Processor anonymizer is compromised due to outdated software components, which require careful examination. Contrarily, extensively documented Python tools can be used to process DICOM files before they are transmitted or utilized by relevant institutions. Subsequently, data can be derived from these images and stored in machine-readable formats. While this perspective does not extensively delve into data storage techniques, it is crucial in the field of medical imaging AI to preserve image resolution. Managing the size of databases becomes a challenging task due to their capacity for rapid and significant expansion. An often highlighted constraint of automated de-identification methods or scripts is the possibility of permanently embedding protected health information onto imaging files, commonly referred to as "burning in". The implementation of universal guidelines for instruments like the MIRC Clinical Trials Processor to filter regions containing potentially sensitive health information is hindered by manufacturer-specific variations, despite the existence of the DICOM standard. By employing basic machine learning techniques, it is feasible to efficiently address this problem. The heart can be visible within a specific scanning area during an echocardiography procedure. Using machine learning-based optical character recognition technologies is an alternative method for identifying and concealing areas that contain printed text. Figure 11.9 demonstrates the cloud based tools.

Furthermore, DICOM tags can encompass scan-level specifics and modality-specific data. Figure 11.10 demonstrates that crucial scan-stage details, such as acquisition body rates, date, and MRI sequence (T1/T2), can be easily extracted from DICOM metadata in cardiac magnetic resonance imaging (MRI) and echocardiography. To facilitate research projects, it is advantageous to maintain a duplicate of the scans in DICOM format. This allows for direct comparisons between AI systems and physicians, as well as the creation of comprehensive datasets with the assistance of medical annotators. This allows for the use of user-friendly and scalable annotation tools that are based on cloud technology. Scans can be assigned to medical professionals for review using different methods, such as using anatomical segmentation masks specific to the field and important labels at the scan level. MD.ai, a cloud-based annotation system that we have developed, offers inherent compatibility with DICOM data stored on cloud storage services with institutional authorization.

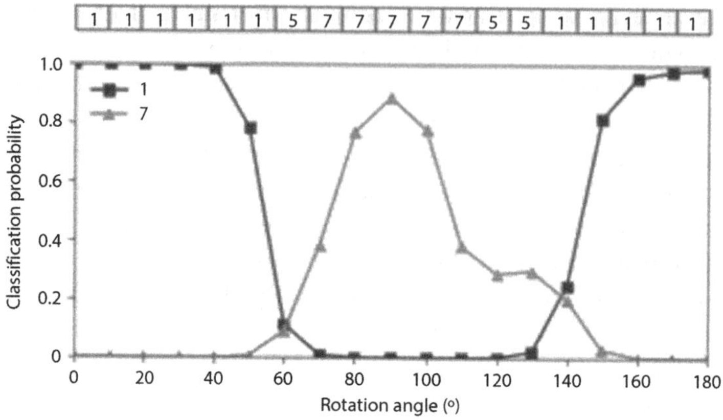

Figure 11.10 Machine learning models trained with standard methods.

Cloud-based annotation preserves the original quality and resolution of the scans, while real-time collaboration replicates the clinical decision-making process. The process of exporting annotations and labels is straightforward, and these technologies can be remotely accessed via any modern web browser. This not only enhances the user experience but also reduces the technological burden on research collaborators. Federated learning and other innovative machine learning training models have the potential to address a range of data-sharing challenges. Kaissis *et al.* examined the core principles, practical obstacles, and security considerations of federated learning. Every institution independently trains its own variations of the models, and only the acquired characteristics of the neural network are exchanged.

The knowledge gathered from each institution's algorithm is aggregated and disseminated at predefined intervals, leading to faster training of systems recognizing COVID-19 in chest CT images. Despite the effectiveness of supervised learning in medical imaging, clinical deployment still faces technological challenges. In large image learning systems, increasing network latency due to transmitting and updating learned weights from multiple centers becomes a significant hurdle in training more extensive neural networks. Researchers must ensure that training weights are securely encrypted across institutions to mitigate network latency. Evaluating datasets for quality and consistency becomes challenging without access to source data. Although many distributed learning systems are similar, access to source data remains essential.

11.8 Computational Architectures

Most modern medical machine-learning architectures have been developed for image or video recognition tasks. These architectures are highly robust, even with fine-grained categorization challenges involving minor intraclass variations. With proper pretraining on large datasets, "off-the-shelf" architectures outperform custom classifiers. These architectures can be utilized with frameworks like TensorFlow and PyTorch, which integrate ImageNet pre-trained parameters for various neural network architectures, enabling researchers to adapt them to medical imaging workloads quickly.

Unlike static images, most medical imaging modalities produce dynamic sequences. For example, echocardiograms provide 2D ultrasonograms of the heart from multiple views, offering a comprehensive examination. Similarly, CT and MRI images resemble 2D snapshots that must be analyzed to discern organ interactions. Video-based neural net algorithms outperform their 2D counterparts in echocardiography, CT, and MRI examinations, especially when incorporating multiple unique view planes to add dimension to current frames.

Video algorithms lack the same level of support as pre-trained image-based networks, which benefit from access to comprehensive libraries. To incorporate newer designs, researchers will likely need to undergo pre-training stages using large, publicly available video datasets like Kinetics and UCF101. Furthermore, the costs of computational resources required for training video networks can be significantly increased. While pre-training enhances performance, especially on smaller datasets, its efficacy diminishes with larger training datasets.

The 2018 roadmap of the National Institutes of Health highlighted the lack of dedicated architectures for medical imaging as a significant issue. In order to effectively apply these models in real-world scenarios, it is advisable to train them on more extensive and contextually relevant objectives. Current medical imaging AI systems primarily focus on detecting a small set of diseases within a background of normal cases, often using binary classifications (disease: 1; normal: 0). However, medical trainees are taught how to interpret imaging investigations by using various diagnostic labels. Novel methodologies have been proposed to train 3D medical imaging-based artificial intelligence systems through self-supervised pre-training, employing extensive unlabeled medical imaging datasets. These methods strive to provide a more profound "clinical comprehension" in contrast to conventional pretraining methods that depend on natural images or videos.

The integration of scan data and physician reports using AI techniques has proven to be highly effective, particularly in the domain of chest X-rays. The content of the reports is analyzed using modern natural language processing algorithms, while the visual network is trained to distinguish between diseases with greater accuracy, thus enhancing neural networks with supplementary knowledge. These methods can greatly reduce the amount of annotated data required for subsequent classification.

Unlabeled imaging studies, alone or combined with text reports, can be used for pretraining, followed by fine-tuning specific supervised learning tasks using high-quality ground truth data.

Building unique architectures for specific applications requires skill, but these methods enable the adaptation of neural net architectures for medical imaging, enhancing their performance. Model architecture, akin to the brain, and learned weights—optimized mathematical functions—are like the mind. Evolutionary search methods utilize machine learning to generate job-specific designs, creating structures that outperform human-made ones. GPUs facilitate deep learning's massively parallel matrix multiplications, making them indispensable for training complex neural networks.

Researchers can leverage cloud computing pay-as-you-go GPUs and consumer GPUs with large memory capacities to build machine learning algorithms for medical imaging. While training network topologies on extensive video data still takes weeks, robust abstraction layers allow research teams to organize their work modularly, facilitating the integration of subcomponents for unexpected advancements in system capabilities.

11.9 Timing and Uncertainty

As clinical AI frameworks evolve from "diagnostic" to "predictive" functions, the importance of time-to-event predictions in the medical context becomes increasingly significant. This shift highlights the need to forecast occurrences over time rather than providing binary predictions. Unlike binary classifiers, which can only predict events at a specific point in time, time-to-event analyses have the ability to estimate the probabilities of events occurring over a period of time. To address the individuals who were not available for further observation or did not experience the event of interest within the specified time frame, these analyses include data censoring.

Survival analyses are crucial in developing treatment recommendations based on empirical evidence, a common practice in medical research. Machine learning techniques that are video- and image-based can improve the understanding of how to integrate Cox proportional-hazards loss

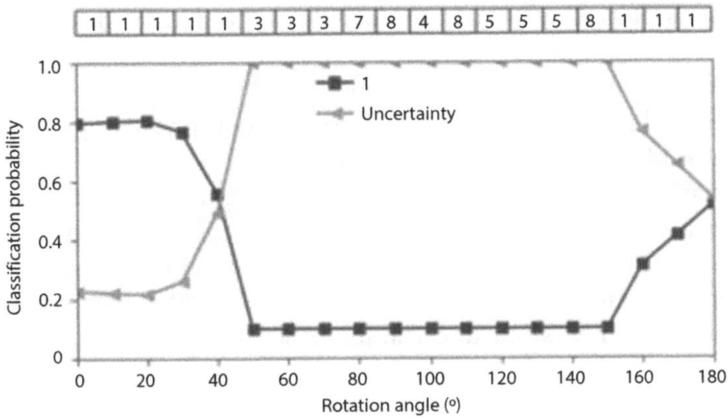

Figure 11.11 Account for classification uncertainty.

functions into neural network architectures, histological segments, and clinical scans. The exclusive integration of histopathology slides enhances the accuracy and efficacy of cancer diagnosis and prognosis. The Figure 11.11 shows that essential scan-stage details, including acquisition body rates, date, and MRI sequence (T1/T2), can be readily extracted from DICOM metadata in cardiac magnetic resonance imaging (MRI) and echocardiography.

Moreover, transparent networks help identify periods when medical practitioners might have overlooked signs and indications of advanced cancer, enabling timely intervention and improving patient outcomes. Instead of simply recommending how care should be administered, these advanced AI systems empower healthcare professionals to make informed decisions based on comprehensive and accurate predictions derived from sophisticated analyses of medical data.

Time-to-event research is becoming increasingly crucial, particularly in diseases where symptoms may manifest slowly, and early stages are asymptomatic before rapidly progressing after a certain period. For instance, symptoms of macular degeneration may not manifest for years, and early signs of illness may be perceived as "normal," posing challenges for neural networks to accurately predict the risk of macular degeneration. By incorporating censoring and survival concepts, these systems can be trained to distinguish between healthy individuals and those at risk of developing the disease.

Visual networks used in time-to-event studies can also aid lung cancer screening by predicting the risk of aggressive spread based on lesions detected in chest CT scans. These translational efforts require well-tested adaptations of machine learning algorithms, particularly those based on the Cox regression model. In recent years, deep learning applications have seen the integration of the Cox model, with researchers extending proportional and non-proportional Cox model extensions to improve survival algorithms like DeepSurv and DeepHit.

Estimating time-to-event outcomes poses significant challenges, especially in medical contexts where lesions detected in imaging scans can provide insights into survival rates with and without treatment. Clinicians may benefit from understanding the confidence level of machine learning predictions, mainly when uncertainty exists. However, many diagnostic machine-learning models cannot express uncertainty or indicate when unsure about a prediction. Addressing this issue, studies have explored deep learning uncertainty quantification techniques using various loss functions to prevent overconfident yet inaccurate predictions.

Uncertain quantification becomes imperative in scenarios involving human clients, such as healthcare. Confidence measures, like those used in AlphaFold2's breakthrough accuracy in the CASP14 challenge, enable users to gauge the reliability of predictions. Open-licensed implementations of uncertainty quantification algorithms are available and compatible with widely used machine learning frameworks. By integrating uncertainty assessment, high-stakes clinical imaging machine learning systems can enhance interpretability and trustworthiness while mitigating the risk of automated bias.

11.10 AI and Risk of Harm

Understanding how advanced algorithms generate predictions is crucial for both system designers and users. Saliency maps and activation maps are commonly used to visualize machine learning predictions. However, it is essential to be cautious in interpreting these visualizations. Saliency maps may seem contextually meaningful but misleading, as specific approaches for constructing them may behave similarly to "edge detectors." Moreover, saliency maps for good and bad predictions can be similar, indicating that they reveal little beyond "where" the algorithms are looking. Serial occlusion tests, where essential areas are occluded, can help ensure that AI focuses on the suitable topics. Activation maps can provide insights into the relative importance of different imaging phases in high-dimensional medical imaging studies. By examining how algorithms perform when specific regions are occluded, researchers can understand the crucial patterns picked up by machine learning models.

Visualization studies offer a unique opportunity to gain biological insights from machine learning algorithms, but variations across activations in clinically essential regions may indicate that networks are capturing non-specific information, reducing their generalizability. Addressing bias in machine learning systems is crucial, and techniques such as model-agnostic methods to evaluate feature importance, incorporating demographic inputs, and using constrained optimization can help make machine learning models fairer and uncover hidden biases.

11.11 Conclusion

In order to develop translatability learning structures for advanced imaging modalities, it is essential to dedicate sufficient time to comprehensively grasp the "video-like" nature of the data and consider factors such as bias, uncertainty, and explainability right from the outset of model construction. To enhance the utility of AI models in medical imaging, researchers can improve the representation of temporal data and consider factors such as bias and ambiguity. Given the ongoing progress in medical imaging and AI, it is crucial to approach new advancements with a prudent level of skepticism and thorough examination. Incorporating functionalities that enable the assessment of clinical proficiency, hospital incorporation, physician connections, and socio-demographic vulnerability can significantly impact the utilization of AI in healthcare environments. The perspective provided in this discussion can be valuable for academics as it highlights potential hurdles in clinical application and offers implied recommendations on overcoming them. By addressing these challenges and adopting best practices early in the development process, researchers can enhance the effectiveness and applicability of AI in medical imaging, ultimately leading to improved patient care and outcomes.

References

1. Rajpurkar, P. *et al.* Deep learning for chest radiograph diagnosis: a retrospective comparison of the CheXNeXt algorithm to practicing radiologists. *PLoS Med.*, 15, e1002686 (2018).
2. Rajpurkar, P. *et al.* AppendiXNet: deep learning for diagnosis of appendicitis from a small dataset of CT exams using video pretraining. *Sci. Rep.*, 10, 3958 (2020).

3. Huang, S.-C. *et al.* PENet is a scalable deep-learning model for automated diagnosis of pulmonary embolism using volumetric CT imaging. *NPJ Digit. Med.*, 3, 61 (2020).
4. Kumar Mohan, Senthil, A. John, and Ananth Kumar Tamilarasan. "Evolutionary Computing and Swarm Intelligence for Hyper Parameters Optimization Problem in Convolutional Neural Networks." In *Soft Computing Approach for Mathematical Modeling of Engineering Problems*, pp. 157-169. CRC Press, 2021.
5. Ghorbani, A. *et al.* Profound learning interpretation of echocardiograms. *NPJ Digit. Med.*, 3, 10 (2018).
6. McKinney, S. M. *et al.* International evaluation of an AI system for breast cancer screening. *Nature*, 577, 89–94 (2020).
7. Yim, J. *et al.* Predicting conversion to wet age-related macular degeneration using deep learning. *Nat. Med.*, 26, 892–899 (2020).
8. Beede, E. *et al.* A human-centered evaluation of a deep learning system deployed in clinics for the detection of diabetic retinopathy. In *Proc. 2020 CHI Conference on Human Factors in Computing Systems* 1–12 (ACM, 2020.
9. Allen, B. *et al.* A road map for translational research on artificial intelligence in medical imaging: from the 2018 National Institutes of Health/RSNA/ACR/Te Academy Workshop. *J. Am. Coll. Radiol.*, 16, 1179–1189 (2019).
10. Kannan, S., P. Pugazhendiran and N. Rishi Keshav. "Energy optimization mechanism using metastable-smart grid (MSSG)." In *J. Phys. Conf. Ser.*, vol. 2466, no. 1, p. 012024. IOP Publishing, 2023.
11. Abadi, M. *et al. TensorFlow: large-scale machine learning on heterogeneous distributed systems.* Preprint at https://arxiv.org/abs/1603.04467v2 (2016).
12. Langlotz, C. P. *et al.* A roadmap for foundational research on artificial intelligence in medical imaging: from the 2018 NIH/RSNA/ACR/Te Academy Workshop. *Radiology*, 291, 781–791 (2019).
13. Ulloa Cerna, A. E. *et al.* Deep-learning-assisted analysis of echocardiographic videos improves predictions of all-cause mortality. *Nat. Biomed. Eng.* https:// doi.org/10.1038/s41551-020-00667-9 (2021).
14. S. R. Burri, A. Kumar, A. Baliyan and T. A. Kumar, "Transforming Payment Processes: A Discussion of AI-Enabled Routing Optimization," *2023 2nd International Conference on Smart Technologies and Systems for Next Generation Computing (ICSTSN)*, Villupuram, India, 2023, pp. 1-7, doi: 10.1109/ICSTSN57873.2023.10151455
15. Oren, O., Gersh, B. J. & Bhatt, D. L. Artificial intelligence in medical imaging: switching from radiographic pathological data to clinically meaningful endpoints. *Lancet Digit. Health*, 2, e486–e488 (2020).
16. Mildenberger, P., Eichelberg, M. & Martin, E. Introduction to the DICOM standard. *Eur. Radiol.*, 12, 920–927 (2002).
17. Mesterhazy, J., Olson, G. & Datta, S. *High performance on-demand de-identifcation of a petabyte-scale medical imaging data lake.* Preprint at https://arxiv.org/abs/2008.01827 (2020).

18. Mason, D. *et al.* pydicom/pydicom: pydicom 2.1.0. Zenodo https://doi.org/10.5281/ZENODO.4197955 (2020).
19. Harris, C. R. *et al.* Array programming with NumPy. *Nature,* 585, 357–362 (2020).
20. Rubin, D. L. *et al.* Automated tracking of quantitative assessments of tumor burden in clinical trials. *Transl. Oncol.,* 7, 23–35 (2014).
21. Kaissis, G. A., Makowski, M. R., Rückert, D. & Braren, R. F. Secure, privacy-preserving and federated machine learning in medical imaging. *Nat. Mach. Intell.,* 2, 305–311 (2020).
22. N. Mahsuda, C. Ananth, N. Isok-Jon, Y. Rayimjon and T. A. Kumar, "Virtual Science is a New Scientific Paradigm," *2023 IEEE Renewable Energy and Sustainable E-Mobility Conference (RESEM),* Bhopal, India, 2023, pp. 1-5, doi: 10.1109/RESEM57584.2023.10236372.
23. Balachandar, N., Chang, K., Kalpathy-Cramer, J. & Rubin, D. L. Accounting for data variability in multi-institutional distributed deep learning for medical imaging. *J. Am. Med. Inform. Assoc.,* 27, 700–708 (2020).
24. Xu, Y. *et al. A collaborative online AI engine for CT-based COVID-19 diagnosis.* Preprint at medRxiv https://doi.org/10.1101/2020.05.10.20096073 (2020).
25. Kaissis, G. *et al.* End-to-end privacy-preserving deep learning on multi-institutional medical imaging. *Nat. Mach. Intell.,* 3, 473–484 (2021).
26. Burri, Srinivasa Rao, Sachin Ahuja, Abhishek Kumar, and Anupam Baliyan. "Exploring the Effectiveness of Optimized Convolutional Neural Network in Transfer Learning for Image Classification: A Practical Approach." In *2023 International Conference on Advancement in Computation & Computer Technologies (InCACCT),* pp. 598-602. IEEE, 2023.
27. Krizhevsky, A., Sutskever, I. & Hinton, G. E. ImageNet classification with deep convolutional neural networks. *Commun. ACM,* 60, 84–90 (2017).
28. Padmapriya, N., T. Ananth Kumar, R. Rajmohan, M. Pavithra and P. Kanimozhi. "Secure Vehicular Communication Using Blockchain Technology." In *Blockchain, Artificial Intelligence, and the Internet of Things,* pp. 141-162. Springer, Cham, 2022.
29. He, K., Zhang, X., Ren, S. & Sun, *J. Identity mappings in deep residual networks.* Preprint at https://arxiv.org/abs/1603.05027 (2016).

12

A Review of Computational Intelligence-Based Biometric Recognition Methods

T. IlamParithi[1]*, K. Antony Sudha[2] and D. Jessintha[3]

[1]*Government Arts and Science College, Sankarankovil, India*
[2]*Einstein College of Engineering, Tirunelveli, India*
[3]*Easwari Engineering College, Chennai, India*

Abstract
In recent years, technology has grown rapidly and technology usage also increased massively. With the help of technology, pupils started to think and act much smarter. A biometric system consists of a device, a sensor, methods, techniques, etc. To find a match to a person, the system uses his physical features such as iris, palm, fingerprint, face, etc. Computational intelligence (CI) methods are commonly used to create biometric identity and overcome non-idealities that are frequent in datasets. Common types include sample augmentation, feature extraction, categorization, indexing, fusion, normalization, and anti-spoofing. Computational intelligence plays a vital role in conducting sophisticated nonlinear calculations by developing models from training data in this environment. These methods employ both supervised and unsupervised training procedures. This work presents a review of computational intelligence-based biometric recognition methods.

Keywords: Neural networks, biometrics, face, fingerprint, iris, computational intelligence

12.1 Introduction

The field of study known as biometrics looks into methods of identifying students that do not rely on something the student possesses, such as a password or token, but rather on aspects of the student's appearance or

**Corresponding author*: iparithy@gmail.com

T. Ananth Kumar, E. Golden Julie, Venkata Raghuveer Burugadda, Abhishek Kumar and Puneet Kumar (eds.) Computational Intelligence: Theory and Applications, (263–280) © 2024 Scrivener Publishing LLC

behavior. Because the characteristics that make up a biometric profile are so specific, it is believed that biometric profiles cannot be forged and cannot be stolen, and it is tough to replicate them [1]. Physiological, behavioral, and soft characteristics are the three subcategories that can be used to divide biometric characteristics further. Physiological attributes are physical characteristics of an individual's body, such as a fingerprint, iris, or face. Individual activities, such as movement, signature, and voice, are associated with behavioral traits. Finally, soft biometric traits are characteristics that have a lower level of unicity, distinctiveness, and permanence than physiological and behavioral traits. Height, weight, and dress color are examples of soft biometric features. A unique approach is utilized to acquire a sample of the biometric attribute in a digital format during the acquisition phase. For example, the user touches his or her finger against a surface, and the system captures the image of the fingerprint. The sample is then split to maintain only the biometric information-containing region, and the system does a quality evaluation to see if the sample was accurately acquired and is of good enough quality to be processed further. Following that, an enhancement process is employed to improve sample quality. The distinguishing features are obtained and recorded in a template, which is then compared to an already registered template to verify if they relate to the very same person [2, 3]. In addition, A biometric classification could be used by the biometric system to quicken the computation process by comparing templates only from the same class.

12.1.1 Objective

Technologies for computational intelligence (CI) are robust, effective at solving difficult problems, effectively adaptive, and typically feature a parallel computing architecture. Due to these technological improvements, society now needs authentication systems that are effective, safe, and trusted. Systems for biometric authentication are faster and more effective in comparison. The primary goal of producing a review is to compile the best literature about computational intelligence-based biometric recognition methods for a significant research question or an active area of study into an easily understandable synthesis.

12.2 Computational Intelligence

Today, the world had moved into a technologically intelligent community. Computational intelligence is one of the most powerful data processing tools to solve nonlinear complex problems. In the year 1994, Bezdek defined computational intelligence. He considers computational intelligence to be one of the components of artificial intelligence [1]. Marks made a clear definition between artificial intelligence and computational intelligence. Marks said that artificial intelligence was formed from the hard-computing techniques and computational intelligence was formed from the soft computing techniques [2].

The main advantage of computational intelligence is that it can adapt to various conditions with the help of soft computing techniques. Basically, hard computing totally relies on the Boolean values that are unable to elucidate the natural language but the soft computing techniques can easily overcome this issue. Generally, computational intelligence can be categorized (Figure 12.1) into the following techniques: (i) Neural Network, (ii) Fuzzy Logic, (iii) Evolutionary Computing, (iv) Computational Learning Theory, and (v) Probabilistic Methods. This section discusses the most often used Computational Intelligence methods in biometrics, such as fuzzy systems, neural networks, and kernel methods. An artificial neural network, often known as a neural network, is a computer program that uses artificial intelligence to solve problems. It is a network of artificial neurons or nodes that is based on biological neural networks. Artificial neural networks can also be used for regression or classification modeling to predict and remote control [23]. Using limited datasets, a significant number of simulations were run. Deep learning, which excels at representation learning, is built on this structure. As a result, artificial neural networks use distributed information processing systems to process and learn information from data [8]. Fault tolerance is one of the most significant features of artificial neural networks, which is modeled by how the human brain functions [6].

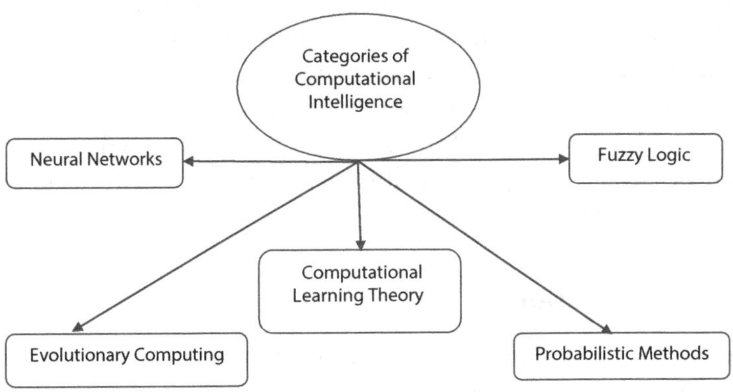

Figure 12.1 Computational intelligence categories.

One of the subclasses of pattern analysis is the Kernel technique, which employs the nonlinear data from kernel into a wide space for improving the skills. The universal kernel technique is Support Vector Machine (SVM). The main advantages of SVM are it requires only a limited set of parameters to configure and it also avoids the optima stagnation and optimizes the convex surface [8]. Kernel approaches are commonly used for biometric fusion, matching, and quality assessment in the field of biometrics. Multi-valued logic defines fuzzy logic [10], which can be considered as a formulation. Moreover, the real value of the formulated variables can be any value that ranges from zero (0) to one (1) and it is necessary that the value must be either 0 or 1. It is frequently used to handle problems with uncertainty, such as when the truth value is not entirely true or false. Fuzzy systems, in particular, have the advantages of being able to use language notions, as well as being robust against imprecise or inaccurate data. Adaptation to conflicting inputs, contradictory inputs, objectives, or the ease with which knowledge may be modified bases. Fuzzy systems are defined by these properties. Biometric recognition has a variety of applications including biometric matching and fusion approaches.

12.3 CI-Based Biometric Recognition

For each step of the biometric recognition process, Figure 12.2 shows the most recent CI-based techniques and Table 12.1 shows the summary of various biometric steps of CI-based methods in this section.

12.3.1 Acquisition

The first and foremost point in the acquisition phase is to gather the biometric data. The biometric data can be gathered by using various biometric sensors such as optimal scanners. These perfect scanners are mostly used to acquire biometric data from iris, fingerprints, and palm [25]. The Computation Intelligence techniques can be implemented in automatic detection of flaws, finding an identity of a device to achieve robust and adaptable acquisition.

12.3.2 Segmentation

The true biometric feature is separated from the background in the segmentation process. This stage is crucial for achieving a high identification rate, and it can be influenced by a variety of parameters such as image

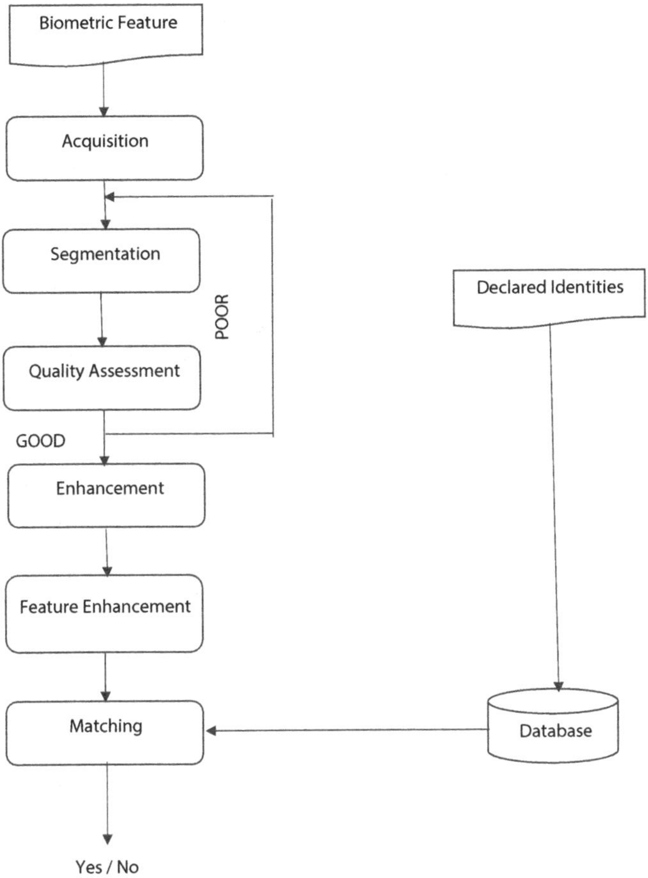

Figure 12.2 An overview of biometric recognition system.

orientation, occlusions, and lighting conditions. Furthermore, each feature may present unique segmentation issues. The segmentation process isolates the face from the background in face recognition; it might be compounded by stance shifts, background variables, or facial expression [15]. In this regard, neural networks [11, 12], as well as fuzzy logic and SVM are some of the most often used techniques for face segmentation.

It is also possible that face landmarks will be required [4]. SVMs or neural networks are used in many of the techniques used for these purposes [14]. The segmentation of the ridge pattern in fingerprint identification avoids the extraction of erroneous characteristics from the background, and because the fingerprint is a striated pattern, this process can be complex, and using global or local criteria can produce unsatisfactory results.

Table 12.1 Overview of biometric steps of based on computational intelligence methods [10].

S. no.	Steps of biometric operation	Fuzzy systems	Kernel methods	Neural networks
1	Acquisition	---	---	Self-calibration, error detection
2	Segmentation	Boundary detection, threshold adaption	Boundary detection, landmark location	Boundary detection, occlusion detection, threshold adaption, landmark location
3	Quality assessment	————	Illumination quality, focus assessment	Problem detection
4	Enhancement	————	————	Artifact Elimination, image reconstruction, rotation correction
5	Feature Extraction	————	————	Automatic deep learning features, candidate filtering.
6	Matching	Coping with distortion, robust matching	Attribute alignment, robust matching	Attribute alignment, robust matching
7	Fusion of various biometrics	Fusion of score level	Fusion of feature and score level	Fusion of sensor level

(*Continued*)

Table 12.1 Overview of biometric steps of based on computational intelligence methods [10]. (*Continued*)

S. no.	Steps of biometric operation	Fuzzy systems	Kernel methods	Neural networks
8	Normalization of score	______	Imposter optimization and valid distributions	______
9	Anti-spoofing	Physiological features detection	Physiological features detection, motion and texture analysis	Physiological features detection
10	Privacy protection	______	Attribute encryption	Attribute encryption

As a result, neural networks [16] and Fuzzy techniques have been offered as strategies to increase segmentation accuracy.

12.3.3 Quality Assessment

The level of accuracy of the biometric information used has a considerable influence on the performance of biometric systems. Then, quality metrics are used to forecast a sample's recognition performance, with higher-quality values related to better individual recognition [7] on the other hand, roughly calculating the relationship among a instance and its potential to recognize something can be difficult. As a result, CI methods are utilized frequently when investigating the relationship between the quality of a sample and the sample itself. Some studies evaluate picture quality in the context of facial identification by using generic image qualities that include contrast, sharpness, and light intensity.

Kernel approaches are employed in particular in [12] to forecast lighting quality, to link illumination quality to sample originality, and to assess illumination quality based on holistic face characteristics [13]. Poor skin conditions, filthy fingers, user inexperience, and ergonomic considerations can all affect sample quality in fingerprint recognition. In this context, self-organizing maps [16] and feed forward neural networks [15] are employed in the most widely used quality assessment techniques.

In addition to finding the quality of touchless and 3D fingerprint samples, the neural networks had been used to pinpoint the issues created by low-quality fingerprint images [24]. Occlusions, off-angle gazing, environmental, and camera influences can affect the quality of the iris image in iris identification systems.

12.3.4 Enhancement

The quality of biometric samples, particularly fingerprint images, has been enhanced through CI techniques. Difference in the location and the fingers force on the sensor can cause fingerprint characteristics, particularly ridges and valleys, to be unclear in certain areas of the image. This can make it difficult to identify a person's fingerprints. The image is subjected to pre-processing so that any differences in quality can be ironed out before the features are extracted [25].

Traditionally, the process of improving fingerprints involved three distinct steps: ridge thinning, image binarization, and ridge enhancement. A Convolutional Deep Belief Network (CDBN) is used in the method that is described in [14], which is trained on fingerprint data taken from a database and chosen for its higher quality [14]. After that, the network begins to work directly on the fingerprint image's pixels to improve it by reconstructing properties comparable to those in the training images. In addition, in the method outlined in [16], ridge thinning is accomplished using (PCNNs) Pulse-Coupled Neural Networks (PCNNs).

The network is trained using a collection of successful thinning efforts in order to avoid the artifacts that some thinning algorithms are well-known.

12.3.5 Feature Extraction

The process of feature extraction is used to obtain the most distinctive properties of the biometric trait, which are then matched for identity comparison. Following this, the process is referred to as feature extraction. In the training phase, the method described employs supervised auto encoders to identify people from a single image, and it is necessary to extract reliable features from photos that are sensitive to differences in stance, attitude, and illumination [23]. This enables the method to identify individuals from a single image—identical techniques to those based on deep learning that are utilized to extract characteristics. It is now possible to take available facial photographs using a variety of multimedia applications as well as in natural settings [14]. The characteristics of fingerprints that are employed most commonly in fingerprint recognition systems are the direction of the ridges, the positioning of single points, tiny points, sweaty pores, and incipient ridges [4]. Other prominent characteristics include the direction of the ridges, the location of single points, tiny points, sweat pores, and the orientation of emerging ridges.

In order to locate the Principal Singular Point (PSP) in both touch-based and touchless images, the research article referred to as [7] employs the feed forward neural network. The process begins with the generation of a list of candidate points, which is followed by the selection of the PSP from among the candidates by means of a trained neural network. The final step in this procedure is the generation of output. Furthermore, utilizing CNNs trained on noise affected rolled images, and the method proposed in [3] recovers the position of the ridges from concealed fingerprint images.

Finally, from touchless fingerprint photos, the approach described in [17] derives the positions of sweat pores. Feed forward neural networks are used in this method, which are trained with characteristics derived from local picture regions centered on manually assessed pore positions [10]. A method is proposed for extracting robust features from iris photos collected in unconstrained instances created by combining Haar Wavelet decomposition with neural networks. Furthermore, the method suggested in [11] uses unsupervised PCNNs to generate binary pictures from iris samples and then compared with Hamming distance.

12.3.6 Matching

To verify whether an actual sample and a previously enrolled template are from the same individual, the matching method compares the characteristics of the real sample and those of the template. The completion of this method results in the generation of a similarity score. At long last, a threshold is applied to decide whether the matching should be approved or declined. It is necessary for matching algorithms to handle variations in the retrieved characteristics [4], which may arise due to shifts in the presentation of the trait or noise. Matching is one of the most common applications for CI methods because of their robustness in the face of imprecision and ambiguity.

Alignment of faces is the first and foremost step in face recognition, and it significantly influences how well the recognition process works. In addition, computational intelligence strategies that do not really depend on particulars but rather on the bigger picture show potential [7]. Standard iris recognition features are typically encoded as binary strings; consequently, fundamental matching methods such as Hamming distance are typically utilized. Despite this, various researchers [1] have utilized computational intelligence approaches to achieve iris matching, particularly with pictures that are not ideal. For instance, deep learning is used to match different iris patterns, but in [5], support vector machines (SVMs) are used to improve performance by making use of photographs taken in an independent environment.

12.3.7 Classification

Classification algorithms are utilized in biometric systems to divide a set of biometric data into various classes, allowing matching to be performed using only samples from the same class, lowering the time needed for recognition. The PCASYS, which is based on neural classifiers, is the most widely used classification approach in fingerprint identification. Furthermore, the work provided in [14] looks at the similarities and dissimilarities between neural and SVM classifiers employing Gabor filtering features. Furthermore, the method proposed in [15] evaluates pseudo-Zernike moments to categorize fingerprints using neural networks [12]. The genetic algorithm is used to gain a huge proficiency with a set of traits from unfair data.

12.3.8 Score Normalization

The post-processing of the primary identical results of the recognition systems is the better way to increase the accuracy before processing the recognition systems. The majority of these algorithms employ training datasets to learn and improve the distributions of impostors and genuine ones with the help of supervised learning techniques like SVM, as well as techniques for calculating normalization functions from both real and impostors [9], cohort normalization processes that exclusively evaluate the impostor distribution [6], and matching score classification approaches.

12.3.9 Anti-Spoofing

The submission of a false biometric to the sensor, such as a phony finger, face photos, or a contact lens with a printed iris pattern, is known as a spoofing attack. Anti-spoofing technologies that identify the liveness of the biometric sample should be implemented as soon as possible to ensure the security of biometric systems [10]. Most face recognition algorithms work with two-dimensional pictures, which can be exploited with photos, movies, make-up, masks, or mannequin heads [9]. To counter these attacks, the research in [6] analyzes the motion with SVMs, assuming that a 2D object moves differently than a real 3D face.

SVMs are also employed in [9] to assess the image's texture pattern and detect lip movements. Fake fingers made of gelatine, silicone, or other materials, as well as dead fingers, can be used to assault fingerprint recognition systems [2]. Several strategies have been developed to identify these assaults, including fuzzy matching, which exploits textural differences between real and phoney fingerprints. Artificial eyes, printed iris pictures, contact lenses, and displays can all be used to fool iris identification systems [16]. Using SVMs, some strategies for preventing these attacks try to detect physiological traits such as eye movements or pupillary contraction. Jaishanker [17] also uses SVM classifiers to identify between fake and real irises based on their optical features under various lighting situations.

12.3.10 Privacy

In comparison to traditional recognition methods, biometric technologies provide greater assurance that the individual is who he claims to be [19]. However, as in the instance of biometric data theft [20], the repercussions of misusing biometric information might be dangerous. Many people are concerned about this issue because they believe their data are being misused to follow their actions. As a result, designing privacy-compliant biometric systems is critical, considering both technological and sociological concerns. CI techniques are frequently utilized in this situation [18] because they allow for robust encryption and good accuracy. SVM and neural networks have been used to propose privacy-preserving biometric recognition systems.

12.4 Applications

Biometric applications and technologies are constantly being employed across broad aspects of public life, such as the business, education, government, and military, for both logical and physical security, as security requirements increase, system performance improves, and costs decrease.

12.4.1 Business

Using a high-tech iris scan to gain access to a resource requires a high level of discretion. This is very cool, and the fingerprint scan is an excellent office security measure. If a low-cost fingerprint biometric sensor is installed on the entrance gates, only authorized individuals will be able to gain entry to the building. In addition, biometrics can be incorporated into multi-factor authentication processes to increase the security of computer sign-ins. In this way, biometrics protect your business's physical location and contribute to its online security. The beauty of biometrics lies in its enhancing security without requiring additional effort from users. In all honesty, employees will have little difficulty learning how to use biometrics. They only need to present themselves to establish their identity; the procedure could not be simpler.

Through the implementation of biometric authentication, long-term cost and time savings could be realized. If employees register their fingerprints on the system, they will never have to waste time attempting to remember new passwords or searching for replacement smartcards. Because biometric technology frees employees from mundane office tasks, they can better focus on their work. A claim that a person is who they say they are is something that can be verified with the aid of biometrics. Employers will therefore know precisely who was present in the office at a given time in the event of a security breach or other emergency. It is vital information during a crisis, but it also has the potential to aid in the resolution of workplace disputes. The use of biometrics has the potential to simplify matters. Similarly, attendance at work can be reliably and automatically recorded using a biometric-based entry system. Biometric solutions are becoming increasingly prevalent in our personal lives, providing us with day-to-day benefits such as enhanced levels of convenience and security.

12.4.2 Education

Several academic institutions are experimenting with collaborative learning as a mode of teaching. Biometrics in collaborative learning can aid the teaching process and also improves the security by offering a reliable and trustworthy method of authentication. This helps to bridge the gap between standard and collaborative learning as well as give collaborative learning a positive reputation. Biometrics could also be used to introduce new practical and efficient assessment tasks into the teaching practice. Voice identification, iris recognition, face recognition, and other biometric capabilities could be used to authenticate students. A tool for recognizing spoken language is integrated into a learning management system [21]. This instrument is used to verify a student's replies by comparing the student's voice print to a recording of the student's voice during a verbal activity. Oral interactions in online examinations can be authorized and confirmed using this method. Biometric technology has improved recently, resulting in higher accuracy at a lower cost [22]. Biometric technologies are emerging as a foundation for a wide number of exciting secure verifications and individual identification solutions.

12.4.3 Military

Biometrics use in defense and intelligence is not restricted to one or two uses; it is blessed with a wide range of applications towards protecting a variety of military duties and activities. Authentication and access control appear to be the most popular aspects of biometrics in defense [23]. It will not only safeguard the armed forces and facilitate military operations, but also preserve a balance between personal freedoms and national security, because the process of recruiting army soldiers is so important, when an efficient, dependable, and durable technology is to be implemented. As a result, biometric facial recognition systems, iris and fingerprint scanners, etc. must be used to verify the candidate's or applicant's identification. Besides that, biometric technology aids the government of any nation in placing restrictions on adversaries' entry and, if their biometric data are already stored, in recognizing the spied individual.

Figure 12.3 provides the use of biometric in the Department of Defense. Moreover, by improving real-time data of the invaders, authorities may be able to increase border protection information. The advantages of using biometric technology in military and intelligence are numerous, including accurate identification of military personnel and detection like any unauthorized intrusion. It can aid national defense by quickly identifying an unlawful entry within the facilities. Furthermore, it safeguards private locations, data, and other sensitive data. It also maintains biometric

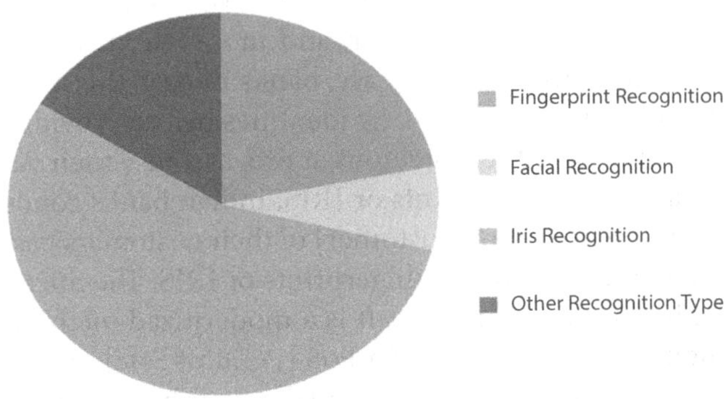

Figure 12.3 Military biometric market revenue in the year of 2019.

information acquired from combat commanders and military branches in an encrypted format.

12.4.4 Health Care

Biometric technology has the potential to increase the healthcare industry's efficiency while also preventing fraud and theft [24]. It has the capability of replacing armbands and barcode scanning as patient identification, reducing the risk of cheating in nations with widespread health insurance. Rather than traditional health cards, biometric tools can be used. One of the most important advantages of biometric data is an authentication method. Instead of filling in forms and providing validation at the office, patients simply place their fingers on a reader, which completes the entire operation of health care access. It has become easy to centralize patient information by reducing duplicate patient records and their health-oriented records using biometric technology. It also increases the medical record's correctness, as well as the accuracy of the healthcare system, and, most importantly, it prevents improper treatment methods.

12.4.5 Banking

With technology advancements, the times of ordinary passwords were gone, as banks around the nation were started using new biometric identification methods. Know your Customer [KYC], Payment Authentication Systems [PAS], Micro ATMs, and other banking applications use biometrics [25]. The process KYC [Know Your Customer] is an important factor of the authorization process for banks to recognize their account holders/customers and ensure that their services are also not exploited. In many countries, the financial institutions are currently employing biometric identification technologies to execute their customers' KYC procedures, doing the job more accurately, faster, and more user-friendly. However, as incidences of identity fraud increase, banks must gather biometric data from consumers to authenticate their identities before providing financial services. After obtaining their previous approval to use their Aadhaar and biometric data such as fingerprints or IRIS, Indian banks conduct a quick eKYC [Electronic Know Your Customer] of their customers based on their Aadhaar and biometric data like fingerprints or IRIS. The micro ATMs are based on the biometric technology. It is a modernized method of making payments digitally with the help of a PoS [Point of Sale] device. Here, the customers can easily make their payments to their businessman by simply placing their fingers or iris. Nowadays, the PoS device is commonly used as a micro ATM that enables the users to make payments to their vendors. The PoS device authenticates the user to transfer the money to the vendor bank account from his account in a secured manner within a few seconds.

12.5 Conclusion

Individual recognition via biometric technology is becoming more common in security applications. However, designing such systems necessitates addressing multiple technological areas at once and addressing all components in a holistic manner. Various biometric steps of CI-based methods are all covered in this paper. According to the review's findings, computational intelligence techniques enable technologies that can boost accuracy and robustness to non-idealities. Furthermore, the review found that diverse CI approaches can complete all tasks involved in the biometric recognition process. This was found in contrast to the typical algorithmic approaches, which led to the realization that CI techniques are enabling technologies. Deep learning and convolutional neural networks are two recent techniques that will receive additional research shortly to improve the overall performance of existing biometric systems. This research will be conducted to make existing biometric systems more accurate.

References

1. N. Siddique, H. Adeli, Computational Intelligence: Synergies of Fuzzy Logic, *Neural Networks and Evolutionary Computing*. Hoboken, NJ: Wiley, 2013.
2. Priya Batta, Sachin Ahuja., Abhishek Kumar 'Future Directions for Secure IoT Frameworks: Insights from Blockchain based Solutions' *Wirel. Pers. Commun.*, 130, 1549–1574 (2023). https://doi.org/10.1007/s11277-023-10344-0.
3. A. Genovese, V. Piuri and F. Scotti, *Touchless Palmprint Recognition Systems*, Springer, 2014.
4. E. Marasco and A. Ross, A survey on antispoofing schemes for fingerprint recognition systems, *ACM Comput. Surv.*, pp. 1-36, 2014.
5. Ilyas, Benkhaddra, Abhishek Kumar, Mohamed Ali Setitra, ZineEl Abidine Bensalem, and Hang Lei. "Prevention of DDoS attacks using an optimized deep learning approach in blockchain technology." *Trans. Emerging Telecommun. Technol.*, 34, no. 4 (2023): e4729.
6. PriyankaBorude, Dr.S.T.Gandhe, Pravin A. Dhulekar, S.J.Pawar, "Identification and Tracking of Facial Features", Elsevier *International Conference on*

Advances In Computing,Communicationand Control (ICAC3 '15), 1st-2nd April 2015.
7. Yu Guan "On Reducing the Effect of Covariate Factors in Gait Recognition: A Classifier Ensemble Method", *IEEE Trans. Pattern Anal. Mach. Intell.*, Vol. 37, No. 7, July 22015.
8. Khary,Popplewell, Multispectral Iris Recognition Utilizing Hough Transform and Modified LBP, *IEEE International Conference on Systems, Man, And Cybernetics*, San Diego, CA, USA, 2014.
9. M. De Marsico, A. Petrosino and S. Ricciardi, Iris recognition through machine learningtechniques: a survey, *Pattern Recognit. Lett.*, 2016.
10. Saravanan, Jayalakshmi, T. Ananth Kumar, Andrew C. Nwanakwaugwu, Sunday Adeola Ajagbe, Ademola T. Opadotun, Deborah D. Afolayan, and Oluwafemi O. Olawoyin. "Detection of COVID-19 Using Denoising Autoencoders and Gabor Filters." In *International Conference on Applied Informatics*, pp. 252-266. Springer, Cham, 2022.
11. Vincent S. Tseng, Josh Jia-Ching Ying, Stephen T.C. Wong, Computational Intelligence Techniques for Combating Covid-19: A Survey, *IEEE Comput. Intell. Mag.*, November 2020.
12. Burri, Srinivasa Rao, Sachin Ahuja, Abhishek Kumar, and Anupam Baliyan. "Exploring the Effectiveness of Optimized Convolutional Neural Network in Transfer Learning for Image Classification: A Practical Approach." In *2023 International Conference on Advancement in Computation & Computer Technologies (InCACCT)*, pp. 598-602. IEEE, 2023.
13. L. Livi, A. Rizzi, A. Sadeghian, Granular modelling and computing approaches for intelligentanalysis of non-geometric data. *Appl. Soft Comput.*, 27, 567–574, 2015.
14. Benkhaddra, Ilyas, Abhishek Kumar, Mohamed Ali Setitra, and Lei Hang. "Design and Development of Consensus Activation Function Enabled Neural Network-Based Smart Healthcare Using BIoT." *Wireless Pers. Commun.*, 130, no. 3 (2023): 1549-1574.
15. Kumar, Tamilarasan Ananth, Rajendrane Rajmohan, Muthu Pavithra, Sunday Adeola Ajagbe, Rania Hodhod, and Tarek Gaber. "Automatic face mask detection system in public transportation in smart cities using IoT and deep learning." *Electronics*, 11, no. 6 (2022): 904.
16. Ilyas, Benkhaddra, Abhishek Kumar, Mohamed Ali Setitra, ZineEl Abidine Bensalem, and Hang Lei. "Prevention of DDoS attacks using an optimized deep learning approach in blockchain technology." *Trans. Emerging Telecommun. Technol.*, 34, no. 4 (2023): e4729.
17. Jaishanker, K. Pillai "Cross-Sensor Iris Recognition through Kernel Learning", *IEEE Trans. Pattern Anal. Mach. Intell.*, Vol. 36, No. 1, January 2014.
18. Kanimozhi, P., S. Parkavi and T. Ananth Kumar. "Predicting Mortgage-Backed Securities Prepayment Risk Using Machine Learning Models." In *2023 2nd International Conference on Smart Technologies and Systems for Next Generation Computing (ICSTSN)*, pp. 1-8. IEEE, 2023.

19. Kumar, T. Ananth, R. Rajmohan, Sunday Adeola Ajagbe, Tarek Gaber, Xiao-Jun Zeng, and Fatma Masmoudi. "A novel CNN gap layer for growth prediction of palm tree plantlings." *PLoS One,* 18, no. 8 (2023): e0289963.
20. S. Kang, D. Lee and C. D. Yoo, Face attribute classification using attribute-aware correlation map and gated convolutional neural networks, in *Proceedings of the IEEE International Conference on Image Processing ICIP'* 2015.
21. Mohamed Sayed, FaridJradi, Biometrics: Effectiveness and Applications within the Blended Learning Environment, *Comput. Eng. Intell. Syst.*, vol.5, No.5, 2014.
22. S. R. Burri, A. Kumar, A. Baliyan and T. A. Kumar, "Transforming Payment Processes: A Discussion of AI-Enabled Routing Optimization," *2023 2nd International Conference on Smart Technologies and Systems for Next Generation Computing (ICSTSN),* Villupuram, India, 2023, pp. 1-7, doi: 10.1109/ICSTSN57873.2023.10151455.
23. Sh. Al-seddek, H. Soliman, M. Morsy, *Sh.* Kishk "A Palmprint-Based Identification System using Radon Transform", *Egypt. Comput. Sci. J.*, Vol.38, No. 3, ISSN 1110-2586, September 2014.
24. Acharya U Rajendra, Hagiwara Yuki, Deshpande Sunny Nitin, Suren S, Koh Joel En Wei, Oh Shu Lih, Arunkumar N Ciaccio Edward J, Lim Choo Min," Characterization of focal EEG signals: a review", *Future Gener. Comput. Syst.*, vol 91, pp 290-299, 2019.
25. Gayathri, M.; Malathy, C. A Deep Learning Framework for Intrusion Detection and Multimodal Biometric Image Authentication. *J. Mob. Multimed.*, 1, 393–420, 2021.

13

Seeing the Unseen: An Automated Early Breast Cancer Detection Using Hyperspectral Imaging

Sravan Kumar Sikhakolli[1], Suresh Aala[1], Sunil Chinnadurai[1] and Inbarasan Muniraj[2]*

[1]*Department of Electronics and Communication Engineering, SRM University AP, Andhra Pradesh, India*
[2]*LiFE Lab, Department of ECE, Alliance School of Applied Engineering, Alliance University, Bengaluru, Karnataka, India*

Abstract
Hyperspectral imaging (HSI) has gained prominence in various fields of science. In particular, it has spurred much interest in biomedical imaging especially cancer (such as skin, breast, oral, colon, pancreatic, and prostate) detecting applications. Of them, breast cancer (BC) is known to be the second-largest cause of mortality throughout the world. According to the Cancer Registry Program, over 1.3 million people in India are suffering from BC, and more recently, the numbers seem to be growing exponentially. Currently, no permanent cure for metastatic BC is reported; nevertheless, detecting it at an earlier stage and treating accordingly is shown to reduce its severity, i.e., increasing the survival rate. To effectively detect BC, several optical techniques including mammography, ultrasound imaging, computed tomography, positron emission tomography, and magnetic resonance imaging are widely used. Note that these methods have their own merits and demerits such as the false-negative results, usage of higher-energy radiation, and poor soft tissue contrast, to name a few. Therefore, to validate the imaging results, a biopsy (using surgical excisions) is often performed, which is painful, troublesome, and may cause discomfort for a longer period. For this reason, cancer detection via non-invasive imaging methods is highly sought. Techniques such as thermal imaging, photo-acoustic imaging, and, more recently, HSI are shown to be providing satisfactory results at the laboratory scale. This chapter comprehensively reviews the

**Corresponding author*: inbarasan.muniraj@alliance.edu.in

T. Ananth Kumar, E. Golden Julie, Venkata Raghuveer Burugadda, Abhishek Kumar and Puneet Kumar (eds.) Computational Intelligence: Theory and Applications, (281–300) © 2024 Scrivener Publishing LLC

utilization of HSI technique for the detection of various stages of breast cancer. We also review the state-of-the-art deep learning frameworks that are employed for automated breast cancer detection.

***Keywords*:** Hyperspectral imaging, breast cancer, cancer imaging, non-invasive imaging, and deep learning

13.1 Introduction

Breast cancer (BC) [1–3] is one of the most dreadful diseases as the 5-year survival rate for women who are diagnosed with localized breast cancer is 99%. According to the American Cancer Society [4], in the year 2020, about 2.3 million women were diagnosed with BC, with approximately 0.7 million deaths reported. By the end of 2020, the numbers increased to 7.8 million infections, making it the world's most common cancer. In India, according to the Cancer Registry Program (CRP) [5], over 1.3 million people are currently suffering from BC, and more recently, the numbers have been growing alarmingly.

Types and Stages of Breast Cancer: At Which Stage Can We Call It Early?
BC can be broadly classified into 5 stages such as Stage 0, I, II, III, and IV [6–8]. Stages 0 and I are generally known as the initial stages as the tumor size is relatively low and detecting cancer at these stages helps to avoid the severity; i.e., the chance of survival is relatively higher [45]. Table 13.1 compares the stages of BC with the size of the tumor and its corresponding survival rate of the patients.

Stage 0: Tumors usually occur/form in the milk ducts or glands of the breast and will remain there.
Stage I: At this stage, the tumor will have a local spread and affects the neighboring ducts. Precisely when tumor spreads to the fatty tissues of the breast is known as Stage IA, and during Stage IB, tumor has broken out from the ducts to the nearby lymph nodes. The size of the tumor, in this stage, is usually similar to that of a peanut.
Stage II: In this stage, the cancer has grown or moved to other parts of the breast. Stage IIA refers to when a breast tumor is found in the tissues but in a similar size to that presented at Stage I. In such cases, lymph nodes may not have been affected, i.e., tumor free. Alternatively, Stage IIB cancer is usually considered as an advanced form of the disease.
Stage III: At this stage, cancer is harsher and tougher to treat; however, it may not have spread to the bones or other organs. Stage IIIA implies

Table 13.1 Types and stages of breast cancer.

Stages	Types	Approximate tumor size (in cm)	Survival rate
0	Ductal carcinoma *in situ* (DCIS)	0–1	99% (Non-invasive)
I	Invasive carcinoma (ICS)	1–2.5	95% (Localized)
II	Invasive lobular carcinoma (ICS)	2.5–5	86% (Regional)
III	Invasive carcinoma (ICS)	>5	57% (Regionally expanded)
IV	Invasive carcinoma (ICS)	Broke through the skin attached to breast	29% (Became distinct)

malignancy of up to nine armpit–collarbone lymph nodes or its spread to the breast lymph nodes. Stage IIIB denotes the tumor has migrated to the chest wall or breast skin, but not the lymph nodes. Stage IIIC in general refers to the fact that 10 or more lymph nodes are infected.

Stage IV: This stage defines that cancer cells from the breast have spread to every other part of the body, including all the lymph nodes that are located closer to the breast, bones, lungs, liver, brain, etc. This stage is often referred to as a metastatic state.

As can be seen from Table 13.1, early detection of breast cancer is crucial to avoid being fatal. In this next section, we describe the different imaging modalities used in literature for the detection of BC.

13.1.1 Conventional Imaging Methods for Detecting BC

Mammography is one of the earliest techniques used for BC imaging. This method involves passing (potentially harmful) X-rays through the breast and collecting the responses with a detector. Mammography [9] is considered a gold-standard method for detecting BC as this method can detect malignant tumors even before they become clearly visible. However, this test detects only the abnormalities but fails to prove whether or not cancer is present. Thus, if other symptoms of cancer are suspected (at a later stage), a biopsy of the breast tissue is often recommended for histopathology and molecular analysis. The other limitation of mammography is the prediction of false-negative results [10].

Breast ultrasonography uses relatively safer acoustic waves and their echoes to produce the images of breast tissues [46]. These images are capable of showing certain changes in tissues such as fluid-filled cysts that are harder to image using mammograms [47–49]. Although this method is comparatively safer, its poor spatial resolution limits its usage as it becomes harder to delineate the tumors of closure proximity.
Magnetic resonance imaging (MRI) [10] employs strong magnetic fields and low-energy electromagnetic waves to capture higher-quality BC images. Thus, breast MRI has many distinct advantages over other conventional techniques. Nevertheless, it does not always distinguish between cancerous and non-cancerous abnormalities, which may lead to unnecessary breast biopsies.
Positron emission tomography (PET) and **computed tomography (CT)** play an important role in BC localization, monitoring treatment response and early detection of recurrences [11]. However, one of the main limitations of PET or CT is that it fails to detect small breast carcinomas.
Breast-specific gamma imaging (BSGI) employs a radiotracer imaging technique using a specialized camera [12], which can be customized according to the patient's breast characteristics. This method is shown to be useful when delineating lesions that are less than 1 cm. However, the main limitation of this method is the usage of gamma rays that can harm the neighboring healthy tissues.
Breast thermography or **thermal imaging** is one of the safest and non-invasive imaging techniques to detect BC. This technique uses an ultra-sensitive sensor to record the infrared or heat images [13] of the breast. One of the main limitations is that these images fail to confirm whether or not cancer is present. Alternatively, thermal images confirm the abnormalities in the breast tissues that need further investigations. Therefore, for validation purposes, biopsies are often performed.

13.1.2 Optical Imaging Techniques to Detect BC

To overcome the limitations of the conventional imaging modalities, several new optical imaging techniques have been proposed in the literature [14], such as optical coherence tomography (OCT), confocal microscopy, multiphoton microscopy [15], multispectral and hyperspectral endoscopy, and light field microscopy, to name a few [39]. In this chapter, we discuss a recently developed optical imaging technique i.e., hyperspectral imaging

(HSI) [16], which records both spatial and spectral information of the object. To note, spectral information is unique to types of tissues (which correspond to the stages of cancer); therefore, a better detection is possible using hyperspectral imaging.

13.2 Hyperspectral Imaging (HSI)

HSI stands for "hyperspectral imaging", which is a spectroscopic-based imaging technique [17]. It is known that the human eye is sensitive to the three primary colors, i.e., red, green, and blue (RGB), from the electromagnetic spectrum. HSI, on the other hand, can record both the spatial and spectral information of hundreds of wavelengths with smaller band gaps [18]. The synthesized HS data are usually represented in the form of a three-dimensional (3D) cube represented as (x, y, λ). The two spatial dimensions are denoted as x and y, and λ represents the spectral information, i.e., wavelength [19]. Figure 13.1 compares the multispectral and hyperspectral imaging modalities. As can be seen, HSI records hundreds of

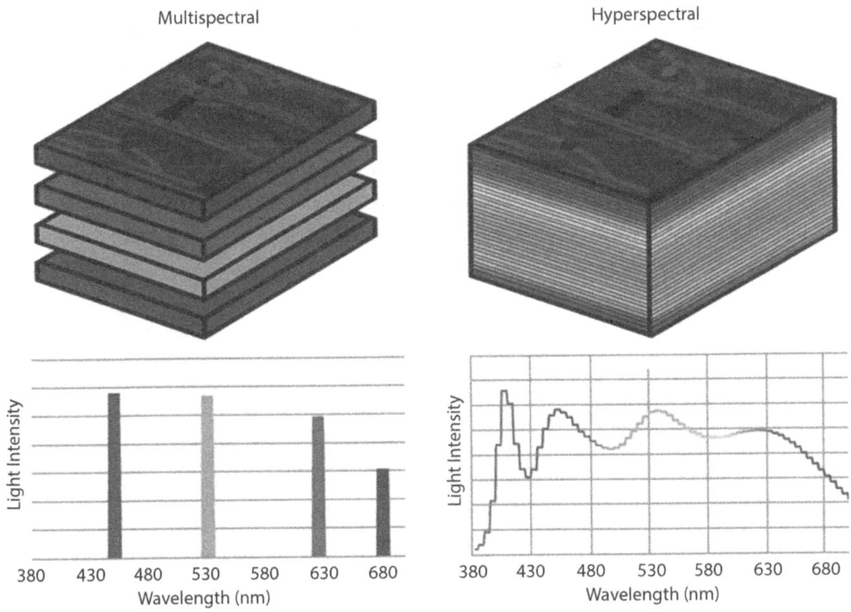

Figure 13.1 Comparison of multispectral and HSI. In this example, a multispectral image contains four distinct spectral bands (left) and an HSI cube contains many more spectral bands (between 380 and 700 nm) (right) [50]. In the following section, an imaging setup to capture the hyperspectral imaging dataset is described.

wavelengths. Thus, HSI is shown to be useful in a wide range of use cases [20] in various scientific areas including remote sensing [21], molecular biology [22], biomedical imaging [23], agriculture and food processing [24], and crime scene investigations [25], to name a few.

13.2.1 How Does HSI Setup Look Like?

Figure 13.2 shows a general hyperspectral imaging system under laboratory conditions.

1. **Moving Stage**: To capture HS images, samples are preferred to be placed on a moving stage as it can assist in moving samples with greater precision. It is also useful to adjust the viewing angles; thus, the entire scene (extended field of view) can be captured. It has the flexibility to move vertically and horizontally.
2. **White Reference Panel**: It is a standard small piece of white-board used in experiments to enable and verify the capture of total reflectance of incident light.
3. **Illumination Source:** Figure 13.2 shows the usage of halogen sources to capture the HSI dataset. It is known that halogen gas and tungsten combine to form halogen light, which can be classified under incandescent light source. For HSI data recording, halogen bulbs are preferred as they cover a wide spectrum such as from the visible and near-infrared (VNIR) range. This spectral bandwidth is suitable for performing investigations in the area of biomedical imaging.

Figure 13.2 Actual laboratory HSI setup.

4. **Sensors:** Several types of hyperspectral sensors are being produced by various manufacturers. Figure 13.2 shows the usage of a Specim IQ Hyperspectral imager that records images from both the visible and near-infrared spectral images, i.e., 400–1000 nm. The spectral resolution of this camera is around 7 nm, and the spatial resolution is 512 × 512 [25].

13.3 State-of-the-Art Techniques for BC Detection

Lately, HSI has been extensively employed to detect BC. Based on organ isolation from their usual biological surroundings, biological imaging can be broadly classified into three types. They are *in vivo*, *ex vivo*, and *in vitro* [38]. Of them, *in vivo* refers to the study that deals with living organisms in their normal and intact state, thus often eliminating the need for painful biopsies [39]. *Ex vivo* examinations, on the other hand, are performed when the tissues are taken outside the body under a more controlled environment. Such investigations therefore need a biopsy. Similarly, *in vitro* studies are also performed when the tissues are taken out from the living organism (after a biopsy) and stored/processed under a controlled laboratory environment. In this examination, tissues can be grown externally as needed and thus experiments can be conducted for multiple days. It is evident from this section that *in vivo* imaging is non-invasive and thus convenient for many examinations as it is better suited for observing the overall effects in a living organism.

13.3.1 Breast Cancer *Ex Vivo* Analysis

The two most preferred imaging setups for *ex vivo* (with excised human tissues) analysis is given in Figure 13.3. Of them, Figure 13.3a shows the reflection imaging setup where the light reflected off from the tissues is captured and Figure 13.3b shows the transmission imaging setup where the light source is kept at the bottom of the tissue and the hyperspectral sensor captures the light that is transmitted through the tissues. Such a setup is preferred for a thin and transparent sample. In either case, captured images must be processed to get the desired result. Figure 13.4. depicts the standard HSI post-processing techniques.

The first two blocks denote the image acquisition processes, i.e., imaging breast tissues by selecting proper illumination sources. Imaging is done as discussed in Section 13.2.1. Illumination sources are chosen based on

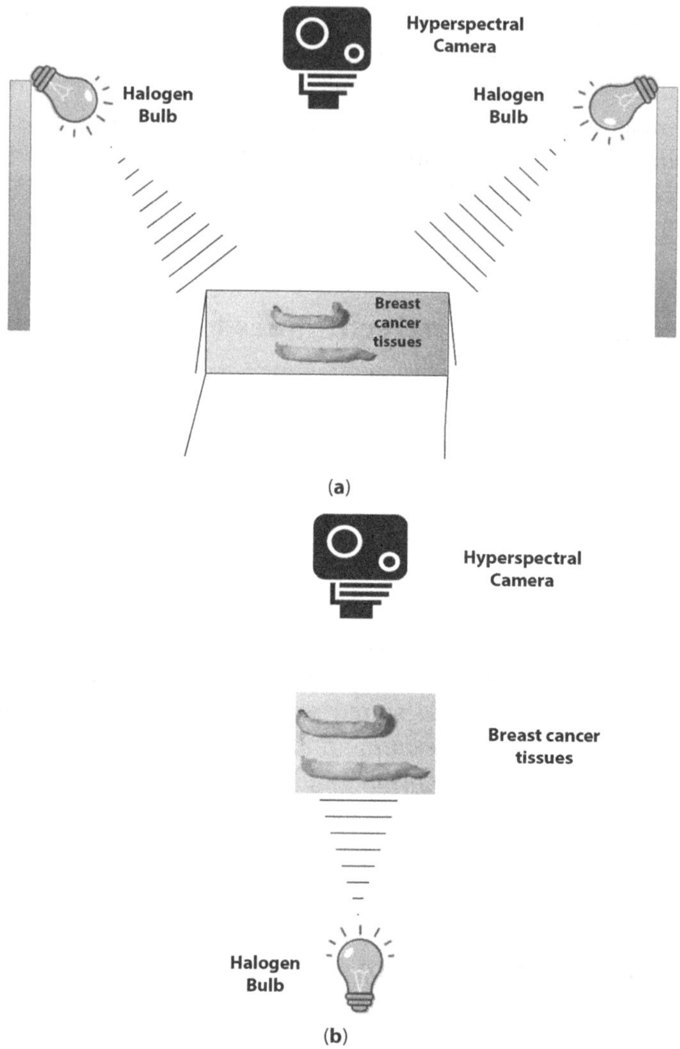

Figure 13.3 (a) Reflection imaging and (b) transmission imaging.

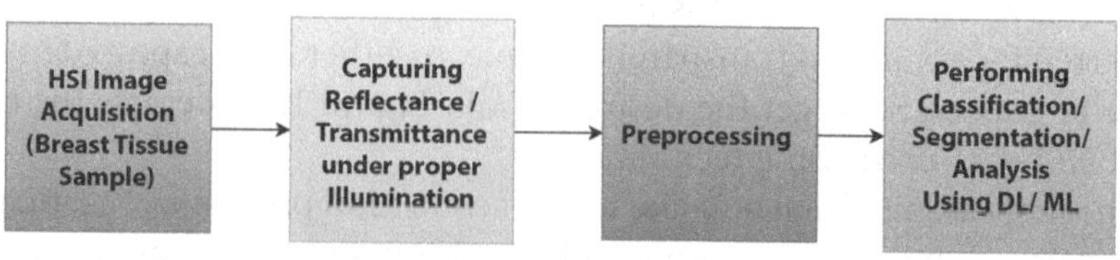

Figure 13.4 HSI *ex vivo* image processing techniques.

experiments and note that the Specim IQ is capable of capturing images under normal room light [25]. The third block, i.e., pre-processing block, refers to the processes such as dimensionality reduction, band selection [54], denoising [55], and image enhancement by filtering [56], to name a few. Finally, image segmentation or classification is performed to delineate the different classes of the tissues. In Section 13.4, we also discuss some of the recent machine and deep learning implementations on HSI datasets. In the following, we review some of the recent investigations using *ex vivo* investigations performed on the HSI dataset.

In [28], Aboughaleb *et al.* demonstrated an *ex vivo* examination for detecting BC using HSI. The authors showed that the K-means clustering algorithm can be used to classify the benign and malignant tissues by extracting the spectral signatures from both the malignant and healthy tissues. It was reported that 95% for sensitivity and 96% for precision can be achieved. It is well known that identifying the resection margin or surgical margin is a crucial aspect of cancer treatment. To address that, Kho *et al.* [29] developed a technique to identify the resection margins for breast-conserving surgery. In their experiments, the authors collected a dataset (i.e., tissue slices) from 18 patients. It was reported that approximately 22,000 spectra were recorded from the resection surfaces of six lumpectomy specimens and a support vector machine (SVM) algorithm was used to classify the tissues. To note, authors delineated tissues such as invasive carcinoma (ICS), ductal carcinoma *in situ* (DCIS) [32], and connective and adipose tissues with an accuracy of 93%, 84%, 70%, and 99%, respectively [29]. In addition to this, the same group of researchers has demonstrated that by using a wider spectrum, i.e., 450–1650 nm, a better classification performance can be achieved. In this work, the authors have chosen 58 and 26 images for training and testing, respectively. A bespoke DL model, i.e., a combined linear discriminant analysis (LDA) and U-Net, was developed to achieve an accuracy of 98% and 99% for specificity and sensitivity, respectively [30]. In another study [31], the authors demonstrated that recording spectra at 550 nm malignant and normal tissue can be differentiated by using the K-means clustering algorithm. In [33], Dawson *et al.* used the HSI to examine the optical characteristics of breast tissue. The results of Transmission Mode (for light transmission) and Reflection Mode (to evaluate diffuse light reflectance) were compared. It was estimated that the optimum wavelength for light transmission and reflection spectra is around 600 and 640 nm, respectively. The authors claimed that, in these bands, normal and malignant tissues can be differentiated [33].

In [34], Kabatznik *et al.* developed a support vector machine (SVM) technique to detect the malignant cells from the BC dataset. In addition to this, the authors used Artificial Neural Network (ANN) to make a single decision for the entire test image. In their study, accuracy for the SVM algorithm was shown to be between 73% and 88.9% and around 87.4% was achieved for ANN [34].

13.3.2 Breast Cancer *In Vivo* Analysis

In vivo analysis, i.e., imaging tissues in living organisms without taking it outside the body, is given in Figure 13.6. Note that *in vivo* BC detection using HSI is still primitive, and the examinations were so far carried out on mice by artificially injecting the cancer cells to it.

As can be seen from Figure 13.6, the processes that are followed for *in vivo* analysis are similar to that of *ex vivo* analysis presented in Figure 13.4. However, the main difference is, as mentioned earlier, how the imaging is being done. In the following, we review some of the recent investigations

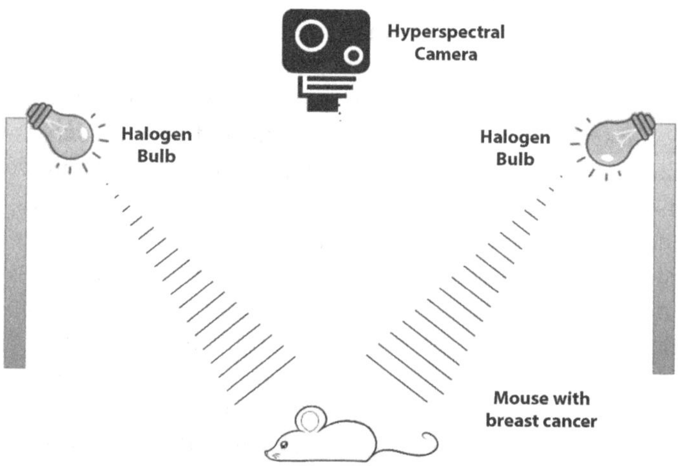

Figure 13.5 Typical *in vivo* examinations.

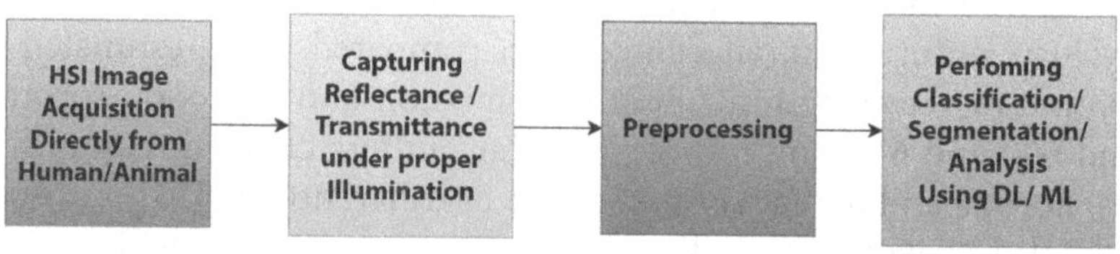

Figure 13.6 *In vivo* image analysis.

using *in vivo* investigations performed on the HSI dataset. Figure 13.5 shows the classical *in vivo* examination.

Panasyuk *et al.* proposed a method to facilitate residual tumor identification during the surgery [35]. In their study, the authors performed *in vivo* imaging using HSI to classify the tumorous and normal breast tissue. This was done using an experimental Dimethylbenz[a]anthracene (DMBA)-induced rat breast tumor model. Initially, for rats with tumors, surgery and HSI imaging were combinedly performed. Later, by partially removing the tumor, HSI imaging was conducted on the excision bed. Finally, the complete removal of the tumors and glands that appeared normal to the naked eye followed by gross examinations, such as both HSI imaging and histopathological investigations, were combinedly performed to authenticate the proposed method.

Sorge *et al.* [36] proposed a system to create *in vivo* serial–spatial maps of hemoglobin saturation at the microvascular level of blood oxygenation. Note that this experiment was carried out on a labeled mouse mammary cancer cell. Similarly, McCormack *et al.* [37] measured the dynamic changes that occur in tumor micro-vessel density and hemoglobin oxygenation (sO_2), when the trastuzumab drug was applied to a mouse with HER2 status. It was reported for 2, 5, 9, and 14 days after treating it with the necessary antibodies, and the results were confirmed with a gold standard immunochemistry.

13.4 Artificial Intelligence in BC Detection Using HSI

For several scientific problems, artificial intelligence [i.e., machine learning (ML), deep learning] techniques have been widely applied [26, 27]. Thereafter, to classify the HSI dataset, several ML techniques, such as support vector machines (SVM), k-nearest neighborhood (k-NN), decision trees, random forest, linear regression, and neural networks, are often used. More recently, deep learning (DL) frameworks have shown themselves to be performing well and thus preferred over ML algorithms, because of their unique structure.

13.4.1 Deep Learning in HSI

Deep learning (DL) is used in various scientific fields of science that infer decisions using images e.g., biomedical imaging [40]. Thus, several DL networks such as convolutional neural networks (CNNs), recurrent neural networks (RNNs), and U-Net have already been shown to be useful methodologies [51–53] for HSI dataset processing and analysis. The latest DL frameworks such as generative adversarial networks (GAN), conditional GANs, gated recurring units (GRU), and long short-term memory networks (LSTM) are also examined [56]. In the following section, we briefly overview some of the DL networks that opted for HSI data processing.

13.4.2 Convolutional Neural Networks

Convolutional neural network (CNN) is a commonly used DL model [41] as it provides good results when it comes to imaging datasets. Figure 13.7 shows the hybrid spectra net that is used to classify the benign and malignant tissues [42]. This structure uses both two-dimensional (2D) and three-dimensional (3D) CNN structures. Here, principal component analysis (PCA) takes the original dataset and identifies the key features, i.e., bands that need to be processed.

Ortega *et al.* [57] developed a hyperspectral microscopic imaging system for the detection of BC in digitized histological images. The proposed system consists of a HS push-broom camera that is combined with a standard optical microscope. This system is capable of imaging at 20× magnification. In their experiments, a total of 112 HS images from histologic samples were recorded. A pathologist then makes a cell-level note on the digitized slides, which are then compared with the captured HS images. For image classification, a bespoke DL network with nine 2D convolutional layers was developed. In their experiments, the area under the curve (AUC) was shown to be more than 0.89.

Similarly, in [59], researchers proposed to use the one-dimensional (1D) CNN to classify healthy and unhealthy (cancerous) breast tissues. In their experiments, breast samples from 20 patients were initially taken to get a Raman spectrum. Further, the Fisher discrimination analysis (FDA), and

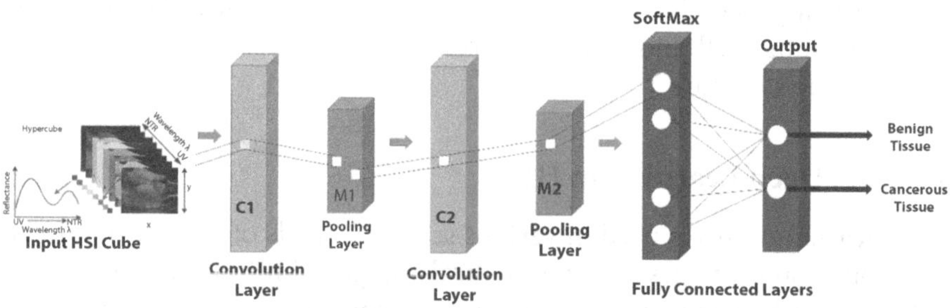

Figure 13.7 Hybrid spectra net.

support vector machine (SVM) classifiers were also used for comparison purposes. From their analysis, the authors concluded that the 1D-CNN achieved a diagnostic accuracy of 92%, a sensitivity of 98%, and a specificity of 86%.

13.4.3 Deep Belief Networks Using HSI

Mughees *et al.* [58] proposed a new spectral adaptive segmented-deep belief network (SAS-DBN) for HSI dataset classification. The proposed network uses deep abstract features by dividing the original spectral bands into several small subgroups and processing each group individually with local DBNs. With these results, data abstraction was shown to be performing better, thus resulting in an accurate HSI classification. Note that applying DBN-based feature extraction to each subgroup nullifies the computational complexity and leads to a better feature extraction.

13.4.4 Residual Networks

A spectral–spatial residual network (SSRN) [43, 44] was developed to extract spectral and spatial properties of the HSI dataset with higher accuracy. Batch normalization was used in spatial–spectral squeeze-and-excitation residual network (SSSERN) to control the layer distribution and to speed up the training process. It is known that the residual networks are easy to optimize as they have very few parameters when compared with conventional deep learning networks.

13.5 Discussion and Conclusion

It is estimated that many cases of breast cancer are over-treated. Therefore, a more personalized approach is highly required to avoid unnecessary (harmful) treatments for thousands of women and men globally, each year. Attempts are underway to reduce rates of biopsies and radiation by employing precise biomarkers. In this chapter, we reviewed several non-invasive imaging techniques (that nullify the need for biopsy) to carry out breast cancer detection that can further help in better diagnosis and therapy. As aforementioned, hyperspectral imaging (HSI) was found to be useful when imaging cancer tissues. In this regard, several investigations have been carried out to demonstrate the imaging capability of HSI using *ex vivo* and *in vitro* examinations. However, *in vivo* analysis is far away from reality; however, such investigation strives to decrease the dependency on pathologists who are very meager to find. Thus, we foresee that the *in vivo* HSI will be a game-changer when it comes to breast cancer imaging.

In addition to this, developing a bespoke deep learning model to train and classify tissues from the HSI dataset will greatly assist surgeons in identifying the resection margins and also aid in a better prognosis. It was shown that the HSI dataset can be classified using a variety of deep neural networks for the detection and diagnosis of breast cancer. We also note that due to a lack of dataset availability, investigations into new deep learning models have not yet been published. We foresee that making the collected spectral datasets publicly available would attract researchers who can then use them for the development of superior learning algorithms that can achieve higher diagnostic sensitivities.

It is worth mentioning that there are very few pre-processing techniques (such as filtering, denoising, and image enhancement) examined in the literature; therefore, novel techniques for hyperspectral datasets are also an open area for exploration. Finally, we expect to see that HS imaging sensors will be produced at cost-effective rates so that they will be more accessible.

References

1. Green, David R., Jason J. Hagon, Cristina Gómez, and Billy J. Gregory. "Using low-cost UAVs for environmental monitoring, mapping, and modelling: Examples from the coastal zone." In *Coastal management*, pp. 465-501. Academic Press, 2019.
2. *Statistics of Breast Cancer in India* https://cytecare.com/blog/statistics-of-breast-cancer/. (Accessed on 04th Aug 2022)
3. Ilyas, Benkhaddra, Abhishek Kumar, Mohamed Ali Setitra, ZineEl Abidine Bensalem, and Hang Lei. "Prevention of DDoS attacks using an optimized deep learning approach in blockchain technology." *Trans. Emerg. Telecommun. Technol.*, 34, no. 4 (2023): e4729.
4. Bala, P. Manju, S. Usharani, R. Rajmohan, T. Ananth Kumar and A. Balachandar. "Bioinspired CNN Approach for Diagnosing COVID-19 Using Images of Chest X-Ray." In *Smart Computer Vision*, pp. 181-201. Cham: Springer International Publishing, 2023.
5. Chatterjee, Sharmila, Amit Chattopadhyay, Surendra Nath Senapati, Dipti Rani Samanta, Leslie Elliott, Dana Loomis, and Lesly Mery. "Cancer registration in India-current scenario and future perspectives." *Asian Pacific J. Cancer Prev.*, 17, no. 8 (2016): 3687-3696.
6. *What are stages and Grades of BC.* https://www.webmd.com/breast-cancer/stages-grades-breast-cancer. (Accessed 06th Aug 2022.)

7. Saslow, Debbie, Carla Boetes, Wylie Burke, Steven Harms, Martin O. Leach, Constance D. Lehman, Elizabeth Morris *et al.* "American Cancer Society guidelines for breast screening with MRI as an adjunct to mammography." *CA: Cancer J. Clin.* 57, no. 2 (2007): 75-89.
8. Shi, Yanlong, Wei Wei, Li Li, Qian Wei, Fei Jiang, Guozhi Xia, and Hongzhu Yu. "The global status of research in breast cancer liver metastasis: a bibliometric and visualized analysis." *Bioengineered,* 12, no. 2 (2021): 12246-12262.
9. Li, Tong, Michael Luke Marinovich, and Nehmat Houssami. "Digital breast tomosynthesis (3D mammography) for breast cancer screening and for assessment of screen-recalled findings: review of the evidence." *Expert Rev. Anticancer Ther.,* 18, no. 8 (2018): 785-791.
10. Radhakrishna, Selvi, S. Agarwal, Purvish M. Parikh, K. Kaur, Shikha Panwar, Shelly Sharma, Ashish Dey, K. K. Saxena, Madhavi Chandra, and Seema Sud. "Role of magnetic resonance imaging in breast cancer management." *South Asian J. Cancer,* 7, no. 02 (2018): 069-071.
11. Paydary, Koosha, Siavash Mehdizadeh Seraj, Mahdi Zirakchian Zadeh, Sahra Emamzadehfard, Sara Pourhassan Shamchi, Saeid Gholami, Thomas J. Werner, and Abass Alavi. "The evolving role of FDG-PET/CT in the diagnosis, staging, and treatment of breast cancer." *Mol. Imaging Biol.,* 21, no. 1 (2019): 1-10.
12. N. Mahsuda, C. Ananth, N. Isok-Jon, Y. Rayimjon and T. A. Kumar, „Virtual Science is a New Scientific Paradigm," *2023 IEEE Renewable Energy and Sustainable E-Mobility Conference (RESEM),* Bhopal, India, 2023, pp. 1-5, doi: 10.1109/RESEM57584.2023.10236372.
13. Fernandes, Steven Lawrence, Venkatesan Rajinikanth, and Seifedine Kadry. "A hybrid framework to evaluate breast abnormality using infrared thermal images." *IEEE Consum. Electron. Mag.,* 8, no. 5 (2019): 31-36.
14. Godavarty, Anuradha, Suset Rodriguez, Young-Jin Jung, and Stephanie Gonzalez. "Optical imaging for breast cancer prescreening." *Breast Cancer: Targets Ther.,* 7 (2015): 193.
15. Sorrells, Janet E., Rishyashring R. Iyer, Lingxiao Yang, Elisabeth M. Martin, Geng Wang, Haohua Tu, Marina Marjanovic, and Stephen A. Boppart. "Computational Photon Counting Using Multithreshold Peak Detection for Fast Fluorescence Lifetime Imaging Microscopy." *ACS Photonics,* (2022).
16. Ortega, Samuel, Himar Fabelo, Dimitris K. Iakovidis, Anastasios Koulaouzidis, and Gustavo M. Callico. "Use of hyperspectral/multispectral imaging in gastroenterology. Shedding some–different–light into the dark." *J. Clin. Med.,* 8, no. 1 (2019): 36.
17. Yoon, Jonghee. "Hyperspectral Imaging for Clinical Applications." *BioChip J.,* (2022): 1-12.
18. Dietrich, M., S. Marx, M. von der Forst, T. Bruckner, F. C. F. Schmitt, M. O. Fiedler, F. Nickel *et al.* "Bedside hyperspectral imaging indicates a microcirculatory sepsis pattern-an observational study." *Microvasc. Res.,* 136 (2021): 1041645.

19. Brugger, Anna, Patrick Schramowski, Stefan Paulus, Ulrike Steiner, Kristian Kersting, and Anne-Katrin Mahlein. "Spectral signatures in the UV range can be combined with secondary plant metabolites by deep learning to characterize barley–powdery mildew interaction." *Plant Pathol.*, 70, no. 7 (2021): 1572-1582.
20. Wang, Zheli, Shuxiang Fan, Jingzhu Wu, Chi Zhang, Fengying Xu, Xuhai Yang, and Jiangbo Li. "Application of long wave near infrared hyperspectral imaging for determination of moisture content of single maize seed." *Spectrochim. Acta, Part A,* 254 (2021): 119666.
21. Subbulakshmi, N., R. Manimegalai, G. Rajakumar, T. Ananth Kumar, and Umadevi Kosuri. "A novel design of low-cost hearing aid devices using an efficient lifting filter bank with a modified variable filter." *Expert Rev. Med. Devices,* 19, no. 12 (2022): 991-999.
22. Zimmermann, Timo, Jens Rietdorf, and Rainer Pepperkok. "Spectral imaging and its applications in live cell microscopy." *FEBS Lett.*, 546, no. 1 (2003): 87-92.
23. Batshev, Vladislav, Alexander Machikhin, Grigoriy Martynov, Vitold Pozhar, Sergey Boritko, Milana Sharikova, Vladimir Lomonov, and Alexander Vinogradov. "Polarizer-free AOTF-based SWIR hyperspectral imaging for biomedical applications." *Sensors,* 20, no. 16 (2020): 4439.
24. Lu, Bing, Phuong D. Dao, Jiangui Liu, Yuhong He, and Jiali Shang. "Recent advances of hyperspectral imaging technology and applications in agriculture." *Remote Sens.*, 12, no. 16 (2020): 2659.
25. *Forensics with hyperspectral imaging* https://www.specim.fi/forensics-with-hyperspectral (Accessed on 10th Aug 2022)
26. Jia, Sen, Shuguo Jiang, Zhijie Lin, Nanying Li, Meng Xu, and Shiqi Yu. "A survey: Deep learning for hyperspectral image classification with few labeled samples." *Neurocomputing,* 448 (2021): 179-204.
27. Li, Shutao, Weiwei Song, Leyuan Fang, Yushi Chen, Pedram Ghamisi, and Jon Atli Benediktsson. "Deep learning for hyperspectral image classification: An overview." *IEEE Trans. Geosci. Remote Sens.*, 57, no. 9 (2019): 6690-6709.
28. Aboughaleb, Ibrahim H., Mohamed Hisham Aref, and Yasser H. El-Sharkawy. "Hyperspectral imaging for diagnosis and detection of *ex-vivo* breast cancer." *Photodiagnosis Photodyn. Ther.*, 31 (2020): 101922.
29. Kho, Esther, Lisanne L. de Boer, Koen K. Van de Vijver, Frederieke van Duijnhoven, Marie-Jeanne TFD Vrancken Peeters, Henricus JCM Sterenborg, and Theo JM Ruers. "Hyperspectral Imaging for Resection Margin Assessment during Cancer SurgeryHyperspectral Imaging for Resection Margin Assessment." *Clin. Cancer Res.*, 25, no. 12 (2019): 3572-3580.
30. Kho, Esther, Behdad Dashtbozorg, Lisanne L. De Boer, Koen K. Van de Vijver, Henricus JCM Sterenborg, and Theo JM Ruers. "Broadband hyperspectral imaging for breast tumor detection using spectral and spatial information." *Biomed. Opt. Express,* 10, no. 9 (2019): 4496-4515.

31. Khouj, Yasser, Jeremy Dawson, James Coad, and Linda Vona-Davis. "Hyperspectral imaging and K-means classification for histologic evaluation of ductal carcinoma in situ." *Front. Oncol.*, 8 (2018): 17.
32. Lu, Guolan, and Baowei Fei. "Medical hyperspectral imaging: a review." *J. Biomed. Opt.*, 19, no. 1 (2014): 010901.
33. Aref, Mohamed, Ibrahim H. Aboughaleb, Abou-Bakr Youssef, and Yasser El-Sharkawy. "Novel approach exploiting the hyperspectral imaging system for breast cancer therapy and diagnosis." *Arch. Breast Cancer,* 7, no. 4 (2020): 189-201.
34. Burri, Srinivasa Rao, Sachin Ahuja, Abhishek Kumar, and Anupam Baliyan. "Exploring the Effectiveness of Optimized Convolutional Neural Network in Transfer Learning for Image Classification: A Practical Approach." In *2023 International Conference on Advancement in Computation & Computer Technologies (InCACCT)*, pp. 598-602. IEEE, 2023.
35. Panasyuk, Svetlana V., Shi Yang, Douglas V. Faller, Duyen Ngo, Robert A. Lew, Jenny E. Freeman, and Adrianne E. Rogers. "Medical hyperspectral imaging to facilitate residual tumor identification during surgery." *Cancer Biol. Ther., 6*, no. 3 (2007): 439-446.
36. Ewerlöf, Maria, Marcus Larsson and E. Göran Salerud. "Spatial and temporal skin blood volume and saturation estimation using a multispectral snapshot imaging camera." In *Imaging, Manipulation, and Analysis of Biomolecules, Cells, and Tissues XV*, vol. 10068, pp. 105-116. SPIE, 2017.
37. McCormack, Devin R., Alex J. Walsh, Wesley Sit, Carlos L. Arteaga, Jin Chen, Rebecca S. Cook, and Melissa C. Skala. "*In vivo* hyperspectral imaging of microvessel response to trastuzumab treatment in breast cancer xenografts." *Biomed. Opt. Express,* 5, no. 7 (2014): 2247-2261.
38. Halicek, Martin, Himar Fabelo, Samuel Ortega, Gustavo M. Callico, and Baowei Fei. "*In-vivo* and *ex-vivo* tissue analysis through hyperspectral imaging techniques: revealing the invisible features of cancer." *Cancers,* 11, no. 6 (2019): 756.
39. U. S. Sekhar, N. Vyas, V. Dutt and A. Kumar, "Multimodal Neuroimaging Data in Early Detection of Alzheimer's Disease: Exploring the Role of Ensemble Models and GAN Algorithm," *2023 International Conference on Circuit Power and Computing Technologies (ICCPCT)*, Kollam, India, 2023, pp. 1664-1669, doi: 10.1109/ICCPCT58313.2023.10245177.
40. Luo, Yanan, Jie Zou, Chengfei Yao, Xiaosong Zhao, Tao Li, and Gang Bai. "HSI-CNN: a novel convolution neural network for hyperspectral image." *In 2018 International Conference on Audio, Language and Image Processing (ICALIP)*, pp. 464-469. IEEE, 2018.
41. Manni, Francesca, Fons van der Sommen, Himar Fabelo, Svitlana Zinger, Caifeng Shan, Erik Edström, Adrian Elmi-Terander, Samuel Ortega, Gustavo Marrero Callicó, and Peter HN de With. "Hyperspectral imaging for glioblastoma surgery: Improving tumor identification using a deep spectral-spatial approach." *Sensors,* 20, no. 23 (2020): 6955.

42. Mughees, Atif, and Linmi Tao. "Multiple deep-belief-network-based spectral-spatial classification of hyperspectral images." *Tsinghua Sci. Technol.*, 24, no. 2 (2018): 183-194.
43. Ozdemir, Akin, and Kemal Polat. "Deep learning applications for hyperspectral imaging: a systematic review." *J. Inst. Electron. Comput.*, 2, no. 1 (2020): 39-56.
44. Liang, Miaomiao, Licheng Jiao, and Zhe Meng. "A superpixel-based relational auto-encoder for feature extraction of hyperspectral images." *Remote Sens.*, 11, no. 20 (2019): 2454.
45. Bhushan, A., A. Gonsalves and J. U. Menon. "Current state of breast cancer diagnosis, treatment, and theranostics. *Pharmaceutics 13 (5): 723.*" (2021).
46. *International Agency for Research on BC WHO* https://gco.iarc.fr/tIoday/data/factsheets/cancers/20-Breast-fact-sheet.pdf (Accessed on 15th Aug 2022.
47. Krupnik, Diana, Shuhab Khan, Unal Okyay, Preston Hartzell, and Hua-Wei Zhou. "Study of Upper Albian rudist buildups in the Edwards Formation using ground-based hyperspectral imaging and terrestrial laser scanning." *Sediment. Geol.*, 345 (2016): 154-167.
48. Zahavi, Ali, Andrei Palshin, Dhanushka Chamara Liyanage, and Mart Tamre. "Influence of illumination sources on hyperspectral imaging." In *2019 20th International Conference on Research and Education in Mechatronics (REM)*, pp. 1-5. IEEE, 2019.
49. *Multispectral (vs)hyperspectral image* https://www.photonics.com/Articles/Multispectral Lighting A Practical Option for/a66251 (Accesed on 20th Aug 2022)
50. Benkhaddra, Ilyas, Abhishek Kumar, Mohamed Ali Setitra, and Lei Hang. "Design and Development of Consensus Activation Function Enabled Neural Network-Based Smart Healthcare Using BIoT." *Wirel. Pers. Commun.*, 130, no. 3 (2023): 1549-1574.
51. Kulcke, Axel, Amadeus Holmer, Philip Wahl, Frank Siemers, Thomas Wild, and Georg Daeschlein. "A compact hyperspectral camera for measurement of perfusion parameters in medicine." *Biomed. Eng./Biomed. Tech.*, 63, no. 5 (2018): 519-527.
52. Ozdemir, Akin, and Kemal Polat. "Deep learning applications for hyperspectral imaging: a systematic review." *J. Inst. Electron. Comput.*, 2, no. 1 (2020): 39-56.
53. Fabelo, Himar, Samuel Ortega, Adam Szolna, Diederik Bulters, Juan F. Piñeiro, Silvester Kabwama, Aruma JO'Shanahan et al. "*In-vivo* hyperspectral human brain image database for brain cancer detection." *IEEE Access*, 7 (2019): 39098-391165.
54. Reshma, R., V. Sowmya and K. P. Soman. "Dimensionality reduction using band selection technique for kernel based hyperspectral image classification." *Proc. Comput. Sci.*, 93 (2016): 396-4025.

55. Rasti, Behnood, Paul Scheunders, Pedram Ghamisi, Giorgio Licciardi, and Jocelyn Chanussot. "Noise reduction in hyperspectral imagery: Overview and application." *Remote Sens.*, 10, no. 3 (2018): 482.
56. Saichandana, B. "Hyperspectral image enhancement using evolutionary algorithm." *Int. J. Adv. Res.*, 3, no. 4 (2016): 934-938.
57. Samuel Ortega, Martin Halicek, Himar Fabelo, Raul Guerra, Carlos Lopez, Marylene Lejeune, Fred Godtliebsen, Gustavo M. Callico, Baowei Fei, "Hyperspectral imaging and deep learning for the detection of breast cancer cells in digitized histological images," *Proc. SPIE 11320, Medical Imaging 2020: Digital Pathology*, 113200V (16 March 2020).
58. A. Mughees and L. Tao, "Multiple deep-belief-network-based spectral-spatial classification of hyperspectral images," in *Tsinghua Sci. Technol.*, vol. 24, no. 2, pp. 183-194, April 2019.
59. Danying Ma, Linwei Shang, Jinlan Tang, Yilin Bao, Juanjuan Fu, Jianhua Yin, Classifying breast cancer tissue by Raman spectroscopy with one-dimensional convolutional neural network, *Spectrochim. Acta, Part A.*

14

Shedding Light into the Dark: Early Oral Cancer Detection Using Hyperspectral Imaging

Suresh Aala[1], Sravan Kumar Sikhakolli[1], Inbarasan Muniraj[2] and Sunil Chinnadurai[1]*

[1]SRM University, Andhra Pradesh, India
[2]Alliance University, Bengaluru, India

Abstract

Cancer is one of the leading causes of mortality in the world with 9.6 million deaths recorded globally for the year 2018 alone. It involves uncontrolled cell division due to the activation of carcinogen genes and causes disorders in the growth of the tissue, which can occur in any part of the human body. Oral cancer (OC) is one of the prominent cancer types, especially in India, where 11.54% of new cases and 10.16% of deaths are caused by OC. To date, there is no promising treatment to cure cancer. Early detection of cancer can increase the chances of survival and quality of life after the treatment. Nowadays, various imaging and non-imaging diagnosis techniques are available. Imaging techniques became popular due to their non-invasiveness, nonpainful nature, and repetitiveness. X-ray, ultrasound, magnetic resonance imaging (MRI), computed tomography (CT), positron emission tomography (PET), and fluorescence imaging are some of those techniques. Fluorescence imaging uses fluorescence contrast agents, whereas all other techniques use ionizing radiation, which is harmful when repetitive imaging is required. However, all these techniques have their pros and cons. Recently, the research community has been working on thermal imaging, photoacoustic imaging, and hyperspectral imaging (HSI) to overcome such limitations. HSI is a promising technique for *in vivo* diagnosis, due to its multi-band capturing capability. It can capture the same location tissue with a higher spatial and spectral resolution, for a wide range of wavelengths from visible to near-infrared (NIR). It provides an ionization-free diagnosis, is less dependent on skilled pathologists,

**Corresponding author*: sunil.c@srmap.edu.in

T. Ananth Kumar, E. Golden Julie, Venkata Raghuveer Burugadda, Abhishek Kumar and Puneet Kumar (eds.) Computational Intelligence: Theory and Applications, (301–320) © 2024 Scrivener Publishing LLC

and produces quick results, and it is even safe for one to undergo this procedure many times. HSI can also be used for the effective identification of resection margin while operating to remove the OC tumor. It normally generates a huge three-dimensional data cube, where the effective processing of these data can produce good results. Currently, the research community is working on the OC HSI data using deep learning techniques like CNN, 3DCNN, R-CNN, Mask R-CNN, Customized CNN, etc. In this chapter, we present state-of-the-art works employing HSI with deep learning techniques for the early detection of OC and propose future research directions to the OC research community.

Keywords: Hyperspectral imaging, head and neck cancer, oral cancer, deep learning, and medical imaging

14.1 Introduction

Oral cancer (OC) stands first in the list of prevalent cancers in India in males and stands third in females. In the world, it takes eighth place on the most common cancer list [1]. OC and other cancers observed in the oropharynx, nasopharynx, laryngopharynx, and neck fall under the head and neck cancer (HNC) category. To date, there is no promising treatment to cure cancer. Early detection can only reduce the mortality rate by up to

Table 14.1 Different stages of head and neck cancer.

Tumor size	Involvement of lymph nodes		Metastasis	Combination	Stage
T1—2 cm or less	N0—no involvement of lymph nodes		M0—no metastases	T1 N0 M0	Stage I
T2—2 to 4 cm	N0—no involvement of lymph nodes		M0—no metastases	T2 N0 M0	Stage II
T3—greater than 4 cm, without local invasion	N0—no involvement of lymph nodes	N1—single ipsilateral node < 3 cm	M0—no metastases	T3 N0 M0 or any N1	Stage III
T4—greater than 4 cm, with local invasion	N2—ipsilateral >3 cm but <6 cm or bilateral nodes	N3—any node >6 cm	M1—metastases	T4, N2, or N3, M1	Stage IV

70%. The severity of the HNC is divided into four stages based on the size of the tumor, involvement of nodes, and metastasis [2]. The staging of head and neck cancer is shown in Table 14.1 [3–5].

Cancer that spreads to lymph nodes indicates the third stage of cancer even though the size of the tumor is smaller and there is no metastasis. Treatment at this advanced stage is not effective, which causes less survival rates. Therefore, detection of cancer in the early stage will greatly help to increase the survival rate and the quality of life after the treatment. Conventional techniques like X-ray, ultrasound, magnetic resonance imaging (MRI), computed tomography (CT), positron emission tomography (PET), and fluorescence imaging are available for the detection of head and neck cancer. These techniques have some drawbacks like harmful radiation, injecting contrast agents, not being advisable for metal implant patients, and not being good for repetitive tests. Moreover, all these techniques will provide information at a particular wavelength only. Hyperspectral image (HSI) emerged as a technique to overcome all these drawbacks and can capture information for a wide range of wavelengths. The capabilities of light absorption and reflection is varying from object to object based on their chemical properties. HSI is a three-dimensional image. HSI cube is shown in Figure 14.1. Length and height represent the spatial resolution and width represents the spectral resolution. Reflectance variations along the HSI cube's spectral dimension give the object's spectral signature. Studying the OC spectral signatures will help doctors in the

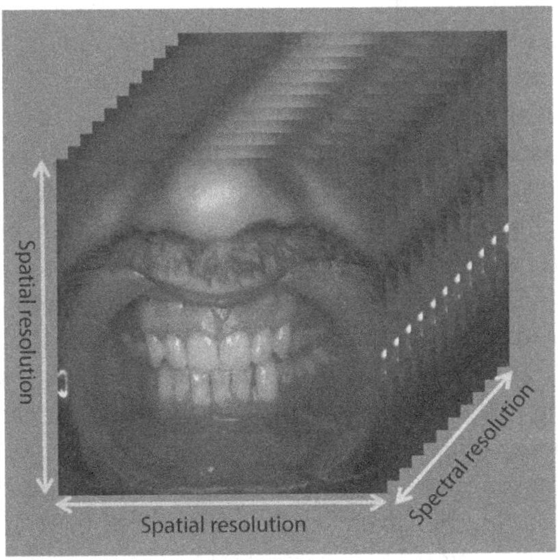

Figure 14.1 HSI cube.

early detection of cancer. Resection margin identification is also important to remove the affected region completely. Cancer recurrence is recorded at 55% after the surgery.

This HSI study can also be useful for accurately identifying resection margins. It saves the normal tissues and also helps to remove the infected tissues completely while operating to remove the malignant tissues. HSI can be used in both the methods of diagnosis *ex vivo* and *in vivo* in the HNC. This is limited to capturing the images of internal organs like the nasopharynx and laryngopharynx because the wavelength it captures cannot penetrate through the body. Endoscopic HSI techniques can be helpful for capturing the internal organs of the head and neck portion. While capturing the images in *in vivo* process by the endoscope, different noises will be added to the image due to the movement of tissues. Preprocessing techniques should apply to remove the noise. HSI shows that it was an effective method for the identification of cancerous tissue and healthy tissue in HNC diagnosis [6]. HSI is also having a few challenges to solve, like huge size images, spectral similarity, less publicly available data sets, etc. HSI can capture the images for every 2 to 3 nm wavelength, based on the spectral resolution. Hundreds of band images will form for a single HSI Data Cube, which results in a huge size. The spectrum was obtained for various tissues like malignant, benign, and normal, which look similar in shape, and sometimes only the reflectance values differ. In extracting meaningful information from these images, conventional image processing techniques are not enough to handle these challenges. Machine learning (ML) is a subset of artificial intelligence (AI), which became popular in processing the HSI to extract meaningful information from it. Several ML algorithms are used for the analysis of medical HSI. ML algorithms are divided into supervised and unsupervised, where there is minimal or no human intervention. These algorithms are prone to evolve into increasingly complicated models. Then, researchers delve into deep learning (DL), which was developed by the inspiration of the human brain's structure and working. DL is also a subset of ML, which has proven its efficiency in the diagnosis of HNC. The research community also got better classification accuracy from the deep learning techniques than the support vector machine (SVM) and kNN [7]. In this chapter, we present state-of-the-art works employing HSI with deep learning techniques for early detection of HNC and propose future research directions to the HNC research community. The remainder of the chapter is outlined as follows. Section 14.2 demonstrates a comprehensive overview of the HSI in HNC with conventional methods. In Section 14.3, we presented the state-of-the-art research work on deep learning in HNC using HSI, followed by a conclusion and significant future research directions given for the improvement of cancer detection using deep learning and HSI in Section 14.4.

14.2 HSI in HNC Detection

Human tissues are a turbid, inhomogeneous, optical medium that has a refractive index higher than air. These tissues have different optical properties like absorption, scattering, total attenuation, effective attenuation, exponential attenuation, etc.; from all these parameters, absorption and scattering are important in optical diagnosis in the biomedical field. These properties are responsible for the light penetration into the tissue and light absolute reflection. The light penetration depth is from 8 to 10 mm, which is varied with the wavelength of the light. The absorption coefficient and scattering coefficient will change with the light wavelength. Hence, penetration depth increases with an increase in the incident light wavelength. The light that penetrates into the tissue will not change its wavelength due to the elastic scattering events. The human tissue contains water, nuclei, nucleolus, lipids, hemoglobin, etc. These human tissues provide two windows for optical diagnosis and treatment. The first window is from 650 to 950 nm, and the second window is from 1000 to 1350 nm, as shown in Figure 14.2 [8].

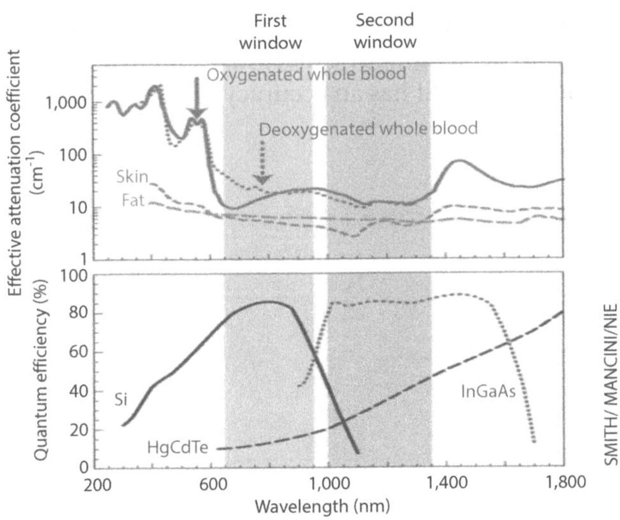

Figure 14.2 Two diagnosis and therapeutic windows of the spectrum.

Table 14.2 Biological differences between cancer tissue and normal tissue.

S. no.	Normal tissue	Cancer tissue
1	Large cytoplasm	Small cytoplasm
2	Single nuclei	Multiple nuclei
3	Single nucleolus	Multiple and large nucleolus
4	More hemoglobin	Less hemoglobin
5	Regular shape	Irregular shape

It is a challenge for doctors to find the deep margin of the tumor during HNC surgery. Thus, HSI can help to find the deep margin of the tumor and diagnose oral cancer [9]. The hyperspectral imaging system contains a light source that emits light onto the sample and the hyperspectral sensor will capture the light reflected from the tissue. The light reflection and absorption properties vary from normal tissue to cancer tissue as they are different in the cell structure and its content. Some of the differences are shown in Table 14.2. For example, light absorption is directly proportional to the Hb levels in the tissue.

This Hb absorption can be noticed from 450 to 600 nm in a hyperspectral spectrum. The absorption coefficient of different biological tissues at different wavelengths is shown in Figure 14.3.

Lu *et al.* studied different imaging methods like HSI, autofluorescence, fluorescence, etc. to detect tongue cancer in both *in vivo* and *ex vivo* techniques. They found that HSI has an accuracy of 75% ± 5% and a specificity

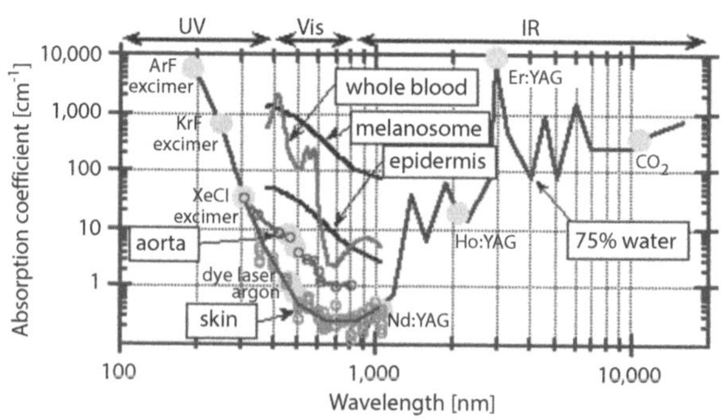

Figure 14.3 Absorption coefficient of biological tissues at different wavelengths [10].

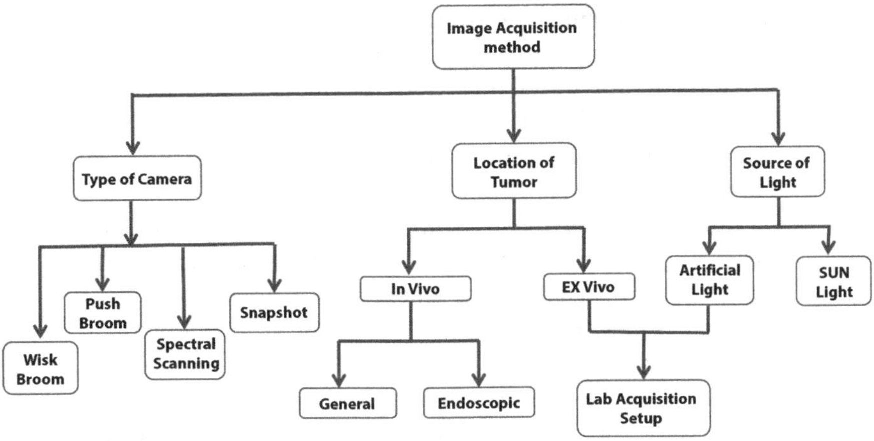

Figure 14.4 HSI imaging methods.

of 78% ± 5% in the *in vivo* technique. An accuracy of 86% ± 6% and a specificity of 79% ± 5% in *ex vivo* are again better than fluorescence and autofluorescence [11].

i. **Hyperspectral Image Acquisition Process**

The hyperspectral image acquisition process is quite important for getting better and more accurate results. The selection of the acquisition method is based on tumor locations, source of light, type of camera scanning, etc. as shown in Figure 14.4. Acquisition methods vary based on different causes like tumor location, light source, and camera scanning.

The hyperspectral imaging lab setup we have in our lab is shown in Figure 14.5. The setup consists of two halogen light sources, a SPECIM IQ camera, a moving platform, a white reference tile, and a specim studio software with Intel Xeon Server for data processing.

A. **Halogen lamps**: Halogen lamps are used as light sources when we are taking images in indoor laboratories. These light sources will produce light with a wide range of wavelengths. These lights require a proper heatsink to cool down the filament of tungsten.
B. **Camera**: Specim IQ hyperspectral camera is used, which has the capability to capture 450 to 1000 nm reflectance. The captured images can be stored and processed by the specim studio. Its spatial and spectral resolution is 520 × 520 pixels and 2 nm, respectively.

C. **Moving platform**: One more important tool in this setup is the moving platform. It is useful to adjust the sample in vertical and horizontal directions. It will help to have a good field of view, and comfort to take the perfect images.
D. **Specim studio**: It is a freely available software, which is provided by SPECIM and compatible with specim cameras. It is helpful to load the images from the devices to the local computer. We can extract the spectral signatures, compare the signatures, and classify the images using these signatures. Generated files from this software can be accessed by other software like Matlab.
E. **Reference tile**: Reference tiles are required in hyperspectral imaging for the correct illumination measurements. White or black reference tiles can be used, but with the SPECIM IQ camera, a specially designed tile is provided, which we can be used as a reference tile.

Cancer that affects the tissues that are visible from the outside like the tongue, lips, gums, cheeks, etc. could undergo the *in vivo* procedure for diagnosis. For cancers that are affected at the internal tissues that are not visible to the outside, the *ex vivo* process of diagnosis or *in vivo* by endoscope procedure is possible. However, these hyper spectral imaging techniques have limitations in medical diagnosis due to the dimensionality curse, less availability of publicly available data sets, and less availability of labeled data sets for training. These limitations can be overcome by using deep learning techniques in HSI [12].

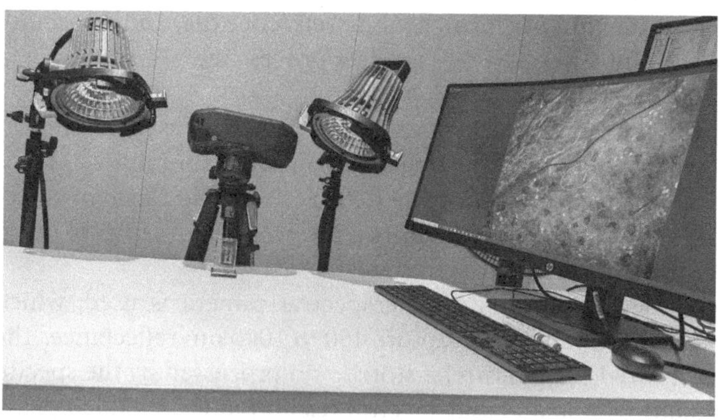

Figure 14.5 HSI laboratory imaging setup.

b. DL Methods for HNC detection using HSI

Adding artificial intelligence to head and neck cancer will increase the accuracy of interpretation of the images. Currently, 25% of articles were found using the DL, 69% using the ML, and 6% using both DL and ML for better accuracy as shown in Figure 14.6 [13].

DL is not only used for low-level tasks like detection, classification, and segmentation. It can also be used for giving treatment optimality and progression prediction [14]. These methods also reduce the delay in cancer detection [15]. Deep learning techniques are gaining attention due to HSI analysis detecting HNC. These are proven by achieving higher sensitivity, specificity, and accuracy than the ML algorithms. DL is a neural network that has more than two layers. The first layer is an input layer and the last layer is an output layer, and all the other layers in between these two are hidden layers. This DL structure is inspired by the structure and function of neurons in the human brain. The input image will feed into the input layer and is forwarded to the hidden layers where the feature extraction and selection take place. These features are related to the logical outputs represented by the class labels. The prediction possibilities are extracted from it. DL methods showed their higher capability in detection, segmentation, classification, and object detection in other medical imaging techniques even for dental diseases [16]. The research community uses these higher capabilities of DL in HSI medical imaging. This effective combination is used in *ex vivo*, *in vivo*, and endoscopic methods in both animal and human samples. The most widely used DL model for the detection of HNC is the convolutional neural network (CNN). This technique is used for both *ex vivo* and *in vivo* mode of detection purposes.

Halicek *et al.* worked on human sinus and thyroid cancer. They used the *ex vivo* diagnosis mode and compared the deep learning model CNN with

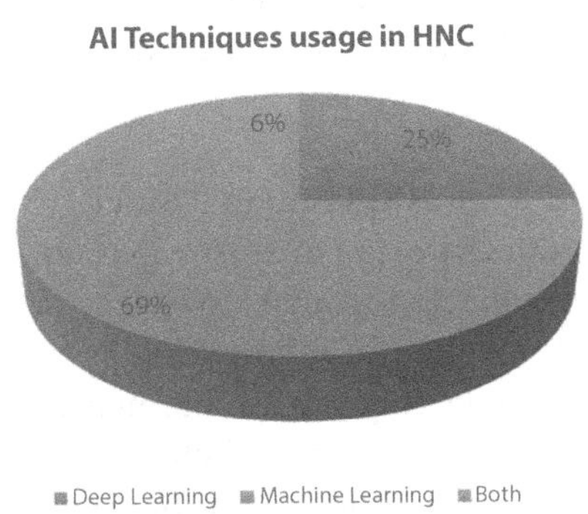

Figure 14.6 AI techniques usage in HNC research.

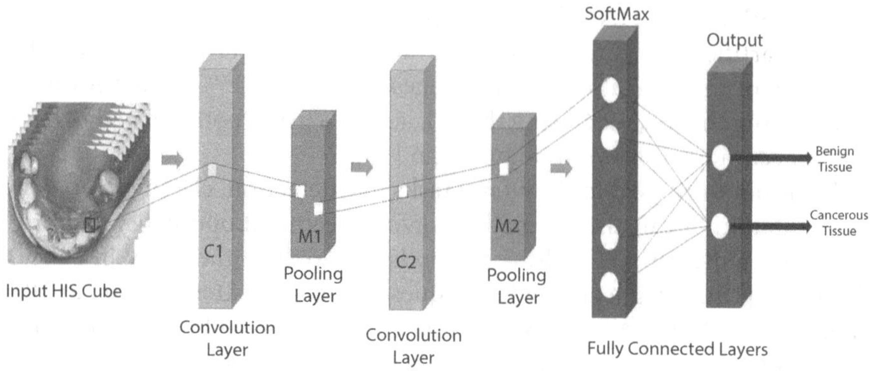

Figure 14.7 CNN architecture for HNC.

SVM and kNN for the detection of sinus and thyroid cancer tissues. They achieved better results with CNN than the other ML models. They constructed the CNN architecture with 6 convolution layers and 3 fully connected layers [17]. The CNN architecture for HNC is shown in Figure 14.7.

In machine learning models, SVM performs better where the procedure is complex. Zhou *et al.* captured polarized hyperspectral images of the histological slides of cancer tissues. They performed classification using different machine learning models by giving Stokes vector parameters. They found that Stoke parameters will increase the performance of the classifiers. Out of all ML algorithms, SVM performed better. This study was conducted on 20 images taken from 10 patients, which totally had 4500 patches. A total of 2250 patches are from normal tissue and the remaining 2250 are from squamous cell carcinoma [18]. In Ref. [19], the authors experimented on 12 mice that have HNC and they trained the model with the sample images of 11 mice. The results were tested by the sample taken from the 12th mice. Principal component analysis (PCA) and SVM were used for the tissue classification and achieved a sensitivity of 93.7% and specificity of 91.3%.

i. Deep Learning in *Ex Vivo* HSI Human Model

Trajanovski *et al.* conducted experiments on tongue squamous cell carcinoma *ex vivo* tissues collected from 14 patients. They used U-Net deep learning architecture for semantic segmenting of the cancer tissue. They presented that instead of selecting all the channels of the spectrum, selecting a few important channels will give better results. They achieved an AUC of 0.924 ± 0.036. They demonstrated that the visual spectrum (VIS) provides more information than the near-infrared spectrum (NIS) [20].

Halicek *et al.* [21] found that HSI-limiting factors including spectral glare, noise, and blur will affect the efficiency of deep learning classification in a medical image. The CNN classification efficiency will improve due to the data pre-processing techniques. They tried different combinations of DL techniques. The better performance is given by the combination of CNN,

Table 14.3 *Ex vivo* head and neck cancer.

S. no.	Rf. no.	HNC sub-type	Deep learning technique	Accuracy	AUC
1	1	HN SCC	CNN	96.40%	-
2	3	SCC	CNN	-	0.82
		Thyroid		92%	-
3	5	Larynx, hypopharynx, buccal mucosa, and floor of the mouth	HSI CNN/RGB CNN	89%	-
4	12	Tongue	U-Net	-	0.924±0.036
5	14	Tongue, larynx, pharynx, and mandible	CNN+HELICoiD+KNN	-	0.81
6	19	Larynx and hypopharynx	CNN	82.40%	0.94
7	21	Larynx and hypopharynx	U-Net	83%	0.88
9	22	Cheek/flour of the mouth	CNN	>80%	-
8	24	Oral	3D CNN	81	0.86
		Thyroid		89%	0.94
9	25	Tongue	ML	-	0.92
10	42	Thyroid	v4 CNN	-	0.9
		Salivary glands			0.92
11	50	H&N	v4-CNN	-	0.82

HELICoiD algorithm, and KNN, achieving and area under the ROC curve (AUC) of 0.81. Halicek *et al.* [22] conducted experiments on classifying the normal tissue and cancer tissue of SCC and thyroid cancer. They took samples from 21 patients and trained the CNN and achieved 92% accuracy, 92% specificity, and 92% sensitivity for thyroid classification and 0.82 AUC for the SCC. Ma *et al.* studied oral carcinoma histological slides of HSI on 20 patients; they identified the nuclei of cancer tissue and normal tissue. They tested the performance of RGB-CNN and HSI-CNN, where the first one was trained by the RGB images of cancer, and the second one is trained by the HSI spectral features. They found that HSI-CNN performed better than RGB-CNN with 89% accuracy [23]. The performance of different deep learning models for the *ex vivo* mode of diagnosis using HSI is shown in Table 14.3.

Histological slides were collected from 15 patients who have already been confirmed to have SCC. Identification of the cancer tissue is identified by the classification of nuclei. SVM and CNN were used for the classification; CNN performed better with an average accuracy of 82.4% [24]. Ma *et al.* [25] studied 25 *ex vivo* surgical images taken from 20 patients. These images are of 3 types, which are normal tissue, tumor tissue, and tumor normal tissues. In traditional methods, the required surgical margin varies from 5 to 25 mm. In this study, using the 3-layered U-Net, they achieved less than a 2-mm margin in 17 patients. They achieved an average AUC of 0.83 and an average accuracy of 83%. Thiem *et al.* studied 316 samples of healthy human oral fat, muscle, and mucosa from 174 patients. They collected fat and muscle from the cheek, and mucosa from the floor of the mouth. The signatures extracted for those three tissues have notable differences throughout from 500 to 1000 nm. Muscle signature showed higher variations when compared with the others. Cancer tissue classification is done by six layered lightweight CNNs, which had more than 80% accuracy [26]. The work in [27] studied oral cancer and thyroid cancer to identify the surgical margin. They classified the tissues as tumor tissue and the tissue nearer and around it was categorized as tumor-normal tissue. These tissues are collected from 20 patients. The spectral signatures of the normal oral and thyroid tissues have a large gap between them, whereas the gap between the SCC tissue and thyroid cancer is not much. The 3D CNN deep learning model provides better results with an accuracy of 90% for thyroid cancer and 81% for oral cancer. The authors in [28] experimented on 1157 pathology images taken from 10 mice. Nuclei and cytoplasm are extracted from the features like color, texture, morphology, and topology, which are analyzed by artificial intelligence techniques for the classification of cancer and normal tissue.

14.3 Deep Learning in *In Vivo* HSI

A. Animal Model

In [29], the authors did research on 12 mice with HNC of M4E and used the CRI *in vivo* imaging model to capture the images of the target. They used the pixel feature extraction and trained the CNN, and achieved a satisfactory average accuracy, specificity, and sensitivity of 91.36%, 93.36%, and 99.41%, respectively. In [30], the authors conducted experiments on 4-NQO-treated tongue cancer in the mouse, and they found that the spectra obtained are very much different between 600 and 850 nm. They compared the performance of different algorithms to classify the treated cancer and the normal portion of the tongue. Random Forest performs better than the other algorithms with an AUC of 0.89. The work in [31] compared the performance of different deep learning architectures like FCN, U-Net, SegNet, and Auto Encoders on *in vivo* cancer classification in 12 mice. They used autoencoders for pixel-wise prediction of cancer being malignant or benign. Adaptive learning can improve the performance of classification. It will happen because misclassified pixels can be recorrected by the adaptive weights. Autoencoders classified the tissues better than the other techniques with an average accuracy of 91.33%.

B. Human Model

Roblyer *et al.* found that intensity and line space between the spectra of the same anatomic location will be the same and differ for different anatomic locations. Reflectance peak, depth, intensity, or line space vary when spectra are collected from the same anatomic location and if the tissue varies between malignant and normal [32]. Liu *et al.* studied 65 human tongue images, with 34 images containing partial tumor and the remainder containing full tumor. They developed a sparse representation method for detecting cancer tissue and they achieved a 96.5% recognition rate [33].

14.3.1 Endoscopic

Current endoscopic techniques like white light endoscopy face some limitations like an unclear boundary and thin white coating on the mucosa of reddish lesions, where these limitations can be overcome by HSI endoscopy [34]. However, HSI also encounters problems such as misregistration, image noise, and specular reflection. These limitations can be overcome by effective pre-processing techniques, then the classification accuracy will

Table 14.4 *In vivo* head and neck cancer.

S. no.	Rf. no.	Endoscopy	Model	HNC sub-type	Deep learning technique	Accuracy	AUC
1	2	No	Animal	HN SCC	CNN	0.9136	-
2	4	Yes	Human	Laryngeal	3D CNN	0.81	-
3	8	No	Animal	HN SCC	AI	89.1	-
4	15	Yes	Human	Laryngeal	3D CNN	0.81	-
5	18	No	Animal	Tongue	AI RF	-	0.89
6	23	No	Animal	HN SCC	Auto encoder	0.9133	-
7	31	Yes	Human	Laryngeal	ML RF	0.88	-

increase [35]. The performance of different deep learning models for the *in vivo* mode of diagnosis using HSI is shown in Table 14.4.

The HSI endoscopic equipment is also added with some tunable filters like the liquid crystal tunable filter, etc. [36]. Researchers are working hard to develop real-time endoscopic equipment like an image mapping spectroscopy endoscope [37]. Some other works on HSI endoscopic research are presented as follows.

Regeling *et al.* found honeycomb-like patterns while studying HS imaging of the larynx. These patterns are observed in some bands only. These honeycombs appeared due to the optical fibers arranged hexagonally in the endoscope. These honeycombs are removed by the pre-processing technique. It increases the accuracy of the classification technique [38]. The real-time use of HSI in minimal invasive surgery is restricted due to the long acquisition time, missing video, large setup, and various interferences in imaging. However, using HSI in minimal invasive surgery can minimize intra-operative and post-operative complications [39]. Bengs *et al.* developed an endoscopic *in vivo* technique, using spatio-spectral 3D CNN architecture for the detection of laryngeal cancer. They observed that spatio-spectral analysis provides better results than the individual analysis either spatial or spectral. They achieved 82% accuracy for cancer detection [40]. Eggert *et al.* conducted experiments on 98 patients to find the *in vivo* diagnosis capability of HSI in medical diagnosis. They followed the endoscopy procedure to classify the head and neck cancer tissues from normal tissues. They developed and tested the HSI 3D CNN, HSI 2D CNN, and

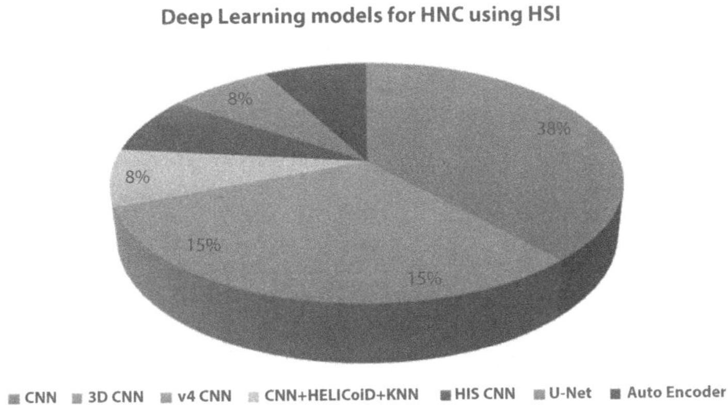

Figure 14.8 Deep learning models for the HNC using HSI.

RGB CNN on 24 patients. Comparatively, the HSI 3D CNN gives an average of 81% accuracy, which is better than the HSI 2D CNN and RGB CNN [41]. Popular deep learning models used for the HNC via HSI are shown in Figure 14.8.

14.4 Conclusion and Future Research Directions

In this comprehensive chapter, we summarized the state-of-the-art research works, mostly deliberating the HSI problems in HNC and some of the solution methods using deep learning. By studying the key literature on deep learning in HNC using HSI, we are presenting some unanswered problems while capturing and processing the HS image. Overall, the deep learning and hyperspectral combination can become a promising tool for the early detection of head and neck cancer.

Head and neck cancer's hyperspectral image analysis using deep learning has started, and only a few models like CNN and U-Net were used. The research community can also use advanced and powerful modules like transformers, generative adversarial networks (GANs), etc.

Hyperspectral imaging for medical applications encounters small-data issues. In this regard, the researchers can think of techniques like synthetic data generation. These techniques can improve the data set, which can further improve the performance of the system. HS capturing will not be perfect in the *in vivo* model of imaging, due to the involuntary movement of the target organ of the patient like the tongue, lips, etc. Some methods should be developed to remove these errors in the HSI, and an in-depth

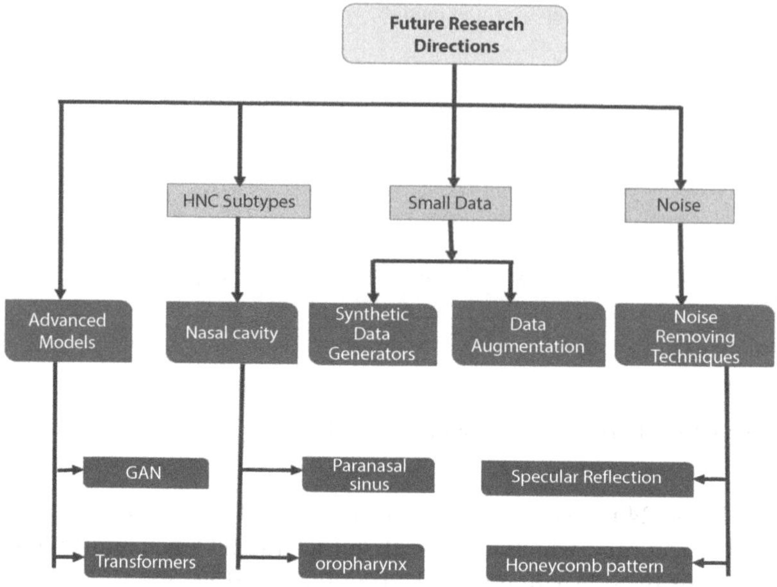

Figure 14.9 Future research directions.

study should be done to identify the different noises like specular reflection and honeycomb-like patterns added to the image during image capture.

Future research directions are given in Figure 14.9. Currently, there is ongoing research on the detection, classification, and segmentation of cancer. The staging of cancer can also be a target for researchers, and all the subtypes of head and neck cancers were not studied by HSI. Cancers of the nasal cavity, paranasal sinus, oropharynx, etc. can also be studied. Inter-patient and intra-patient studies can also be possible, and whether the DL model developed based on one patient's images will work for the other patients will be known. Time-series data analysis is also possible and may help to achieve better and more accurate results.

References

1. Shajahan Ahamed, Mehreen, and Amsalu Degu. "Health-related quality of life among cervical cancer patients at Kenyatta National Hospital." *J. Oncol. Pharm. Pract.*, (2022): 10781552211073886.
2. Shin, Dongsuk, Nadarajah Vigneswaran, Ann Gillenwater, and Rebecca Richards-Kortum. "Advances in fluorescence imaging techniques to detect oral cancer and its precursors." *Future Oncol.*, 6, no. 7 (2010): 1143-1154.

3. Halicek, Martin, James D. Dormer, James V. Little, Amy Y. Chen, and Baowei Fei. "Tumor detection of the thyroid and salivary glands using hyperspectral imaging and deep learning." *Biomed. Opt. Express,* 11, no. 3 (2020): 1383-1400.
4. Shin, Dongsuk, Nadarajah Vigneswaran, Ann Gillenwater, and Rebecca Richards-Kortum. "Advances in fluorescence imaging techniques to detect oral cancer and its precursors." *Future Oncol.,* 6, no. 7 (2010): 1143-1154.
5. S. R. Burri, A. Kumar, A. Baliyan and T. A. Kumar, "Transforming Payment Processes: A Discussion of AI-Enabled Routing Optimization," *2023 2nd International Conference on Smart Technologies and Systems for Next Generation Computing (ICSTSN),* Villupuram, India, 2023, pp. 1-7, doi: 10.1109/ICSTSN57873.2023.10151455.
6. Lu, Guolan, James V. Little, Xu Wang, Hongzheng Zhang, Mihir R. Patel, Christopher C. Griffith, Mark W. El-Deiry, Amy Y. Chen, and Baowei Fei. "Detection of Head and Neck Cancer in Surgical Specimens Using Quantitative Hyperspectral ImagingHyperspectral Imaging for Head and Neck Cancer Detection." *Clin. Cancer Res.,* 23, no. 18 (2017): 5426-5436.
7. Crowson, Matthew G., Jonathan Ranisau, Antoine Eskander, Aaron Babier, Bin Xu, Russel R. Kahmke, Joseph M. Chen, and Timothy CY Chan. "A contemporary review of machine learning in otolaryngology–head and neck surgery." *Laryngoscope,* 130, no. 1 (2020): 45-51.
8. Burri, Srinivasa Rao, Sachin Ahuja, Abhishek Kumar, and Anupam Baliyan. "Exploring the Effectiveness of Optimized Convolutional Neural Network in Transfer Learning for Image Classification: A Practical Approach." In *2023 International Conference on Advancement in Computation & Computer Technologies (InCACCT),* pp. 598-602. IEEE, 2023.
9. de Koning, SG Brouwer, A. W. M. A. Schaeffers, W. Schats, M. W. M. van den Brekel, T. J. M. Ruers and M. B. Karakullukcu. "Assessment of the deep resection margin during oral cancer surgery: A systematic review." *Eur. J. Surg. Oncol.,* 47, no. 9 (2021): 2220-2232.
10. Keiser, Gerd, and Fu-Jen Kao. "Biophotonic applications of optical communication devices." In *Biophotonics: Photonic Solutions for Better Health Care,* vol. 6991, pp. 249-256. SPIE, 2008.
11. Lu, Guolan, Dongsheng Wang, Xulei Qin, Susan Muller, Xu Wang, Amy Y. Chen, Zhuo Georgia Chen, and Baowei Fei. "Detection and delineation of squamous neoplasia with hyperspectral imaging in a mouse model of tongue carcinogenesis." *J. Biophotonics,* 11, no. 3 (2018): e201700078.
12. Signoroni, Alberto, Mattia Savardi, Annalisa Baronio, and Sergio Benini. "Deep learning meets hyperspectral image analysis: A multidisciplinary review." *J. Imaging,* 5, no. 5 (2019): 52.
13. Mahmood, Hanya, Muhammad Shaban, Nasir Rajpoot, and Syed A. Khurram. "Artificial Intelligence-based methods in head and neck cancer diagnosis: An overview." *Br. J. Cancer,* 124, no. 12 (2021): 1934-1940.

14. N. Mahsuda, C. Ananth, N. Isok-Jon, Y. Rayimjon and T. A. Kumar, "Virtual Science is a New Scientific Paradigm," *2023 IEEE Renewable Energy and Sustainable E-Mobility Conference (RESEM)*, Bhopal, India, 2023, pp. 1-5, doi: 10.1109/RESEM57584.2023.10236372.
15. Ilhan, Betul, Pelin Guneri, and Petra Wilder-Smith. "The contribution of artificial intelligence to reducing the diagnostic delay in oral cancer." *Oral Oncol.*, 116 (2021): 105254.
16. Bala, P. Manju, S. Usharani, R. Rajmohan, T. Ananth Kumar and A. Balachandar. "Bioinspired CNN Approach for Diagnosing COVID-19 Using Images of Chest X-Ray." In *Smart Computer Vision*, pp. 181-201. Cham: Springer International Publishing, 2023.
17. Halicek, Martin, Guolan Lu, James V. Little, Xu Wang, Mihir Patel, Christopher C. Griffith, Mark W. El-Deiry, Amy Y. Chen, and Baowei Fei. "Deep convolutional neural networks for classifying head and neck cancer using hyperspectral imaging." *J. Biomed. Opt.*, 22, no. 6 (2017): 060503.
18. Zhou, Ximing, Ling Ma, William Brown, James V. Little, Amy Y. Chen, Larry L. Myers, Baran D. Sumer, and Baowei Fei. "Automatic detection of head and neck squamous cell carcinoma on pathologic slides using polarized hyperspectral imaging and machine learning." In *Medical Imaging 2021: Digital Pathology*, vol. 11603, pp. 165-173. SPIE, 2021.
19. Lu, Guolan, Luma V. Halig, Dongsheng Wang, Xulei Qin, Zhuo Georgia Chen, and Baowei Fei. "Spectral-spatial classification for noninvasive cancer detection using hyperspectral imaging." *J. Biomed. Opt.*, 19, no. 10 (2014): 106004.
20. Trajanovski, Stojan, Caifeng Shan, Pim JC Weijtmans, Susan G. Brouwer de Koning, and Theo JM Ruers. "Tongue tumor detection in hyperspectral images using deep learning semantic segmentation." *IEEE. Trans. Biomed. Eng.*, 68, no. 4 (2020): 1330-1340.
21. Halicek, Martin, Himar Fabelo, Samuel Ortega, James V. Little, Xu Wang, Amy Y. Chen, Gustavo Marrero Callico, Larry Myers, Baran D. Sumer, and Baowei Fei. "Hyperspectral imaging for head and neck cancer detection: specular glare and variance of the tumor margin in surgical specimens." *J. Med. Imaging*, 6, no. 3 (2019): 035004.
22. Halicek, Martin, James V. Little, Xu Wang, Amy Y. Chen, and Baowei Fei. "Optical biopsy of head and neck cancer using hyperspectral imaging and convolutional neural networks." *J. Biomed. Opt.*, 24, no. 3 (2019): 036007.
23. Ma, Ling, James V. Little, Amy Y. Chen, Larry Myers, Baran D. Sumer, and Baowei Fei. "Automatic detection of head and neck squamous cell carcinoma on histologic slides using hyperspectral microscopic imaging." *J. Biomed. Opt.*, 27, no. 4 (2022): 046501.
24. Benkhaddra, Ilyas, Abhishek Kumar, Mohamed Ali Setitra, and Lei Hang. "Design and Development of Consensus Activation Function Enabled Neural Network-Based Smart Healthcare Using BIoT." *Wirel. Pers. Commun.*, 130, no. 3 (2023): 1549-1574.

25. Ma, Ling, Maysam Shahedi, Ted Shi, Martin Halicek, James V. Little, Amy Y. Chen, Larry L. Myers, Baran D. Sumer, and Baowei Fei. "Pixel-level tumor margin assessment of surgical specimen with hyperspectral imaging and deep learning classification." In *Medical Imaging 2021: Image-Guided Procedures, Robotic Interventions, and Modeling*, vol. 11598, pp. 269-278. SPIE, 2021.
26. Thiem, Daniel GE, Paul Römer, Matthias Gielisch, Bilal Al-Nawas, Martin Schlüter, Bastian Plaß, and Peer W. Kämmerer. "Hyperspectral imaging and artificial intelligence to detect oral malignancy–part 1-automated tissue classification of oral muscle, fat and mucosa using a light-weight 6-layer deep neural network." *Head Face Med.*, 17, no. 1 (2021): 1-9.
27. Halicek, Martin, James V. Little, Xu Wang, Mihir Patel, Christopher C. Griffith, Amy Y. Chen, and Baowei Fei. "Tumor margin classification of head and neck cancer using hyperspectral imaging and convolutional neural networks." In *Medical Imaging 2018: Image-Guided Procedures, Robotic Interventions, and Modeling*, vol. 10576, pp. 17-27. SPIE, 2018.
28. Lu, Guolan, Dongsheng Wang, Xulei Qin, Susan Muller, James V. Little, Xu Wang, Amy Y. Chen, Georgia Chen, and Baowei Fei. "Histopathology feature mining and association with hyperspectral imaging for the detection of squamous neoplasia." *Sci. Rep.*, 9, no. 1 (2019): 1-13.
29. Ma, Ling, Guolan Lu, Dongsheng Wang, Xu Wang, Zhuo Georgia Chen, Susan Muller, Amy Chen, and Baowei Fei. "Deep learning based classification for head and neck cancer detection with hyperspectral imaging in an animal model." In *Medical imaging 2017: Biomedical applications in molecular, structural, and functional imaging*, vol. 10137, pp. 632-639. SPIE, 2017.
30. Lu, Guolan, Xulei Qin, Dongsheng Wang, Susan Muller, Hongzheng Zhang, Amy Chen, Zhuo Georgia Chen, and Baowei Fei. "Hyperspectral imaging of neoplastic progression in a mouse model of oral carcinogenesis." In *Medical Imaging 2016: Biomedical Applications in Molecular, Structural, and Functional Imaging*, vol. 9788, pp. 252-259. SPIE, 2016.
31. Ma, Ling, Guolan Lu, Dongsheng Wang, Xulei Qin, Zhuo Georgia Chen, and Baowei Fei. "Adaptive deep learning for head and neck cancer detection using hyperspectral imaging." *Visual Computing for Industry, Biomedicine, Art* 2, no. 1 (2019): 1-12.
32. Roblyer, Darren, Cristina Kurachi, Ann M. Gillenwater, and Rebecca Richards-Kortum. "In vivo fluorescence hyperspectral imaging of oral neoplasia." In *Visual Computing for Industry, Biomedicine, Art* 2, vol. 7169, pp. 96-105. SPIE, 2009.
33. Benkhaddra, Ilyas, Abhishek Kumar, Mohamed Ali Setitra, and Lei Hang. "Design and Development of Consensus Activation Function Enabled Neural Network-Based Smart Healthcare Using BIoT." *Wirel. Pers. Commun.*, 130, no. 3 (2023): 1549-1574.
34. Wu, I., Hao-Yi Syu, Chun-Ping Jen, Ming-Yen Lu, Yi-Ting Chen, Ming-Tsang Wu, Chie-Tong Kuo, Yu-Yuan Tsai, and Hsiang-Chen Wang. "Early

identification of esophageal squamous neoplasm by hyperspectral endoscopic imaging." *Sci. Rep.*, 8, no. 1 (2018): 1-10.

35. Regeling, Bianca, Wiebke Laffers, Andreas OH Gerstner, Stephan Westermann, Nina A. Müller, Kai Schmidt, Jörg Bendix, and Boris Thies. "Development of an image pre-processor for operational hyperspectral laryngeal cancer detection." *J. Biophotonics,* 9, no. 3 (2016): 235-245.
36. Martin, Matthew E., Musundi B. Wabuyele, Masoud Panjehpour, Mary N. Phan, Bergein F. Overholt, and Tuan Vo-Dinh. "Hyperspectral fluorescence imaging system for biomedical diagnostics." In *Advanced Biomedical and Clinical Diagnostic Systems IV*, vol. 6080, pp. 136-144. SPIE, 2006.
37. Kester, Robert T., Noah Bedard, Liang S. Gao, and Tomasz S. Tkaczyk. "Real-time snapshot hyperspectral imaging endoscope." *J. Biomed. Opt.,* 16, no. 5 (2011): 056005.
38. Regeling, Bianca, Boris Thies, Andreas OH Gerstner, Stephan Westermann, Nina A. Müller, Jörg Bendix, and Wiebke Laffers. "Hyperspectral imaging using flexible endoscopy for laryngeal cancer detection." *Sensors,* 16, no. 8 (2016): 1288.
39. Köhler, Hannes, Axel Kulcke, Marianne Maktabi, Yusef Moulla, Boris Jansen-Winkeln, Manuel Barberio, Michele Diana, Ines Gockel, Thomas Neumuth, and Claire Chalopin. "Laparoscopic system for simultaneous high-resolution video and rapid hyperspectral imaging in the visible and near-infrared spectral range." *J. Biomed. Opt.*, 25, no. 8 (2020): 086004.
40. Bengs, Marcel, Stephan Westermann, Nils Gessert, Dennis Eggert, Andreas OH Gerstner, Nina A. Mueller, Christian Betz, Wiebke Laffers, and Alexander Schlaefer. "Spatio-spectral deep learning methods for *in-vivo* hyperspectral laryngeal cancer detection." In *Medical Imaging 2020: Computer-Aided Diagnosis,* vol. 11314, pp. 369-374. SPIE, 2020.
41. Chalopin, C., Nickel, F., Pfahl, A., Köhler, H., Maktabi, M., Thieme, R., ... & Gockel, I. (2022). Künstliche Intelligenz und hyperspektrale Bildgebung zur bildgestützten Assistenz in der minimal-invasiven Chirurgie. *Die Chirurgie,* 1-8.

15

Machine Learning Techniques for Glaucoma Screening Using Optic Disc Detection

V. Subha[1]*, S. Niraja P. Rayen[2] and Manivanna Boopathi[3]

[1]*Department of CSE, Manonmaniam Sundaranar University, Tirunelveli, India*
[2]*Department of Computer Science, St. Xavier's College, Tirunelveli, India*
[3]*Department of EIE, Saveetha Engineering College, Chennai, India*

Abstract

Since the major aspect of an information processing system is to facilitate inbuilt intelligence to manage tremendous amounts of data in any form, computers play an essential role in data processing with image files. In ophthalmology, image processing plays a crucial role in recognizing an issue belonging to a human's eye. Most of the visual problems have been caused by frequent use of computers or some discomfort related to the eyes. The optic disc (OD) holds cardinal aspects in the human visual system to diagnose retinal diseases. It is represented as a bright region using the blood vessel's high fractal dimension. The disc's location is used to diagnose various eye diseases, such as glaucoma, diabetic retinopathy, and macular degeneration. The present screening system provides a way to detect glaucoma with optic disc segmentation.

An abnormality in the eye termed vision loss results in glaucoma, a chronic disease that eventually leads to blindness. The detection process includes important features like the optic disc (OD), the optic cup (OC), and the neuroretinal rim (NRR) for the identification of glaucoma. The cardinal objective is to obtain an improved way to proceed with the OD detection using a combination of multiple segmentation algorithms. The present work analyses some algorithms for optic disc segmentation and OD detection in a fundus image. Optic disc detection is utilized for determining the location of the disc centre with a directional matched filter by applying the green channel image from the input.

**Corresponding author*: subha_velappan@msuniv.ac.in

T. Ananth Kumar, E. Golden Julie, Venkata Raghuveer Burugadda, Abhishek Kumar and Puneet Kumar (eds.) Computational Intelligence: Theory and Applications, (321–348) © 2024 Scrivener Publishing LLC

The main vessels are detected on the OD with the green channel image. The approximate direction of the main vessel is aligned vertically over the OD region. Then, the kernel size of the OD region is the maximum width of the central vessel presented in OD. The cup boundary is encompassed by the blood vessel's density and is detected by various features based on the colour information belonging to the cup region, and it is followed by a clinical convention method for evaluating the CDR value. This value is used to examine whether the cup area has increased and to reduce a gradual loss of vision using an automatic glaucoma diagnosis system with machine learning algorithms. Hence, this method can recognize a high correlation using supervised classification with ground truth segmentation results in the retinal image.

Keywords: Fundus image, glaucoma, optic disc, optic cup, INST, segmentation, cup–disc ratio, image processing

15.1 Introduction

Since computers can easily store enormous amounts of data and analyze information rapidly and intelligently, automation has played a vital part in automating any kind of procedure in every element of computer usage. The deliberation level can be varied on different platforms to ensure its utility. Along with its utility, health problems, too, have come into existence with the use of computers in day-to-day life. People who work on computers develop eye problems. Most probably, problems related to the visual system are caused by working on computers continuously. This section explains the major parts of the eye used in visual creation and further explicates the problems related to the eye. The inner surface of the eye has a layer called the retina, where the vessels are located, forming a thin membrane, which is more likely to break up into the interior of the vascular membrane.

The image retention of the retina has similar features to light-sensitive photography images. Then, the fundus part of the image can exist on the back side of the retina. The human retina consists of an optic nerve and a large artery. Using this, the location of the optic disc is identified, and it can be used as an origin reference for identification. On the back side of the eye, every optic nerve is connected to the retina via a circular origin called the optic disc. Optic disc detection can be used to diagnose many eye diseases, such as glaucoma, diabetes, and macular degeneration. In this way, an essential technique for OD segmentation is detected by the development of visual identification systems and ophthalmologic diagnostic systems. This screening system furnishes a way to detect glaucoma with optic disc segmentation. When the optic nerve gets worse, it causes a problem known as glaucoma, which is linked to high pressure and its inherited level. It cannot be restored to prevent vision loss. Even if glaucoma is incurable, early detection of the disease may stop further development. To diagnose certain diseases of the retina, imaging techniques use the main features of the retina, such as the optic disc (OD), the optic cup (OC), and the neuroretinal rim (NRR). Therefore, the diagnosis of glaucoma is analyzed by a vital factor called OD. The optic disc is composed of blood vessels and nerves, and the disc originates from them [1]. Optic discs can be isolated from other bright cells, such as solids and artifacts, using higher-level measurements of blood vessels. The primary objective is to acquire an improved optic disc location by using several predictive algorithm combinations based on detection instructions and location-sharing algorithms in the fundus image. Optic disc recognition can be performed with filter-oriented segmentation to determine the origin of the disc.

For this purpose, the study was performed with a target filter. The image was separated from the green channel input before applying the target filter. Then, the matched filter is rotated with the green channel image to show the optic disc's main deck. The vessel orientation must be aligned along the *y*-axis to approximate the direction of the major vessels passing through the optic cup. The core size depends on the center's maximum width inside the optic disc. In order to increase the success rate of the optic disc detection, vessel features were used with each optic disc candidate for filtering the vertical matching. The distribution of the optic cup is more difficult than the optic disc distribution because of the boundaries of cup extension with high blood vessel density. It leads to blurred boundaries between the optic disc and the optic cup, making it difficult to separate them. The cup color information can be used to detect an optic cup. The cup region was found with similar occurrences and contrasting occurrences from the background color of the image plane. After locating the disc and cup, various metrics can be calculated at different levels to detect the glaucoma effect by the cup–disc ratio (CDR). Vision impairment is gradually changed by overwhelming the optic cup area. CDR values are estimated to examine the incremented level of the cup area. The cup–disc ratio was calculated to represent the glaucoma diagnostic system. Hence, the method recognizes a highly correlated way of detecting glaucoma retina images, which is capable of producing a potential system for the screening process.

15.1.1 Ophthalmic Process

Retinal funds can exist in the particular domain as an internal structure node; thus, the input images act as microscopic elements relating to the components of the eye, like the lens, retina, optic disc, and posterior chamber. Most optometrists, ophthalmologists, and trained medical professionals are capable of screening the disease variance by using the captured input images with the combination of tomography, so that the diagnosis of the disease can be forwarded to selected monitoring schemes for reference purposes. Then, the clinical section widely uses the automatic process to find further ways to analyze or categorize the diagnosis method relating to identifying several disease types, such as diabetic retinopathy or glaucoma. For the identified disease, treatment can be preceded by various retinal fundus images as a primary source through the clinical background, which can quickly assist the clinician in achieving the highest throughput and efficiency in a screening process.

Most ophthalmic pathologies are relatively new causes of blindness, with glaucoma being the most common and severe form among those affecting adults in their working years. It is reactivated by complications such as diabetes mellitus, though a necessary affection for vision impairment following diabetes. Based on the survey about the disorder of the patients, 2% were affected by blind factors and vision degradation has been undergone with 10% primary elements. Then, degradation is concerned about glaucoma complications after 15 years of diabetic consequences.

15.1.2 Digital Imaging

Based on the binary ranges (0/1), digital imaging is a way to represent an encoded object that the visual creation of the given background environment will detect. It denotes the object's presence by distinguishing the characteristics of the intensity value with a gray scale rather than an RGB scale. In order to localize the object, image identification corresponds to its infrared radiation. Chiefly, infrared illumination and low dimensions are the two constraints that generate the encoded vision in digital imaging. Hence, the thermal images act as a source of grayscale radiation in digital vision technologies, and then the variation of grayscale depth is indicated between 0 and 1. However, some different temperatures help identify image variation with a color object while using thermal cameras.

Medical imaging applications follow a designed software platform architecture. It has been increasingly prioritized as a sophisticated image for health image. With this, a new platform was developed in a classic and object-oriented design with some design patterns. The forum incorporates common algorithms for processing and analyzing medical images in a framework that includes reconstruction and division of visual inscriptions and provides powerful tools for scientists and engineers. It comprises general frameworks and some key technologies to describe the process.

Computed tomography (CT), ultrasound images, or a combination of medical imaging technologies can be used to represent an image in the form of molecules [2]. It has been followed by the development of various medical imaging methods, and medical imaging will make a significant difference in managing various medical problems in the future by allowing physicians to choose the corresponding treatment based on the patient's specific needs. By having this, the amelioration of health is monitored. Regardless of the exact way, it is depicted vividly, which continues to improve medical care by diagnosing acne and planning the treatment. It should be suited for each patient, providing the structure or function to understand the complexity of the onset and progression of the disease. Thus, the development process concludes with the best drugs and other therapies to tackle and cure the disease. It is activated by innovative research in the field of an application detection system belonging to medical diagnosis [3]. In particular, medical IR (Interventional Radiology) is a mathematical research field that has supported theory and practical experience for two decades. Conventionally, medical IRs consider a set of procedures to diagnose diseases relating to the nervous system via the numerical optimization method, which is likely to be concentrated on an optimal basis. The success of the ultimate advanced search approach is to provide accurate evaluation of medical results with image-guided rules and have the potential to create an efficient and effective decision-making environment. This contribution aims to establish the most recognized medical clinical experiments along with eye problems that combine evolution and measurement algorithms. In order to achieve this, the IR framework was demonstrated by providing a detailed description of the components involved, such as vascular and neuron. After that, many proposals were considered. Eventually, it follows one of the most representative methods for finding the comparison of two sets of three-dimensional images in medical scenarios.

15.1.2.1 Image Processing

Image processing is a method to enhance the qualities of an image with respect to pixel resolution by performing related operations within the image to extract improved qualities from the given properties belonging to it. It processes the image using signal values in the binary range 0 and

1, associating the particular features or characteristics of the pixel with the corresponding region in the input image and producing an output image. Improve digital image processing routines in the application of thermal image processing. Develop special image processing approaches based on the features of thermal images. Thermal image processing is another recent technique to carry over digital signal conversion by representing an image as a digital frame. It accepts an input image as a pixel frame, like a picture or video file of thermal type. Each type may consist of either a specific set of parameters or characteristics relating to the production of output, from which medical ultrasound is implemented to offer real diagnostic options at a graphical orientation [4]. This system discusses the appropriateness of using the Graphics Processing Unit (GPU) as the main signal for future ultrasound systems. This case study demonstrates the promise of using a high-performance graphics processor in such a system. In the same vein, processing an image can be composed of various submodules with some application. It can be categorized as the following:

- Classification
- Feature extraction
- Pattern recognition
- Projection
- Segmentation
- Compression

15.1.3 Eye and Its Parts

For a human being, the visuals become possible by seeing through the eye. The visual field can be described by its factors, such as how far you can see to the side. Visual perception of the human eye consists of major elements for view projection.

The image can be figured out in the retina by the optic parts like the cornea and lens; then, the visual is reflected on the retina, whose function is akin to the film in a camera. Nerve impulses are activated through a chemical and electrical formulation at the retina, and a light-striking cascade initiates them. Thus, visuals are emulated in the brain with the help of optic nerve fibers. Then, the important nerve tissue can originate, which leads to outgrowth development in the nervous component system. The following section describes each element in detail.

15.1.3.1 *Optic Disc*

The optical or optical head is the point where the nucleic cells of the eye enter the optical nerve. At this point, no light or cone clipping responds to light emission. It can stop the sight of a vision called a "blind spot." The optic disc shows the onset of the optic nerve (the nerve fibers, the second), and the cells of the cellular cavities are collected. The optic disc is also a point for the large arteries that supply the retina. An optical nerve lies in the human eye, with a range of millions beyond the region between the brain and the eye. The optic disc is placed from 3 to 4 mm in y-axis orientation, with average values between 1 and 2 mm. Thus, the orientation varies at different depression levels, which are known to form an area called the optical cup.

15.1.3.2 *Aqueous Humor*

It appears as a liquid-like plasma to support the lens' structure with the posterior and anterior chambers and is located between the lens and retina with oxygen and nutrients. It flows into the bloodstream through the cell network.

15.1.3.3 *Choroid*

It is an outlier artery portion located at the eye's rearview, providing blood supply to the retina with arteries between the retina and sclera to de-generate central vision as a connective layer.

15.1.3.4 *Ciliary Body*

It is identified as the lens shape of the human eye, and the movement of the lens is controlled when there is aqueous detection.

15.1.3.5 *Ciliary Muscle*

The ciliary muscle enables the view by changing the shape of the lens. For instance, focusing on the fine font or moon over a million miles. It relaxes the remote view by the lens for narrow sight.

15.1.3.6 Iris

It appears behind the cornea and in the center of the pupil as an adjustable circular form comprising various eye colors such as brown, cyan, and blue. Located behind the eyelid and in front of the eye, it is a muscle-fibrous ring that shrinks and extends the visual response with respect to the surrounding light.

15.1.3.7 Pupil

The pupil is a hole in the middle of the iris that can capture the visited sight through the light-passing method. The muscular body controls its size.

15.1.3.8 Retina

The retina transmits signals to the brain via the nerve cells by converting the captured illumination (visual) into electric rays. Therefore, the retina is responsible for making vision through central-based visibility with good color vision at the origin of the macula. Most of the vision problems originate in one place called the retina.

15.1.3.9 Photoreceptor Cells

The radiation cells can exist in the retinal area to transmit the information to the brain, recollecting it from an electric light signal source that can cause some chemical transformation to enable the reaction. Cells can impart the retina to provide vision. Three signals, such as red, green, and blue, are used to represent the cells. General cells react to light with rods and cons. They incurred a light to detect motion in the vision. Therefore, rods are the periphery element to deliver vision.

15.1.3.10 Retinal Blood Vessels

Irregular artery growth and vascular leakage cause vision loss in the forms of diabetes, chronic diseases, and eye disease. It is regulated by the arteries to protect against blockage.

15.1.3.11 Sclera

The sclera acts as a wall of the eye and appears in white liquid, preventing the shape of the eye with some kind of inner pressure, so it can be used to protect the eye's delicate interior.

15.1.3.12 Uvea

It is a well-known middle layer of the eye. It consists of three parts: the iris, choroid, and ciliary. It contains inflammation with some degree of adjustment to retain an object at a long distance.

15.1.3.13 Visual Axis

A line that intersects the centers of both regions of the pupil and fovea is termed the visible axis. It supports the eye's visual system on the center axis, where a view can be created. The condition of the eye called strabismus occurs when the eye muscle cannot keep up. It leads to serious sight loss at the axis level due to the damage to the vessel structure.

15.1.3.14 Visual Cortex

It is the primary region that integrates visibility in the brain, processing the information from the eyes and relaying it back to the retina. If any causes occur in this region, visible canals lead to a disease called blindness.

15.1.3.15 Visual Fields

Nasal and temporal are important fields of the retina combined with different segment levels that represent the main visual to the eye.

15.1.3.16 Vitreous

It is a fluid portion that prevents vision impairment by covering the full portion of the eye. As one ages, the level of its function declines from one form to another (gel to fluid), and it undergoes gradual changes in the retina. Therefore, people develop darkness in their vision. In some cases, vitamin levels are released to represent the normal signs at the same age.

15.1.3.17 Zonules

Zonule encompasses hundreds of threads that retain the lens by changing its shape concerning vision level, both near and far.

15.1.3.18 Macula (Yellow Spot)

It is a sensitive part of the retina rounded between inches or about an inch in diameter. It gives 20/20 vision to the responding central vision for reading or viewing. Vision impairment can be sought by a vision of 20/200 to 20/800.

15.1.3.19 Optic Nerve

Each optic nerve has a collection of 1.2 million neurons. It acts as a medium to connect the eye with the brain.

15.1.4 Eye Diseases

15.1.4.1 Myopia

The retina can refract the light rays incorrectly, thereby causing a condition known as myopia. In the short-sighted, the image is not focused precisely in the lens, causing the distance value to blur. In short, the more short-sighted vision leads to a more blurred view of the distant object.

15.1.4.2 Hyperopia

Hyperopia is a condition in which nearby objects are blurry. Generations at a young age can easily overcome it with their correspondingly focused tissues to make clear images. It gets harder when they get older.

15.1.4.3 Astigmatism

Astigmatism is a problematic condition that occurs due to an error in the shape of the cornea. The distant object looks blurry, and this is caused by distorted vision.

15.1.4.4 *Presbyopia*

The flexibility of the lens inside the eye can be reduced by the natural aging process called presbyopia, which causes blurring of vision when the projection view is at a closer distance. It is possible to affect those who are around the age of 40. Because of presbyopia, vision problems can be retained at a lesser level by the default requirement of spectacles for people.

15.1.4.5 *Strabismus*

Strabismus reflects a point at which the visual defects of two eyes are pointed out in two different directions. When the eye has a normal view in a straight position, it can stay in the existing directions, either up or down or in or out. Hypertropia (when the eye turns up), hypotropia (when the eye turns down), esotropia (when the eye turns in), and exotropia (when the eye turns out) are the four kinds of strabismus. Each of these conditions may cover true assumptions due to simultaneously aiming at the same object, which both eyes cannot regulate. In some cases, stereovision loss may result from a partial or total level of perception depth. This type of problem is identified by vision therapy and surgery when it is required. Most of the children may get affected at 4% of the level.

15.1.4.6 *Amblyopia*

It occurs at lower levels of visual clarity and/or is involved with muscle control in one eye, resulting in stereoscopic vision loss by focusing on binocular depth perception. Following the detection, using vision therapy is essential, which can help reduce this problem. It can be treated as a curable form during a specific period between ages 7 and 8. In some places, this type of visual impairment affected approximately 2 or 3 out of 100 children. The identical problem is to prove a solution for the treatment, corresponding to the age factor. Amblyopia is identified by convincing the treatment of bifocals and patches.

15.1.4.7 *Cataracts*

This type of injury breaks down the protein capability of the eyes while aging, and it becomes opaque via the rays' acceleration. It occurs in the opaque section of the eye, resulting in impaired vision.

15.1.4.8 Glaucoma

Glaucoma is the leading cause of blindness across the continent. The majority of people over the age of 65 are at risk of developing this disease. An early diagnosis system may reduce the effects of glaucoma to a possible minimum rate. Glaucoma comprises various levels of disease. When the eye experiences increased pressure, it may cause optic nerve damage. Visionless spots may grow with the drained fluid, producing some pressure internally. The eye can enter a blind state until the pressure is left untreated.

15.1.5 Indications of Glaucoma

Availability of glaucoma can appear as open-angle and closed-angle glaucoma. It can be identified by the sign of the subsequent loss of vision and the variability of the optical nerve studies (increased cup/disc in a basic asthma study). The 90% factor of presence can account for the seriousness of glaucoma. Closed-angle glaucoma of the eyes narrowed to less than 10% in some cases but almost half in others in other countries. Approximately 10% of patients with closed curves with angles are determined by sudden eye pain, halo around a light, red eyes, intraocular pressure (>30 mm mercury), nausea, and vomiting. It decreases vision at a constant rate for middle-aged people.

15.1.6 Causes of Glaucoma

There are several reasons for glaucoma. Increased blood pressure is the primary risk factor for glaucoma. Fifty percent of people with normal eye disease have high eye pressure due to the following causes:

15.1.6.1 Dietary

There is no clear evidence that vitamin deficiency can cause eye glaucoma. Supplemental vitamins are not the recommended treatment for glaucoma. Caffeine increases blood pressure in people with glaucoma, but it does not seem to affect normal people.

15.1.6.2 Ethnicity and Gender

These are the frequent causes, and they are prone to glaucoma at close corners due to the deepest depth of the anterior chamber, much of which will be behind the cornea. In special cases, women have more than three times the risk of glaucoma compared to their frontal lens. Owing to this factor, people of African descent are more likely to be affected by glaucoma.

15.1.6.3 Genetics

Multiple disorders associated with abnormalities, like high blood pressure in the human body, can be attributed to genetic origins. Similarly, cornea and chronic diseases are categorized by other genetic faults within a human eye structure. It is associated with genetic changes in some areas, like regular stress headaches, including one-third of primary open-angle glaucoma (POAG), which is associated with genetic changes. Family hereditary factors can account for about 6% of glaucoma cases.

15.1.7 Analytical Methods of Glaucoma

The primary aim is to detect glaucoma disease from input retina images, specified by the OD's location, with primary optic disc diameter measured by its cup–disc ratio. Thus, performance analysis can be found with segmentation techniques. The following section emphasizes some of the existing analytical processes.

Aliaa Abdel-Haleim *et al.* developed the Optic Disc (OD) discovery method to automate diagnostic systems for psychiatric disorders. It follows a way to locate OD in the digital image of the retina automatically. The method starts by making brightness and normal light levels in the image by aligning the illumination and the varying histological alignment method. The given algorithm is based on randomizing the expected retinal artery samples. Therefore, a consistent filter is available that responds to the filtering of the noises from the given vessels in each direction of the operational site. The nerve is divided by a standard 2-D filter, and mapping with the smaller pieces of the retina is obtained by using the vessel segments. The diverse vessels were monitored again to locate the candidates, eventually using local intensity. The proposed matching filters are distinguished by their resizing function in four different sizes, and the ship's destination in the vicinity of each OD candidate is measured. It provides the minimum differences to rate coordinates of the OD center [5].

Arturo Aquino *et al.* proposed an optic discovery function to set up a system for automatically diagnosing eye diseases by introducing an advanced method for hardware that enables splitting technology on digital images. It uses the techniques of Morphological Detection and Edge Detection, followed by the Hough Circular, to obtain a circular estimate of the limit with a particular distance. It requires that local pixels be the origin of the information source. In order to do this, a location-based approach is designed using an election algorithm. The algorithms have been verified with 1200 samples of the MESSIDOR database available to the public. It produces the result with a standard deviation at the average calculation time in seconds. Besides, it presents a discussion about the pros and cons of the models that are widely used for division [6].

Chisako Muramatsu *et al.* analyzed the retinal studies to detect glaucoma. Glaucoma is the most prominent cause of blindness. Specialists can diagnose glaucoma by determining the area of the lens, the disc, and the mirror ratio of the disc. Thus, the surface area of the reflected disc will be calculated by a ratio calculation algorithm, and it is proportional to the vertical region of the plotted space in the disc. The edge of the optic disc was found using the edge filter and is received on the origin side of the optic disc. The cup edge is then resolved by the zero-tolerance classification method. Finally, the ratio of cup to disc is calculated with 45 images to verify glaucoma and produces a 0.947 accuracy result to find the correct solution [7].

15.2 Glaucoma Screening with Optic Disc and Classification

This section presents an approach to glaucoma eye discovery based on CDR and ISNT laws for classification. To produce the availability of OD and OC occurrences, these two laws specify the comparison of accuracy features at both Levelset and the SuperPixel method. It ensures the efficiency of the glaucoma screening system. Figure 15.1 depicts the screening glaucoma flow and the suggested method's general state diagram.

The given screening method is simple and effective in using computers and can be used to diagnose glaucoma. It is an effective computation method to diagnose glaucoma based on the high-quality factors associated with its features. More details about these modules are discussed below:

The proposed method has five steps. They are:

1. Optic Disc Detection
2. Cropping ROI
3. Optic Disc Segmentation
4. Optic Cup Segmentation
5. Post Proccssing

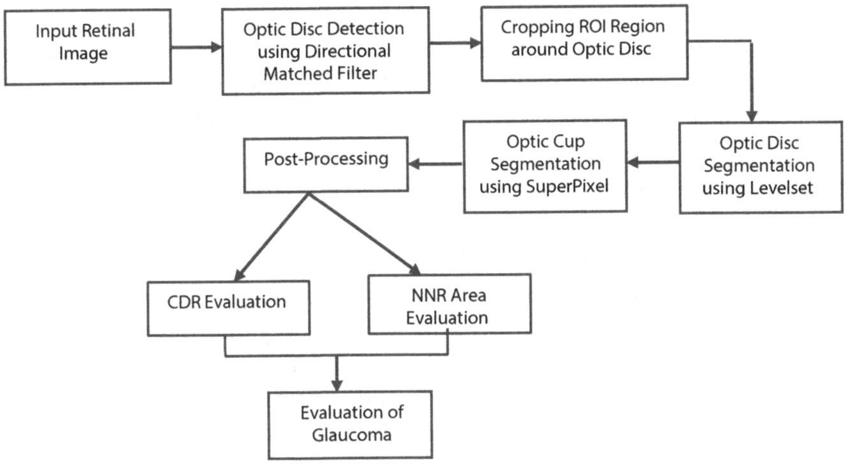

Figure 15.1 Flow diagram of the glaucoma screening.

15.2.1 Optic Disc Detection

The optic disc formulates the position of the dislocation. For this purpose, the system employs target filters. Before applying a matched filter, distribute the green channel image from the input. Then, this matched filter is narrowed with the green image of the channel to find the main OD. In order to locate, the direction corresponds to the y-axis alignment with the transfer of the main element direction through OD. The storage element's size depends on the center's maximum width inside the stream. The OD detection is determined by the success values and each executable region of the candidate that belongs to the rectangular area for vertically matching filters.

Furthermore, OD localization is carried out in a well-known framework representation as sparse classification by a dictionary-based method that embeds a scaling approach [8]. It has been presented by screening automation for conditions like diabetic retinopathy, critically focusing the center point to detect or locate the optic disc (OD). If there are multiple scaling values, they are considered with a fixed size of sub-images to pose OD origin values using a novel dictionary method. Thus, the linear combination of all sub-images is covered as OD dictionary elements to represent the given test image. From these coefficients, a confidence measure is followed to indicate the presence of OD through independent process identification as channel intensity ranges with red and gray scales. The confidence map is constructed to mention the respective measures at the confidence level. From the RIM and DRION databases, the proposed method gives an average computation time in seconds/image, and accuracy is evaluated by comparing the existing techniques for 453/500 test images [9, 10]. Then, the location of OD is responded to at a high peak level by a blob detector through a confidence map.

In order to proceed with channeling, the main focus of the development is to design an algorithm for detecting the rays with mathematical values. Thus, mathematical morphology is selected due to the appearance of normal micro-aneurysms [11]. It has been using the fastest technology to find the health threats in the human eye; the negative one is retinal diabetes. Timely treatment can be performed by detecting electron hormones to overcome the causes of retina. Generally, the algorithm consists of the stages of preliminary treatment, candidate detector, and unused feature removal. This performance is evaluated using DIARETDB1's database, which provides a well-rounded collection of highly skilled experts and protocols. Best practices will be achieved when considering the arrangement of the processing image's green channel size with the histogram's equivalent level of 0.03. Thus, the initial threshold for the edge detection of the uncertain edges is the optimal amount of micro-aneurysm factor, from 5 to 16 pixels.

The automated analysis of retinal diseases emerged as a critical test with the discovery of the OD parameter [12]. The test is done based on the OD section and the splice region derived from the monocular visual forms. A new distribution approach has been proposed, including information about the image area's dimensions at the order of each point that enters into multi-sectional views with selected OD regions. It derives a new cup-based approach based on anatomical data, such as bowling, which is suitable for glaucoma specialists. The curve in the container is automatically detected using the support area ideas that select the correct analysis scale. It follows a strategy with multiple options to derive tilting vessels, referred to as a rocket knee, a shining light in the interior to get the desired boundary. The clinical expert has analyzed the experimental results for the 138 non-glaucoma types and the inputs of the 100 glaucoma types. The distribution result shows a sequence of processes with different geometric variations in the dataset. The error value is estimated with the vertical propositional of the cup diameter to the disc at 0.09/0.08 (mean gap/standard edge) points, while the cup/disc size is 0.12/010. Generally, the quality and quantity of the results show the efficacy of both segments and subsequent classifications of glaucoma.

15.2.2 Cropping ROI

In order to obtain the region of interest (ROI), the OD region is calculated by the cup–disc ratio. The OD region is found using a directly matched filter. Based on the OD location, the ROI region is detected and cropped using the following steps:

1. Extract the image from the given plane.
2. Transform the resolution into binary form.
3. Apply any specific morphology operation to identify the candidate.
4. The directional matched filter is used for smoothing the boundaries.
5. The output ROI extraction is shown in Figure 15.2.

The optic disc's region of interest (ROI) will produce preeminent ROI localization. The new algorithm with a web-based approach adds a step-by-step process before image analysis with ROI detection [13]. It introduces a factor called the disc–cup ratio concerning CDR to diagnose the occurrence of glaucoma by measuring the neuro-retinal optical glass ratio. Glaucoma can be characterized by spectral neurons that change the optic nerve and the visionary sphere. The comparison of fundus input images is to yield an accurate ROI result of 88% and 96%, respectively, through Singapore Eye Research Centre images. The outcomes are aimed at the possibility of glaucoma.

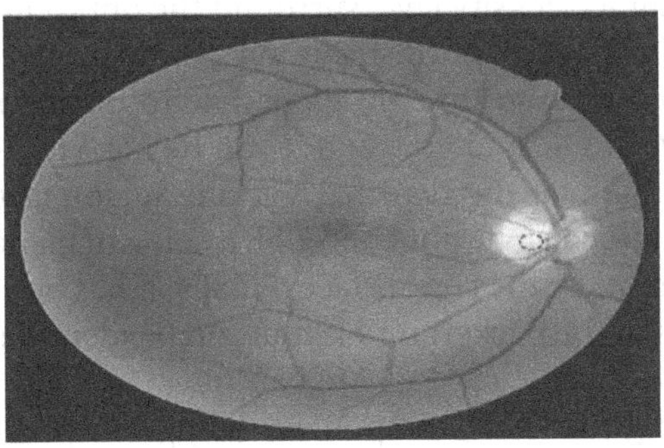

Figure 15.2 ROI extraction.

15.2.3 Optic Disc Segmentation

Segmentation is done at the previously addressed portion using the Level set algorithm. Channel identification, selected to verify several issues, is detected with the help of distracter removal. If the availability of the channel is red, the appearance of the OD contrasts against the background, while candidates appear less prominent. Unfortunately, OD is saturated by the red channel in some images. To avoid this problem, the given method finds the initial ROI statistics based on the red channel saturation. Vascular infiltration is one of the significant difficulties in the absolute part of the OD limit.

Furthermore, a measuring tool is designed to automatically consider the retinal fundus image in terms of a two-dimensional perspective to detect optic disc regions by quantifying peripapillary atrophy [14]. Peripapillary atrophy (PPA) finds a collision of similar retina tissue. The OD region was segmented using this model according to its shape constraint. It evolved with a modified approach that modifies the first-order estimation factor to produce PPA as a cropped region from the original image (OD+PPA). Filtering, thresholding, and region growing are the mechanisms used to refine the boundary subsequently. Strategies of the rare kind with False and True studies define selection analysis of premarital discrimination. Outcome results emulate learning with a negative spread, which is finer than a positive spread. This methodology, constructed on the Biologically Inspired Feature (BIF) project proposal, has achieved more than 90% accuracy in identifying PPAs better than previous approaches. It can be used to maintain eye care and reduce the value of the diagnosis.

15.2.4 Optic Cup Segmentation

Arteries with a higher density level surround the optic cup (OC), so there is a greater possibility that OC distribution can be more critical than OD distribution. From time to time, it is possible to distinguish the unclear boundaries between OC and OD, and it can be hard to detect their existence. Thus, the cup can be detected via one major factor called color information. Isolation can be done through a colorful plane in a dark environment to differentiate the cup surface. Finally, it has been found that the same cup regions in the background layout can be identified using median filtering, as shown in Figure 15.3. Median filters are applied to "aircraft" to delete annoying low-level components using morphological blockage operations to remove vessels. Closing the trend extends the boundaries of

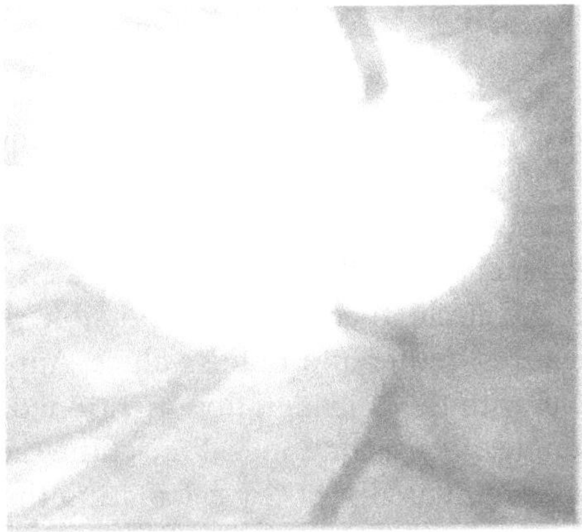

Figure 15.3 Optic cup region from median filtering.

the foreground to the image and minimizes the background holes in such areas.

Therefore, if the storage element has the same size, the direction of the OC is discharged. This will lead to districts that have a small part of the divisional procedure. In addition, if the storage element's size is larger than the frontier boundary, it will increase, leading to a larger OC area. The OC is divided simultaneously using the area of distribution, and the results are combined to produce the final result by removing blood vessels. In most cases, experiments were found to generate accurate segment results for the given datasets containing a radius level below 13. The optic cup region is recognized once the blood vessel is removed, as shown in Figure 15.4.

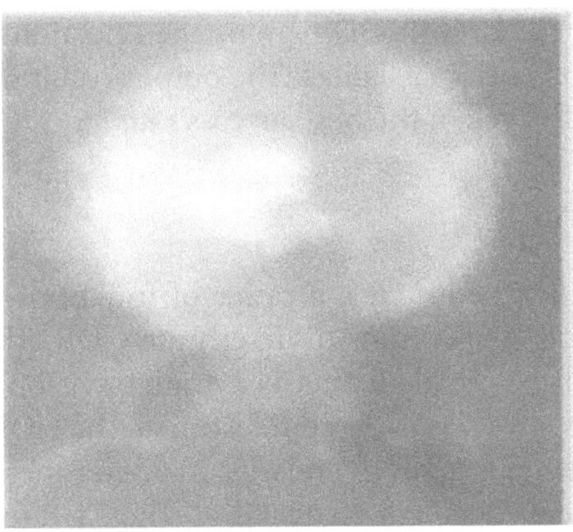

Figure 15.4 Optic cup region after blood vessel removal.

15.2.5 Post-Processing

OD and OC fumes are derived from two combinations to create the final sequel. The result is combined with a logical OR technique. In general, OD and OC are represented by shape estimation, either circular or elliptical. Then, the result is evaluated with a circular estimation because it is comparable to a disc and a cup with the orientation of a circle. By making the evaluation through the circle, there will be a possible requirement corresponding to two features: center and radius values. Applying approximate values at a circle level with the consideration mentioned above can involve a higher level of complexity. Estimation is done at the radius level to determine the centroid of segmented parts by calculating the radius value into half-sections. The processing approach employs both the features of the disc to detect glaucoma when assessment includes increasing the accuracy of the findings.

It has been considered the objective function to isolate the optic disc (OD) by overcoming the failure process to detect the existence of lesions or artifacts in an input image [15]. It originates from the new technique used to locate the OD by distinguishing the occurrence of exudates into large or bright artifacts based on Iterative Brightest Pixels Extraction (IBPE), designed to overcome the occurrence of artifacts. The localization method is integrated by the pixels at a bright level through a series of iterative functions for the extraction and discrimination of geometric features. It follows a binary candidate map constructed to extract the pixels and has high intensity at each iterative process. The purpose of performing the checking process is to differentiate the regions of OD from the candidate set with the help of the geometric features of each employed candidate. The algorithm reconstructs the cluster map from the given retinal database to identify the brightest pixel with a false-hit OD region. The selection is done iteratively to deduct the region with real values. The output result shows that the performance rate is achieved at the best success rate.

15.2.5.1 Cup–Disc Ratio

After discovering discs and cups, a range of functions can be calculated by following clinical conventions to determine CDR. The area of the cup increases the lethargy with glaucoma as a result of vision loss. The enlargement of the cup area was considered to estimate the CDR value. The CDR value is decided depending on the relative diameter measured, which corresponds to a vertical cup and a vertical disc. The CDR rate is derived from the equation below.

$$CDR = VCD/VDD \tag{15.1}$$

where VCD is the vertical cup diameter and VDD is the vertical disc diameter. The CDR value is less than 0.5 for regular OD, while it goes beyond 0.5 if glaucoma exists.

15.2.5.2 Evaluation of the NRR Area in the ISNT Quadrants

The NRR considers a region segment with a significant task in the glaucoma analysis. About the ISNT rule, for the normal Optic Disc Ratio (ODR) area, the NRR is in the row: Inferior ≥ Superior ≥ Nasal ≥ Temporal.

Then, the above fibers, like superior and inferior nerves, temporal, and nasal fibers, are prior to their order, which leads to the identification of the causes known as glaucoma. The violation can be entered into the ISNT rule due to the results of the thinning of the superior and inferior rims. The false ODR area is identified by circular shifts [16] that were assigned to retain the shape of the disc circularly, and simultaneously, the change has been done across the pharmaceutical borders of an image. It has been drawn from the framework for diagnosing false optic disc (OD) by demonstrating accurate and effective techniques to detect the location of optic discs (ODs). At every pixel size of the retina, the variation range of the image is evaluated through a series of flat-angled segments with rounded edges of a certain length. It proves that processing algorithms are faster than the advanced method.

15.2.5.3 Superpixel Method

Using this, the regions are divided into subparts, which are collected together into a whole section, known as a superpixel. Then, generation is started by assigning a label value to each pixel as a subpart with no repetition values [17].

The Superpixel segmentation algorithm

1. Read an image with the expected number of pixels at the starting point to obtain an initial segmentation.
2. Choose the edge value to denote object boundaries in an image by defining the distance factor of each pixel.
3. Continue the iteration until the pixel positions and intensities are updated with the starting point.
4. Finally, a superpixel segmented image is generated.

15.2.5.4 Level Set Method

The transformation of surfaces from one form to another is based on different levels using a partial differential equation. The Level set method represents the surfaces starting at the zero level to the upper-dimensional surface. It can be an affordable technique relating to the frequent changes in the topology structure.

The Level set method has a very high-quality feature to represent the problems of shape manufacturing. Therefore, it is used for many functions close to a mathematical operation. It follows a segmentation technique for periodic alteration with evolution to produce usable results. Thus, it can implement the function that forwards the initialized values repetitively. It is based on the method known as the Level set function to achieve segmentation at the various iteration levels by solving re-initialization using a partial differential with different values [18]. It is achieved through a classification rate with the fewest false negatives. The final results, which only varied corresponding to the features, are to be considered as follows:

1. They are decomposing the image into regions with respect to their mean intensity values.
2. Evolving curves or surfaces processed with topological order.
3. Specify the interface location point using interior and exterior boundary with $0 < \varphi \leq 0$ (φ is the interface location point).
4. Calculate $n = \nabla\varphi/|\nabla\varphi|$ (∇ is the differentiation function with n integers).
5. Finding the mean value by $\kappa = \nabla \cdot n$.

15.3 Experimental Section

15.3.1 Dataset Description

The image dataset is employed with two public datasets of retinal images called RIM and DRION-DB for testing and to analyze comparative studies of segmentation algorithms. It comprises 500 images in addition to those with normal and abnormal (disease) retinal images. For all input images, the location of "OD" is properly identified by glaucoma experts.

15.3.2 Experimental Images

Experiments were conducted on a color image set to validate the efficiency of the given scheme. For the experimental purposes of several standards, 512 × 512 cover images are taken from the given datasets. Sample input images are shown in Figure 15.5.

15.3.3 Experimental Testing Phase

Testing is a sequence of functional steps to produce an expected result corresponding to an error related to a possible false declaration. It derives from some of the test cases to find errors that are in undiscovered mode. Based on the experiments, the test cases can exist in the present system, as shown in Table 15.1.

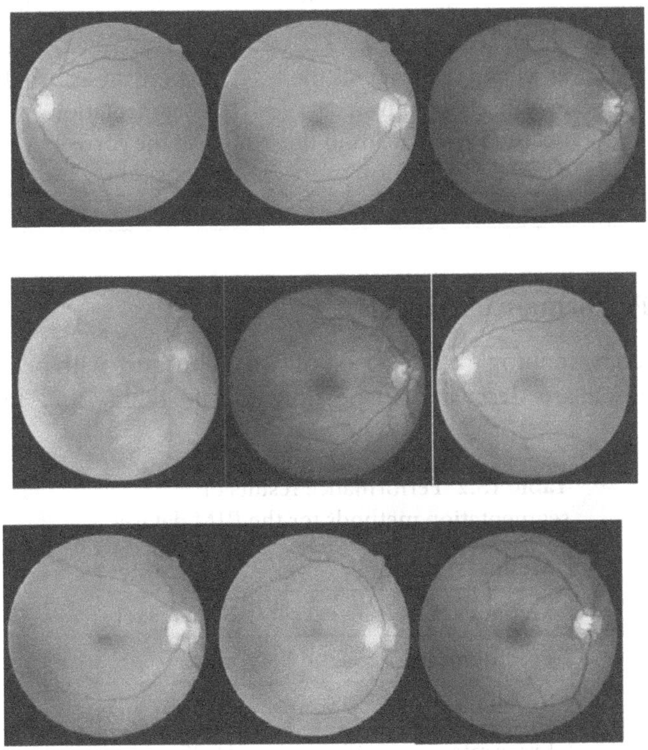

Figure 15.5 Experimental images.

Table 15.1 Test cases for input processes.

Test case no.	Input	Expected output	Obtained output	Test case result
1	Color image	The resolution is converted to a gray image.	The color is converted from RGB to grayscale.	Pass
2	Median filtered image	OD is identified, and it is separated.	Only the identified part is produced as the output.	Pass
3	Direction matched filter image	Detecting the disc's correct appearance.	Location varies from possible orientation.	Pass
4	Level set and superpixel approach	Segments the given data fields in the form of an image.	Making the segmentation at the correct position.	Pass

15.3.4 Performance Analysis

It is analyzed by making a comparison of two techniques with performance metrics, which are described in Section 15.3.4. Table 15.2, Table 15.3,

Table 15.2 Performance results of segmentation methods for the RIM dataset.

Methods		
Metrics	**Level set**	**Superpixel**
Precision rate	54.33	62.42
Recall rate	72.72	78.08
Error rate	10.00	16.00
Specificity	72.73	84.32
Accuracy	90	93

Table 15.3 Performance results of segmentation methods for the DRION dataset.

Methods		
Metrics	**Level set**	**Superpixel**
Precision rate	53.84	60.67
Recall rate	63.63	70.00
Error rate	20.00	27.00
Specificity	63.64	70.32
Accuracy	80	87

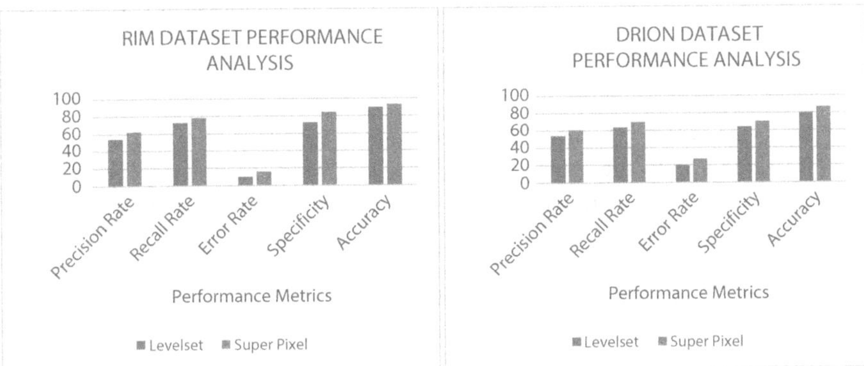

Figure 15.6 Performance analysis of segmentation methods using the RIM and DRION dataset.

and Figure 15.6 show the performance result using two datasets (RIM and DRION DB).

15.4 Conclusion

Continual vision loss can be violated by glaucoma; gradual impairment is monitored through nerves subsequently. Over the decades, millions of people have been injured by the vision impairment caused by glaucoma, a primary reason for blindness. The development of the process guides how to overcome a vision impairment that happens gradually over time. Since symptoms occur only when the disease reaches the final stage, glaucoma can be cured at the earliest stage of treatment. Hence, it is a crucial step to detect glaucoma at an earlier stage. It presents a comparison approach with Level set and Superpixel generation related to Disc ratio and ISNT measurement to identify glaucoma. With the help of two features, the accuracy of the glaucoma discovery increases. Disc and cup values are changed according to the Level set and the Superpixel method. The result analysis shows that the Superpixel method provides a better result than the Level set method based on performance metrics for both datasets using classification. The described approaches are effortless and can be used to discover the problem of glaucoma.

References

1. Sarhan, Abdullah, *et al.* "Glaucoma Detection Using Image Processing Techniques: A Literature Review." *Comput. Med. Imaging Graph.*, vol. 78, Dec. 2019, p. 101657. ScienceDirect, https://doi.org/10.1016/j.compmedimag.2019.101657.
2. Mertz, Leslie. "Medical Imaging: Just What the Doctor (and the Researcher) Ordered: New Applications for Medical Imaging Technology." *IEEE Pulse*, vol. 4, no. 1, Jan. 2013, pp. 12–17. IEEE Xplore, https://doi.org/10.1109/MPUL.2012.2228803.
3. Damas, S., *et al.* "Medical Image Registration Using Evolutionary Computation: An Experimental Survey." *IEEE Comput. Intell. Mag.*, vol. 6, no. 4, Nov. 2011, pp. 26–42. IEEE Xplore, https://doi.org/10.1109/MCI.2011.942582.
4. So, Hayden *et al.* "Medical Ultrasound Imaging: To GPU or Not to GPU?" *IEEE Micro*, vol. 31, no. 5, Sept. 2011, pp. 54–65. IEEE Xplore, https://doi.org/10.1109/MM.2011.65.
5. Youssif, Aliaa, *et al.* "Optic Disc Detection From Normalized Digital Fundus Images using a Vessels' Direction Matched Filter." *IEEE Trans. Med. Imaging*, vol. 27, Feb. 2008, pp. 11–18. ResearchGate, https://doi.org/10.1109/TMI.2007.900326.
6. Aquino, Arturo, *et al.* "Detecting the Optic Disc Boundary in Digital Fundus Images Using Morphological, Edge Detection, and Feature Extraction Techniques." *IEEE Trans. Med. Imaging*, vol. 29, no. 11, Nov. 2010, pp. 1860–69. IEEE Xplore, https://doi.org/10.1109/TMI.2010.2053042.
7. Muramatsu, Chisako, *et al.* "Automated Segmentation of Optic Disc Region on Retinal Fundus Photographs: Comparison of Contour Modeling and Pixel Classification Methods." *Comput. Methods Programs Biomed.*, vol. 101, no. 1, Jan. 2011, pp. 23–32. ScienceDirect, https://doi.org/10.1016/j.cmpb.2010.04.006.

8. Benkhaddra, Ilyas, Abhishek Kumar, Mohamed Ali Setitra, and Lei Hang. "Design and Development of Consensus Activation Function Enabled Neural Network-Based Smart Healthcare Using BIoT." *Wirel. Pers. Commun.*, 130, no. 3 (2023): 1549-1574.
9. Batista, Francisco José Fumero, *et al.* "RIM-ONE DL: A Unified Retinal Image Database for Assessing Glaucoma Using Deep Learning." *Image Anal. Stereol.*, vol. 39, no. 3, 3, Nov. 2020, pp. 161–67. *www.ias-iss.org*, https://doi.org/10.5566/ias.2346.
10. Carmona, Enrique J., *et al.* "Identification of the Optic Nerve Head with Genetic Algorithms." *Artif. Intell. Med.*, vol. 43, no. 3, July 2008, pp. 243–59. *PubMed*, https://doi.org/10.1016/j.artmed.2008.04.005.
11. Whardana, Adithya Kusuma, and Nanik Suciati. "A Simple Method for Optic Disk Segmentation from Retinal Fundus Image." *Int. J. Image Graph. Signal Process.*, vol. 6, no. 11, 2014, pp. 36–42.
12. Joshi, Gopal Datt, *et al.* "Optic Disk and Cup Segmentation From Monocular Color Retinal Images for Glaucoma Assessment." *IEEE Transactions on Medical Imaging*, vol. 30, no. 6, June 2011, pp. 1192–205. IEEE Xplore, https://doi.org/10.1109/TMI.2011.2106509.
13. Zhang, Zhuo, *et al.* "Optic Disc Region of Interest Localization in Fundus Image for Glaucoma Detection in Argali." *2010 5th IEEE Conference on Industrial Electronics and Applications*, IEEE, 2010, pp. 1686–89.
14. Kumar, Abhishek, Swarn Avinash Kumar, Vishal Dutt, S. Shitharth, and Esha Tripathi. "IoT-based arrhythmia classification using the enhanced hunt optimization-based deep learning." *Expert Syst.*, (2023): e13298.
15. Yu, Chun Yuan, and Shyr Shen Yu. "Automatic Localization of the Optic Disc Based on Iterative Brightest Pixels Extraction." *2014 International Symposium on Computer, Consumer and Control*, 2014, pp. 613–16. IEEE Xplore, https://doi.org/10.1109/IS3C.2014.166.
16. Akhatov, A., I. Himmatov, Christo Ananth *and T.* Ananth Kumar. "System of Persons Identification Based on Human Characteristics." In *International Conference on Data Management, Analytics & Innovation*, pp. 1029-1046. Singapore: Springer Nature Singapore, 2023.
17. Srivastav, Arun Lal, Markandeya, Naveen Patel, Mayank Pandey, Ashutosh Kumar Pandey, Ashutosh Kumar Dubey, Abhishek Kumar, Abhishek Kumar Bhardwaj, and Vinod Kumar Chaudhary. "Concepts of circular economy for sustainable management of electronic wastes: challenges and management options." *Environ. Sci. Pollut. Res.*, 30, no. 17 (2023): 48654-48675.
18. Anusorn, Chalinee Burana, *et al.* "Image Processing Techniques for Glaucoma Detection Using the Cup-to-Disc Ratio." *Sci. Tech. Asia*, 2013, pp. 22–34.

16

Role of Artificial Intelligence in Marketing

G. Muruganantham and R.S. Aswanth*

Department of Management Studies, National Institute of Technology, Tiruchirappalli, India

Abstract

Artificial intelligence (AI) is changing the marketing sector by giving marketers a new and creative way to connect with customers. AI can handle a lot of data and provide good customer behavior, preference, trending data, etc., which helps marketers create customer-relevant and sales-boosting marketing tactics. Email marketing, social media management, and ad placement may be automated with AI, saving time and money and improving marketing plans. AI-powered chatbots may immediately assist clients and answer basic questions, freeing marketers to focus on other activities. Moreover, it is transforming marketing through predictive analytics. AI can use client data to anticipate what they will buy and analyze their feedback to improve products and services. By adapting to this new AI approach, marketers can target campaigns to enhance sales. AI is increasingly important as firms aim to create more customized, effective, and measurable marketing tactics. Businesses can stay ahead in the ever-changing digital environment by embracing AI. This chapter focuses on how using AI in marketing might help with efficiency, customer satisfaction, and strategy formulation. Overall, this chapter provides a comprehensive overview of the role of AI in marketing, highlighting both the opportunities and challenges associated with this emerging technology. It is useful for marketing experts, professors, and students who want to learn more about the present and future of "artificial intelligence" in the field.

***Keywords*:** Artificial intelligence, marketing, digital marketing, consumer engagement, customer satisfaction, technology, social media

**Corresponding author*: rsaswanth007@gmail.com

T. Ananth Kumar, E. Golden Julie, Venkata Raghuveer Burugadda, Abhishek Kumar and Puneet Kumar (eds.) Computational Intelligence: Theory and Applications, (349–368) © 2024 Scrivener Publishing LLC

16.1 Introduction

As the digital era continues to advance, it becomes clear that artificial intelligence (AI) is more than a trendy term or a straightforward concept. It is a transformative force affecting nearly every area of our lives, including how we buy and sell products and services. When customers shop in the modern society, they want the items people buy to make their lives easier and more easy; thus, that is what they look for in a product [1]. Many experts have even claimed that "artificial intelligence" will significantly alter the face of marketing in the future [2, 3]. AI is categorized as analytical, human-inspired, and humanized AI based on different kinds of intelligence it possesses (cognitive, emotional, and social intelligence); without a doubt, the beginnings of artificial intelligence can be dated back to the 1940s, and more narrowly to 1942, when American science fiction novelist "Isaac Asimov" wrote a brief novel, *Runaround* [4]. The term "artificial intelligence" (AI) refers to "intelligence displayed by machines" [5]. Artificial intelligence (AI) is defined as "intelligence that gathers input from sensors and then uses that data to change its surroundings" [6]. Alternatively, artificial intelligence (AI) can be defined as "manifested by machines that exhibit aspects of human intelligence" [7]. There are "strong AI and weak AI", which are the two primary sorts of artificial intelligence. Artificial general intelligence (also known as strong AI) is a type of AI in which the algorithm possesses consciousness, sensibility, and mind and is intelligent across multiple domains. Artificial intelligence that is "weak" or "artificial narrow" is limited in its ability to do a wide variety of activities [5].

Gkikas and Theodoridis (2019) defined artificial intelligence in marketing as "the development of artificial agents that, given information about consumers, competitors, and a particular company, suggest and take marketing actions to achieve the best marketing outcome." Experts from earlier studies [9] explain AI as a multidimensional term from the perspective of how it is used by humans and machines together. AI-enabled systems facilitate personalization of customer experiences [10] and help marketers use a wide variety of solicited and unsolicited forms of customer engagement to improve marketing outcomes [11]. Thus, it makes sense to argue that marketing AI is the enactment of "machine learning" and "deep learning" techniques to marketing problems [8].

Using AI in marketing has a lot of benefits, but there are also problems that need to be fixed, such as privacy, security, and lack of openness. Businesses need to make sure that their customers' data are accurate and clear, and that any choices made with the help of AI are fair and unbiased [12]. Concerns and doubts have been raised regarding how artificial intelligence would affect the marketing sector and the economy [13]. Businesses are becoming more aware of the significance of implementing AI developments into their management practices and products. As a consequence of this, businesses have the opportunity to achieve a competitive edge and improve their level of readiness for the subsequent shift in the market [14].

Hence, consumers no longer require a great deal of time or intellectual ability to make the most informed purchasing decisions due to the emergence of AI [15]. Let us look at the current state of marketing AI and how businesses can benefit from this cutting-edge technology to get an advantage over the competition. In this chapter, we will take a closer look at the role of artificial intelligence (AI) in marketing, explore some of the latest trends and best practices, and consider the potential impact of this fast-growing field on businesses and consumers alike.

16.1.1 Impact of AI in Marketing

AI is being used increasingly in marketing because processing power is improving, the cost of computing is going down, huge amounts of data are available, and new methods and models for machine learning are being made [12]. Artificial intelligence (AI) is applied in marketing to automate routine tasks, maximize advertising budgets, and create customized content that caters to the preferences of certain audiences [16]. A variety of sectors will see changes to their sales processes as a result of AI. Using sophisticated voice analysis tools, an AI assistant may be ready to figure out from a customer's voice that a never before mentioned problem still presents itself and make an immediate response to aid the (human) sales representative in planning their succeeding move. AI will eventually affect every part of a brand, but so far, it has had the most important effects on brand fulfillment, customer service, and personalization [17]. Artificial intelligence (AI) impacts marketing activities by eliminating the need for specialized marketers and generating new opportunities for both humans and machines to work together. New methods are required in the age of machines. The marketing industry is rapidly changing due to the development of AI. The marketing environment is expected to undergo fast changes as the rate of change increases [5]. Technology based on user interaction is easy to learn and use, and it speeds up the delivery of information while lowering the need for human labor [18]. Also, they help the person have a more satisfying experience [19]. Lecointre-Erickson *et al.* (2018) found that users have a better time when their emotions are stoked, and this has a good effect on their behavior intentions, such as their intent to buy.

AI development is becoming more and more important in mobile apps and websites because it can help businesses run better and give customers a better experience. AI development services for mobile apps and websites have many advantages, one of which is that they can process huge amounts of data and give people very personalized recommendations. AI could be used by a shopping app to suggest products based on what the user has bought and what pages they have looked at in the past. AI is being used in everything from websites and apps for smartphones to virtual helpers [21]. These AI assistants can make things like planning and food shopping easier, which also give good advantages to the marketers too.

An ever-increasing amount of data, digital collaboration, online social interaction, digital marketing, and e-commerce all appear together in the fashion industry to create and sell a tangible good to a customer base that was born and raised with digital technology. The advent of the most significant shift in the fashion industry since the Industrial Revolution is predicted to occur as a result of the convergence of big data, IoT, the platform economy, and artificial intelligence [22].

16.1.2 Benefits of AI in Marketing

Some of the major benefits were listed below:

- A previous study [23] found stated that "when considering the sharing economy, it is necessary to reevaluate many different types of institutions (including customers, companies and channels, and regulators), processes (including innovation, branding, customer experience, and value appropriation), and the creation of value (including value for consumers, value for firms, and value for society).
- Those in marketing who are already using AI say that it has helped them, especially in terms of customer understanding and efficiency. Jim Yu, CEO of BrightEdge, said that despite the hoopla around AI, the results of this poll prove that AI is very real, and that search and content marketers are adopting AI-first technology at a quicker rate than the industry average [24].

- Emotions are something that artificial intelligence (AI) systems and technologies will soon be able to perceive, analyze, evaluate, and mimic. Currently, market researchers and political pollsters can use a combination of facial analysis, voice pattern analysis, and deep learning to determine human emotions [25].
- Artificial intelligence (AI) and machine learning (ML) have been hailed as potentially game-changing developments in the modern era. Their financial market performance proved that incremental gains might quickly accumulate into enormous wealth if the right actions were taken repeatedly. Since their self-driving cars have been so successful, the laws and ethics governing automation and driving have been reevaluated. These benefits, and likely many more, make AI augmentation an attractive, if not necessary, area for investment, study, and business implementation [26].
- New, more accurate forecasting models are being made possible by the advent of machine learning and big data. It can quickly sift through large amounts of data to reveal actionable insights that boost productivity in businesses. Complex sales trends can be better identified and forecast with the use of AI tools, and the findings are then compared to those of more traditional forecasting methods [27].
- The introduction of new technologies, such as personal computers (PCs), the Internet, and cell phones, causes companies to rethink their long-term goals and operational models. The ability of businesses to anticipate and respond to client requirements and provide them with solutions is boosted by such developments. One of the reasons for AI's success is the tremendous degree of customization it offers. By combining customer data with AI tools, businesses can deliver personalized offerings. The use of AI can enable managers to learn in real time and enhance their customers' lifetime value. The retention of clients and the maintenance of a competitive edge are the twin pillars of a product curation strategy of this type [28].
- With the development of natural language processing, a branch of AI that helps computers comprehend speech, it is now possible to utilize these systems to monitor and respond to simple inquiries from customers [29].

16.1.3 AI in Marketing Functions

Online retailing AI	As a result of AI's improved ability to forecast client preferences, businesses may shift away from the traditional "shop and ship" strategy.
Sales AI	Artificial intelligence bots can automate parts of the sales process, freeing up time and energy for human salespeople to focus on higher-value tasks.
Customer service robots	AI robots that automate tasks are able to handle basic inquiries from customers.
Customer screening AI	The use of AI allowed us to determine which customers would benefit most from monetary discounts.

Source: Compiled from expert analysis [2].

16.1.4 Applications of AI in Marketing

The following table domains and subthemes were provided to illustrate the value that artificial intelligence (AI) brings to digital marketing strategies.

Integrated Digital Marketing	Intelligent search
	Recommender systems
Content Marketing	Programmatic advertising
	Creation and curation of content
	Automated insights
	Narrative science
	Contact personalization
Experiential Marketing	Voice recognition systems
	Virtual transformation
	Image recognition
Marketing Operations	Marketing automation
	Forecasting
	Predictive analytics
	Campaign execution

Marketing Research	Customer segmentation
	Consumer behavior
	Data mining

Source: Compiled by the authors.

To create a unified and well-coordinated marketing strategy, businesses often employ a method known as "integrated digital marketing," which involves the use of several different digital platforms and technologies. One facet of integrated digital marketing is the use of artificial intelligence (AI), intelligent search, and recommender systems, to boost marketing efforts and improve customer experiences by delivering more personalized and relevant experiences to customers. There has been a great deal of study into the effects that developments in web technologies, such as those used in intelligent content marketing, have on various types of communication channels, including business and marketing communications. Content has evolved into one of the most important and effective marketing tools, and AI-powered marketing methods have significantly influenced its creation and management. As more and more content is produced and picked on an hourly basis across nearly all channels of information dissemination, customizing that content is becoming increasingly common. In fact, the need for highly customized content was sparked by the hope of providing automated insights through AI-powered content marketing, and this need has been satisfied through the creation of content recommender systems based on narrative science techniques [30].

When it comes to marketing, experiential is one of the most cutting-edge and well-funded sub-disciplines. Much study has concentrated on speech, reality/transformation, chatbots, and the effects on picture recognition [20]. Other major areas of study have been the manner in which AI is employed in marketing, the methods for uncovering new marketing prospects through the use of chatbots, and the development of more intelligent search engines. Recent studies have been dedicated to the examination of direct marketing analytics through the utilization of support vector data description. Marketing is one of the first procedures to feel the effects of AI, and this has led to a number of exciting developments, including AI-driven environments in branding, a wide range of real-time application scenarios of "AI-powered marketing automation", "AI's integration in marketing", "sales forecasting", and more gradual shifts in sales and marketing positions [30]. One of the fastest-growing industries is marketing technology, or "MARTECH", which is concentrated on marketing automation and digital adoption.

Understanding customer behavior and client segmentation have been important foci of market research studies. In their extensive investigation into the structure of strategic thinking for AI in marketing, a previous study [7] presented a three-pronged approach to "strategic marketing planning". It characterized the current use of AI in marketing into three different groups: mechanical, thinking, and emotional AI, depending on its mode of the usage or function across the entire marketing process [30]. Data mining is a hot topic in the field of data sciences, but studies on the topic are still limited in the marketing industry. This article addresses this gap by discussing data mining strategies via the lens of social media discussion patterns.

16.1.5 Challenges of AI in Marketing

However, utilizing AI in marketing could potentially have certain unintended consequences. According to earlier research [31], the rapid expansion of artificial intelligence and robot-based systems across industries is having a significant impact on the global economy, as well as on society in general and the workplace specifically. A significant area of focus should be placed on protecting the confidentiality of the personal information of customers.

Due to the fact that AI algorithms are able to draw conclusions from vast volumes of data, it is conceivable for data breaches and illicit utilization of personal information to take place. In order to protect against such a risk, strict guidelines and best practices for the protection of personal information are required. A further cause for concern is the possibility that certain marketing responsibilities might one day be handled by artificial intelligence, which might result in the loss of jobs.

As marketers, they have seen a lot of hype cycles come and go. The next big thing, be it a social media fad or the big data revolution, is always just around the corner and then gone. The promise of AI, though, is real and cannot be emphasized. The pace of progress is being hastened by the transformation of corporations like Google and Amazon becoming AI-first companies. In today's world, any marketer can be an AI-first marketer because the most forward-thinking companies are building AI right into their platforms [32].

As they attempt to incorporate ever-more-advanced artificial intelligence into their products, engineers must be careful not to put in too much, too quickly, or handle too many jobs. Many people, especially those in needy professions like day care and health, value human interaction above all else. Experts in the field of technology have been raving about the prospects of artificial intelligence. Customers, on the other hand, are not keen on handing over control of their lives to robots [33]. Even while artificial intelligence (AI) has the potential to boost productivity and accuracy, human marketers still have the upper hand in terms of their creativity and compassion. Companies need to strike the appropriate balance between utilizing the benefits of AI and maintaining a human element in their marketing strategies.

16.1.6 Future of AI in Marketing

In marketing, the future of AI seems promising, with lots of exciting opportunities awaiting to be explored. Customers' experiences, marketing efforts, and content personalization are all being enhanced by artificial intelligence (AI) technology at present. Here, we will show some exciting statistical records where artificial intelligence (AI) makes a huge impact on marketing in the foreseeable future.

- According to previous research [34], the amount of money invested in AI globally will reach $98 billion in 2023, expanding at a rate of 28.4% each year.
- Experts [35] from "McKinsey Analytics" found that 50% of companies have embraced AI in a minimum of one business process, and 75% of businesses that employ AI have witnessed a 10% gain in the experience of customers.
- The best thing about AI is that it can learn from big amounts of data [2, 36]. A recent study [30] says that the return on investment (ROI) for using AI will be 99% in the next 5 years and 187% in the next 10 years.
- Grand View Research forecasts that the worldwide market for AI will grow from $80 billion in 2020 to $266 billion in 2027, or a compound annual growth rate (CAGR) of 35.2%.
- Forbes found that during the next three years, 80% of businesses plan to put money into AI startups.
- Accenture estimates that AI could add $14 trillion to the global economy by 2035, and OpenAI reports that businesses can save an average of $300,000 annually thanks to AI-powered solutions.

These data shed light to the expanding applicability of AI across industries as well as the significant potential economic impact that the technology may have [21]. Moreover, it is expected that artificial intelligence will improve to the point where it will be able to do complicated jobs such as medical diagnosis and automobile navigation. Along with the findings of some experts [2], the incorporation of "artificial intelligence" will be a critical component in the retail industry's continued growth in the next years. From an earlier study [37], Turban *et al.* discovered that when making a purchase, consumers are more likely to use augmented reality, voice assistants, and chatbots.

16.2 New Trends of AI in Marketing

Some further unique AI-driven marketing trends have emerged, as shown below [30].

- Automated Email Marketing: Email marketing campaigns that use AI may examine customer preferences, activities, and history to craft more relevant and engaging communications. This entails the use of algorithms to generate email subject lines and content, as well as sending the messages at peak engagement periods.
- AI-Powered Content Curation: Artificial intelligence algorithms can examine vast quantities of content like articles, blogs, and social media posts in order to curate and recommend relevant stuff to readers. Marketers can now tailor content to specific users based on their preferences and interests.
- Influencer Marketing Optimization: The ideal influencers for a brand's marketing efforts can be found with the help of artificial intelligence. By assessing social media data and user engagement, AI algorithms may pair brands with influencers who are most likely to reach the desired demographic.
- AI-Driven Customer Segmentation: Clustering algorithms and machine learning are just two examples of the artificial intelligence approaches that may be used to analyze customer data and identify meaningful subsets and trends. This paves the way for businesses to target specific customers with tailored messages and deals.

- Voice and Visual Search Optimization: With the proliferation of voice assistants and visual search capabilities, marketers are focusing on tailoring their content and advertisements to these emerging user habits. As part of this process, you will learn how to optimize visual material for search engine algorithms and gain an understanding of the intent behind voice searches.
- AI-Powered Ad Targeting and Optimization: By assessing user data, browsing behavior, and demographic information, AI systems can improve ad targeting and offer customized ads. Benefits include higher ad relevance, higher conversion rates, and a higher return on ad spend (ROAS).
- AI-Powered Customer Service: Chatbots and virtual assistants powered by AI are being used to enhance the support experience for customers. These AI-driven systems can answer customer inquiries, provide timely responses, and fix frequent problems, which boosts customer satisfaction and relieves the burden on human support staff.
- AI-Enhanced Marketing Analytics: Marketers can benefit from AI systems' ability to sift through mountains of data and extract useful information. Predicting sales, finding upsell and cross-sell opportunities, fine-tuning pricing, and assessing the success of marketing initiatives all fall under this category.
- AI-Powered Social Media Marketing: Social media data may be analyzed by AI systems looking for patterns, sentiment, and consumer preferences. Marketers may utilize this information to fine-tune their social media advertising, streamline their interactions with customers, and monitor public opinion of their brands.
- AI-Enabled Marketing Automation: Several marketing tasks, such as lead scoring, campaign management, and customized content delivery, can be automated with the help of AI. While AI takes care of the boring stuff and makes things run more smoothly, marketers are free to focus on strategy and creativity.

16.2.1 Companies Using AI in Marketing

As AI is so complex and changes so quickly, it might be difficult to forecast how it will be employed in the actual world. Some of the world's most successful and well-known firms have been employing AI for some time now, and it has paid off in higher sales, positive press, and brand awareness. Here are a few examples of prestigious companies that use AI and machine learning in their marketing campaigns [38].

- Amazon:

Amazon's technology has evolved since it pioneered tailored product suggestions. Now, ideas consider what anybody bought, what others have bought, how anyone used the Internet, and other factors. AI sets Amazon prices. Price reduction will boost sales. Desire raises prices. The strategy maximizes sales and income. Seattle, Chicago, and San Francisco Amazon stores lack checkouts. These shops utilize AI, cameras, and sensors. This technology tracks purchases and bills customers via the Amazon Go app after they depart. The company introduced Echo Look, an AI-powered personal planner that employs machine-learning algorithms to provide precise outfit ideas and enhance clothing, shoe, and accessory sales.

- Starbucks:

Starbucks has improved its rewards program and personalization since launching its AI and big data plan in 2016. Starbucks has long touted its capacity to be customized. Loyalty cards and smartphone apps are used to track customer spending, location, and purchasing patterns. The company employs predictive analytics to deliver users personalized marketing communications such as store recommendations and incentives. Customers may use the app's AI-powered "virtual barista" to place orders from their phones. Starbucks tracks 90 million transactions per week to optimize shop layout, product development, and customer experience.

- Alibaba:

This year (2023), Alibaba Group opened its first "FashionAI" shop. The store's smart garment tags, smart mirrors, and virtual wardrobe app make it easier for customers to buy fashion items. This is the company's second AI venture. Alibaba's intelligent customer care technology, launched in 2015, has outperformed human customer support staff. Alibaba, like Amazon, employs comparable technologies to provide customized product suggestions, search results, and storefronts that automatically highlight the most intriguing products. Every day, millions of individuals utilize the company's apps and website. The corporation likely has plans for using this massive customer behavioral data, which is ideal for artificial intelligence.

• Nike:
One of the first fitness trackers was created by Nike in 2006. They are working with a marketing giant to improve customer service and product fit. Nike began offering in-store shoe customization last year. This is a terrific approach to promote and collects a lot of data that machine learning algorithms can use to build new products and send more relevant ads. Nike's Chief Digital Officer, Adam Sussman, called Invertex's acquisition "deepening our bench of digital talent and furthering our capabilities in computer vision and artificial intelligence as we create the most compelling Nike consumer experience at every touch point". Nike's ambitions with data are helpful for artificial intelligence now and in the future.

• BMW:
BMW is one of the few automakers that has fully integrated AI into its manufacturing and marketing operations. BMW leverages Big Data for product development, engineering, sales, and customer service. The company's AI-powered sports car learns each driver's preferences and adjusts the settings and interior. BMW's intelligent personal aid debuted this year. It connects cars to the internet, like smartphones. The app can accomplish these and more. It can provide notifications, guide using voice-activated commands, and forecast routes. Each driver's data will increase the company's marketing intelligence. This system could help promote non-company-owned gas stations and parking lots.

• The NineHertz:
For years, NineHertz has been India's AI creation firm. NineHertz's AI engineers, authors, and data scientists provide clients with cutting-edge technology solutions that meet their individual, business, or industry demands. Their AI experts know consumer goals and work hard. They apply this knowledge to build exceptional products that help clients flourish in a fast-paced market. The NineHertz offers a comprehensive range of consulting services to assist companies maximize their AI investments, as well as training sessions for anyone interested in learning about AI's real-world applications. Powerful algorithms and user-friendly software are the company's specialties. It is ideal for introducing users to AI and ML.

• Tata Elxsi:
Tata Elxsi leads the globe in AI-based services. Since 1989, this company has employed industry experts. They also help companies in various industries go digital. AI writers from automotive, industrial, telecom,

and hospitality work together to meet consumer needs using cutting-edge technology. Tata Elxsi provides AI consulting, analytics, and engineering services. Their all-in-one design makes integration with existing infrastructure easy. This is especially helpful for firms trying to keep up with technological advances like streamlining complex operations or automating decision-making.

• Persistent Systems Ltd:
Persistent Systems Ltd. provides enterprise AI solutions. India-based corporation works globally. They offer reliable AI services with over 20 years of research and industrial experience. They offer automated information extraction, speech recognition, natural language processing, autonomous robotics, and more. Persistent Systems helps famous companies optimize their procedures and production. Persistent Systems has completed thousands of AI projects, making it the industry leader.

16.3 Aspects of AI in Marketing across Different Industries

Aspect	Retail	Health care	Financial service
Customer insights	Uses data analysis to learn about customers by looking at their demographics, interests, and past purchases.	Examines patient information, medical history, and treatment results to identify trends and provide individualized healthcare suggestions.	Offers customized investment guidance by assessing a user's profile data, past purchases, and investment preferences.

Personalization	It tailors the shopping experience to the user by recommending items, offering deals, and displaying relevant information.	Individualized treatment plans, medication reminders, and health guidelines are all generated using the patient's medical records and health data.	Offers investment advice suited to each customer's unique situation, as well as financial planning and individualized products.
Chatbots	Customers can get instant responses to their questions about products and guidance during the buying process from chatbots.	Chatbots are utilized to provide round-the-clock assistance to patients by addressing their questions and concerns and providing information about medical conditions and treatments.	Customers can get help with banking questions and receive information about available financial products and services from chatbots.
Marketing campaigns	By studying consumer habits, businesses may better tailor offers, discounts, and loyalty plans to the people most likely to make use of them.	Creates targeted health promotions and preventative care programs based on individual patients' demographic information, health risks, and patterns of health-seeking behaviors.	Marketing strategies for financial products and services are customized for individual consumers depending on their income levels, savings habits, and major life changes.

Customer experience	Uses AI to make suggestions based on a customer's preferences, allowing for virtual trying on and faster checkouts in stores and online.	Improves the patient experience by using AI to speed up scheduling, cut down on wait times, and offer telehealth options for distant appointments.	Offers customized financial guidance, simplifies account maintenance, and opens the door to convenient digital banking to better serve customers.
Data security	Adopts strict security measures to protect customer information, protect transactions, and meet the requirements of data privacy legislation.	When it comes to patient's health records, it is imperative that strict data privacy regulations have adhered to ensure the protection of their information.	In order to safeguard customers' financial information, stop fraud, and guarantee conformity with industry requirements, stringent security measures are used.

Source: Compiled by the authors.

These case studies put an emphasis on the opportunities and usage scenarios that are specific to the retail, healthcare, and financial services industries [2, 39]. The purpose of doing so is to demonstrate how artificial intelligence (AI) in marketing is utilized in each of these areas.

16.4 Conclusion

In recent years, AI has become an increasingly significant component of marketing. Artificial intelligence (AI) has the ability to help marketers by sifting through mountains of data, taking care of ordinary tasks automatically, and providing actionable insights and predictions. From content creation to training and development, the technology is shaping the direction of the industry. AI is set to drive personalization in marketing and advertising. By improving the connectivity and integrating insights from various applications, which are often deployed on different platforms, marketers can leverage AI to gain a more holistic understanding of their customers and create more personalized and smarter customer experiences. AI is used in advertising in several ways, including, but not limited to, personalization, prediction analytics, chatbots, content production, picture/video recognition, and fraud detection. Artificial intelligence (AI) could look at client data and behavior to create customized marketing messages and offers, predict customer behavior, and find trends that could be used to guide marketing strategy. Chatbots with artificial intelligence help customers and can make content like reviews, headlines, and social media updates. AI can evaluate and tag pictures and videos, in addition to spotting fraud. AI can give more customized and useful information to customers, which can improve the effectiveness of marketing, the return on investment, and customer satisfaction. There has been some impact that AI has already had on marketing, but there will be an even greater impact in the future, and as a result, there is a significant amount more to learn. It is important, however, to use AI in an honest and open way, protecting users' privacy and making choices based on data. AI in marketing will provide the customer experience and it will bring competitive advantage to the firm.

References

1. K. Seiders, G. B. Voss and A. L. Godfrey, "Original empirical research servcon: Development and validation of a multidimensional service convenience scale," *J. Acad. Mark. Sci.*, vol. 35, no. 1, pp. 144-56, 2007, doi: 10.1007/s11747-006-0001-5.
2. T. Davenport, A. Guha, D. Grewal, T. Bressgott and T. Davenport, "How artificial intelligence will change the future of marketing," *J. Acad. Mark. Sci.*, vol. 48, pp. 24-42, 2020.
3. R. T. Rust, "The future of marketing," *Int. J. Res. Mark.*, vol. 37, no. 1, pp. 15-26, 2019.
4. M. Haenlein and A. Kaplan, "A Brief History of Artificial Intelligence:," *Calif. Manage. Rev.*, vol. 61, no. 4, pp. 1-10, 2019, doi: 10.1177/0008125619864925.
5. K. L. Siau and Y. Yang, "Impact of artificial intelligence, robotics, and machine learning on sales and marketing," *Proc. Twelfth Midwest Assoc. Inf. Syst. Conf.*, p. 48, 2017.
6. S. J. Russell and P. Norvig, *Artificial Intelligence A Modern Approach*, Third. New Jersey: Pearson, 2010.

7. M. Huang and R. T. Rust, "Artificial Intelligence in Service," *J. Serv. Res.*, vol. 21, no. 2, pp. 155-172, 2020, doi: 10.1177/1094670517752459.
8. D. C. Gkikas and P. K. Theodoridis, "Artificial Intelligence (AI) Impact on Digital Marketing Research," *Strateg. Innov. Mark. Tour.*, pp. 1251-1259, 2019, doi: https://doi.org/10.1007/978-3-030-12453-3_143.
9. P. van Esch, J. S. Black and J. Ferolie, "Marketing AI recruitment: The next phase in job application and selection," *Comput. Hum. Behav.*, vol. 90. pp. 215-222, 2019. doi: 10.1016/j.chb.2018.09.009.
10. S. Kumar, "Artificial intelligence divulges effective tactics of top management institutes of India," *Benchmarking An Int. J.*, vol. 26, no. 7, pp. 2188-2204, 2019, doi: 10.1108/BIJ-08-2018-0251.
11. R. Perez-vega, V. Kaartemo, C. R. Lages and N. Borghei, "Reshaping the contexts of online customer engagement behavior via artificial intelligence : A conceptual framework," *J. Bus. Res.*, vol. 129, no. November 2020, pp. 902-910, 2021, doi: 10.1016/j.jbusres.2020.11.002.
12. M. Huang and R. T. Rust, "A strategic framework for artificial intelligence in marketing," *J. Acad. Mark. Sci.*, vol. 49, pp. 30-50, 2021.
13. C. Cath, S. Wachter, B. Mittelstadt, M. Taddeo and L. Floridi, "Artificial Intelligence and the 'Good Society': the US, EU, and UK approach," *Sci. Eng. Ethics*, vol. 24, no. 2, pp. 505-528, 2018, doi: 10.1007/s11948-017-9901-7.
14. S. Han and H. Yang, "Understanding adoption of intelligent personal assistants: A parasocial relationship perspective," *Ind. Manag. Data Syst.*, vol. 118, no. 3, pp. 618-636, 2018, doi: 10.1108/IMDS-05-2017-0214.
15. P. Klaus and J. Zaichkowsky, "AI voice bots : a services marketing research agenda," *J. Serv. Mark.*, pp. 1-10, 2020, doi: 10.1108/JSM-01-2019-0043.
16. E. Hermann and E. Hermann, "Leveraging Artificial Intelligence in Marketing for Social Good - An Ethical Perspective," *J. Bus. Ethics*, vol. 179, no. 1, pp. 43-61, 2022, doi: 10.1007/s10551-021-04843-y.
17. A. West, J. Clifford and D. Atkinson, "'Alexa, build me a brand' An Investigation into the impact of Artificial Intelligence on Branding," *Bus. Manag. Rev.*, vol. 9, no. 3, pp. 9-10, 2018.
18. P. B. Brandtzaeg and A. Følstad, "Why people use chatbots," *Int. Conf. Internet Sci.*, vol. 10673 LNCS, pp. 377-392, 2017, doi: 10.1007/978-3-319-70284-1_30.
19. C. M. Chen and Y. N. Tsai, "Interactive augmented reality system for enhancing library instruction in elementary schools," *Comput. Educ.*, vol. 59, no. 2, pp. 638-652, 2012, doi: 10.1016/j.compedu.2012.03.001.
20. Burri, Srinivasa Rao, Sachin Ahuja, Abhishek Kumar, and Anupam Baliyan. "Exploring the Effectiveness of Optimized Convolutional Neural Network in Transfer Learning for Image Classification: A Practical Approach." In *2023 International Conference on Advancement in Computation & Computer Technologies (InCACCT)*, pp. 598-602. IEEE, 2023.
21. D. Herald, "Top Artificial Intelligence Companies in India," *The Printers (Mysore) Private Ltd.*, 2023. https://www.deccanherald.com/brandspot/

pr-spot/top-artificial-intelligence-companies-in-india-1189155.html (accessed May 10, 2023).

22. Textile World, "How Fashion Became A Digital Industry," *Textile World*, 2018. https://www.textileworld.com/textile-world/features/2018/03/how-fashion-became-a-digital-industry/ (accessed May 12, 2023).
23. C. Moorman, H. J. Van Heerde, C. P. Moreau and R. W. Palmatier, "Challenging the Boundaries of Marketing," *J. Mark.*, vol. 83, no. 5, pp. 1-4, 2019, doi: 10.1177/0022242919867086.
24. F. Text, "United States : 60 % of Enterprise Marketers Set To Use Artificial Intelligence (AI) in Content Marketing Strategy This Year," *Asia News Monitor*, Bangkok, pp. 1-4, Mar. 19, 2018. [Online]. Available: https://www.proquest.com/docview/2014758443?accountid=49696&parentSessionId=E-OPSh53p5Dk17Ag%2FG1psGHbYDNniK3bMpCC8aiCD%2BIc%3D
25. Sophie Kleber, "3 Ways AI Is Getting More Emotional," *Harv. Bus. Rev.*, 2018. https://hbr.org/2018/07/3-ways-ai-is-getting-more-emotional (accessed May 13, 2023).
26. R. Smith, "The 21st-Century Printing Press," *Res. Manag.*, vol. 60, no. 1, pp. 57-59, 2017, doi: 10.1080/08956308.2017.1255061.
27. A. Mehendale and N. S. H. R, "Application of artificial intelligence (AI) for effective and adaptive sales forecasting," *J. Contemp. Manag. Res.*, vol. 12, no. 2, pp. 17-35, 2018.
28. V. Kumar, B. Rajan, R. Venkatesan and J. Lecinski, "Understanding the role of artificial intelligence in personalized engagement marketing," *Calif. Manage. Rev.*, vol. 61, no. 4, pp. 135-155, 2019, doi: 10.1177/0008125619859317.
29. Jonathan Vanian, "Hello, This Is Artificial Intelligence. How Can I Help You? Eye on A.I.," *Fortune*, 2019. https://fortune.com/2019/08/27/customer-service-artificial-intelligence/ (accessed May 13, 2023).
30. S. Chintalapati, "Artificial intelligence in marketing : A systematic literature review," *Int. J. Mark. Res.*, vol. 64, no. 1, pp. 38–68, 2022, doi: 10.1177/14707853211018428.
31. D. Acemoglu and P. Restrepo, "Robots and Jobs : Evidence from US Labor," *J. Polit. Econ.*, 2019, doi: 10.1086/705716.
32. F. Text, "60 % of Enterprise Marketers Set To Use Artificial Intelligence (AI) in Content Marketing Strategy This Year : Over 500 surveyed marketers provide insight on AI-adoption tipping point, with key benefits aligned around personalization and customer exper," *PR Newswire*; New York, New York, pp. 1-4, Mar. 06, 2018. [Online]. Available: https://search.proquest.com/docview/2010764090?accountid=49696
33. Qi Huang, "Application of Artificial Intelligence in Mechanical Engineering Qi Huang," *Adv. Comput. Sci. Res.*, vol. 74, pp. 855–860, 2017, [Online]. Available: http://creativecommons.org/licenses/by-nc/4.0/
34. Kumar, Abhishek, Swarn Avinash Kumar, Vishal Dutt, S. Shitharth, and Esha Tripathi. "IoT based arrhythmia classification using the enhanced hunt optimization-based deep learning." *Expert Syst.* (2023): e13298.

35. T. Balakrishnan, M. Chui and N. Henke, "Global Survey: The State of AI in 2020," *McKinsey Digit.*, no. November, pp. 1-14, 2020, [Online]. Available: https://www.mckinsey.com/business-functions/mckinsey-analytics/our-insights/global-survey-the-state-of-ai-in-2020
36. D. Shah and E. Shay, "How and Why Artificial Intelligence, Mixed Reality and Blockchain Technologies Will Change Marketing We Know Today," *Handb. Adv. Mark. an Era Disruptions Essays Honour Jagdish N. Sheth*, no. February, pp. 377-390, 2020, doi: 10.4135/9789353287733.n32.
37. E. Turban, J. Outland, T.-P. Liang, J. K. Lee, D. King and D. C. Turban, *Electron. Commer.*, vol. 16, no. 3-4. 2018. doi: 10.1080/02564602.1999.11416851.
38. Mark Wood, Adam Park, Kate Burns, and Eric Wilkinson, "5 Brands That Are Successfully Leveraging AI for Marketing," *Concured*, 2023. https://concured.com/blog/5-brands-that-are-successfully-leveraging-ai-for-marketing/ (accessed May 09, 2023).
39. S. R. Burri, A. Kumar, A. Baliyan and T. A. Kumar, "Predictive Intelligence for Healthcare Outcomes: An AI Architecture Overview," *2023 2nd International Conference on Smart Technologies and Systems for Next Generation Computing (ICSTSN)*, Villupuram, India, 2023, pp. 1-6, doi: 10.1109/ICSTSN57873.2023.10151477.

About the Editors

T. Ananth Kumar, PhD is an associate professor in the Indo French Educational Trust College of Engineering, Anna University, Chennai, India. He has presented papers in various national and international conferences and journals, as well as may book chapters. Additionally, he is a lifetime member of the Indian Society of Technical Education and has many patents spanning across various domains.

E. Golden Julie, PhD is currently working as a Senior Assistant Professor in the department of Computer Science and Engineering, Anna University, Tirunelveli, India. She has more than 12 years of experience in teaching, has published more than 34 papers in various international journals, presented more than 20 papers in both national and international conferences, and written ten book chapters. She has given many guest lectures on various subjects such as multicore architecture, operating systems, and compiler design in premier institutions. Additionally, she is an active lifetime member in Indian Society of Technical Education.

Venkata Raghuveer Burugudda is a senior solution architect and technology leader with over 16 years of experience across the United States and India in product delivery and technology transformation, driving growth for a global network in remittances and payments. He modernized a point of sale solution with new and organizational common architecture to deliver a fast and efficient user experience and allow easy integration of new capabilities through the adoption of cloud migration, devops, test driven principles, and user-centric solutions.

Abhishek Kumar, PhD is currently working as an associate professor and the assistant director of the Computer Science & Engineering Department at Chandigarh University, Punjab, India. He more than 11 years of teaching experience and has been a session chair and keynote speaker for many international conferences and webinars. In addition to his experience, he has more than 100 publications in reputed, peer reviewed national and international journals, books, and conferences, has authored or co-authored seven books published, and edited and additional 27 books.

Puneet Kumar, PhD is a professor and the head of the Department of Computer Science & Engineering at the University Institute of Engineering, Chandigarh University, Mohali, India. He has more than 18 years of teaching, research, and industrial experience and has published various research papers and articles in national and international journals, many of which are widely cited across the world. He is also the recipient of several software copyrights from the Ministry of Human Resource and Development, Government of India.

Index

Also of Interest

Check out these other related titles from Scrivener Publishing

Artificial Intelligence-Enabled Digital Twin for Smart Manufacturing, Edited by Amit Kumar Tyagi, Shrikant Tiwari, Senthil Kumar Arumugam, and Avinash Kumar Sharma, ISBN: 9781394303571. An essential book on the applications of AI and digital twin technology in the smart manufacturing sector.

Quantum Computing and Artificial Intelligence: The Industry Use Cases, Edited by Pethuru Raj, B. Sundaravadivazhagan, Mariya Ouaissa, V. Kavitha and K. Shantha Kumari, ISBN: 9781394242368.

Artificial Intelligence-Based System Models in Healthcare, Edited by A. Jose Anand, K. Kalaiselvi and Jyotir Moy Chatterjee, ISBN: 9781394242498. Artificial Intelligence-Based System Models in Healthcare provides a comprehensive and insightful guide to the transformative applications of AI in the healthcare system.

Artificial Intelligence Enabled Businesses: How to Develop Strategies for Innovation, Edited by Sweta Dixit, Mohit Maurya, Vishal Jain and Geetha Subramaniam, ISBN: 9781394233977.

INTEGRATED DEVICES FOR ARTIFICIAL INTELLIGENCE AND VLSI: VLSI Design, Simulation and Applications, Edited by Balwinder Raj, Suman Lata Tripathi, Tarun Chaudhary, K. Srinivasa Rao, and Mandeep Singh, ISBN: 9781394204359. With its in-depth exploration of the close connection between microelectronics, AI, and VLSI technology, this book offers valuable insights into the cutting-edge techniques and tools used in VLSI design automation, making it an essential resource for anyone seeking to stay ahead in the rapidly evolving field of VLSI design.

DECENTRALIZED SYSTEMS AND DISTRIBUTED COMPUTING, Edited by Sandhya Avasthi, Suman Lata Tripathi, Namrata Dhanda, and Satya Bhushan Verma, ISBN: 978139420436. This book provides a comprehensive exploration of next-generation internet, distributed systems, and distributed computing, offering valuable insights into their impact on society and the future of technology.

EXPLAINABLE MACHINE LEARNING MODELS AND ARCHITECTURES: Real-Time System Implementation, Edited by Suman Lata Tripathi and Mufti Mahmud, ISBN: 9781394185849. This cutting-edge new volume covers the hardware architecture implementation, the software implementation approach, and the efficient hardware of machine learning applications.

MACHINE LEARNING TECHNIQUES FOR VLSI CHIP DESIGN, Edited by Abhishek Kumar, Suman Lata Tripathi, and K. Srinivasa Rao, ISBN: 9781119910398. This cutting-edge new volume covers the hardware architecture implementation, the software implementation approach, and the efficient hardware of machine learning applications with FPGA or CMOS circuits, and many other aspects and applications of machine learning techniques for VLSI chip design.

Printed in the USA/Agawam, MA
September 16, 2026

910661.123